Fodor's

NAPA A
SONOM

Welcome to Napa and Sonoma

In California's premier wine region, the pleasures of eating and drinking are celebrated daily. It's easy to join in at famous wineries and rising newcomers off country roads, or at trendy in-town tasting rooms. Chefs transform local ingredients into feasts, and gourmet groceries sell perfect picnic fare. Yountville, Healdsburg, and St. Helena have small-town charm as well as luxurious inns, hotels, and spas, yet the natural setting is equally sublime, whether experienced from a canoe on the Russian River or the deck of a winery overlooking endless rows of vines.

TOP REASONS TO GO

★ **Fine Wine:** Rutherford Cabernets, Carneros Chardonnays, Russian River Pinots.

★ **Spectacular Food:** Marquee Napa chefs, farmers' markets, Sonoma cheese shops.

★ **Cool Towns:** From chic Healdsburg to laid-back Calistoga, a place to suit every mood.

★ **Spas:** Mud baths, herbal wraps, couples' massages, and more in soothing settings.

★ **Winery Architecture:** Stone classics like Buena Vista, all-glass dazzlers like Hall.

★ **Outdoor Fun:** Biking past bright-green vineyards, hot-air ballooning over golden hills.

Contents

1 **EXPERIENCE NAPA**
  AND SONOMA 6
  15 Ultimate Experiences 8
  What's Where 14
  What to Eat and Drink
  in Napa and Sonoma 16
  Best Bars in Napa and Sonoma 18
  Ten Things to Buy in Napa and Sonoma .. 20
  Art Lover's Guide to Napa and Sonoma ... 22
  Top Napa Wineries 24
  Top Sonoma Wineries 25
  What to Read
  and Watch Before Your Trip 26
  Kids and Families 28

2 **TRAVEL SMART** 29
  Getting Here and Around 30
  Before You Go 32
  Essentials 33
  Great Itineraries 36
  Contacts 42
  On the Calendar 43

3 **VISITING WINERIES**
  AND TASTING ROOMS 45

4 **NAPA VALLEY** 65
  Welcome To Napa Valley 66
  Planning 69
  Napa 73
  Yountville 94
  Oakville 107
  Rutherford 109
  St. Helena 116
  Calistoga 132

5 **SONOMA VALLEY**
  AND PETALUMA 145
  Welcome To
  Sonoma Valley and Petaluma 146
  Planning 149
  Sonoma 151
  Glen Ellen 169
  Kenwood 174
  Petaluma 179

6 **NORTHERN SONOMA,**
  RUSSIAN RIVER,
  AND WEST COUNTY 183
  Welcome To
  Northern Sonoma,
  Russian River, and West County 184
  Planning 186
  Healdsburg 189
  Geyserville 213
  Forestville 218
  Guerneville 221
  Jenner 224
  Bodega Bay 225
  Occidental 227
  Sebastopol 228
  Graton 234
  Santa Rosa 235

INDEX 247

ABOUT OUR WRITERS 256

MAPS

Appellations 58–59
Southern Napa Valley 76
Downtown Napa 84
Yountville 96
Northern Napa Valley 113
Downtown St. Helena 120
Sonoma Valley and Petaluma 154–155
Downtown Sonoma 162
Healdsburg and Northern Sonoma 191
Downtown Healdsburg 195
West County 219
Santa Rosa 242–243

Did You Know?

The average acre of grapes yields just under 4,000 bottles of wine. It takes 740 pounds of grapes to fill a barrel, 2.4 pounds to make one bottle.

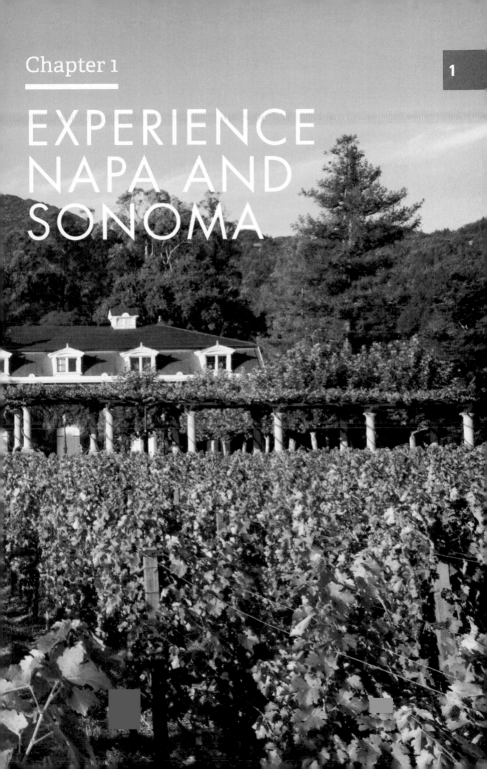

Chapter 1

EXPERIENCE NAPA AND SONOMA

15 ULTIMATE EXPERIENCES

Napa and Sonoma offers terrific experiences that should be on every traveler's list. Here are Fodor's top picks for a memorable trip.

1 Take to the Skies

It's worth waking before sunrise for a hot-air balloon ride over the vineyards. The experience is breathtaking, and oh-so-romantic for couples. Most flights end with a champagne breakfast back on the ground. *(Ch. 4, 6)*

2 Ogle the Art

Museum-quality artworks enhance a visit to several wineries, but you can also ogle street art and visit artists studios and arts centers. *(Ch. 4, 5, 6)*

3 Ride the Rails

The romance of the rails and vineyard views make for a crowd-pleasing excursion on the Napa Valley Wine Train, often with winery stops. *(Ch. 4)*

4 Sip Sparkling Wine

A few wineries focus on sparkling wines. Schramsberg and Korbel have good tours; sip in style at Domaine Carneros, Gloria Ferrer, and Iron Horse. *(Ch. 4, 5, 6)*

5 Paddle a River

Several outfits offer guided or self-guided kayaking or canoe trips on the Napa and Russian rivers. Pack a picnic, and you're ready to go! *(Ch. 4, 6)*

6 Splurge on a Meal

Celebrated chefs operate Wine Country restaurants, often using ingredients grown steps from the kitchen. Food this refined is worth at least one splurge. *(Ch. 4, 5, 6)*

7 Shop Till You Stop

Among the Wine Country's charms is that it's not overrun with cutesy boutiques or chains. Healdsburg earns top honors for its diverse shopping opps. *(Ch. 4, 5, 6)*

8 Play Winemaker

Learn to blend wine at entertaining sessions exploring the winemaker's art. At some wineries you'll even bottle and label your creation to take home. *(Ch. 4, 6)*

9 Sample Spirits

At distillery tasting rooms you can sample spirits and learn about the production process and how it differs from wine and beer making. *(Ch. 4, 5, 6)*

10 Taste on a Hilltop

That Cab or Chard tastes all the better with hilltop valley vistas; in Napa, try Barnett or Pride, in Sonoma, Kunde, Jordan, or Trattore Farms. *(Ch. 4, 5, 6)*

11 Be a Pinot Pilgrim

To get a feel for the climate and terrain that foster world-class Pinot Noir, explore the Carneros District, Russian River Valley, and Sonoma Coast. *(Ch. 4, 5, 6)*

12 Hone Your Skills

Instructors and guest chefs beguile students and visitors during cooking demonstrations at two Culinary Institute of America campuses in the Napa Valley. *(Ch. 4)*

13 Luxuriate at a Spa

For pure unadulterated luxuriating, Wine Country spas rank among the world's finest, with the emphasis on wellness as much as working out kinks. *(Ch. 4, 5, 6)*

14 Bike Past Vines

The Wine Country's many valleys make for leisurely guided or self-guided bike rides past gently rolling vineyards and sometimes through them. *(Ch. 4, 5, 6)*

15 Hit the Beach

Windswept, photogenic beaches and dramatically craggy cliffs are the norm along the Sonoma Coast. The drive north from Bodega Bay to Fort Ross is breathtaking. *(Ch. 6)*

WHAT'S WHERE

1 Napa Valley. By far the best known of the California wine regions, Napa is home to some of the biggest names in wine, many of which still produce the same bottles of Cabernet Sauvignon that first put the valley on the map. Densely populated with winery after winery, especially along Highway 29 and the Silverado Trail, it's also home to luxury accommodations, some of the country's best restaurants, and spas with deluxe treatments, some incorporating grape seeds and other wine-making by-products.

2 Sonoma Valley and Petaluma. Centered on the historic town of Sonoma, the Sonoma Valley goes easier on the glitz but contains sophisticated wineries and excellent restaurants. Key moments in California and wine-industry history took place here. Part of the Carneros District viticultural area lies within the southern Sonoma Valley. Those who venture into the Carneros and west of the Sonoma Valley into the Petaluma Gap appellation will discover wineries specializing in Pinot Noir and Chardonnay. Both grapes thrive in the comparatively cool climate. Farther north, Cabernet Sauvignon and other warm-weather varietals are grown.

3 Northern Sonoma, Russian River, and West County. Ritzy Healdsburg is a popular base for exploring three important grape-growing areas, the Russian River, Dry Creek, and Alexander valleys. Everything from Chardonnay and Pinot Noir to Cabernet Sauvignon, Zinfandel, and Petite Sirah grows here. In the county's western parts lie the Sonoma Coast wineries, beloved by connoisseurs for European-style wines from cool-climate grapes.

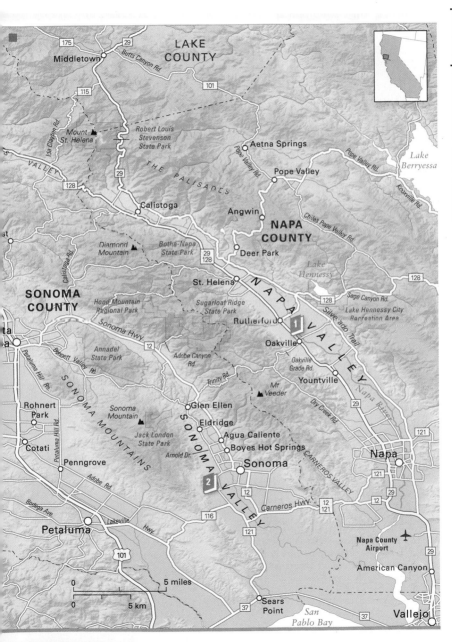

What to Eat and Drink in Napa and Sonoma

DAY BOAT SCALLOPS AT VALETTE

Sublime execution and heavenly ingredients—butter, fresh local fennel and leeks, Pernod, fennel butter, scallops flown in from Maine, caviar, Champagne beurre blanc (more butter), and a light, fluffy pastry—make chef Dustin Valette's signature day boat scallops *en croûte* a Healdsburg must-try.

COCKTAILS AT LAS ALCOBAS

Invented at Las Alcobas Napa Valley's Mexico City sister hotel and the perfect antidote to a day of Cabernets, the Las Alcobas Margarita refreshes palates with sea-salt foam and lime-skin shavings. A homegrown favorite is the Acacia Cocktail—gin, honey, crème de violet, sparkling wine.

STEAK AND A LIBRARY CAB AT PRESS

St. Helena's outstanding steak house Press can purchase beef anywhere in the world, but the purveyor of choice for an exquisitely marbled dry-aged steak is Northern California's Flannery Beef. Maximize your bliss with a late-1990s Cabernet from the restaurant's extensive wine library.

MAD FRITZ ALE

Master brewer Nile Zacherle and wife Whitney Fisher made a lot of wine for boutique wineries before opening their craft brewery specializing in "origin-specific beers," with the source of each ingredient acknowledged on the back label. Tales from a Renaissance-era Aesop's Fables edition provide most of the beers' names and all the front-label illustrations.

MUSHROOMY MUSHROOM SOUP AT KITCHEN DOOR

"It's so mushroomy, how does he do it?" ask many patrons at star chef Todd Humphries's the Kitchen Door in downtown Napa's Oxbow Public Market. His soup's secrets of success? A heavy stock, his mushroom combo, and a splash of marsala, says Humphries.

Chris Killar's Red Wine Truffle

RED WINE TRUFFLES AT KOLLAR CHOCOLATES

Chocolatier Chris Kollar installed an open kitchen in his shop at downtown Yountville's V Marketplace so patrons could see him and his crew at work, experimenting with new confections or whipping up another batch of red wine truffles, made from Napa Valley Zinfandel.

CHARLIE PALMER'S LOBSTER CORN DOG

Chef Charlie Palmer's trademark lobster corn dog is simple in conception—a lump of lobster surrounded by deep-fried cornbread, served on a stick with pickled-ramp remoulade—yet somehow much more than the sum of its parts. Enjoy one or more at the Archer Hotel Napa's Sky & Vine rooftop bar.

MODEL BAKERY ENGLISH MUFFINS

Three parts English muffin and one part doughnut, the Model Bakery's fluffy, doughy, orgasmically delicious signature baked good seduces on every level. Even Oprah swoons for these muffins, available at the bakery's Napa, Yountville, and St. Helena locations.

SORBET BRUNCH MIMOSA

One of the principals in Calistoga's Lovina restaurant is also involved with a beloved San Francisco spot where brunch isn't brunch without a zesty mimosa with a divine scoop of blood-orange sorbet. The tradition continues in Calistoga.

SCREAMING EAGLE BY THE GLASS

With a mile-long waiting list for the right to pay thousands for a bottle, Screaming Eagle is the holy grail of cult Cabernets. Jump the line at the Fairmont Sonoma Mission Inn's 38° North Lounge, where you can savor the latest vintage for $500 by the half glass or $900 for a standard pour. An inconceivable splurge? Perhaps, but at least you can say you tried it.

Best Bars in Napa and Sonoma

SIGH
Quotes from Dom Perignon, Coco Chanel, and Churchill extolling champagne's virtues are painted on mirrors at Sigh, a downtown Sonoma bar devoted to sparkling wine. The festive space exudes mid-century style. The centerpiece oval bar's taps dispense bubblies from as near as Sonoma's Gloria Ferrer, 6 miles away, and as far afield as France, Argentina, and Australia.

DUKE'S SPIRITED COCKTAILS
Happy hour is active in Healdsburg as winery employees unwind and visitors transition from wine-tasting to dining mode. Among the liveliest spots downtown is Duke's, whose elaborate "farm-to-bar" cocktails cleanse weary palates. Duke's Common next door serves delectable bites.

ERNIE'S TIN BAR
Roadside Ernie's is as famous for its no-cellphone policy—use your phone, and the next round's on you—as its 20 brews on tap and convivial vibe. The Petaluma watering hole, basically a long narrow bar with a few tables inside and an outdoor patio, shares a corrugated-tin building with a garage. Warning: the dude with the Stetson is as apt to be a millionaire as a ranch hand.

THE ROOFTOP
The boutique Harmon Guest House's rooftop bar earns rave reviews for its eco-friendly style and views of downtown Healdsburg and beyond to 991-foot Fitch Mountain. The specialty cocktail lineup changes regularly to suit the season and complement the seafood-leaning food menu.

GOOSE & GANDER

A Craftsman bungalow off St. Helena's Main Street houses this popular eatery and its cool basement bar. The low ceiling and subdued lighting add speakeasy appeal G&G comes by honestly: the bungalow's original owner allegedly used the cellar for Prohibition-era bootlegging.

GEYSERVILLE GUN CLUB

Historic, retro, and au courant, this bar occupies a ground-floor sliver of Geyserville's circa-1900 Odd Fellows Hall. The cocktails change seasonally but if you like gin, try a signature Gun Club Gibson (Plymouth Gin, dry vermouth, orange bitters, and pickling spices).

EL BARRIO

Guerneville's hole-in-the-wall with south-of-the-border flair specializes in craft cocktails based on tequila and mescal. Adventurous types should consider the challenge of El Viejo, featuring both; if you're not sure what to order, La Casa, the house margarita, is a safe bet.

Sky & Vine

SKY & VINE

Among the Wine Country's best cocktail perches, the Archer Hotel Napa's sixth-floor rooftop bar seduces with valley views, snappy libations, and snacks and bites from chef Charlie Palmer and crew. If zero proof's your thing, try the beet kombucha—delicious, and so good for you. During "reverse happy hour" (9 pm–closing), Sky & Vine is almost a bargain.

NAPA PALISADES SALOON

"Be here, drink beer," is the motto of this regular ole place, an excellent downtown Napa spot to throw back a few brews or bourbons and take in the game. Nothing fancy here, just 30-plus craft beers on tap, a full bar, a whiskey bar, and eight large-screen TVs.

SUSIE'S BAR

A good scrubbing down a few years back erased decades of divey patina, but Calistoga's low-key Susie's remains fun, affordable, and endearingly downscale. It's hardly a destination bar, but with good pours and reasonable prices for top-shelf spirits, you'll get the biggest bang here for your liquor dollar.

Ten Things to Buy in Napa and Sonoma

OLIVE OIL

By tradition dating to antiquity, grapes and olives have supplied two staples of the southern European diet: wine and olive oil. Visitors to several wineries with olive mills, including Petaluma's McEvoy Ranch, can taste and purchase extra virgin oils produced entirely on-site.

POTTERY

For their farm-to-plate cuisine some Wine Country restaurants extend their support of local purveyors to the second part of the equation, serving meals on elegant ceramic dinnerware sometimes crafted within a few miles. Napa Valley artisans of note include Amanda Wright and Richard Carter, both with studios in St. Helena, and Jeff and Sally Manfredi of Calistoga.

WINE GLASSES

High-end wineries take pride in serving wines in high-quality stemware. After a few tastings, you might catch on that the quality and shape of a glass really do enhance wines' aromatics and other attributes. Some winery gift shops sell the brand featured in the tasting room.

FASHION JEWELRY

"Everyday wearable chic" is the goal of many local jewelry artisans, some of whom put a bohemian spin on their output by incorporating leather or oxidized metals. Look for jewelry at winery gift shops and in downtown Sonoma, St. Helena, Healdsburg, Yountville, and Napa.

WINE

Yes, this one is obvious— buy wine in the Wine Country—but perhaps for reasons you haven't considered. Familiar brands have a few widely distributed wines you can easily purchase back home. At the winery, though, the focus will be on higher-quality small-production offerings sold only in the tasting room. Wines in a custom box make an excellent gift for someone back home.

GIFT BOOKS

With their photogenic mountains, valleys, vineyards, and architecture, the Napa Valley and Sonoma County inspire large-format gift books devoted to wine, food, and other topics. Perennial favorites include titles about winery dogs and cats or containing aerial photography.

GOURMET COOKING TOOLS AND UTENSILS

Should your Wine Country trip awaken your inner gourmet chef, well-curated shops here carry every type of cooking tool and utensil imaginable. Two spots not to miss are the Spice Islands Marketplace at St. Helena's Culinary Institute of America at Greystone and the Store at CIA Copia in Napa. Packed to the gills, the Marketplace is the kind of place you can while away hours.

WINE-BARREL FURNITURE AND ACCESSORIES

What happens to oak barrels after they're used to make wine? Most are sold off, their staves, metal hoops, and lids transformed into Adirondack chairs, barstools, planters, wine racks, lazy Susans, chandeliers, swings, jewelry, and anything else enterprising artisans dream up.

WINE-BOTTLE CANDLES

Wine bottles are even more ubiquitous than barrels as a wine-making by-product in need of recycling and reuse. Many bottles are indeed recycled, with others finding a second life as water glasses, chandeliers, and vessels for candles. Feast it Forward in Napa carries wine-scented candles made from natural soy wax, as do numerous winery gift shops.

TERROIR-DRIVEN BEAUTY PRODUCTS

"Terroir" is the French term for soil, climate, and related conditions that make a vineyard, and therefore its wines, unique. Several Napa and Sonoma companies apply this concept to sourcing ingredients for beauty and skin-care products found throughout the Wine Country.

Art Lover's Guide to Napa and Sonoma

THE HESS COLLECTION
Artworks by heavy hitters like Robert Rauschenberg fill the Hess Collection's two-floor gallery west of downtown Napa. Swiss-born vintner Donald Hess acquired the pieces over several decades. Gallery admission is free, but you're welcome to (for a fee) taste some wine, too.

THE DONUM ESTATE
It's fitting that most of The Donum Estate's three dozen–plus large-scale outdoor sculptures grace the winery's lush vineyards, where winegrower Anne Moller-Racke's mastery of precision farming yields Pinot Noirs and Chardonnays that are works of art themselves. The visual feast begins with Jaume Plensa's marble Sanna, Giant Head, which looms over the driveway leading to the board-and-batten hospitality center, itself a stylish set piece by San Francisco–based architect Matt Hollis. Collection highlights include Chinese artist-activist Ai Weiwei's bronze Circle of Animals/ Zodiac Heads, displayed in a grassy meadow. A Louise Bourgeois spider occupies its own indoor pavilion.

HALL ST. HELENA
Lawrence Argent's 35-foot polished-stainless-steel sculpture of a leaping rabbit marks the entrance to Hall St. Helena, which devotes a whole tour (reservations required, tasting included) to the contemporary artworks collected by owners Kathryn and Craig Hall. You can view most of the collection before or after a standard tasting or on other tours. Hall is known for Cabernet Sauvignons, a few of which have earned 100-point scores from major wine critics.

DI ROSA CENTER FOR CONTEMPORARY ART
The late Rene di Rosa founded this Carneros District art park that focuses on Northern California works from the mid-20th century to the present. Two galleries display some of the permanent collection and host temporary exhibitions, and the Sculpture Meadow and the area around di Rosa's former residence contain outdoor sculptures.

MUMM NAPA
Visitors to the French champagne producer Mumm's outpost in Rutherford can sip sparkling wines while viewing photographs in two galleries. One contains the Poetry of Light exhibition of images by Ansel Adams, among them his famous shot of Half Dome in Yosemite National Park. The other gallery presents the works of respected contemporary photographers.

RAD NAPA
Full-scale murals adorn warehouse and other structures in Napa courtesy of artists funded by RAD Napa (Rail Arts District Napa). One of the flashiest examples, painted on the two-story CIA at Copia building, was inspired by the culinary gardens out front. Napa Valley Wine Train passengers and hikers and bikers along the Napa Valley Vine Trail have the best views. RAD Napa's website has a touring map.

di Rosa

SOFA SANTA ROSA ARTS DISTRICT

Street murals along Art Alley are the showstoppers of this small arts district centered around South A Street in downtown Santa Rosa. You can view artworks and artists at work at the adjacent Santa Rosa Arts Center. Nearby JaM JAr carries the jewelry and paintings of its two owners. On First Fridays (of the month) the district's members stay open between 5 pm and 8 pm, and many galleries have openings attended by the featured artists.

PATRICK AMIOT JUNK ART

All over Sonoma County you'll see the sculptures Sebastopol resident Patrick Amiot fashions out of sheet metal and found objects, rendered all the more whimsical by the wild colors his wife, Brigitte Laurent, paints on them. For the most significant concentration of sculptures, head two blocks west of Main Street to Florence Avenue, where many residents, including the two artists, proudly display the fanciful fabrications.

CA' TOGA GALLERIA D'ARTE

For sheer exuberance it's hard to imagine anything topping Italian artist Carlo Marchiori's storefront Ca' Toga Galleria d'Arte in downtown Calistoga. This place is all about Marchiori's creativity, as expressed in everything from paintings and sculptures to ceramic housewares. Be sure to look up—the ceiling's a trip. The pièce de résistance is the artist's over-the-top Palladian-style villa. Heavy on the trompe l'oeil, it's open for visits on a limited basis.

FRANCIS FORD COPPOLA WINERY

The Movie Gallery at the famous director's Geyserville winery doesn't display much art per se, but its collection contains props and other items related to his films, among them some of late-20th-century cinema's defining works. Among the selfie stars are Don Corleone's desk from *The Godfather* and the namesake 1948 vehicle from *Tucker: The Man and His Dream*. Ever twirling on a car-showroom platform and one of only 51 produced, the auto is worth more than a million dollars. The gallery's supporting cast includes costumes from Bram Stoker's *Dracula*, models from daughter-director Sofia Coppola's films, five FFC Oscars, and hundreds of other items.

Top Napa Wineries

ASHES AND DIAMONDS
Record producer Kashy Khaledi opened this winery whose splashy glass-and-metal tasting space evokes classic midcentury-modern California architecture. In their restrained elegance, the all-Bordeaux wines by two much-heralded pros hark back to 1960s Napa, too.

DOMAINE CARNEROS
The main building of this Napa winery was modeled after an 18th-century French château owned by the Champagne-making Taittinger family, one of whose members selected the site Domaine Carneros now occupies. On a sunny day, the experience of sipping a crisp sparkling wine on the outdoor terrace feels noble indeed.

INGLENOOK
History buffs won't want to miss Inglenook, which was founded in the 19th century by a Finnish sea captain and rejuvenated over the past several decades by filmmaker Francis Ford Coppola. You can learn all about this fabled property on a tour or while tasting in an opulent salon—or just sip peacefully at a wine bar with a picturesque courtyard.

JOSEPH PHELPS VINEYARDS
In good weather, there are few more glorious tasting spots in the Napa Valley than the terrace at this St. Helena winery. Phelps is known for its Cabernet Sauvignons and Insignia, a Bordeaux blend. The wine-related seminars here are smart and entertaining.

SCHRAMSBERG
The 19th-century cellars at sparkling-wine producer Schramsberg hold millions of bottles. On the fascinating tour you'll learn how the bubblies at this Calistoga mainstay are made using the *méthode traditionelle,* and how the bottles are "riddled" (turned every few days) by hand.

SMITH-MADRONE WINERY
Step back in time at this Spring Mountain winery where two brothers named Smith make wines in a weathered, no-frills redwood barn. Founder Stu has been doing the farming and Charlie has been making the wines for more than four decades at this place with splendid valley views.

STONY HILL VINEYARD
The winemakers at this winery on Spring Mountain's eastern slope craft old world–style, mostly white wines in a low-tech cellar that looks like something out of *The Hobbit.* The dense woods on the drive up to the winery and the steeply banked vineyards surrounding it reinforce the sense of timeless perfection each bottle expresses.

TREFETHEN FAMILY VINEYARDS
The main tasting space at Trefethen, a three-story wooden former winery building dating to 1886, was completely renovated following the 2014 Napa earthquake. A half-century old itself, Trefethen makes Riesling, Chardonnay, and Merlot in addition to Cabernet Sauvignon and a Malbec-oriented red blend.

VENGE VINEYARDS
Kirk Venge consults on the blending of several exclusive wineries' Cabernets and other wines, but his own winery is delightfully casual, and the cost of both tastings and bottles is reasonable given the quality. With its vineyard views, the ranch-house tasting room's porch is a magical perch. Book ahead to visit here.

VGS CHATEAU POTELLE
Small bites from an acclaimed Napa restaurant and Cabernet and other reds made from mountain fruit pair perfectly in Chateau Potelle's whimsically decorated St. Helena bungalow. In good weather, tastings take place under an open-air Moroccan tent. In either setting, owner Jean-Noel Fourmeaux's hospitality shines.

Top Sonoma Wineries

THE DONUM ESTATE

Single-vineyard Pinot Noirs exhibiting "power yet elegance" made the reputation of this Carneros District winery also known for smooth, balanced Chardonnays. The three dozen–plus large-scale, museum-quality outdoor sculptures by the likes of Anselm Kiefer add a touch of high culture to a visit.

IRON HORSE VINEYARDS

Proof that tasting sparkling wine doesn't have to be stuffy, this winery on the outskirts of Sebastopol pours its selections outdoors, with tremendous views of vine-covered hills that make the top-notch bubblies (and a few still wines) taste even better.

LIMERICK LANE

This winery's tasting room, in a restored stone farm building, is hardly Sonoma County's grandest, but the Zinfandel, Syrah, and Petite Sirah are arguably among the entire state's best. If you're curious about Zinfandel, don't miss Limerick Lane, whose oldest vines date back a century-plus.

MERRY EDWARDS WINERY

Serious Pinot Noir lovers seek out this Sebastopol spot to experience wines celebrating the singular characteristics of the Russian River Valley appellation. Tastings are offered several times daily.

PATZ & HALL

This winery is known for single-vineyard Chardonnays and Pinot Noirs made by James Hall, who consistently surpasses peers who have access to the same high-quality fruit. At Salon Tastings in a stylish ranch house a few miles south of Sonoma Plaza, the wines are paired with gourmet bites.

RIDGE VINEYARDS

Oenophiles will be familiar with Ridge, which produces some of California's best Cabernet Sauvignon, Chardonnay, and Zinfandel. You can taste wines made from grapes grown here at Ridge's Healdsburg vineyards, and some from its neighbors, along with wines made at its older Santa Cruz Mountains winery.

ROBERT YOUNG ESTATE WINERY

Guests to the hilltop tasting room of this longtime grower enjoy views down the Alexander Valley while sipping Chardonnay and other whites and Bordeaux-style reds. The first Youngs settled in Geyserville in 1858; the complete history of local agriculture unfolded on this historic site.

SCRIBE

Two sons of walnut growers established this winery on land in Sonoma first planted to grapes in the late 1850s by a German immigrant. Their food-friendly wines include Riesling, Sylvaner, Chardonnay, Pinot Noir, Syrah, and Cabernet Sauvignon.

SILVER OAK

"Only one wine can be your best," was cofounder Justin Meyer's rationale for Silver Oak's decision to focus solely on Cabernet. The winery pours its two yearly offerings (one from Napa, the other from Sonoma) in a glass-walled eco-friendly tasting room in the Alexander Valley.

THREE STICKS WINES

The chance to make Pinots and Chardonnays from Three Sticks's prized Durell and Gap's Crown vineyards lured Bob Cabral from his longtime post at an exclusive Sonoma County winery. Guests taste Cabral's gems at the lavishly restored Adobe, west of Sonoma Plaza.

What to Read and Watch Before Your Trip

Books

COOKBOOKS

Bouchon Bakery (2012), by Thomas Keller and Sebastien Rouxel. The legendary Keller and his executive pastry chef share recipes that made Yountville's Bouchon Bakery an instant hit.

The Essential Thomas Keller: The French Laundry Cookbook & Ad Hoc at Home (2010), by Thomas Keller. Recipes inspired by Keller's upscale and down-home Yountville establishments show the chef's great range.

Mustards Grill Napa Valley Cookbook (2001), by Cindy Pawlcyn and Brigid Callinan. Pawlcyn describes her iconic eatery as "a cross between a roadside rib joint and a French country restaurant." She shares recipes and expounds on her culinary philosophy.

Plats du Jour: The Girl & the Fig's Journey Through the Seasons in Wine Country (2011), by Sondra Bernstein. The chef behind Sonoma County's two "fig" restaurants reveals her cooking secrets and adapts some of her signature dishes.

Wine Country Women of Napa Valley (2017), by Michelle Mandro and Dona Kopol Bonik. Winemakers, chefs, executives, and women holding other key positions share insights and recipes in this large-format volume filled with photography.

FICTION

Murder Uncorked (2005), *Murder by the Glass: A Wine-Lover's Mystery* (2006), and *Silenced by Syrah* (2007), by Michele Scott. Vineyard manager Nikki Sands is the protagonist of this light and humorous mystery series that unfolds in the Napa Valley.

Nose: A Novel (2013), by James Conaway. A fictitious Northern California wine-making region—couldn't be Napa or Sonoma, could it?—is the setting for a mystery.

NONFICTION

Appellation Napa Valley: Building and Protecting an American Treasure (2016), by Richard Mendelson. An industry lawyer describes the Napa Valley's evolution into a major wine region, from a legal and business standpoint.

Crush: The Triumph of California Wine (2018), by John Briscoe. Napa and Sonoma are key players in this tale of five high and four low points for the state's wine industry during the past two centuries.

The Emperor of Wine: The Rise of Robert M. Parker, Jr. and the Reign of American Taste (2005), by Elin McCoy. Examination of the American critic's enormous influence considers the sources and worldwide impact of his wine rating system's dominance.

Harvests of Joy: How the Good Life Became Great Business (1999), by Robert Mondavi and Paul Chutkow. Wine tycoon Robert Mondavi tells his story.

The House of Mondavi: The Rise and Fall of an American Wine Dynasty (2007), by Julia Flynn Siler. The author ruffled many a Napa feather when she published this tell-all book.

Judgment of Paris: California vs. France and the Historic 1976 Paris Tasting That Revolutionized Wine (2005), by George M. Taber. The journalist who originally broke the story of the pivotal event analyzes its history and repercussions.

Napa at Last Light: America's Eden in an Age of Calamity (2018), by James Conaway. The author of two previous bestsellers (Napa, 1990; The Far Side of Eden, 2002) about the Napa Valley reflects on current challenges.

Napa County (2009), by Todd L. Shulman. Old postcards of Krug, Inglenook, and other historic wineries add visual spice to this county chronicle.

Napa Valley: The Land, the Wine, the People (2011), by Charles O'Rear. A former National Geographic photographer portrays the valley in this lush book.

Napa Valley Then & Now (2015), by Kelli A. White. A well-regarded sommelier's encyclopedic book details the valley's wines, wineries, and history.

The New California Wine: A Guide to the Producers and Wines Behind a Revolution in Taste (2013), by Jon Bonné. A former local wine critic profiles the leaders of the movement to create "wines that show nuance, restraint, and a deep evocation of place."

A New Napa Cuisine (2014), by Christopher Kostow. The much-lauded chef of the Restaurant at Meadowood in St. Helena describes his evolution as a chef and his land-focused approach to cooking.

A Perfect Score: The Art, Soul, and Business of a 21st-Century Winery (2016), by Craig and Kathryn Hall. The owners of Hall Wines describe their path to achieving a 100-point Wine Advocate score.

Sonoma Wine and the Story of Buena Vista (2013), by Charles L. Sullivan. California's first winery provides the hook for this survey of Sonoma County's winemaking history.

Tangled Vines: Greed, Murder, Obsession, and an Arsonist in the Vineyards of California (2015), by Frances Dinkelspiel. Rare vintages by the author's great-great-grandfather were among the 4½ million bottles destroyed in a deliberately set warehouse fire were.

When the Rivers Ran Red: An Amazing Story of Courage and Triumph in

America's Wine Country (2009), by Vivienne Sosnowski. The author chronicles the devastating effect of Prohibition on Northern California winemakers.

Films and TV

Bottle Shock (2008). Filmed primarily in the Napa and Sonoma valleys, Randall Miller's fictionalized feature about the 1976 Paris tasting focuses on Calistoga's Chateau Montelena.

Burn Country (2016). Sonoma County seems downright sinister (especially at night) in this indie drama about an Atghani exile who becomes a reporter for a local paper and falls into danger pursuing leads on a murder case. Melissa Leo and James Franco are among the stars.

Falcon Crest (1981–90). This soap opera centered on a winery in the fictional "Tuscany Valley" (aka Napa) may not have aged as well as wines made during its era, but it has acquired a nostalgic patina. At its best it's pulpy good fun.

Napa Valley Dreams (2013). Rodney Vance wrote and directed this contemplative love note to the Napa Valley; the 41-minute documentary includes juicy location shots and interviews with major winemakers and other valley residents.

Somm, Somm into the Bottle, Somm 3 (2012–2018). The Napa Valley plays a role in each of these documentaries about, respectively, the master sommelier exam, the world of wine through ten bottles, and three influential experts.

Wine Country (2019). Calistoga has a star turn in this comedy about a 50th-birthday celebration in Northern California; Amy Poehler directed and co-stars (with Tina Fey).

Kids and Families

The Wine Country isn't a particularly child-oriented destination. Don't expect to find tons of activities organized with kids in mind. That said, you'll find plenty of playgrounds (there's one in Sonoma Plaza, for instance), as well as the occasional family-friendly attraction.

CHOOSING A PLACE TO STAY

If you're traveling with kids, always mention it when making your reservations. Most of the smaller, more romantic inns and bed-and-breakfasts discourage or prohibit children, and those places that do allow them may prefer to put such families in a particular cottage or room so that any noise is less disruptive to other guests. Larger hotels are a mixed bag. Some actively discourage children, whereas others are more welcoming. Of the large, luxurious hotels, Meadowood tends to be the most child-friendly.

EATING OUT

Unless your kid is a budding Thomas Keller, it's best to call ahead to see if a restaurant can accommodate those under 12 with a special menu. You will find inexpensive cafés in almost every town, and places like Gott's Roadside, a retro burger stand in St. Helena, are big hits with kids.

FAMILY-FRIENDLY ATTRACTIONS

One especially family-friendly attraction is the Charles M. Schulz Museum in Santa Rosa. Its intelligent exhibits generally appeal to adults; younger kids may or may not enjoy the level of detail. The sure bets for kids are the play area outside and the education room, where they can color, draw, and create their own cartoons. Another place for a family outing, also in Santa Rosa, is Safari West, an African wildlife preserve on 400 acres. The highlight is the two-hour tour of the property in open-air vehicles that sometimes come within a few feet of giraffes, zebras, and other animals. You can spend the night in tent-cabins here. At Sonoma Canopy Tours, north of Occidental, families zip-line through the redwoods together. A mile south of Sonoma Plaza, Sonoma TrainTown Railroad dazzles the under-10 set with a 4-mile ride on a quarter-scale train, a petting zoo, and amusement rides.

AT THE WINERIES

Children have become a common sight at many wineries, and well-behaved children will generally be greeted with a smile. Some wineries offer a small treat—grape juice or another beverage, or sometimes coloring books or a similar distraction.

When booking a tour, ask if kids are allowed (for insurance and other reasons, wineries sometimes prohibit children under a certain age), how long it lasts, and whether there's another tour option that would be more suitable. Robert Mondavi Winery welcomes children to its 30-minute Discovery Tour—it's a good length for little ones.

A few particularly kid-friendly wineries include Calistoga's Castello di Amorosa (what's not to like about a 107-room medieval castle, complete with a dungeon?) and Sterling Vineyards, where a short aerial tram ride whisks visitors from the parking lot to the tasting room. In Sonoma County, Benziger conducts vineyard tours in a tractor-pulled tram, and its picnic grounds are kid-friendly.

You'll find plenty of kids poolside at the Francis Ford Coppola Winery in Geyserville, and Honig Vineyard & Winery in Rutherford prides itself on making sure kids enjoy a visit as much as their parents do.

Chapter 2

TRAVEL SMART NAPA AND SONOMA

★ **CAPITAL:**
Sacramento

♟ **POPULATION:**
40.1 million

💬 **LANGUAGE:**
English

€ **CURRENCY:**
U.S. dollar

✉ **AREA CODE**
707

⚠ **EMERGENCIES:**
911

🚗 **DRIVING**
On the right

⚡ **ELECTRICITY:**
120–240 v/60 cycles; plugs have two or three rectangular prongs

🕐 **TIME:**
Three hours behind New York

🌐 **WEB RESOURCES:**
www.visitnapavalley.com,
www.sonomacounty.com,
www.visitcalifornia.com,
travel.state.gov

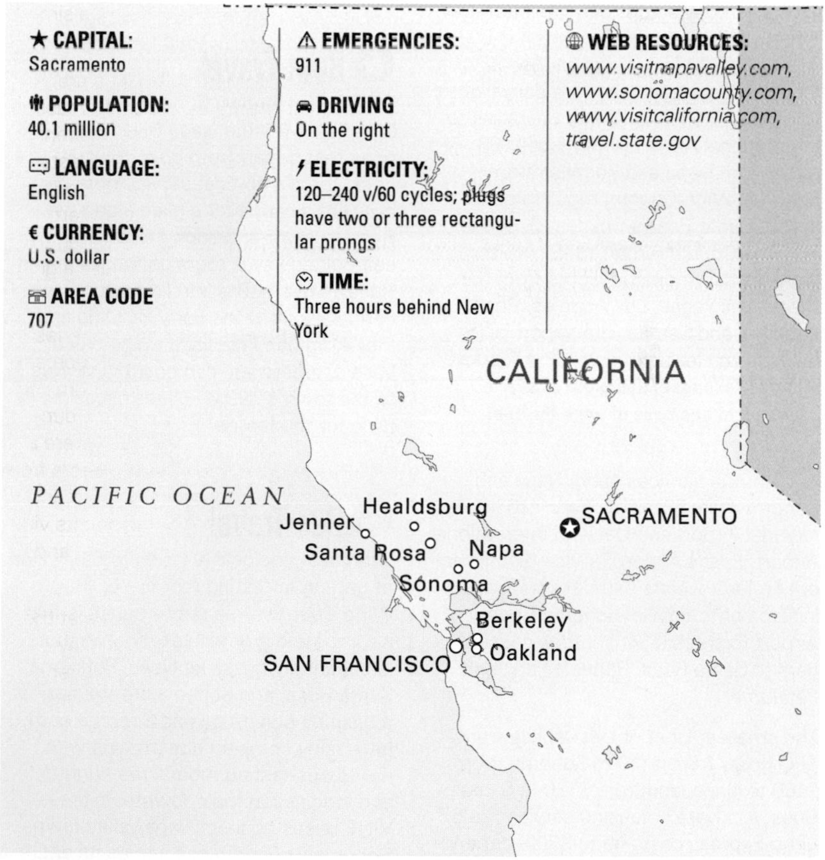

CALIFORNIA

PACIFIC OCEAN

Healdsburg

Jenner

Santa Rosa

Napa

Sonoma

⊗ SACRAMENTO

Berkeley

Oakland

SAN FRANCISCO

Getting Here and Around

✈ Air Travel

Nonstop flights from New York to San Francisco take about 6½ hours, and with the three-hour time change, it's possible to leave JFK by 8 am and be in San Francisco before noon. Some flights require changing planes midway, making the total excursion between 8 and 9½ hours.

AIRPORTS

The major gateway to the Wine Country is San Francisco International Airport (SFO), 60 miles from the city of Napa. Oakland International Airport (OAK), almost directly across San Francisco Bay, is actually closer to Napa, which is 50 miles away. Most visitors choose SFO, though, because it has more daily flights. Another option is to fly into Sacramento International Airport (SMF), about 68 miles from Napa and 76 miles from Sonoma. Wine Country regulars often fly into Santa Rosa's Charles M. Schulz Sonoma County Airport (STS), which receives daily nonstop flights from San Diego, Las Vegas, Los Angeles, Phoenix, Portland, and Seattle. The airport is 15 miles from Healdsburg. ■TIP→ Alaska allows passengers flying out of STS to check up to one case of wine for free.

AIRPORT TRANSFERS

Two shuttle services serve Napa and Sonoma from both San Francisco International Airport and Oakland International Airport. Evans Airport Service ($40) is an option for travelers without cars staying in Napa or Yountville. Sonoma County Airport Express ($34) shuttles passengers to Santa Rosa, Rohnert Park, and Petaluma.

The smallest Uber or Lyft vehicle from SFO costs from $140 to Sonoma, from $160 to Napa, and from $130 to Santa Rosa. A private limousine service like SF Limo Express costs up to $300, depending on how far north you are going.

⊛ Bicycle Travel

Much of the Wine Country is flat—most of the Napa Valley and Sonoma Valley floors, for instance, along with swaths of Healdsburg and Geyserville in Northern Sonoma. With all the vineyard scenery, if you're fit at all you can spend a great day touring the countryside by bike. You can rent bicycles or book guided tours in Napa, Yountville, St. Helena, and Calistoga; in Sonoma County you'll find places in Healdsburg, Santa Rosa, and many other towns.

◎ Boat Travel

Except for Gondola Servizio's romantic 30- and 50-minute Napa River gondola rides that depart from downtown Napa's dock, there's no boat service here. You can rent a canoe for a glide along the Russian River and book guided and self-guided kayak tours on the Napa and Russian rivers. The San Francisco Bay Ferry sails from the Ferry Building and Pier 41 in San Francisco to the city of Vallejo, where you can board VINE Bus 11 to the town of Napa. Buses occasionally fill in for the ferries.

⊜ Bus Travel

The knee-jerk local reaction to the notion of getting to tasting rooms—or the Wine Country—via public transit is that it's impossible or will take forever, but it's definitely possible. Napa, Petaluma, Santa Rosa, and Sonoma are the easiest to visit by bus. Napa and Sonoma both have fairly compact downtowns with numerous tasting rooms, restaurants, and lodgings in their downtown areas. VINE buses connect Napa Valley towns; Sonoma County Transit serves its entire county. Golden Gate Transit Bus 101 heads north from San Francisco to Petaluma and Santa Rosa.

🚗 Car Travel

A car is the most convenient way to navigate Napa and Sonoma. If you're flying into the area, it's almost always easiest to pick up a car at the airport. You'll also find rental companies in major Wine Country towns. A few rules to note: Smartphone use for any purpose is prohibited, including mapping applications unless the device is mounted to a car's windshield or dashboard and can be activated with a single swipe or finger tap. A right turn after stopping at a red light is legal unless posted otherwise.

If you base yourself in the Napa Valley towns of Napa, Yountville, or St. Helena, or in Sonoma County's Healdsburg or Sonoma, you can visit numerous tasting rooms and nearby wineries on foot or by bicycle on mostly flat terrain. The free Yountville trolley loops through town, and ride-sharing is viable there and in Napa. Sonoma County sprawls more, but except for far west the public transit and ride-sharing generally work well.

PARKING

Parking is rarely a problem, as wineries have ample free lots, as do most hotels (some do charge). In some communities, street parking is limited to two or three hours during the day, but reasonably priced municipal lots are usually available.

ROAD CONDITIONS

Roads in the Wine Country are generally well maintained and, except on weekdays between 7 and 9:30 am and 4 and 6 pm and on some weekends, scenic and relatively uncrowded.

🚘 Ride-Sharing

Lyft and Uber are generally dependable, though rides are sometimes difficult to get after 10 pm or if you're far from one of the towns.

🚕 Taxi Travel

Traditional taxis aren't common in the Wine Country, and the few remaining companies provide so-so service. A better option is to use limousine or car services that charge by the hour or trip. Concierges and innkeepers will know the best choices in the area where you are staying.

Executive Car Service Napa Valley is a solid Napa outfit. In Sonoma County try Eco Quick Service or Vern's Taxi, which serves the Sonoma Valley (Sonoma, Glen Ellen, Kenwood, Santa Rosa).

🚆 Train Travel

SMART (Sonoma-Marin Area Rail Transit) trains travel between San Rafael in Marin County north to Santa Rosa's Aiport, with Sonoma County stops that include Petaluma, Rohnert Park, and downtown Santa Rosa. If you're carless and traveling light, you can take Golden Gate Transit Bus 101 and then a SMART train from San Francisco into Sonoma County. Trains don't run late, though. Napa has no commuter train service, but the Napa Valley Wine Train plies former passenger and freight tracks between Napa and St. Helena, offering meals and wine tasting aboard its historic cars, with some excursions including stops at area wineries.

Before You Go

Passport

All foreign nationals must possess a valid passport to enter the United States. This includes infants and small children. In most cases the passport must be valid for at least six months beyond your scheduled return date. Keep in mind that having a valid passport and visa does not guarantee entry to the United States. The final decision about eligibility is made at your place of entry by a U.S. Customs and Border Protection agent.

Visa

Foreign citizens visiting the United States must have a visa—among the most common being the Nonimmigrant Visitor Visa—unless they belong to one of the three dozen or so nations participating in the Visa Waiver Program. To qualify for the waiver program, visitors need an e-passport with an embedded electronic identification chip and must have an updated Electronic System for Travel Authorization (ESTA). ESTA is the automated system used by the U.S. Department of Homeland Security to determine whether an individual traveler qualifies for the waiver program. Note that even if your home country participates in the waiver program, you may not be eligible if you have recently visited a country on the U.S. terror-prevention list.

Immunizations

The United States has no traveler vaccination requirements. The U.S.-based Centers for Disease Control and Prevention (CDC) maintains a list of current infectious-disease outbreaks within the country. The CDC recommends that prospective U.S. travelers from abroad rely on resources within their home country for health recommendations.

When to Go

The weather in Napa and Sonoma is pleasant nearly year-round. Daytime temperatures average about 55°F in winter up into the 80s in summer, when readings in the 90s and higher are typical. April, May, and October are milder but still warm. The rainiest months are usually from December through March.

HIGH SEASON $$$$

High season extends from April through October. Hotel rates are highest during peak harvest, in September and October, with weekends from June through August also busy. Then, and in summer, book lodgings well ahead.

LOW SEASON $$

The Wine Country is more or less a year-round destination, but except for holiday weekends, the first three months of the year qualify as low season. You'll find the least expensive lodging rates at this time.

VALUE SEASON $$

April and May, after the rains have tapered off and vineyards have begun to turn vivid green, can be excellent times to visit Napa and Sonoma. The sky is often sunny, and reasonable rates can often be found even at pricey hotels and inns. Although in some years November and December can be rainy, these two months are also fine times to visit.

Essentials

🛏 Lodging

Inns and hotels range from low-key to sumptuous, with the broadest selection of moderately priced rooms in Napa, Petaluma, and Santa Rosa. Reservations are a good idea, especially during the fall harvest season and on weekends. Minimum stays of two or three nights are common, though some lodgings are flexible about this in winter. Some places aren't suitable for kids, so ask before you book.

APARTMENT AND HOUSE RENTALS
You'll find listings for Airbnb and similar rentals throughout the Wine Country.

INNS
Many inns occupy historic Victorian-era buildings. When rates include breakfast the preparations often involve fresh, local produce. Most have Wi-Fi, but some may not have air-conditioning—be sure to ask if visiting in July or August, when temperatures can reach 90°F.

HOTELS
Newer hotels tend to have a more modern, streamlined aesthetic and spalike bathrooms, and many have excellent restaurants. Most hotels have Wi-Fi, sometimes free. Most large properties have pools and fitness rooms; those without usually have arrangements with nearby facilities, sometimes for a fee.

What it Costs			
$	$$	$$$	$$$$
HOTELS			
under $201	$201–$300	$301–$400	over $400

🍴 Dining

What it Cost			
$	$$	$$$	$$$$
RESTAURANTS			
under $16	$16–$22	$23–$30	over $30

Top Wine Country chefs tend to apply French and Italian techniques to dishes incorporating fresh, local products. Menus are often vegan- and vegetarian-friendly, with gluten-free options.

DISCOUNTS AND DEALS
Stopping for lunch or brunch can be a cost-effective strategy at pricey restaurants, as can sitting at the bar and ordering appetizers rather than entrées. Some places eliminate corkage fees one night a week or more.

MEALS AND MEALTIMES
Lunch is typically served from 11 or 11:30 to 2:30 or 3, with dinner service starting at 5 or 5:30 and lasting until 9 or 10. Restaurants that serve breakfast usually open by 7, sometimes earlier, with some serving breakfast through the lunch hour. Most weekend brunches start at 10 or 11 and go at least until 2.

PAYING
Most restaurants take cash or credit cards, though a few don't accept the latter. In most establishments tipping is the norm, but some include the service in the menu price or add it to the bill. *For guidelines on tipping see Tipping, below.*

RESERVATIONS AND DRESS
Where reservations are indicated as essential, book a week or more ahead in summer and early fall. Except as noted in individual listings, dress is informal.

Essentials

Shopping

Fine wine attracts fine everything else—dining, lodging, and spas—and shopping is no exception. Sonoma County's Healdsburg and Sonoma and the Napa Valley's Napa, St. Helena, and Yountville stand out for quality, selection, and their walkable downtowns.

Hands-down the Wine Country's best shopping town, Healdsburg supports establishments selling one-of-a-kind artworks, housewares, and clothing. South 37 miles in Sonoma, shops and galleries ring its historic plaza and fill adjacent arcades and side streets.

Nightlife

The Wine Country's two largest cities, Santa Rosa and Napa, offer the most in the way of nightlife, with Healdsburg and Petaluma two additional possibilities. Healdsburg has a sophisticated bar scene—and like Napa a popular rooftop hotel bar—though beer lovers might favor the Russian River Brewing Company's original Santa Rosa pub or its full-scale brewpub and beer garden in Windsor (between Santa Rosa and Healdsburg). The pub at Lagunitas Brewing Co. in Petaluma is among the other options for a fresh Sonoma County brew (if in Napa, try Stone Brewing Co.). If you're into sparkling wine, Sigh in downtown Sonoma pours an international selection of bubbles.

Performing Arts

Most A-list talents who perform in the Napa Valley do so as part of one of several festivals, most notably BottleRockNapa (major and indie bands), Festival Napa Valley (opera, theater, dance, and classical music), and the Napa Valley Film Festival (more to promote a film than to perform). Because of the city of Napa's size and proximity to San Francisco, a few downtown venues, among them Blue Note Napa and the Uptown Theatre, attract big-name musical acts, as does smaller, more intimate Silo's. Over in Sonoma County, the Luther Burbank Center for the Arts in Santa Rosa and the Green Music Center in nearby Rohnert Park draw top musicians in all genres and present plays and musicals. Healdsburg's the Raven Theater hosts community theater and the homegrown jazz festival.

Activities

Driving from winery to winery, you may find yourself captivated by the incredible landscape. To experience it up close, hop on a bike, paddle a canoe or a kayak, or hike a trail. Balloon rides depart early in the morning and usually include a post-ride champagne toast and brunch. Packages at bicycle outfitters may include bikes, winery tours, and a guide—or you can rent a bike and head off on your own. The Napa and Russian Rivers provide serene settings for canoe and kayaking trips past trees, meadows, vineyards, and small towns. Half- and full-day self-guided trips are the norm. Among the area state parks with hiking trails are Robert Louis Stevenson in the Napa Valley and Jack London and Armstrong Woods in Sonoma County.

Health/Safety

The Wine Country is generally a safe place for travelers who observe all normal precautions. Most visitors will feel safe walking at night in all the smaller towns and the downtown area of towns like Sonoma. Still, the largest cities, such as Napa and Santa Rosa, have a few rougher sections (typically far from the tourist spots), so you should check with a local before you go wandering in unknown neighborhoods. Car break-ins are not particularly common here, although it's always best to remove valuables from your car, or at least keep them out of sight. The main danger you face in the Wine Country is the threat of drunk drivers. Keep an eye out for drivers who may have had one too many glasses of wine, as well as for bikers who might be hidden around the next bend in the road.

🍷 Shipping Wine

Because individual states regulate alcoholic beverages, shipping wine back home can be easy or complicated, depending on where you live. Some states prohibit all direct shipments from wineries. Others allow the shipment of limited quantities—a certain number of gallons or cases per year—if a winery has purchased a permit to do so. The penalties for noncompliance can be steep: it's a felony, for instance, to ship wines to Utah (this includes shipping the wines yourself). Since selling wine is their business, tasting room hosts are well versed in the regulations. If you decide to send wines back home, keep in mind that most states require that someone 21 or older sign for the delivery.

💲 Money

The sweet life costs a pretty penny in the Wine Country, where even a motel room can cost $200 a night in high season. That said, it is possible to stick to a lower budget if you're willing to stay in fairly basic lodgings, eat at less expensive restaurants, and take advantage of the many picnicking opportunities. Sales tax is 7¾% in Napa County and 8⅛%–9⅛% in Sonoma County. The tax on hotel rooms adds 12%–14% to your bill in Sonoma County and 14% in Napa County. Prices for attractions and activities are given for adults. Reduced fees are almost always available for children, students, and senior citizens.

💲 Tipping

Tipping Guidelines for Napa and Sonoma

Bartender	15%–20%, starting at $1 per drink at casual places
Bellhop	$2–$5 per bag, depending on the level of the hotel
Hotel concierge	$5 or more, if he or she performs a service for you
Hotel doorman, room service, or valet	$3–$5
Hotel maid	$4–$6 a day (either daily or at the end of your stay, in cash)
Taxi driver	15%–20%, but round up the fare to the next dollar amount
Tour guide	10%–15% of the cost of the tour
Waiter	18%–22%, with 20% being the minimum at high-end restaurants; nothing additional if a service charge is added to the bill

🧳 Packing

Dressy-casual attire is the norm at most wineries, restaurants, and accommodations, though except at resorts and fine-dining establishments no one will pay much attention to what you wear. Pack a sweater or light jacket even in summer—it gets chilly when the fog rolls in.

Great Itineraries

First-Timer's Napa Tour

On this two-day Napa Valley survey you'll tour key wineries, taste fine wine, learn some history, and shop and dine.

DAY 1: HISTORY, TASTING, SHOPPING, DINING

Start your first morning at downtown Napa's **Oxbow Public Market.** Down a brew at Ritual Coffee Roasters, or if in need of something more substantial drop by C Casa for tacos, quesadillas, and other gluten-free breakfast items or nearby Model Bakery, for a doughy English muffin. Afterward, tour the culinary garden at the adjacent **CIA at Copia** campus and pop inside and peruse the bronze Wine Hall of Fame plaques on the ground floor. The hall's inductees include Gustave Niebaum and John Daniel of the day's first stop, Inglenook, and Joseph Phelps, whose namesake winery is an afternoon alternate.

From the market drive north on Highway 29 to Rutherford, where film director Francis Ford Coppola spent decades acquiring and restoring **Inglenook,** one of the 19th-century Napa Valley's grand estates. The winery's tour and exhibits provide a fascinating overview of area wine making, and the Cabernets, most notably the flagship Rubicon, are superb.

Departing Inglenook, continue north 3¾ miles on Highway 29 to St. Helena for lunch at **Farmstead at Long Meadow Ranch,** where many ingredients and some of the wines come from the ranch's properties in Rutherford and elsewhere.

Plan your after-lunch tasting based on your preferences in wine and atmosphere. The Super Tuscan wines at Calistoga's always lively **Castello di Amorosa,** off Highway 29 about 6½ miles north of Farmstead, are as over-the-top as the medieval-style architecture. All tastings here include a tour of at least part of the 107-room structure, but you'll see more as part of the higher-end experiences. More serene in both setting and wines is **Joseph Phelps Vineyards.** Off the Silverado Trail about 3 miles from Farmstead, the St. Helena operation serves its collector-worthy wines, including the Cabernet-heavy Insignia Bordeaux red blend, in a masterfully restored redwood building from the 1970s or outside on a terrace overlooking grapevines and oaks. Reach Phelps from Farmstead by heading north briefly on Highway 29, east on Pope Street, south on the Silverado Trail, and east on Taplin Road.

Check into your St. Helena lodgings—the luxurious **Meadowood Napa Valley,** on the Silverado Trail not far from Phelps, and Main Street's pleasant **Inn St. Helena** are two good options. Poke around St. Helena's shops until dinner, perhaps at Meadowood, **Cook St. Helena,** or **Goose & Gander.**

DAY 2: TASTINGS, A TOUR, LUNCH, AND A TOAST

If your lodging doesn't serve breakfast, begin your day in downtown St. Helena with a pastry, quiche, or granola parfait at the original **Model Bakery** location.

After breakfast, drive about 6 miles (south on Highway 29, east on Zinfandel Lane, south on the Silverado Trail, and west on Highway 128, also signed as Conn Creek Road) to **Frog's Leap.** The Rutherford winery's guided tour is educational and entertaining, but you can also taste Sauvignon Blanc, Cabernet Sauvignon, and other wines without the tour.

Spend the afternoon in the Carneros District, known for Chardonnay, Pinot Noir, and sparkling wine. From Frogs Leap,

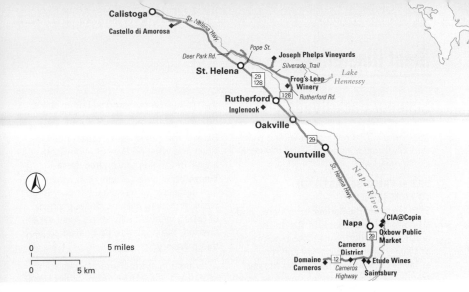

head south on Conn Creek Road and east on Skellenger Lane to the Silverado Trail, where you'll turn south. After about 8 miles, turn west on Oak Knoll Road, which in 2 miles runs into Highway 29. Drive south 7 miles, then turn west on Highway 121 (aka Carneros Highway) for 1¾ miles to reach your lunchtime stop, the **Boon Fly Café.** Part of the Carneros Resort and Spa, the casual café serves fried chicken, gourmet pizzas, and burgers.

From Boon Fly, backtrack ¼-mile east on Highway 121 to Cuttings Wharf Road, which leads south (turn right) to Etude Wines, known for Chardonnay, Pinot Noir, and Cabernet Sauvignon. If you're not hungry, visit Etude's first and then stop by Boon Fly for a late lunch—they serve food all day. Nearby Saintsbury, where reservations are always required, is another famed Pinot house that merits a visit if you have time.

From Etude (or Boon Fly), continue west on Highway 121 to **Domaine Carneros,** whose stately château is modeled after one in France by the winery's founders, the makers of Taittinger champagne. The winemaker here is fond of comparing the sophisticated sparkling wines she

crafts to "Audrey Hepburn in a little black dress." If the weather's fine, sit on the vineyard-view outdoor terrace; if not, repair inside to the Louis XV–inspired salon.

After your tasting, take the scenic route—Old Sonoma Road, north off Highway 121 less than ¼-mile east of Domaine Carneros—to downtown Napa. In town, turn north on Jefferson Street and east on 1st Street. Consider **Angèle** (French), **Compline** (Modern American), or **Miminashi** (Japanese) for dinner.

Great Itineraries

Sonoma Back Roads Tour

Stay strictly rural on this easygoing trek through forests, vineyards, and the occasional meadow.

DAY 1: FROM SEBASTOPOL TO FORESTVILLE

Start Day 1 at **The Barlow** food, wine, and art complex in Sebastopol; it's on the north side of Highway 12 two blocks east of Main Street. Have coffee and a pastry at **Taylor Lane Organic Coffee** and mosey around. Most of the shops won't be open yet, but you can catch a whiff of the complex's maker vibe and plot a return visit.

From The Barlow pick up the Gravenstein Highway (also signed as Main Street and Highway 116 just west of The Barlow), heading north 3½ miles to Graton Road and **Dutton-Goldfield Winery.** The winery, a collaboration between a major grape grower, Steve Dutton of Dutton Ranch, and Dan Goldfield, a celebrated winemaker, built its reputation on Chardonnay and Pinot Noir grown in Russian River Valley and other vineyards that benefit from coastal fog and wind. Dutton-Goldfield also makes a few other whites and reds.

If your tasting goes quickly, without even getting into your car you can sample more cool-climate Chardonnays and Pinot Noirs (Syrahs, too) at nearby **Red Car Wines**—the two spaces share the same parking lot. When you're ready to move on, take Graton Road west half a mile to Graton. Browse the shops and gallery on the hamlet's one-block main drag and have lunch at the **Willow Wood Market Cafe.** The creamy polenta with roasted-vegetable ragout is a signature dish.

After lunch, walk some of the **West County Regional Trail** north from Graton Road a block west of the restaurants—the trailhead is just past Ross Road. Look for the plaques with historical tidbits about the railroad that once operated here.

Back in the car, drive northeast on Ross Road and west on Ross Station Road a total of 3 miles to visit **Iron Horse Vineyards,** known for sparkling wines. The barnlike tasting space has only three walls, providing patrons closeup views of rolling vineyard hills steps away. When needed, the hosts fire up heaters to keep things toasty.

After tasting at Iron Horse, backtrack to Highway 116 and turn north. At Martinelli Road hang a right to reach Forestville's **Hartford Family Winery,** which produces Chardonnay, and Pinot, and old-vine Zinfandel.

Splurge on a night's rest at Forestville's **The Farmhouse Inn** and dine at its stellar restaurant. (A less-expensive option: stay in Guerneville at **AutoCamp Russian River** or **boon hotel + spa** and have dinner at **boon eat + drink.**)

DAY 2: HEALDSBURG AND GEYSERVILLE

Have a leisurely breakfast at your lodging or start Day 2 with a stop at **Pascaline Patisserie & Café,** a treat as much for its French-country ambience as the exquisite pastries. (If you stayed in Guerneville, head downtown to Big Bottom Market.) On weekdays you can dawdle because the first stop, **MacRostie Estate House,** doesn't open until 11 (tastings start at 10 on weekends). From River Road head north on Wohler Road (which begins across from The Farmhouse Inn) and then Westside Road, a 6½-mile drive. Owner Steve MacRostie has grown grapes for decades. His Healdsburg winery sources Chardonnay and Pinot Noir from his vineyards but also many other all-star sites.

After tasting, continue on Westside to West Dry Creek Road, proceed north, and turn east at Lambert Bridge Road. Drive a little past your next stop, **Dry Creek Vineyard,** to the **Dry Creek General Store** and assemble a picnic. After sampling some of the Sauvignon Blanc, Zinfandel, Merlot, and Cabernet Sauvignon made at Dry Creek, the first winery to open (in 1972) in these parts since Prohibition, choose a wine to have with your picnic under the redwoods.

End the day with a Cabernet at the day's final stop, Geyserville's **Robert Young Estate Winery.** From the general store head south on Dry Creek Road ¾-mile, turning left onto Lytton Springs Road, left again (after 2¾ miles) on Lytton Station Road, left again onto Alexander Valley Road 1½ miles later, and left once more onto Highway 128 after 2 miles. When the highway curves sharply right after about ½-mile, continue straight onto Geysers Road and turn right onto Red Winery Road. The namesake founder has two Chardonnay clones named for him, but the robust Cabernet Sauvignons and other wines from red Bordeaux grapes are the reason to come here. Oh yes, and the view down the entire Alexander Valley from the winery's knoll-top hospitality center.

Departing Robert Young, backtrack to U.S. 101 and head south to Healdsburg for a cocktail from the fourth-story rooftop bar of the **Harmon Guest House.** Have dinner with a view here or at nearby **Chalkboard** or **Valette.**

Great Itineraries

The Ultimate Wine Trip, 4 Days

On this four-day extravaganza, you'll taste well-known and under-the-radar wines, bed down in plush hotels, and dine at restaurants operated by celebrity chefs.

DAY 1: NORTHERN SONOMA

Begin your tour in **Geyserville,** about 78 miles north of San Francisco off U.S. 101. Get your bearings and smart advice at the small downtown area's **Locals Tasting Room,** which pours the wines of superlative boutique wineries. Have lunch at nearby Diavolo or Catelli's, then head south on Geyserville Avenue to the French-style château of Healdsburg's **Jordan Vineyard & Winery.** (After 4 miles on Geyserville Avenue, look for the arrowed Jordan signs instructing you to turn left on Lytton Springs Road, Lytton Station Road, and Alexander Valley Road to reach the winery's yellow entrance.) Jordan produces one Russian River Valley Chardonnay and one Alexander Valley Cabernet Sauvignon each year. Enjoy a 2 pm Library Tasting of the current releases and a library (older) red, then head southwest on Alexander Valley Road and Healdsburg Avenue to **Healdsburg Plaza.** Explore the nearby shops; if you're up for more tasting, Siduri and Thumbprint Cellars are good options. **Hôtel Les Mars** and **Harmon Guest House** are two spots near the plaza to spend the night; stay at the Honor Mansion or Camellia Inn for a more traditional bed-and-breakfast experience. The Harmon's rooftop bar is a swank spot for a predinner cocktail before moving on to a meal at **Chalkboard, Bravas Bar de Tapas,** or **Campo Fina,** all close by.

DAY 2: HEALDSBURG AND GLEN ELLEN

Wineries dot the Dry Creek Valley countryside, among them **Comstock Wines** and **Ridge Vineyards,** which open at 10:30 and 11 respectively. In the afternoon head south on U.S. 101 and east on scenic Highway 12 to the Sonoma Valley town of **Glen Ellen.** Hike the trails at **Jack London State Historic Park** and visit the memorabilia-filled museum dedicated to the famous writer, who grew grapes and wrote some of his later works here. To reach the park head west on Jack London Drive from Arnold Drive. If you're itching to taste more wine, Laurel Glen Vineyards and Kivelstadt Cellars downtown and Benziger Family Winery, on the way to the park, are all excellent choices. Dine at **Glen Ellen Star** and stay at the **Olea Hotel** or the **Gaige House + Ryokan.**

DAY 3: NORTHERN NAPA VALLEY

Head east 11 miles from Glen Ellen on Trinity Road, which twists and turns over the Mayacamas Mountains, eventually becoming the Oakville Grade. If you see a new home or construction on the Sonoma County–side slopes, it's likely to replace a residence lost during the 2017 wildfires. Unless you're the one driving, bask in the stupendous **Napa Valley** views as you descend into Oakville. At Highway 29, drive 7½ miles north through downtown **St. Helena** to **Charles Krug Winery,** where Napa Valley wine making got its start in 1861. After tasting here, take lunch downtown at **Market** or **Cook St. Helena** and check out Main Street's shops before heading south on Highway 29 to **Hall St. Helena** (high-scoring Cabernets, impressive art collection) or its homey neighbor, Prager Winery & Port Works. When you're done tasting, continue south on Highway 29 to Yountville for more shopping. Start at **Hunter Gatherer,** at Madison and Washington Streets, and work your way south on Washington past **RH Yountville,** whose The Wine Vault

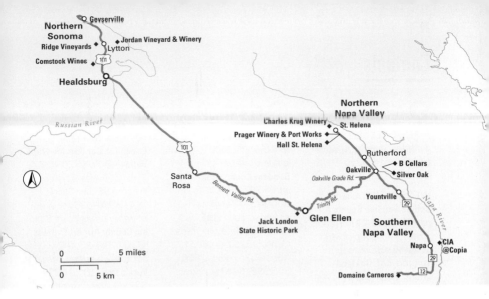

at the Historic Ma(i)sonry Building is a classy sipping stop, as is Stewart Cellars across the street.

Stay overnight at **Bardessono** or the **North Block Hotel,** both within walking distance of Yountville's famous restaurants. A meal at **The French Laundry** is many visitors' holy grail, but dining at **Bistro Jeanty** or Keller's **Bouchon Bistro** will also leave you feeling well served.

DAY 4: SOUTHERN NAPA VALLEY

After breakfast at your lodging or South-side Yountville at Stewart Cellars, head north 3 miles on Highway 29 to **Oakville,** where sipping wine at **Silver Oak, Nickel & Nickel,** or **B Cellars** will make clear why collectors covet Oakville Cabernet Sauvignons. Nickel & Nickel is on Highway 29; Silver Oak and B Cellars are east of it on Oakville Cross Road. After your tasting, have a picnic at **Oakville Grocery,**

in business on Highway 29 since 1881, or have lunch at **Mustards Grill.** After your meal, head south on Highway 29, exiting at 1st Street to visit downtown Napa's **CIA at Copia** food and wine complex (don't miss the museum of culinary equipment upstairs). Backtrack on 1st Street to Highway 29 and head south to Highway 121. Turn west to reach the Carneros District, whose **Domaine Carneros** makes French-style sparkling wines. There's hardly a more elegant way to bid a Wine Country adieu than from the château's vineyard-view terrace.

Contacts

✈ Air Travel

AIRLINE SECURITY Transportation Security Administration. ☏ 866/289–9673 ⊕ www. tsa.gov.

INFORMATION Charles M. Schulz Sonoma County Airport (STS). ✉ 2200 Airport Blvd. ☏ 707/565–7240 ⊕ www.sonomacountyairport.org. **Oakland International Airport** (OAK). ✉ 1 Airport Dr., Oakland ☏ 510/563–3300 ⊕ www. oaklandairport.com. **Sacramento International Airport** (SMF). ✉ 6900 Airport Blvd. ☏ 916/929–5411 ⊕ www.sacramento. aero/smf. **San Francisco International Airport** (SFO). ✉ McDonnell and Links Rds., San Francisco ☏ 800/435–9736, 650/821–8211 ⊕ www. flysfo.com.

AIRLINES Alaska Airlines. ☏ 800/252–7522 ⊕ www. alaskaair.com. **Allegiant.** ☏ 702/505–8888 ⊕ www. allegiantair.com. **American Airlines.** ☏ 800/433–7300 ⊕ www.aa.com. **Sun Country Airlines.** ☏ 651/905–2737 ⊕ www.suncountry. com.

⛴ Boat Travel

San Francisco Bay Ferry. ☏ 707/643–3779, 877/643–3779 ⊕ sanfranciscobayferry.com.

🚌 Bus Travel

Golden Gate Transit. ☏ 415/455–2000 ⊕ www. goldengatetransit.org **Sonoma County Transit.** ☏ 707/576–7433, 800/345–7433 ⊕ www. sctransit.com **VINE.** ✉ Soscol Gateway Transit Center, 625 Burnell St., Napa ☏ 707/251–2800, 800/696–6443 ⊕ www. ridethevine.com.

🚗 Car Travel

American Automobile Association (AAA). ☏ 800/222–4357 ⊕ www.aaa.com. **511 SF Bay Traffic/Transit Alerts.** ⊕ 511.org.

RENTAL AGENCIES Alamo. ☏ 800/462–5266 ⊕ www.alamo.com. **Avis.** ☏ 800/633–3469 ⊕ www.avis.com. **Budget.** ☏ 800/218–7992 ⊕ www. budget.com. **Exotic Car Collection by Enterprise.** ☏ 415/542–6023, 866/458–9227 ⊕ exoticcars.enterprise.com/ sanfrancisco. **Hertz.** ☏ 800/654–3131 ⊕ www. hertz.com. **National Car Rental.** ☏ 877/222–9058 ⊕ www.nationalcar.com.

CAR SERVICES, SHUTTLES, TAXIS Eco Quick Service. ☏ 707/280–3337 ⊕ www.ecoquicktransportation.com . **Evans Airport Service.** ✉ Napa Office and Airport Terminal, 4075 Solano Ave., Napa ☏ 707/255–1559 ⊕ www. evanstransportation.com **Executive Car Service Napa Valley.** ☏ 707/479–4247 ⊕ executivecarservicenapa.com **SF Limo Express.** ☏ 415/990–6364 ⊕ www. sflimoexpress.com. **Sonoma County Airport Express.** ☏ 707/837–8700 ⊕ www. airportexpressinc.com. **Vern's Taxi.** ☏ 707/938–8885 ⊕ www.vernstaxi. com.

🚆 Train Travel

SMART (Sonoma-Marin Area Rapid Transit). ☏ 707/794–3330 ⊕ sonomamarintrain.org.

➕ Health/Safety

Ambulance, fire, police. ☏ 911 emergency.

On the Calendar

January

Winter Wineland. In mid-January, wineries in the Alexander, Russian River, and Dry Creek valleys—including many not generally open to the public—offer tastings, seminars, and entertainment. ⊕ *www.wineroad.com*.

March

Flavor! Napa Valley Several days of dinners, cooking demonstrations, and wine-and-food tastings—many involving top chefs and winemakers—take place in late March. The event benefits the California campus of the Culinary Institute of America. ⊕ *www.flavornapavalley.com*.

Wine Road Barrel Tasting Weekends. In early March, more than 100 wineries open their cellars for two weekends of tastings straight from the barrel. More wineries participate on the first weekend than the second one. ⊕ *www.wineroad.com*.

May

BottleRock Napa Valley. An end-of-May three-day food, wine, and music festival, BottleRock gets summer rolling (and rocking) with acts headlined by the likes of Bruno Mars, the Red Hot Chili Peppers, and Halsey. Tickets sell out in early January when the lineup is announced. ⊕ *www.bottlerocknapavalley.com*.

June

Auction Napa Valley. Dozens of events culminate in the Napa Valley's glitziest night—with an opulent dinner and an auction of rare wines and other coveted items to benefit nonprofit health and other programs. It's held on the first full weekend in June. ⊕ *auctionnapavalley.org*.

July

Festival Napa Valley. This acclaimed mid-July event attracts international opera, theater, dance, and classical-music performers to Castello di Amorosa and other venues. ⊕ *www.festivalnapavalley.org*.

August

West of West Wine Festival. Wineries and grape growers along Sonoma County's coastline sponsor this early-August festival. You can sample Chardonnays, Pinot Noirs, Syrahs, and other wines of small producers with no tasting rooms of their own. ⊕ *www.westsonomacoast.com*.

September

Sonoma County Harvest Fair. This early fall festival at the county fairgrounds in Santa Rosa celebrates Sonoma agriculture with wine and olive-oil competitions, cooking demos, flower and livestock shows, carnival rides, and local entertainers. ⊠ *Santa Rosa* ⊕ *www.harvestfair.org*.

Taste of Sonoma. Chefs, grape growers, and winemakers team up to celebrate Sonoma County food and wine on the first Saturday in September. Dozens of wineries pour current and library releases in the main, tented area and in outdoor VIP lounges, and there are seminars and presentations about wine-related topics. ⊕ *tasteofsonoma.com*.

October

Pinot on the River. Pinot Noir fans flock to the Russian River Valley in late October for a weekend of tastings, seminars, and lively discourse about what makes a great Pinot. ⊕ *www.pinotfestival.com.*

November

A Wine & Food Affair. For this November event, always a sellout, wineries prepare a favorite recipe and serve it with wine. Participants travel from winery to winery to sample the fare. ⊕ *www.wineroad.com.*

Chapter 3

VISITING WINERIES AND TASTING ROOMS

3

Whether you're a serious wine collector making your annual pilgrimage to Northern California's Wine Country or a newbie who doesn't know the difference between Merlot and Mourvèdre but is eager to learn, you can have a great time touring Napa and Sonoma wineries. Your gateway to the wine world is the tasting room, where staff members—and occasionally even the winemaker—are almost always happy to chat with curious guests.

Tasting rooms range from the grand to the humble, offering everything from a few sips of wine to in-depth tours of the wine-making facilities and vineyards. First-time visitors frequently enjoy the history-oriented tours at Beaulieu, Beringer, Charles Krug, and Inglenook, or the ones at Mondavi and Korbel that highlight process as well. The environments at some wineries reflect their founders' other interests: horses at Nickel & Nickel and Tamber Bey, movie-making at Francis Ford Coppola and Frank Family, art and architecture at Artesa and Hall St. Helena, and medieval history at the Castello di Amorosa.

To prepare yourself for your winery visits, we've covered the fundamentals: tasting rooms and what to expect, how to save money on tasting fees, and the types of tours typically offered by wineries. A list of common tasting terms will help you interpret what your mouth is experiencing as you sip. We've also described the major grape varietals, as well as the specific techniques employed to craft white, red, sparkling, and rosé wines. Because great wines begin in the vineyard, we've included a section on soils, climates, and organic and biodynamic farming methods. A handy Wine Lover's Glossary of terms, from *acidity* to *zymology,* covers what you may come across in the tasting room or on a tour.

Wine Tasting 101

Don't be intimidated by sommeliers who toss around esoteric adjectives as they swirl their glasses. At its core, wine tasting is simply about determining which wines you like best. Nevertheless, knowing a few basic guidelines can make your winery visit much more enjoyable.
■ TIP➜ Above all, follow your instincts at the tasting bar: there is no right or wrong way to describe wine.

If you watch the pros, you'll probably notice that they take the time to inspect, swirl, and sniff the wine before they get around to sipping it. Follow their lead and take your time, going through each of the following steps. Starting with the pop of the cork and the splashing of wine into a glass, all of your senses play a part in wine tasting.

USE YOUR EYES

Before you taste it, take a good look at the wine in your glass. Holding the glass by the stem, raise it to the light. Whether it's white, rosé, or red, your wine should be clear, without cloudiness or sediments, when you drink it. Some unfiltered wines may seem cloudy at first, but they will clear as the sediments settle.

In natural light, place the glass in front of a white background such as a blank sheet of paper or a tablecloth. **Check the color.** Is it right for the wine? A California white should be golden: straw, medium, or deep, depending on the type. Rich, sweet, dessert wine will have more intense color, but Chardonnay and Sauvignon Blanc will be paler. A rosé should be a clear pink, from pale to deep, without too much red or any orange. Reds may lean toward ruby or garnet coloring; some have a purple tinge. They shouldn't be pale (the exception is Pinot Noir, which can be quite pale yet still have character). In any color of wine, a brownish tinge is a flaw that indicates the wine is too old, has been incorrectly stored, or has gone bad.

BREATHE DEEP

After you have looked at the wine's color, **sniff the wine once or twice** to see if you can identify any aromas. Then gently move your glass in a circular motion to swirl the wine around. Aerating the wine this way releases more of its aromas. (It's called "volatilizing the esters," if you're trying to impress someone.) Stick your nose into the glass and take another long sniff.

Wine should smell good to you. You might pick up the scent of apricots, peaches, ripe melon, honey, and wildflowers in a white wine; black pepper, cherry, violets, and cedar in a red. Rosés (which are made from red wine grapes) smell something like red wine, but in a scaled-back way, with hints of raspberry, strawberry, and sometimes a touch of rose petal. You might encounter surprising smells, such as tar—which some people actually appreciate in certain (generally expensive) red wines.

For the most part, a wine's aroma should be clean and pleasing to you not "off." If you find a wine's odor odd or unpleasant, there's probably something wrong. A vinegar smell indicates that the wine has started to spoil. A rotten wood or soggy cardboard smell usually means that the cork has gone bad, ruining the wine. It's extremely rare to find these faults in wines poured in the tasting rooms, however, because staffers usually taste from each bottle before pouring from it.

JUST A SIP

Once you've checked its appearance and aroma, **take a sip**—not a swig or a gulp—of the wine. As you sip a wine, **gently swish it around in your mouth**—this releases more aromas for your nose to explore. Do the aroma and the flavor complement each other, improve each other? While moving the wine around in your mouth, also think about the way it feels: silky or crisp? Does it coat your tongue or is it thinner? Does it seem to fill your mouth with flavor or is it weak? This combination of weight and intensity is referred to as *body*: a good wine may be light-, medium-, or full-bodied.

The more complex a wine, the more flavors you will detect in the course of tasting. You might experience different things when you first take a sip (*up front*), when you swish (*in the middle* or *midpalate*), and just before you swallow (*at the end* or *back-palate*).

SPIT OR SWALLOW?

You may choose to spit out the wine (into the dump bucket or a plastic cup) or swallow it. The pros typically spit, because they want to preserve their palates (and sobriety!) for the wines to come, but you'll find that swallowers far outnumber spitters in the winery tasting rooms. Either way, **pay attention to what happens after the wine leaves your mouth**—this is the finish, and it can be spectacular. What sensations stay behind or appear? Does the flavor fade away quickly or linger pleasantly? A long finish is a sign of quality; wine with no perceptible finish is inferior.

Tasting Rooms and Winery Tours

At most wineries you'll have to pay for the privilege of tasting. Fees in the Napa Valley range from $25 to $50 for a tasting of current releases and from $50 to $100 or more to taste reserve, estate, or library wines. In Sonoma County tastings generally cost from $15 to $25 for the former and $25 to $60 for the latter. To experience wine making at its highest level, consider splurging for a special tasting at one winery at least.

In tasting rooms tipping is the exception rather than the rule. Most frequent visitors to the Wine Country never tip those pouring the wines in the tasting rooms, though if a server has gone out of his or her way to be helpful—by pouring special wines not on the list, for example—leaving $5 or $10 would be a nice gesture.

Many wineries are open to the public, usually daily from around 10 or 11 am to 5 pm. They may close as early as 4 or 4:30, especially in winter, so it's best to get a reasonably early start if you want to fit in more than a few spots. ■TIP→ **Most wineries stop serving new visitors from 15 to 30 minutes before the posted closing**

Wine Clubs

If several of a winery's offerings appeal to you and you live in a state that allows you to order wines directly from wineries, consider joining its wine club. You'll receive offers for members-only releases, invitations to winery events, and a discount on all your purchases.

time, so don't expect to skate in at the last moment.

IN THE TASTING ROOM

In most tasting rooms, a list of the wines available that day will be on the bar or offered by the server. The wines will be listed in a suggested tasting order, generally starting with the lightest-bodied whites and progressing to the most intense reds. Dessert wines will come at the end.

You'll usually find an assortment of the winery's current releases. There might also be a list of reserve (special in some way) or library (older) wines you can taste for a higher fee.

Don't feel the need to try all the wines you're offered. Many wineries limit the number of pours to four or five, so don't waste a taste on something you know you don't prefer.

The server will pour you an ounce or so of each wine you select. There might be a plate of crackers on the bar; nibble them when you want to clear your palate before tasting the next selection. If you don't like a wine, or you've tasted enough, pour the rest into one of the dump buckets on the bar (if you don't see one, just ask).

TAKING A TOUR

Even if you're not a devoted wine drinker, seeing how grapes become wine can be fascinating. Tours tend to be most exciting in September and October, when

Filmmaker Francis Ford Coppola owns Inglenook, one of the Nap Valley's great wine estates.

the harvest and crush are under way. Depending on the size of the winery, tours range from a few people to large groups and typically last 30 minutes to an hour. ■ TIP→ **Wear comfortable shoes, because you might be walking on wet floors or stepping over hoses or other equipment.**

Some winery tours are free, in which case you usually pay a separate fee to taste the wine. If you've paid for the tour—often from $20 to $40—your wine tasting is usually included in the price.

At large wineries, introductory tours are typically offered several times daily. Less frequent are specialized tours and seminars focusing on such subjects as growing techniques, sensory evaluation, wine blending, and food-and-wine pairing. These events typically cost from $30 to $100.

Top California Grape Varietals

Several dozen grape varietals are grown in Napa and Sonoma, from favorites like Chardonnay and Cabernet Sauvignon to less familiar types like Albariño and Tempranillo. You'll likely come across many of the following varietals as you visit the wineries.

WHITE

Albariño. One of the most popular wine grapes in Spain (it's also a staple of Portuguese wine making), this cool-climate grape creates light, citrusy wines, often with overtones of mango or kiwi.

Chardonnay. A grape originally from relatively cool Burgundy, France, Chardonnay in Napa and Sonoma can be fruit-forward or restrained, buttery or highly acidic, depending on where it's grown, when during harvest it's picked, and the wine-making techniques applied.

Silver Oak's Healdsburg winery and tasting room are models of energy efficiency.

Gewürztraminer. Cooler California climes such as the Russian River Valley are great for growing this German-Alsatian grape, which is turned into a boldly perfumed, fruity wine.

Marsanne. A white-wine grape of France's northern Rhône Valley, Marsanne can produce a dry or sweet wine depending on how it is handled.

Pinot Gris. Known in Italy as Pinot Grigio, this varietal in Napa and Sonoma yields a more deeply colored, less acidic wine with medium to full body.

Riesling. Also called White Riesling, this cool-climate German grape has a sweet reputation in America. When made in a dry style, though, it can be crisply refreshing, with lush aromas.

Roussanne. This grape from the Rhône Valley makes an especially fragrant wine that can achieve a balance of fruitiness and acidity.

Sauvignon Blanc. Hailing from Bordeaux and the Loire Valley, this white grape does very well almost anywhere in Napa and Sonoma. Sauvignon Blancs display a range of personalities, from herbaceous to tropical-fruity.

Viognier. A grape from France's Rhône Valley, Viognier is usually made in a dry style. The best Viogniers have an intense fruity or floral bouquet.

RED

Barbera. Prevalent in California thanks to 19th-century Italian immigrants, Barbera yields low-tannin, high-acid wines with big fruit.

Cabernet Franc. Most often used in blends, often to add complexity to Cabernet Sauvignon, this French grape can produce aromatic, soft, and subtle wines.

Cabernet Sauvignon. The king of California reds, this Bordeaux grape is at home in well-drained soils. On its own it can require an extended aging period, so it's often softened with Cabernet Franc, Merlot, and other red varieties for earlier drinking.

Grenache. This Spanish grape, which makes some of the southern Rhône Valley's most distinguished wines, ripens best in hot, dry conditions. Done right, Grenache is dark and concentrated and improves with age.

Merlot. This blue-black Bordeaux varietal makes soft, full-bodied wines. Often fruity, it can be complex even when young.

Mourvèdre. A native of France's Rhône Valley, this grape makes wine that is deeply colored, very dense, and high in alcohol. When young it can seem harsh, but it mellows with aging.

Petite Sirah. Unrelated to the Rhône grape Syrah, Petite Sirah produces a hearty wine that is often used in blends.

Pinot Noir. The darling of grape growers in cooler parts of Napa and Sonoma, including the Carneros region and the Russian River Valley, Pinot Noir is also called the "heartbreak grape" because it's hard to cultivate. At its best it has a subtle but addictive earthy quality.

Sangiovese. Dominant in the Chianti region and much of central Italy, Sangiovese can, depending on how it's grown and vinified, be made into vibrant, light- to medium-bodied wines or complex reds.

Syrah. Another big California red, this grape originated in the Rhône Valley. With good tannins it can become a full-bodied, almost smoky beauty.

Tempranillo. The major varietal in Spain's Rioja region, sturdy Tempranillo makes inky purple wines with a rich texture. Wines from this grape are great on their own but often excel paired with red-meat and game dishes.

Zinfandel. Celebrated as California's own (though it has distant old-world origins), Zinfandel is rich and spicy. Its tannins can make it complex and well suited for aging.

How Wine Is Made

THE CRUSH

The process of turning grapes into wine generally starts at the **crush pad,** where the grapes are brought in from the vineyards. Good winemakers carefully monitor their grapes throughout the year, but their presence is critical at harvest, when ripeness determines the proper day for picking. Once that day arrives, the crush begins.

Wineries pick their grapes by machine or by hand, depending on the terrain and the type of grape. Harvesting often takes place at night with the help of powerful floodlights. Why at night? In addition to it being easier on the workers (daytime temperatures often reach 90°F [32°C] or more in September), the fruit-acid content in the pulp and juice of the grapes peaks in the cool night air. The acids—an essential component during fermentation and aging, and an important part of wine's flavor—plummet in the heat of the day.

Grapes arrive at the crush pad in large containers called gondolas. Unless the winemaker intends to ferment the entire clusters, which is generally done only for red wines, they are dropped gently onto a conveyor belt that deposits them into a **stemmer-crusher,** which separates the grapes from their stems. Then the sorting process begins. At most wineries this is done by hand at sorting tables, where workers remove remaining stems and leaves and reject any obviously damaged berries. Because anything not sorted out will wind up in the fermenting tank, some wineries double or even triple sort to achieve higher quality. Stems, for instance, can add unwanted tannins or, if not sufficiently ripe, "greenness" to a finished wine. On the other hand, winemakers sometimes desire those tannins and allow some stems through. A few high-end wineries use electronic optical grape sorters that scan and assess the fruit. Berries deemed too small or otherwise defective are whisked away, along with any extraneous vegetal matter.

No matter the process used, the sorted grapes are then ready for transfer to a press or vat. After this step the production process goes one of four ways, depending on whether a white, red, rosé, or sparkling wine is being made.

WHITE WINES

The juice of white-wine grapes first goes to **settling tanks,** where the skins and solids sink to the bottom, separating from the free-run juice on top. The material in the settling tanks still contains a lot of juice, so after the free-run juice is pumped off, the rest goes into a **press.** By one of several methods, additional liquid is squeezed from the solids. Like the free-run juice, the press juice is usually pumped into a stainless-steel **fermenter.**

During fermentation, yeast feeds on the sugar in grape juice and converts it to alcohol and carbon dioxide. Wine yeast dies and fermentation naturally stops in two to four weeks, when the alcohol level reaches between 13% and 15% (or sometimes more).

To prevent oxidation that damages wine's color and flavor, winemakers almost always add sulfur dioxide, in the form of sulfites, before fermenting. A winemaker may also encourage **malolactic fermentation** (or simply *malo*) to soften a wine's acidity or deepen its flavor and complexity. This is done either by inoculating the wine with lactic bacteria soon after fermentation begins or right after it ends, or by transferring the new wine to wooden vats that harbor the bacteria.

For richer results, free-run juice from Chardonnay grapes, as well as some from Sauvignon Blanc grapes, might be fermented in oak barrels. In many cases the barrels used to make white wines, especially Sauvignon Blanc, are older, "neutral" barrels previously used to make other wines. These neutral barrels

can add fullness to a wine without adding any wood flavors. In recent years wineries have begun using "concrete eggs" (egg-shaped fermenting tanks made out of concrete), mostly to make white wines. Bigger than a barrel but smaller than most stainless tanks, the eggs, like barrels, are porous enough to "breathe," but unlike wood don't impart flavors or tannins to wines. The notion of fermenting wines in concrete receptacles may sound newfangled, but their use dates back to the 19th century (and some say even further).

When the wine has finished fermenting, whether in a tank or a barrel, it is generally **racked**—moved into a clean tank or barrel to separate it from any remaining grape solids. Sometimes Chardonnay and special batches of Sauvignon Blanc are left "on the lees"—atop the spent yeast, grape solids, and other matter that were in the fermenting tank—for extended periods of time before being racked to pick up extra complexity. Wine may be racked several times as the sediment continues to settle out.

After the first racking the wine may be **filtered** to take out solid particles that can cloud the wine and any stray yeast or bacteria that can spoil it. This is especially common for whites, which may be filtered several times before bottling. Most commercial producers filter their wines, but many fine-wine makers don't, as they believe it leads to less complex wines that don't age as well.

White wine may also be **fined** by mixing in a fine clay called bentonite, albumen from egg whites, or other agent. As they settle out, they absorb undesirable substances that can cloud the wine. As with filtering, the process is more common with ordinary table wines than with fine wines.

New wine is stored in stainless-steel, oak, or concrete containers to rest and develop before bottling. This stage, called maturation or **aging,** may last anywhere from a few months to more than a year. Barrel rooms are kept dark to protect the wine from both light and heat, either of which can be damaging. Some wineries keep their wines in air-conditioned rooms or warehouses; others use long, tunnel-like caves bored into hillsides, where the wine remains at a constant temperature.

Before bottling (sometimes earlier), wine-makers typically blend several batches of wine together to balance flavor. Careful **blending** gives them an extra chance to create a perfect single-varietal wine or to combine several varietals that complement each other. Premium vintners also make unblended wines that highlight the attributes of grapes from a single vineyard.

If wine is aged for any length of time before bottling, it will be racked and perhaps filtered several times. Once it is bottled, the wine is stored for **bottle aging.** This is done in a cool, dark space to prevent the corks from drying out; a shrunken cork allows oxygen to enter the bottle and spoil the wine. In a few months most white wines will be ready for release.

RED WINES

Red-wine production differs slightly from that of white wine. Red-wine grapes are crushed in the same way, but the juice is not separated from the grape skins and pulp before fermentation. This is what gives red wine its color and flavor. After crushing, the red-wine **must**—the thick slurry of juice, pulp, and skins—is fermented in vats. The juice is "left on the skins" for varying amounts of time, from a few days to a few weeks, depending on the type of grape and on how much color and flavor the winemaker wants to extract.

Fermentation also extracts chemical compounds such as **tannins** from the skins and seeds, making red wines more robust than whites. In a red designed for drinking soon after bottling, tannin levels are kept down; they should have a greater presence in wine meant for aging. In a young red not ready for drinking, tannins feel dry or coarse in your mouth, but they soften over time. A wine with well-balanced tannins will maintain its fruitiness and backbone as its flavor develops. Without adequate tannins and acidity, a wine will not age well.

Creating the **oak barrels** that age the wine is a craft in its own right. At Demptos Napa Cooperage, a French-owned company that employs French barrel-making techniques, the process involves several elaborate production phases. The staves of oak are formed into the shape of a barrel using metal bands, and then the rough edges of the bound planks are smoothed. Finally, the barrels are literally toasted to give the oak its characteristic flavor, which will in turn be imparted to the wine.

At the end of fermentation, the free-run wine is drained off. The grape skins and pulp are sent to a press, where the remaining liquid is extracted. As with white wines, the winemaker may blend a little of the press wine into the free-run wine to add complexity. Otherwise, the press juice goes into bulk wine—the lower-quality, less expensive stuff.

Next up is **oak-barrel aging,** which takes from a half year to a year or longer. Oak, like grapes, contains natural tannins, and the wine extracts these tannins from the barrels. The wood also has countless tiny pores through which water slowly evaporates, making the wine more concentrated. To ensure the aging wine does not oxidize, the barrels are regularly **topped off** with wine from the same vintage, reducing oxygen exposure.

New, or virgin, oak barrels impart the most tannins to a wine. With each successive use the tannins are diminished, until the barrel is said to be "neutral."

3

Visiting Wineries and Tasting Rooms

It's All on the Label

A wine's label will tell you a lot about what's inside. To decode the details, look for the following information:

■ **Alcohol content:** In most cases, U.S. law requires bottles to list the alcohol content, which typically hovers around 13% or 14%, but big red wines from California, especially Zinfandel, can soar to 16% or more.

■ **Appellation:** At least 85% of the grapes must have come from the AVA (American Viticultural Area) listed on the bottle. A bottle that says "Mt. Veeder," for example, contains mostly grapes that are grown in the compact Mt. Veeder appellation, but if the label says "California," the grapes could be from anywhere in the state.

■ **Estate or Estate Grown:** Wines with this label must be made entirely of grapes grown on land owned or farmed by the winery.

■ **Reserve:** An inexact term meaning "special" (and therefore usually costing more), *reserve* can refer to how or where the grapes were grown, how the wine was made, or even how long it was aged.

■ **Varietal:** If a type of grape is listed on the label, it means that at least 75% of the grapes in this wine are of that varietal. If there's none listed, it's almost certainly a blend of various types of grapes.

■ **Vineyard name:** If the label lists a vineyard, then at least 95% of the grapes used must have been harvested there.

■ **Vintage:** If a year appears on the label, it means that at least 95% of the grapes were harvested in that year (85% if the wine is not designated with an AVA). If no vintage is listed, the grapes may come from more than one year's harvest.

Depending on the varietal, winemakers might blend juice aged in virgin oak barrels with juice aged in neutral barrels. In the tasting room you may hear, for instance, that a Pinot Noir was aged in 30% new oak and 70% two-year-old oak, meaning that the bulk of the wine was aged in oak used for two previous agings.

SPARKLING WINES

Despite the mystique surrounding them, sparkling wines are nothing more or less than wines in which carbon dioxide is suspended, making them bubbly. Good sparkling wine will always be fairly expensive because a great deal of work goes into making it.

White sparkling wines can be made from either white or black grapes. In France, champagne is traditionally made from Pinot Noir or Chardonnay grapes,

and that's mostly the case in Napa and Sonoma.

The freshly pressed juice and pulp, or must, is **fermented with special yeasts** that preserve the characteristic fruit flavor of the grape variety used. Before bottling, this finished "still" wine (without bubbles) is mixed with a *liqueur de tirage,* a blend of wine, sugar, and yeast. This mixture causes the wine to ferment again—in the bottle, where it stays for up to 12 weeks. **Carbon dioxide,** a by-product of fermentation, is produced and trapped in the bottle, where it dissolves into the wine (instead of escaping into the air, as happens during fermentation in barrel, vat, or tank). This captive carbon dioxide transforms a still wine into a sparkler.

New bottles of sparkling wine are stored on their sides. The wine now ages *sur lie,* or "on the lees" (the dead yeast cells and other deposits trapped in the bottle). This aging process enriches the wine's texture and increases the complexity of its bouquet. The amount of time spent sur lie has a direct relation to its quality: the longer the aging, the more complex the wine.

The lees must be removed from the bottle before a sparkling wine can be enjoyed. This is achieved in a process whose first step is called **riddling.** In the past, each bottle, head tilted slightly downward, was placed in a riddling rack, an A-frame with many holes of bottle-neck size. Riddlers gave each bottle a slight shake and a downward turn—every day, if possible. This continued for six weeks, until each bottle rested upside down in the hole and the sediment had collected in the neck, next to the cork. Today most sparkling wines are riddled in ingeniously designed machines called gyro palettes, which can handle 500 or more bottles at a time, though at a few wineries, such as Schramsberg, the work is still done by hand.

After riddling, the bottles are **disgorged.** The upside-down bottles are placed in a very cold solution, which freezes the sed-iments in a block that attaches itself to the crown cap that seals the bottle. The cap and frozen plug are removed, and the bottle is topped off with a wine-and-sugar mixture called **dosage** and recorked with the traditional champagne cork. The dosage ultimately determines the sparkler's sweetness.

Most sparkling wines are not vintage dated but are *assembled* (the term sparkling-wine makers use instead of *blended*) to create a **cuvée,** a mix of different wines and sometimes different vintages consistent with the house style. Nevertheless, sparkling wines may be vintage dated in particularly great years.

Sparkling wine may also be made by time- and cost-saving bulk methods. In the **Charmat process,** invented by Eugene Charmat early in the 20th century, the secondary fermentation takes place in large tanks rather than individual bottles. Basically, each tank is treated as one huge bottle. This comes at a price: although the sparkling wine may be ready in as little as a month, it has neither the complexity nor the bubble quality of traditional sparklers.

ROSÉ WINES

Rosé or blush wines are made from red-wine grapes, but the juicy pulp is left on the skins for a matter of hours—typ-ically from 12 to 36—rather than days. When the winemaker decides that the juice has reached the desired color, it is drained off and filtered. Yeast is added, and the juice is left to ferment. Because the must stays on the skins for a shorter time, fewer tannins are leached from the skins, and the resulting wine is not as full flavored as a red. You might say that rosé is a lighter, fruitier version of red wine, not a pink version of white.

The range of tastes and textures is remarkable. Depending on how it's made, rosé of Cabernet Sauvignon, for instance, can have a velvety and almost savory taste, while rosé of Pinot Noir or Syrah might have a crisp and mineral taste.

Grape Growing: The Basics

Most kinds of wine grapes are touchy. If the weather is too hot, they can produce too much sugar and not enough acid, resulting in overly alcoholic wines. Too cool and they won't ripen properly, and some will develop an unpleasant vegetal taste. And rain at the wrong time of year can wreak havoc on vineyards, causing grapes to rot on the vine. These and many other conditions must be just right to coax the best out of persnickety wine grapes, and Napa and Sonoma have that magical combination of sun, rain, fog,

Pinot Noir and Chardonnay are widely grown in the Russian River Valley.

slope, and soil that allows many varieties of wine grape to thrive.

APPELLATIONS: LOCATION, LOCATION, LOCATION

California growers and winemakers generally agree that no matter what high-tech wine-making techniques might be used after the grapes are picked, in fact the wine is really made in the vineyard. This emphasis on *terroir* (a French term that encompasses a region's soil, micro-climate, and overall growing conditions) reflects a belief that the quality of a wine is determined by what happens before the grapes are crushed.

In the United States, the Alcohol and Tobacco Tax and Trade Bureau (TTB) designates **appellations of origin** based on political boundaries or unique soil, climate, or other characteristics. California, for instance, is an appellation, as are Napa and Sonoma counties. More significantly to wine lovers, the TTB can designate a unique grape-growing region as an American Viticultural Area (AVA), more commonly called an appellation.

Whether the appellation of origin is based on politics or terroir, it refers to the source of a wine's grapes, not to where it was made.

Different appellations are renowned for different wines. The Napa Valley is known for Cabernet Sauvignon, for example, the Russian River Valley for Chardonnay and Pinot Noir, and the Dry Creek Valley for Zinfandel. As of 2019, the Napa Valley contained 16 subappellations and Sonoma County 18, with a 19th, the West Sonoma Coast AVA, expecting approval by spring at the latest. Wineries can indicate the appellation or AVA on a bottle's label only if 85% of the grapes were grown within it.

What makes things a little confusing is that appellations often overlap, allowing for increased levels of specificity. The Napa Valley AVA is, of course, part of the California appellation, but the Napa Valley AVA is itself divided into 16 smaller subappellations, the Oakville and Rutherford AVAs being among the most famous of these. Another well-known

AVA, Los Carneros, overlaps Napa and Sonoma counties, and there are even subappellations within subappellations. Sonoma County's Russian River Valley AVA, for example, contains the smaller Green Valley of the Russian River Valley AVA, which earned status as a separate viticultural area by virtue of its soils and a climate cooler and foggier than much of the rest of the Russian River Valley.

GEOLOGY 101

"Site trumps everything," says longtime Frank Family Vineyards winemaker Todd Graff, by which he means that the specific land where vines grow is more significant than grape clones, farming techniques, and even wine making. In other words, geology matters. Grapevines are among the few plants that give their best fruit when grown in poor, rocky soil. On the other hand, they don't like wet feet: the ideal vineyard soil is easily permeable by water for good drainage.

Different grape varieties thrive in different types of soil. For instance, Cabernet Sauvignon does best in well-drained, gravelly soil. If it's too wet or contains too much heavy clay or organic matter, the soil will give the wine an obnoxious vegetative quality. Merlot, however, can grow in soil with more clay and still be made into a delicious, rich wine. Chardonnay likes well-drained vineyards but will also take heavy soil.

The soils below Napa Valley's crags and in the valleys of Sonoma County are dizzyingly diverse, which helps account for the unusually wide variety of grapes grown in such a small area. Some of the soils are composed of dense, heavy, sedimentary clays washed from the mountains; others are very rocky clays, loams, or silts of alluvial fans. These fertile, well-drained soils cover much of the valleys' floors. Other areas have soil based on serpentine, a rock that rarely appears aboveground. In all there are about 60 soil types in the Napa and Sonoma valleys.

DOWN ON THE FARM

Much like a fruit or nut orchard, a vineyard can produce excellent grapes for decades—with varietals like Zinfandel even a century or more—if given the proper attention. The growing cycle starts in winter, when the vines are bare and dormant. While the plants rest, the grower works to enrich the soil and repair the trellising system (if there is one) that holds up the vines. This is when **pruning** takes place to regulate the vine's growth and the crop size.

In spring the soil is aerated by plowing, and new vines go in. The grower trains established vines so they grow, with or without trellising, in the shape most beneficial for the grapes. **Bud break** occurs when the first bits of green emerge from the vines, and a pale green veil appears over the winter's gray-black vineyards. A late frost can be devastating at this time of year. Summer brings the flowering of the vines, when clusters of tiny green blossoms appear, and **fruit set,** when the grapes form from the blossoms. As the vineyards turn luxuriant and leafy, more pruning, along with leaf pulling, keeps foliage in check so the vine directs nutrients to the grapes, and so the sun can reach the fruit. As summer advances, during what's known as **veraison,** grapes begin to change color from green to yellow (for most whites) or purple (for reds). Before or after veraison, the grower will **thin the fruit,** cutting off (or "dropping") some bunches so the remaining grapes intensify in flavor.

Fall is the busiest season in the vineyard. Growers and winemakers carefully monitor the ripeness of the grapes, sometimes with equipment that tests sugar and acid levels and sometimes simply by tasting them. As soon as the grapes are ripe, **harvest** begins. In Napa and Sonoma this generally starts in August and continues through October. Once grapes are ripe, picking must be done as quickly as possible, within just a day or two, to

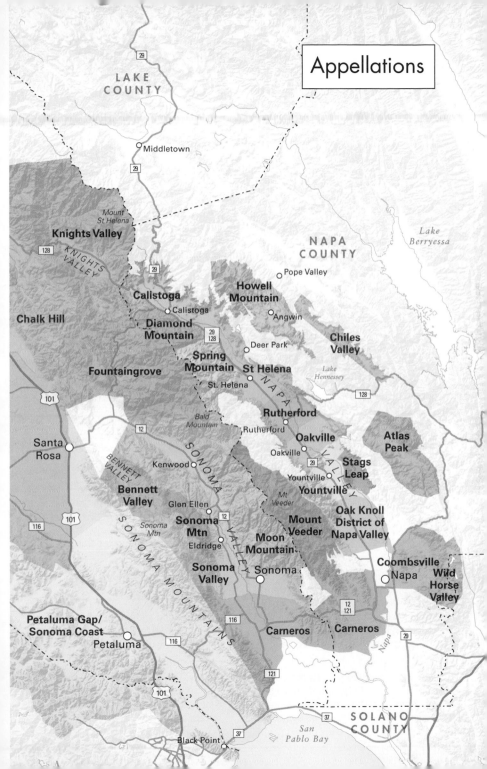

keep the grapes from passing their peak. Most grapes are harvested mechanically, but some are picked by hand. After harvest, the vines start to regenerate for the next year.

Many winemakers purchase at least some of their grapes. Some have negotiated long-term contracts with top growers, buying grapes from the same supplier year after year. This way, the winemaker can control the consistency and quality of the fruit, just as if it came from the winery's own vineyard. Other wineries buy from several growers, and many growers sell to more than one winery.

ORGANIC AND BIODYNAMIC

If, as many grape growers insist, a wine is only as good as the vineyard it comes from, those who have adopted organic and biodynamic agricultural methods may be on to something. But when using terms like *organic* and *biodynamic,* what do vintners mean? Although organic viticulture is governmentally recognized and regulated, it is vaguely defined and its value is hotly debated—just like the rest of organic farming. It boils down to a rejection of chemical fertilizers, pesticides, and fungicides. Biodynamic farmers also reject these artificial agents, and their vineyard maintenance involves metaphysical principles as well.

Even rarer than wines produced from organically grown grapes are completely organic wines. For a wine to be certified as organic, not only do the grapes have to come from organic vineyards, but the processing must use a minimum of chemical additives. Some winemakers argue that it is impossible to make truly fine wine without using additives like sulfur dioxide, an antioxidant that protects the wine's color, aroma, flavor, and longevity.

Very few producers make completely organic wine. To be called organic, a wine must contain certified organic grapes and have no added sulfites.

(Remember that some wines made from certified organic grapes still contain naturally occurring sulfites.)

Biodynamic farmers view the land as a living, self-sustaining organism requiring a healthy, unified ecosystem to thrive. To nurture the soil, for instance, vineyard workers spray specially formulated herbal "teas" (the ingredients include yarrow, dandelion, valerian, and stinging nettle flowers) onto compost spread in the fields. Grazing animals such as sheep maintain the ground cover between the vines (the animals' manure provides natural fertilizer), and natural predators, among them insect-eating bats, control pests that might damage the crop. Biodynamic farmers believe that the movements of the sun and the moon influence plant development, so astronomical calendars play a role in the timing of many vineyard activities.

At its most elevated level, the biodynamic philosophy recognizes a farm as a metaphysical entity that requires its human inhabitants not merely to tend it but to form a spiritual bond with it, a notion that other organic farmers share in theory even if their methods sometimes diverge. Among wineries whose practices have been certified organic are Hall in the Napa Valley, and Preston Family Winery in Northern Sonoma County. The Napa Valley's Robert Sinskey Vineyards is certified both organic and biodynamic, as is the Sonoma Valley's Benziger Family Winery.

Wine Lover's Glossary

Wine making and tasting require specialized vocabularies. Some words are merely show-off jargon, but many are specific and helpful.

Acidity. The tartness of a wine, derived from the fruit acids of the grape. Acids stabilize a wine (i.e., preserve its character), balance its sweetness, and bring out its flavors. Tartaric acid is the primary acid in wine, but malic, lactic, and citric acids also occur.

Aging. The process by which some wines improve over time, becoming smoother and more complex. Wine is often aged in oak vats or barrels, slowly interacting with the air through the pores in the wood. Sometimes wine is cellared for bottle aging.

Alcohol. Ethyl alcohol is a colorless, volatile, pungent spirit that not only gives wine its stimulating effect and some of its flavor but also acts as a preservative, stabilizing the wine and allowing it to age.

American Viticultural Area (AVA). More commonly termed an *appellation*. A region with unique soil, climate, and other conditions can be designated an AVA by the Alcohol and Tobacco Tax and Trade Bureau. When a label lists an AVA—Napa Valley or Mt. Veeder, for example—at least 85% of the grapes used to make the wine must come from that AVA.

Ampelography. The science of identifying varietals by their leaves, grapevines, and, more recently, DNA.

Appellation. *See American Viticultural Area.*

Aroma. The scent of young wine derived from the fresh fruit. It diminishes with fermentation and is replaced by a more complex bouquet as the wine ages. The term may also describe particular fruity odors in a wine, such as black cherry, green olive, ripe raspberry, or apple.

Balance. A quality of wine in which all desirable elements (fruit, acid, tannin) are present in the proper proportion.

Barrel fermenting. The fermenting of wine in small oak barrels instead of large tanks or vats. This method keeps grape lots separate before wine blending. The cost of oak barrels makes this method expensive.

Biodynamic. An approach to agriculture that focuses on regarding the land as a living thing; it generally incorporates organic farming techniques and the use of the astronomical calendar in hopes of cultivating a healthy balance in the vineyard ecosystem.

Blanc de blancs. Sparkling or still white wine made solely from white grapes.

Blanc de noirs. White wine made with red grapes by removing the skins during crush. Some sparkling whites, for example, are made with red Pinot Noir grapes.

Blending. The mixing of several wines to create one of greater complexity or appeal, as when a heavy wine is blended with a lighter one to make a more approachable medium-bodied wine.

Body. The wine's heft or density as experienced by the palate. *See also Mouthfeel.*

Bordeaux blend. A red wine blended from varietals native to France's Bordeaux region. The primary ones are Cabernet Sauvignon, Cabernet Franc, Malbec, Merlot, and Petit Verdot.

Bouquet. The odors a mature wine gives off when opened. They should be pleasantly complex and should give an indication of the wine's grape variety, origin, age, and quality.

Brix. A method of telling whether grapes are ready for picking by measuring their sugars.

Brut. French term for the driest category of sparkling wine. *See also Demi-sec, Sec.*

Cask. A synonym for *barrel*. More generally, any size or shape wine container made from wood staves.

Cellaring. Storage of wine in bottles for aging. The bottles are laid on their sides to keep the corks moist and prevent air leakage that would spoil the wine.

Champagne. The northernmost wine district of France, where the world's only

3

Visiting Wineries and Tasting Rooms

genuine champagne is made. The term is often used loosely in America to denote sparkling wines.

Cloudiness. The presence of particles that do not settle out of a wine, causing it to look and taste dusty or muddy. If settling and decanting do not correct cloudiness, the wine was poorly made or is spoiled.

Complexity. The qualities of good wine that provide a multilayered sensory experience to the drinker. Balanced flavors, harmonious aromas or bouquet, and a long finish are components of complexity.

Cork taint. Describes wine that is flawed by the musty, wet-cardboard flavor imparted by cork mold, technically known as TCA, or 2,4,6-Trichloroanisole.

Crush. American term for the harvest season. Also refers to the year's crop of grapes crushed for wine.

Cuvée. Generally a sparkling wine, but sometimes a still wine, that is a blend of different wines and sometimes different vintages.

Decant. To pour a wine from its bottle into another container either to expose it to air or to eliminate sediment. Decanting for sediment pours out the clear wine and leaves the residue behind in the original bottle.

Demi-sec. French term that translates as "half-dry." It is applied to sweet wines that contain 3.5%–5% sugar.

Dessert wines. Sweet wines that are big in flavor and aroma. Some are quite low in alcohol; others, such as port-style wines, are fortified with brandy or another spirit and may be 17%–21% alcohol.

Dry. Having very little sweetness or residual sugar. Most wines are dry, although some whites, such as Rieslings, are made to be "off-dry," meaning "on the sweet side."

Estate bottled. A wine entirely made by one winery at a single facility. In general the grapes come from the vineyards the winery owns or farms within the same appellation (which must be printed on the label).

Fermentation. The biochemical process by which grape juice becomes wine. Enzymes generated by yeast cells convert grape sugars into alcohol and carbon dioxide. Fermentation stops when either the sugar is depleted and the yeast starves or when high alcohol levels kill the yeast.

Fermenter. Any vessel (such as a barrel, tank, or vat) in which wine is fermented.

Filtering, Filtration. A purification process in which wine is pumped through filters to rid it of suspended particles.

Fining. A method of clarifying wine by adding egg whites, bentonite (a type of clay), or other substances to a barrel. Most wine meant for everyday drinking is fined; however, better wines are fined less often.

Finish. The flavors that remain in the mouth after swallowing wine. A good wine has a long finish with complex flavor and aroma.

Flight. A few wines—usually from three to five—specially selected for tasting together.

Fortification. A process by which brandy or another spirit is added to a wine to stop fermentation and to increase its level of alcohol, as in the case of port-style dessert wines.

Fruity. Having aromatic nuances of fresh fruit, such as fig, raspberry, or apple. Fruitiness, a sign of quality in young wines, is replaced by bouquet in aged wines.

Green. Said of a wine made from unripe grapes, with a pronounced leafy flavor and a raw edge.

Late harvest. Wine made from grapes harvested later in the season than the main lot and thus higher in sugar levels. Many dessert wines are late harvest.

Lees. The spent yeast, grape solids, and tartrates that drop to the bottom of the barrel or tank as wine ages. Wine, particularly white wine, gains complexity when it is left on the lees for a time.

Library wine. An older vintage than the winery's current releases.

Malolactic fermentation. A secondary fermentation, aka *ML* or *malo,* that changes harsh malic acid into softer lactic acid and carbon dioxide. Wine is sometimes inoculated with lactic bacteria or placed in wooden containers harboring the bacteria to enhance this process.

Meritage. A trademarked name for American Bordeaux blends.

Méthode champenoise. The traditional, time-consuming method of making sparkling wines by fermenting them in individual bottles. By agreement with the European Union, sparkling wines made in California this way are labeled *méthode traditionelle.*

Mouthfeel. Literally, the way wine feels in the mouth.

Must. The slushy mix of crushed grapes—juice, pulp, skin, seeds, and bits of stem—produced by the stemmer-crusher at the beginning of the wine-making process.

Neutral oak. The wood of older barrels or vats that no longer pass much flavor or tannin to the wine stored within.

New oak. The wood of a fresh barrel or vat that has not previously been used to ferment or age wine. It can impart desirable flavors and enhance a wine's complexity, but if used to excess it can overpower a wine's true character.

Nonvintage. A blend of wines from different years. Nonvintage wines have no date on their label.

Nose. The overall fragrance (aroma or bouquet) given off by a wine.

Oaky. A vanilla-woody flavor that develops when wine is aged in oak barrels. Leave a wine too long in a new oak barrel and that oaky taste overpowers the other flavors.

Organic viticulture. The technique of growing grapes without the use of chemical fertilizers, pesticides, or fungicides.

Oxidation. Undesirable flavor and color changes to juice or wine caused by too much contact with the air, either during processing or because of a leaky barrel or cork.

pH. Technical term for a measure of acidity. It is a reverse measure: the lower the pH level, the higher the acidity. Most wines range in pH from 2.9 to 4.2, with the most desirable level between 3.2 and 3.5.

Phylloxera. A disease caused by the root louse *Phylloxera vastatrix,* which attacks and ultimately destroys vines' roots.

Racking. Moving wine from one tank or barrel to another to leave unwanted deposits behind; the wine may or may not be fined or filtered in the process.

Residual sugar. The natural sugar left in a wine after fermentation, which converts sugar into alcohol. In general, the higher the sugar levels, the sweeter the wine.

Rhône blend. A wine made from grapes hailing from France's Rhône Valley, such as Grenache, Syrah, Mourvèdre, or Viognier.

Rosé. Pink wine, usually made from red-wine grapes (of any variety). The juice is left on the skins only long enough to give it a tinge of color.

Sec. French for "dry." The term is generally applied within the sparkling or sweet

3

Visiting Wineries and Tasting Rooms

categories, indicating the wine has 1.7%–3.5% residual sugar. Sec is drier than demi-sec but not as dry as brut.

Sediment. Dissolved or suspended solids that drop out of most red wines as they age in the bottle, thus clarifying their appearance, flavors, and aromas. Sediment is not a defect in an old wine or in a new wine that has been bottled unfiltered.

Sparkling wines. Wines in which carbon dioxide is dissolved, making them bubbly. Examples are French champagne, Italian prosecco, and Spanish cava.

Sugar. Source of grapes' natural sweetness. When yeast feeds on sugar, it produces alcohol and carbon dioxide. The higher the sugar content of the grape, the higher the potential alcohol level or sweetness of the wine.

Sulfites. Compounds of sulfur dioxide almost always added before fermentation to prevent oxidation and to kill bacteria and wild yeasts that can cause off flavors.

Sustainable viticulture. A viticultural method that aims to bring the vineyard into harmony with the environment. Organic and other techniques are used to minimize agricultural impact and to promote biodiversity.

Table wine. Any wine that has at least 7% but not more than 14% alcohol by volume. The term doesn't necessarily imply anything about the wine's quality or price—both super-premium and jug wines can be labeled as table wine.

Tannins. You can tell when they're there, but their origins are still a mystery. These natural grape compounds produce a sensation of drying or astringency in the mouth and throat. Tannins settle out as wine ages; they're a big player in many red wines.

Tartaric acid, Tartrates. The principal acid of wine. Crystalline tartrates form on the insides of vats or barrels and sometimes in the bottle or on the cork. They look like tiny shards of glass but are not harmful.

Terroir. French for "soil." Typically used to describe the soil and climate conditions that influence the quality and characteristics of grapes and wine.

Varietal. A wine that takes its name from the grape variety from which it is predominantly made. According to U.S. law, at least 75% of a wine must come from a particular grape to be labeled with its variety name.

Veraison. The time during the ripening process when grapes change their color from green to red or yellow and sugar levels rise.

Vertical tasting. A tasting of several vintages of the same wine.

Vinification. The process by which grapes are made into wine.

Vintage. A given year's grape harvest. A vintage date (e.g., 2018) on a label indicates the year the wine's grapes were harvested rather than the year the wine was bottled.

Viticulture. The cultivation of grapes.

Yeast. A minute, single-celled fungus that germinates and multiplies rapidly as it feeds on sugar with the help of enzymes, creating alcohol and releasing carbon dioxide in the process of fermentation.

Zymology. The science of fermentation.

Chapter 4

NAPA VALLEY

4

👁 **Sights**
★★★★★

🍴 **Restaurants**
★★★★★

🛏 **Hotels**
★★★★★

🛍 **Shopping**
★★★★☆

🍸 **Nightlife**
★★★☆☆

WELCOME TO NAPA VALLEY

TOP REASONS TO GO

★ **Wine tasting:** Whether you're on a pilgrimage to famous Cabernet houses or searching for hidden-gem wineries and obscure varietals, the valley supplies plenty of both.

★ **Fine dining:** It might sound like hype, but a meal at one of the valley's top-tier restaurants can be a revelation—about the level of artistry intuitive chefs can achieve and how well quality wines pair with food.

★ **Art and architecture:** Several wineries are owned by art collectors whose holdings grace indoor and outdoor spaces, and the valley contains remarkable specimens of winery architecture.

★ **Spa treatments:** Work-hard, play-hard types and inveterate sybarites flock to spas for pampering.

★ **Balloon rides:** By the dawn's early light, hot-air balloons soar over the vineyards, a magical sight from the ground and even more thrilling from above. Afterward, enjoy a champagne brunch.

1 Napa. The valley's largest town has plenty of wineries and tasting rooms, and downtown has evolved into a shopping and fine-dining haven.

2 Yountville. Several must-visit restaurants are in this small town whose other delights include its well-groomed main street and downtown tasting rooms; most of Yount-ville's wineries are to the east, with a few to the north and south.

3 Oakville. With a population of less than 100, this town is all about its vineyards, mostly of Cabernet.

4 Rutherford. "It takes Rutherford dust to grow great Cabernet," a legend-ary winemaker once said, and with several dozen wineries in this appella-tion, there are plenty of opportunities to ponder what this means.

5 St. Helena. Genteel St. Helena's Main Street evokes images of classic Americana; its wineries range from valley stalwarts Beringer and Charles Krug to boutique wineries tucked away in the hills.

6 Calistoga. This spa town still has its Old West–style false fronts, but it's now also home to luxurious lodgings and spas with 21st-century panache.

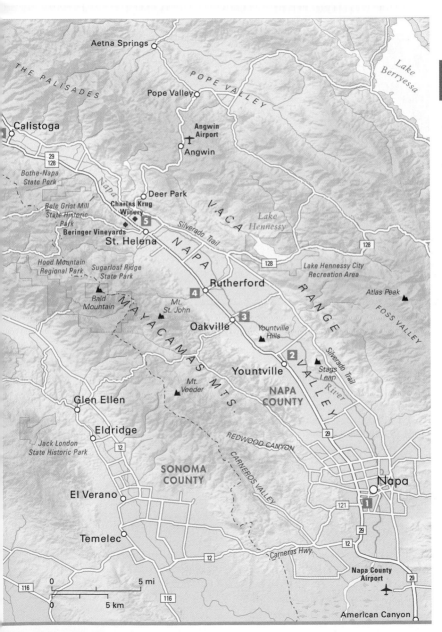

With more than 500 wineries and many of the biggest brands in the business, the Napa Valley is the Wine Country's star. Napa, the largest town, lures visitors with cultural attractions and (relatively) reasonably priced accommodations. A few miles north, compact Yountville is packed with top-notch restaurants and hotels, and Oakville and Rutherford are extolled for their Cabernet Sauvignon–friendly soils. Beyond them, St. Helena teems with elegant boutiques and restaurants, and casual Calistoga, known for its spas and hot springs, has the feel of an Old West frontier town.

The Napa Valley contains only about an eighth of the acreage planted in Bordeaux, but past volcanic and other seismic activity have bequeathed the valley diverse soils and microclimates that provide winemakers with the raw materials to craft wines of consistently high quality. More land is devoted to Cabernet Sauvignon and Chardonnay than any other varietals, but Cabernet Franc, Merlot, Pinot Noir, Petite Sirah, Sauvignon Blanc, Syrah, Zinfandel, and other wines are also made here. In terms of output, though, the valley's reputation far exceeds the mere 4% of California's total wine-grape harvest it represents.

So what makes the Napa Valley one of the state's top tourist destinations and a playground for San Francisco Bay Area residents? For one thing, variety: for every blockbuster winery whose name you'll recognize from the shelves of wine stores and the pages of *Wine Spectator*—Robert Mondavi, Beringer, and Caymus, to name a very few—you'll also find low-frills operations that will warmly invite you into their modest tasting rooms. The local viticulture has in turn inspired a robust passion for food, and several marquee chefs have solidified the valley's position as one of the country's great restaurant destinations. You will also get a glimpse of California's history, from wine cellars dating back to the late 1800s to the flurry of Steamboat Gothic architecture dressing up Calistoga.

Binding all these temptations together is the sheer scenic beauty of the place. Much of Napa Valley's landscape unspools in orderly, densely planted rows of vines. Even the climate cooperates, as the warm summer days and refreshingly cool evenings so favorable for grape growing also make perfect weather for traveling.

MAJOR REGIONS

The Napa Valley has 16 American Viticultural Areas (*see Appellations, below*) but practically speaking can be divided into its southern and northern parts. The southern Napa Valley encompasses the relatively cooler grape-growing areas and the towns of Napa and Yountville, along with slightly warmer Oakville. The northern Napa Valley begins around Rutherford and continues north to even hotter St. Helena and Calistoga.

Planning

When to Go

The Napa Valley is a year-round destination whose charms vary depending on the season. Watching the misty winter fog rising on a rainy day off dark, gnarly grapevines, for example, can be just as captivating a moment as witnessing a summer sunset backlighting flourishing vineyard rows. Because the Napa Valley is the most-visited Wine Country locale, summers draw hordes of tourists, making late spring and early fall, when it's less crowded and temperatures are often cooler, among the best times to come. Harvesttime—from August into November, depending on the grape type and the year's weather—is the best time to visit to see wine making in action. Weekends can be busy year-round. To avoid heavy traffic on summer weekends, it almost always works best to arrive by midmorning, especially if you need to be back in San Francisco by early evening.

Getting Here and Around

BUS TRAVEL

VINE buses, which pick up passengers from the BART (Bay Area Rapid Transit) El Cerrito Del Norte station and the Vallejo Ferry Terminal, run between Napa and Calistoga, with one stop or more in Yountville, Oakville, Rutherford, St. Helena, and Calistoga. Note, though, that buses don't operate on all routes on Sunday. *For more information about arriving by bus, see Bus Travel in the Travel Smart chapter.*

CONTACT VINE. ☎ *707/251–2800, 800/696–6443* ⊕ *www.ridethevine.com.*

CAR TRAVEL

Traveling by car is the most convenient way to tour the Napa Valley. In normal traffic both of the main routes from San Francisco will get you here in about an hour. You can head north across the Golden Gate Bridge and U.S. 101, east on Highway 37 and then Highway 121, and north on Highway 29; or east across the San Francisco–Oakland Bay Bridge and north on Interstate 80, west on Highway 37, and north on Highway 29.

Highway 29 can become congested, especially on summer weekends. Traffic can be slow in St. Helena during morning and afternoon rush hours, though a street-widening project south of downtown has alleviated some of the backup. You might find slightly less traffic on the Silverado Trail, which roughly parallels Highway 29 between Napa and Calistoga. Every few miles, cross streets connect the two highways like rungs on a ladder, making it easy to cross from one to the other.

■TIP→ **Although the Silverado Trail can get busy in the late afternoon, it's often a better option than Highway 29 if you're traveling between, say, St. Helena or Calistoga and the city of Napa.**

4

Napa Valley PLANNING

For information about car services and limos, see Getting Here and Around in the Travel Smart chapter.

Restaurants

Dining out is one of the deep pleasures of a Napa Valley visit. Cuisine here tends to focus on seasonal produce, some of it from gardens the restaurants maintain themselves, and many chefs endeavor to source their proteins locally, too. The French Laundry, the Restaurant at Meadowood, La Toque, Bouchon Bistro, Bistro Jeanty, Solbar, Restaurant at Auberge du Soleil, and Press often appear at the top of visitors' agendas, and rightfully so: in addition to stellar cuisine they all have sommeliers or waiters capable of helping you select wines that will enhance your enjoyment of your meal immeasurably, and the level of service matches the food and surroundings. Another two dozen restaurants provide experiences nearly on a par with those at the above establishments, so if your favorite is booked when you visit, you'll still have plenty of options. *Restaurant reviews have been shortened. For full information, visit Fodors.com.*

Hotels

With the price of accommodations at high-end inns and hotels *starting* at more than $1,000 a night, when it comes to Napa Valley lodging the question seems to be how much are you willing to pay? If you have the means, you can ensconce yourself between plush linens at exclusive hillside retreats with fancy architecture and even fancier amenities, and you're more or less guaranteed to have a fine time. As with Napa Valley restaurants, though, the decor and amenities the most stylish hotels and inns provide have upped the ante for all hoteliers and innkeepers, so even if you're on a budget you can live swell. Many smaller inns

and hotels and even the motels provide pleasant stays for a fairly reasonable price. The main problem with these establishments is that they often book up quickly, so if you're visiting between late May and October, it's wise to reserve your room as far ahead as possible. *Hotel reviews have been shortened. For full information, visit Fodors.com.*

What it Costs			
$	$$	$$$	$$$$
RESTAURANTS			
under $16	$16–$22	$23–$30	over $30
HOTELS			
under $201	$201–$300	$301–$400	over $400

Planning Your Time

First things first: even in a month it's impossible to "do" the Napa Valley— there are simply too many wineries here. Many visitors find that tasting at three or at most four a day and spending quality time at each of them, with a leisurely lunch to rest the palate, is preferable to cramming in as many visits as possible. You can, of course, add variety with a spa treatment (these can take up to a half day), a balloon ride (expect to rise early and finish in the late morning), shopping, or a bicycle ride.

You can maximize your time touring wineries with a few simple strategies. If you'll be visiting a big operation such as Mondavi, Beringer, or Castello di Amorosa, try to schedule that stop early in the day and then smaller wineries after lunch; you're less likely to be held up by the crowds that way. Even during the week in summertime, the afternoon traffic on Highway 29 can be heavy, so after 3 pm try to avoid wineries along this stretch. Plan your visits to wineries on or just off the Silverado Trail for later

Top Tastings and Tours

Tastings

Joseph Phelps Vineyards, St. Helena. Tastings at Phelps unfold like everything else here: with class, grace, and precision—an apt description of the wines themselves.

O'Brien Estate, Napa. The superb wines, self-contained location, and genial hosts make a stop at this Oak Knoll District winery the highlight of many a Wine Country vacation.

Silver Oak, Oakville. The sole wine produced here is a Cabernet Sauvignon blend available for tasting in a stone building constructed of materials from a 19th-century flour mill.

Tours

Beringer Vineyards, St. Helena. Of several Napa wineries with tours focusing on the history of California wine making, Beringer has perhaps the prettiest site.

Schramsberg, Calistoga. Deep inside 19th-century caves created by Chinese laborers, you'll learn all about crafting méthode traditionelle sparkling wines. Back aboveground, you'll taste some.

Setting

Barnett Vineyards, St. Helena. Arrive early at this producer atop Spring Mountain to bask in northern Napa Valley views rivaling those from a balloon.

Hall St. Helena. A glass-walled tasting area perched over the vineyards provides a dramatic setting for sampling award-winning Cabernets.

Food Pairing

B Cellars, Oakville. An open kitchen dominates the B Cellars tasting space, a clear indication that this boutique winery takes the relationship between food and wine seriously.

VGS Chateau Potelle, St. Helena. Sophisticated whimsy is on full display at this tasting room where wines are paired exceedingly well with a top chef's small bites.

4

Napa Valley PLANNING

in the day, though even there you might find the going slow heading south from Rutherford.

The town of Napa is the valley's most affordable base, and it's especially convenient if most of your touring will be in the southern half. If you'll be dining a lot in Yountville, staying there is a good idea because you can walk or take the Yountville Trolley back to your lodging. Calistoga is the most affordable base in the northern Napa Valley, though it's not always convenient for touring southern Napa wineries.

Appellations

Nearly all of Napa County, which stretches from the Mayacamas Mountains in the west to Lake Berryessa in the east, makes up the Napa Valley American Viticultural Area (AVA). This large region is divided into many smaller AVAs, or sub-appellations, each with its own unique characteristics.

Los Carneros AVA stretches west from the Napa River across the southern Napa Valley into the southern Sonoma Valley. Pinot Noir and Chardonnay are the main grapes grown in this cool, windswept region just north of San Pablo Bay, but Merlot, Syrah, and, in the warmer

Napa Valley Wine Train passengers get up-close vineyard views from vintage railcars.

portions, Cabernet Sauvignon, also do well here. Four of the subappellations north of the Carneros District—Oak Knoll, Oakville, Rutherford, and St. Helena—stretch clear across the valley floor. Chilled by coastal fog, the **Oak Knoll District of Napa Valley AVA** has some of the coolest temperatures. The **Oakville AVA,** just north of Yountville, is studded with both big-name wineries such as Robert Mondavi and Silver Oak and awe-inspiring boutique labels, among them the super-exclusive Screaming Eagle. Oakville's gravelly, well-drained soil is especially good for Cabernet Sauvignon.

A sunny climate and well-drained soil make **Rutherford AVA** one of the best locations for Cabernet Sauvignon in California, if not the world. North of Rutherford, the **St. Helena AVA** is one of Napa's toastiest, as the slopes surrounding the narrow valley reflect the sun's heat. Bordeaux varietals are the most popular grapes grown here—particularly Cabernet Sauvignon, but also Merlot. Just north, at the foot of Mt. St. Helena

is the **Calistoga AVA**; Cabernet Sauvignon does well here, but also Zinfandel, Syrah, and Petite Sirah.

The **Stags Leap District AVA,** a small district on the eastern side of the valley, is marked by dramatic volcanic palisades. As with the neighboring **Yountville AVA,** Cabernet Sauvignon and Merlot are by far the favored grapes. In both subappellations, cool evening breezes encourage a long growing season and intense fruit flavors. Some describe the resulting wines as "rock soft" or an "iron fist in a velvet glove." Also on the valley's eastern edge is the **Coombsville AVA.** Cabernet Sauvignon grows on the western-facing slopes of the Vaca Mountains, with Merlot, Chardonnay, Syrah, and Pinot Noir more prevalent in the cooler lower elevations.

The **Mt. Veeder** and **Spring Mountain AVAs** each encompass parts of the mountains that give them their names. Both demonstrate how stressing out grapevines can yield outstanding results; the big winner is Cabernet Sauvignon. Growing grapes on these slopes takes a certain reckless-ness—or foolhardiness, depending on your point of view—since many of the vineyards are so steep that they have to be tilled and harvested by hand.

The great variety of the climates and soils of the remaining subappellations—the **Atlas Peak, Chiles Valley, Diamond Mountain District, Howell Mountain,** and **Wild Horse Valley AVAs**—explains why vintners here can make so many different wines, and make them so well, in what in the end is a relatively compact region.

Napa

46 miles northeast of San Francisco.

After many years as a blue-collar burg detached from the Wine Country scene, the Napa Valley's largest town (population about 80,000) has evolved into its shining star. Masaharu Morimoto and other chefs of note operate restaurants here, several swank hotels and inns can be found downtown and beyond, and nightlife options include the West Coast edition of the famed Blue Note jazz club. A walkway that follows the Napa River has made downtown more pedestrian-friend-ly, and the Oxbow Public Market, a complex of high-end food purveyors, is popular with locals and tourists.

The market is named for the nearby oxbow bend in the Napa River, a bit north of where Napa was founded in 1848. The first wood-frame building was a saloon, and the downtown area still projects an old-river-town vibe. Many Victorian houses have survived, some as bed-and-breakfast inns, and in the original business district a few older buildings have been preserved. Some of these structures, along with a few newer ones, were heavily damaged during a magni-tude 6.0 earthquake in 2014.

Napans are rightly proud of how the city pulled together following the quake and

the wildfires of 2017; visitors to down-town, though, will find little lingering evidence of the temblor or the fires. One cause for celebration in 2018 was the completion of the five-story Archer Hotel Napa and the opening of its rooftop bar (fabulous views). The hotel and the shops and restaurants of the surrounding First Street Napa complex have helped to revitalize a large swath of downtown.

■ **TIP→ If based in Napa, in addition to exploring the wineries amid the surround-ing countryside, plan on spending at least a half day strolling the downtown area.**

GETTING HERE AND AROUND

To get to downtown Napa from Highway 29, take the 1st Street exit and follow the signs for Central Napa. Most of the town's sights and many of its restaurants are clustered in an easily walkable area around Main Street (you'll find street parking and garages nearby). Most win-eries with Napa addresses are on or just off Highway 29 or the parallel Silverado Trail, the exception being the ones in the Carneros District or Mt. Veeder AVA. Most of these are on or just off Highway 121. VINE buses travel between Napa and Calistoga.

VISITOR INFORMATION
CONTACT Do Napa. ☎ *707/257–0322* ⊕ *www.donapa.com.*

Sights

Acumen Wine Gallery
WINERY/DISTILLERY | Highly structured Cabernet Sauvignons from Atlas Peak grapes are the calling card of Acumen, which presents its wines in a combi-nation tasting room and art gallery in downtown Napa. Artist Vincent Xeus designed the hip-elegant space (some of his paintings grace the walls), notewor-thy for its use of glass, brass, copper, and reclaimed wood. It's a plush setting in which to sample the refined output of winemaker Henrik Poulsen. One tasting explores the affordable but very

well-crafted Mountainside wines, another the collector-quality Peak vintages. Guests opting for the Summit Experience wine-and-food pairing receive pours from both tiers, served with gourmet bites prepared by a beloved local caterer. An appointment is required for the Summit tasting and preferred for the Mountainside and Peak ones, though walk-ins are accommodated if possible. ⊠ *1315 1st St. ⊹ Near Randolph St.* ☎ *707/492–8336* ⊕ *acumenwine.com* ⊠ *Tastings from $25* ⊘ *Closed Tues. and Wed. except by appt.*

Artesa Vineyards & Winery

WINERY/DISTILLERY | From a distance the modern, minimalist architecture of Artesa blends harmoniously with the surrounding Carneros landscape, but up close its pools, fountains, and large outdoor sculptures make a vivid impression. So, too, do the wines: mostly Chardonnay and Pinot Noir but also Cabernet Sauvignon, sparkling, and limited releases like Albariño and Tempranillo. You can sample wines without a reservation in the Foyer Bar, but one is required for single-vineyard flights and food pairings. The latter can be enjoyed in the light-filled Salon Bar or outside on a terrace with views of estate and neighboring vineyards and, on a clear day, San Francisco. ⊠ *1345 Henry Rd. ⊹ Off Old Sonoma Rd. and Dealy La.* ☎ *707/224–1668* ⊕ *www.artesawinery. com* ⊠ *Tastings from $35, tour $45 (includes tasting).*

★ Ashes & Diamonds

WINERY/DISTILLERY | Barbara Bestor's sleek white design for this appointment-only winery's glass-and-metal tasting space evokes midcentury modern architecture and with it the era and wines before the Napa Valley's rise to prominence. Two much-heralded pros lead the wine-making team assembled by record producer Kashy Khaledi: Steve Matthiasson, known for his classic, restrained style and attention to viticultural detail, and Diana Snowden Seysses, who draws on experiences in Burgundy, Provence, and California. Bordeaux varietals are the focus, most notably Cabernet Sauvignon and Cabernet Franc but also the white blend of Sauvignon Blanc and Sémillon and even the rosé (of Cabernet Franc). With a label designer who was also responsible for a Jay-Z album cover and interiors that recall the *Mad Men* in Palm Springs story arc, the pitch seems unabashedly to millennials, but the wines, low in alcohol and with higher acidity (good for aging), enchant connoisseurs of all stripes. ⊠ *4130 Howard La. ⊹ Off Hwy. 29* ☎ *707/666–4777* ⊕ *ashesdiamonds.com* ⊠ *Tastings from $40.*

★ Bouchaine Vineyards

WINERY/DISTILLERY | Tranquil Bouchaine lies just north of the tidal sloughs of San Pablo Bay—to appreciate the off-the-beaten-path setting, step outside the semicircular hilltop tasting room and scan the skies for hawks and golden eagles soaring above the vineyards. The alternately breezy and foggy weather in this part of the Carneros works well for the Burgundian varietals Pinot Noir and Chardonnay. These account for most of the wines Chris Kajani, formerly of nearby Saintsbury, makes, but also look for Riesling and Cabernet Sauvignon. ⊠ *1075 Buchli Station Rd. ⊹ Off Duhig Rd., south of Hwy. 121* ☎ *707/252–9065* ⊕ *www.bouchaine.com* ⊠ *Tasting $25, tour (includes tasting) $50.*

★ CIA at Copia

COLLEGE | Full-fledged foodies and the merely curious achieve gastronomical bliss at the Culinary Institute of America's Oxbow District campus, its facade brightened since 2018 by a wraparound mural inspired by the colorful garden that fronts the facility. A restaurant, a shop, a museum, and the Vintners Hall of Fame—not to mention classes and demonstrations involving food-and-wine pairings, sparkling wines, ancient grains, cheeses, pasta, and sauces—make this a spend-a-half-day-here sort of place. One well-attended class for adults explores the Napa Valley's history through eight glasses of wine, and children join their parents for Family Funday workshops about making mac and cheese and nutritious lunches. Head upstairs to the Chuck Williams Culinary Arts Museum. Named for the founder of the Williams-Sonoma kitchenwares chain, it holds a fascinating collection of cooking, baking, and other food-related tools, tableware, gizmos, and gadgets, some dating back more than a century. ⊠ *500 1st St.* ✛ *Near McKinstry St.* ☎ *707/967–2500* ⊕ *www.ciaatcopia. com* ⊠ *Facility free, demonstrations and classes from $15.*

Clos du Val

WINERY/DISTILLERY | A Napa Valley mainstay since the early 1970s, Clos du Val built its reputation on its intense reserve Cabernet Sauvignon, made with estate Stags Leap District fruit. As the winery grew, a shift into higher-production wines using grapes from outside sources occurred, but in recent years the focus has returned to estate-grown small-lot wines. Although known for Cabernet, Clos Du Val also produces Merlot, Petit Verdot, and Pinot Noir, along with whites that include Chardonnay and Sauvignon Blanc. Since late 2018, guests have been sampling these wines in a glass-fronted vineyard's-edge tasting room (reservations recommended but not required) with flashy interiors by St. Helena–based designer Erin Martin. In good weather, hosts retract the glass windows, transforming the tasting room and its patio into a unified space. ⊠ *5330 Silverado Trail* ✛ *Just south of Capps Dr.* ☎ *707/261–5212* ⊕ *www.closduval.com* ⊠ *Tastings from $35.*

Cru @ The Annex

WINERY/DISTILLERY | Prepare for a multisensory, multilabel experience at this tasting room adjacent to the main Oxbow market buildings. The snazzy space successfully integrates Mexican blankets, a backlit laser-etched Napa Valley wall map, outré lighting fixtures, and large monitors screening silent video art. Personable hosts stimulate your taste buds with wines from three labels produced by St. Helena's Vineyard 29 winery. Keith Emerson makes Sauvignon Blanc, Pinot Noir, Merlot, and Cabernet Sauvignon for Cru. Until 2018, Philippe Melka, a preeminent wine-making consultant, crafted the collector-quality estate-grown Cabernets of Aida and Vineyard 29, but Emerson now makes these as well. Tastings are by the glass, flight, or bottle. Walk-ins are welcome, but reservations are recommended on weekends. ■ **TIP➔ In good weather enjoy Napa River and Oxbow Commons views from the outdoor patio.** ⊠ *Oxbow Public Market, 1046 McKinstry St.* ✛ *At 1st St.* ☎ *707/927–2409* ⊕ *www. cruattheannex.com* ⊠ *Tastings from $29* ⊙ *Closed Tues. and Wed.*

Cuvaison Estate Wines

WINERY/DISTILLERY | The flagship Carneros Chardonnay is the star at Cuvaison (pronounced "coo-vay-SAHN"), whose light-filled tasting room (plenty of glass) was constructed from inventively recycled materials. The winery also makes estate-grown Sauvignon Blanc, Pinot Noir, and Syrah under its own label, as well as Brandlin Cabernet Sauvignons, a Zinfandel, and a Malbec from a historic Mt. Veeder estate 1,200 feet above the Napa Valley floor. Some wines can be purchased only at the winery, or sometimes online. All tastings—by appointment only, though hosts usually accommodate short-notice guests—are sit-down style, either indoors or, in good weather, on an outdoor patio whose lounge chairs and vineyard views encourage you to take the time to savor the wines. ⊠ *1221 Duhig Rd.* ✛ *At Hwy. 121* ☎ *707/942–2455* ⊕ *www.cuvaison.com* ⊠ *Tastings from $35, tour and tasting $55.*

Darioush

WINERY/DISTILLERY | The lavish visitor center at Darioush is unlike any other in the valley: 16 freestanding, sand-colored columns loom in front of a travertine

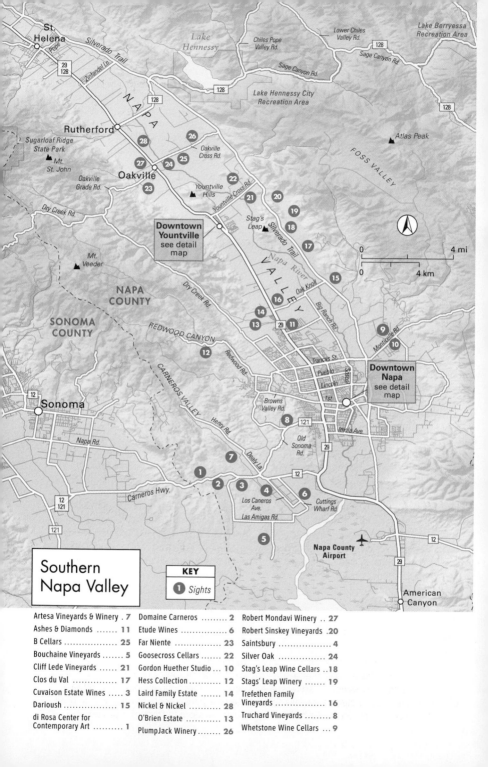

Southern Napa Valley

KEY

1 Sights

Artesa Vineyards & Winery . **7**

Ashes & Diamonds **11**

B Cellars **25**

Bouchaine Vineyards **5**

Cliff Lede Vineyards **21**

Clos du Val **17**

Cuvaison Estate Wines .. **3**

Darioush **15**

di Rosa Center for
Contemporary Art **1**

Domaine Carneros **2**

Etude Wines **6**

Far Niente **23**

Goosecross Cellars **22**

Gordon Huether Studio ... **10**

Hess Collection **12**

Laird Family Estate **14**

Nickel & Nickel **28**

O'Brien Estate **13**

PlumpJack Winery **26**

Robert Mondavi Winery .. **27**

Robert Sinskey Vineyards .**20**

Saintsbury **4**

Silver Oak **24**

Stag's Leap Wine Cellars ..**18**

Stags' Leap Winery **19**

Trefethen Family
Vineyards **16**

Truchard Vineyards **8**

Whetstone Wine Cellars ... **9**

The main château at Domaine Carneros sits high on a hill.

building whose exuberant architecture recalls the ancient Persian capital Persepolis. Exceptional hospitality and well-balanced wines from southern Napa Valley grapes are the winery's hallmarks. The signature Napa Valley Cabernet Sauvignon and other bottlings combine grapes grown high on Mt. Veeder with valley-floor fruit, the former providing tannins and structure, the latter mellower, savory notes. Viognier, Chardonnay, Merlot, Shiraz, and the Duel Cab-Shiraz blend are among the other pours here. ■TIP➔ **On weekdays walk-in parties can taste at the bar, but an appointment is required for them on weekends and always for seated tastings that include cheese-wine pairings.** ⊠ *4240 Silverado Trail* ⚓ *Near Shady Oaks Dr.* ☏ *707/257–2345* ⊕ *www.darioush.com* ☎ *Tastings from $48.*

di Rosa Center for Contemporary Art

MUSEUM | The late Rene di Rosa assembled an extensive collection of artworks created by Northern California artists from the 1960s to the present, displaying them on this 217-acre Carneros District property surrounded by Chardonnay and Pinot Noir vineyards. Two galleries at opposite ends of a 35-acre lake show works from the collection and host temporary exhibitions, and the Sculpture Meadow behind the second gallery holds a few dozen large outdoor pieces. As 2019 dawned, di Rosa's residence, previously a highlight of a visit here, remained closed as conservation efforts continued to restore artworks damaged by smoke during the Wine Country's October 2017 wildfires. ■TIP➔ **Docent-led tours take place daily at 11 and 1.** ⊠ *5200 Sonoma Hwy./Hwy. 121* ⚓ *Near Duhig Rd.* ☏ *707/226–5991* ⊕ *www.dirosaart.org* ☎ *$18* ⊙ *Closed Mon. and Tues.*

★ Domaine Carneros

WINERY/DISTILLERY | A visit to this majestic château is an opulent way to enjoy the Carneros District—especially in fine weather, when the vineyard views are spectacular. The château was modeled after an 18th-century French mansion owned by the Taittinger family. Carved into the hillside beneath the winery, the cellars produce sparkling wines reminiscent of those made by Taittinger, using only Los Carneros AVA grapes. The winery sells flights and glasses of its sparklers, Chardonnay, Pinot Noir, and other wines. Enjoy them all with cheese and charcuterie plates, caviar, or smoked salmon. Seating is in the Louis XV–inspired salon or on the terrace overlooking the vines. The tour covers traditional methods of making sparkling wines. Tours and tastings are by appointment only. ⊠ *1240 Duhig Rd.* ✛ *At Hwy. 121* ☎ *707/257–0101, 800/716–2788* ⊕ *www. domainecarneros.com* 🎟 *Tastings from $12, tour $50.*

Etude Wines

WINERY/DISTILLERY | You're apt to see or hear hawks, egrets, Canada geese, and other wildlife on the grounds of Etude, known for sophisticated Pinot Noirs. Although the winery and its light-filled tasting room are in Napa County, the grapes for its flagship Carneros Estate Pinot Noir come from the Sonoma portion of Los Carneros, as do those for the rarer Heirloom Carneros Pinot Noir. Hosts pour Chardonnay, Pinot Blanc, Pinot Noir, and other wines daily at the tasting bar and in good weather on the patio. Carneros, Sonoma Coast, Willamette Valley, Santa Barbara County, and New Zealand Pinots, all crafted by winemaker Jon Priest, are compared at Study of Pinot Noir sessions (reservations required). ■TIP➜ **Etude also excels at single-vineyard Napa Valley Cabernets; these can be sampled by appointment at seated tastings overlooking the production facility.** ⊠ *1250 Cuttings Wharf Rd.* ✛ *1 mile south of Hwy. 121* ☎ *707/257–5782* ⊕ *www. etudewines.com* 🎟 *Tastings from $25.*

Gordon Huether Studio

MUSEUM | Local multimedia artist Gordon Huether has made a name for himself at home and internationally with his large-scale sculptures and installations. His Napa 9/11 Memorial anchors a section of Main Street downtown, across the street his music-inspired wall installations pep up the Blue Note Napa jazz club, and his sculpture of the late vintner Robert Mondavi and his wife, Margrit, sits atop the CIA at Copia building in the Oxbow District. On weekdays his studio 3 miles northeast of town is open for drop-in visits, where you can see scale models of his latest projects and glimpse his staff (and sometimes the artist himself) at work. ⊠ *1821 Monticello Rd.* ✛ *Near Atlas Peak Rd.* ☎ *707/255–5954* ⊕ *www. gordonhuether.com* 🎟 *Free* ◷ *Closed weekends.*

Hess Collection

WINERY/DISTILLERY | About 9 miles northwest of Napa, up a winding road ascending Mt. Veeder, this winery is a delightful discovery. The limestone structure, rustic from the outside but modern and airy within, contains Swiss owner Donald Hess's world-class art collection, including large-scale works by contemporary artists such as Andy Goldsworthy, Anselm Kiefer, and Robert Rauschenberg. Cabernet Sauvignon is a major strength, with Chardonnays, Albariño, and Grüner Veltliner among the whites. Tastings outdoors in the garden and the courtyard take place from spring to fall, with cheese or nuts and other nibbles accompanying the wines. ■TIP➜ **Among the wine-and-food pairings offered year-round, most of which involve a guided tour of the art collection, is a fun one showcasing locally made artisanal chocolates.** ⊠ *4411 Redwood Rd.* ✛ *West off Hwy. 29 at Trancas St./Redwood Rd. exit* ☎ *707/255–1144* ⊕ *www.hesscollection.com* 🎟 *Tastings from $25, art gallery free.*

John Anthony Vineyards Tasting Room

WINERY/DISTILLERY | Cabernet Sauvignon from Coombsville and Oak Knoll, two southern Napa Valley appellations, is the specialty of John Anthony Truchard, who presents his wines by the glass, flight, or bottle at a rustic-chic storefront tasting room in downtown Napa. As a farmer Truchard emphasizes matching the right varietal and clone, or variant of it, to the right vineyard. Having done so, he creates only 100% single-varietal wines—no blending of Cabernet with Merlot, for instance—meant to be "as beautiful as the vineyards they come from." The Syrah also stands out among the reds. La Dame Michele, a sparkling wine made from Pinot Noir grapes, and the Church Vineyard Sauvignon Blanc are the lighter wines to seek out. ⊠ *1440 1st St.* ✛ *At Franklin St.* ☎ *707/265–7711* ⊕ *www. johnanthonyvineyards.com* 🖪 *Tastings from $10.*

Laird Family Estate

WINERY/DISTILLERY | By its account the Laird family has amassed the Napa Valley's largest vineyard holdings. Nearly all the grapes the Lairds farm are sold to other wineries—the family also makes the wines for some of them—but 3% are withheld for wines that guests can sip at a vineyard-view indoor–outdoor tasting space off Highway 29. Bottlings of note include the Cold Creek Chardonnay from the Carneros District's Sonoma County side, the Phantom Ranch Pinot Noir from the appellation's Napa side, and the Mast Ranch Cabernet Sauvignon, from a hillside property far west in the Yountville AVA. ■**TIP➔ Although pleasant at any hour, the outdoor west-facing patio here is best enjoyed in the late afternoon as the sun sets over the Mayacamas Mountains.** ⊠ *5055 Solano Ave.* ✛ *Off Hwy. 29* ☎ *877/297–4902* ⊕ *www.lairdfamilyestate.com* 🖪 *Tastings from $20.*

Mark Herold Wines

WINERY/DISTILLERY | Mark Herold, whose debut Merus Cabernet vintage led to prestigious wine-making and consulting opportunities, sold that cult brand in 2008 and for the past several years has made collector-quality Cabernets bearing his name. For a few years after the sale, while contractually prohibited from making Cabernet, Herold developed zesty, agreeably priced wines from mostly Spanish and Rhône varietals. Guests sample flights of the winemaker's diverse lineup at a peppy storefront tasting room in Napa's Oxbow District. Walk-ins are welcome, but reserve ahead for a food–wine pairing. ■**TIP➔ The tasting room, which also serves wines by the glass, stays open until 6 or 7 pm, making it a swell last stop of the day, especially if you'll be dining nearby.** ⊠ *710 1st St.* ✛ *At McKinstry St.* ☎ *707/256–3111* ⊕ *www. markheroldwines.com* 🖪 *Tastings from $20.*

Napa Valley Distillery

WINERY/DISTILLERY | Entertaining educators keep the proceedings light and lively at this distillery, which bills itself as Napa's first since Prohibition. NVD makes gin, rum, whiskey, and the flagship grape-based vodka, along with brandies and barrel-aged bottled cocktails that include Manhattans (the top seller), mai tais, and negronis. Visits, always by appointment, begin with a tasting upstairs in the "art deco speakeasy with a tiki twist" Grand Salon, where lesson number one is how to properly sip spirits (spoiler: don't swirl your glass like you would with wine). Back downstairs in the production facility, you'll learn the basics of alcohol and distilling. ■**TIP➔ If you just want to sample the wares, the distillery operates a tasting bar in the main Oxbow Public Market building.** ⊠ *2485 Stockton St.* ✛ *Off California Blvd.* ☎ *707/265–6272* ⊕ *www.napadistillery.com* 🖪 *Tasting $30* ☉ *Closed Wed.*

Napa Valley Wine Train

TOUR—SIGHT | Guests on this Napa Valley attraction, a fixture since 1989, ride the same rails along which, from the 1860s to the 1930s, trains transported passengers as far north as Calistoga's spas and hauled wine and other agricultural freight south toward San Francisco. The rolling stock includes restored Pullman railroad cars and a two-story Vista Dome car with a curved glass roof that travel a leisurely, scenic route between Napa and St.

Helena. Patrons on the Quattro Vino tour enjoy a four-course lunch and tastings at four wineries, with stops at one or more wineries incorporated into other tours. Some rides involve no winery stops, and themed trips are scheduled throughout the year. ■ TIP➤ It's best to make this trip during the day, when you can enjoy the vineyard views. ⊠ 1275 McKinstry St. ⊹ Off 1st St. ☎ 707/253–2111, 800/427–4124 ⊕ www.winetrain.com ⊠ From $149.

★ O'Brien Estate

WINERY/DISTILLERY | Barb and Bart O'Brien live on and operate this 40-acre Oak Knoll District estate, where in good weather guests sip wines at an outdoor tasting area adjoining the vineyard that produces the fruit for them. It's a singular setting in which to enjoy Merlot, Cabernet Sauvignon, Bordeaux-style red blends, Sauvignon Blanc, and Chardonnay wines that indeed merit the mid-90s (sometimes higher) scores they garner from critics. Club members snap up most of the bottlings, with the rest sold at intimate tastings held four times daily (reservations are required; book well ahead). All visits include vineyard and winery tours and an account of Barb and Bart's interesting path to winery ownership. ■ TIP➤ The superb wines and genial hosts make a stop here the highlight of many a Wine Country vacation. ⊠ 1200 Orchard Ave. ⊹ Off Solano Ave. ☎ 707/252–8463 ⊕ www. obrienestate.com ⊠ Tasting $55.

★ Oxbow Public Market

MARKET | The market's two dozen stands provide an introduction to Northern California's diverse artisanal food products. Swoon over decadent charcuterie at the Fatted Calf (great sandwiches, too), slurp oysters at Hog Island, or chow down on vegetarian, duck, or salmon tacos at C Casa. You can sample wine (and cheese) at the Oxbow Cheese & Wine Merchant, ales at Fieldwork Brewery's taproom, and barrel-aged cocktails at the Napa Valley Distillery. Napa Bookmine is among the few nonfood vendors here. ■ TIP➤ If you don't mind eating at the counter, you can select a steak at the Five Dot Ranch meat stand and pay $10 above market price ($14 with two sides) to have it grilled on the spot, a real deal for a quality slab. ⊠ 610 and 644 1st St. ⊹ At McKinstry St. ⊕ www.oxbowpublicmarket.com.

RAD Napa (Rail Arts District Napa)

PUBLIC ART | . An ambitious beautification project also promoting democracy in art, outdoor wellness, and a few other ideals, RAD Napa commissions artists to paint murals on buildings, fences, and utility boxes along or near downtown Napa's railroad tracks. Sculptures and other installations are also involved. Many of the outdoor artworks can be viewed along the Napa Valley Wine Trail pedestrian and biking path or aboard the Napa Valley Wine Train. The CIA at Copia's two-story mural of its garden, painted by Hueman (née Allison Tinati), is part of the project. ⊠ Napa ☎ 707/501–5355 ⊕ www.radnapa.org.

RiverHouse by Bespoke Collection

MUSEUM | Commune with artworks by modern and contemporary masters at this tasting room operated by Aerena Galleries. Hosts pour wines from two labels—Aerena Wines and Blackbird Vineyards—both crafted by Aaron Pott and Kyle Mizuno. Grapes for the Aerena wines, among them Chardonnay, rosé, and Cabernet Sauvignon, come from several appellations, with the ones for Blackbird strictly Napa Valley. Smooth yet complex "Right Bank" Bordeaux reds emphasizing Merlot and Cabernet Franc are Blackbird's calling card. Tastings take place inside the high-ceilinged, vaguely industrial-loft gallery space or on the riverfront patio just outside. ■ TIP➤ "Bespoke" luxury experiences include one tasting that involves next-door neighbor Morimoto Napa's cuisine and another that's conducted airborne in a restored DC-3 plane. ⊠ 604 Main St. ⊹ At 5th St. ☎ 707/252–4440 ⊕ riverhouse.

Both the art and the wine inspire at the Hess Collection.

bespokecollection.com ✉ Tastings from $55.

Saintsbury

WINERY/DISTILLERY | Back in 1981, when Saintsbury released its first Pinot Noir, Los Carneros had yet to earn its current reputation as a setting in which the often finicky varietal could prosper. This pioneer helped disprove the conventional wisdom that only the French could produce great Pinot Noir, and with their subtlety and balance Saintsbury's wines continue to please. In recent years the winery has expanded its reach to the Green Valley of the Russian River Valley, the Sonoma Coast, and Mendocino County's Anderson Valley with equally impressive results. Named for the English author and critic George Saintsbury (he wrote *Notes on a Cellar-Book*), this unpretentious operation also makes Chardonnay. Visits are by appointment only. ■TIP➔ **When the weather cooperates, tastings take place in a rose garden.** ✉ 1500 Los Carneros Ave. ✛ South off Hwy. 121 and east (left) on Withers Rd.

for entrance ☎ 707/252–0592 ⊕ www. saintsbury.com ✉ Tastings from $35.

Stag's Leap Wine Cellars

WINERY/DISTILLERY | A 1973 Stag's Leap Wine Cellars S.L.V. Cabernet Sauvignon put this winery and the Napa Valley on the enological map by placing first in the famous Judgment of Paris tasting of 1976. The grapes for that wine came from a vineyard visible from the stone-and-glass Fay Outlook & Visitor Center, which has broad views of a second fabled Cabernet vineyard (Fay) and the promontory that gives both the winery and the Stags Leap District AVA their names. The top-of-the-line Cabernets from these vineyards are poured at the Estate Collection Tasting. Among the other options are a cave tour and tasting and special wine-and-food pairings, all by appointment. ■TIP➔ **When the weather's right, two patios with the same views as the tasting room fill up quickly.** ✉ 5766 Silverado Trail, at Wappo Hill Rd. ☎ 707/261–6410 ⊕ www.cask23.com ✉ Tasting $45, tours from $75.

The Paris Wine Tasting of 1976

The event that changed the California wine industry forever took place half a world away, in Paris. To celebrate the American Bicentennial, Steven Spurrier, a British wine merchant, sponsored a comparative blind tasting of California Cabernet Sauvignon and Chardonnay wines against Bordeaux Cabernet blends and French white Burgundies. The tasters were French and included journalists and producers.

And the Winners Were...

The 1973 Stag's Leap Wine Cellars Cabernet Sauvignon came in first among the reds, and the 1973 Chateau Montelena Chardonnay edged out the French and other California whites. The so-called Judgment of Paris stunned the wine establishment, as it was the first serious challenge to the supremacy of French wines. When the shouting died down, the rush was on. Tourists and winemakers streamed into the Napa Valley and interest grew so strong it helped revitalize Sonoma County's wine industry as well.

Stags' Leap Winery

WINERY/DISTILLERY | A must for history buffs, this winery was established in 1893 in a bowl-shaped micro valley at the base of the Stags Leap Palisades. Three years earlier its original owners erected the Manor House, which reopened in 2016 after restoration of its castlelike stone facade and redwood-paneled interior. The home, whose open-air porch seems out of a flapper-era movie set, hosts elegant, appointment-only seated tastings of equally refined wines by the Bordeaux-born Christophe Paubert. Estate Cabernet Sauvignons, Merlot, and Petite Sirah, one bottling of the last varietal from vines planted in 1929, are the calling cards. Paubert also makes a blend of these three red grapes, along with Viognier, Chardonnay, and rosé. Some tastings take place on the porch, others inside; all require an appointment and include a tour of the property and tales of its storied past. ✉ *6150 Silverado Trail ✛ ¾ mile south of Yountville Cross Rd.* ☎ *707/257-5790* ⊕ *stagsleap.com* 🍷 *Tastings from $65.*

★ St. Clair Brown Winery & Brewery

WINERY/DISTILLERY | Tastings at this women-run "urban winery"—and, since 2017, nanobrewery—a few blocks north of downtown take place in an intimate, light-filled greenhouse or a colorful culinary garden. Winemaker Elaine St. Clair, well regarded for stints at Domaine Carneros and Black Stallion, produces elegant wines—crisp yet complex whites and smooth, French-style reds whose stars include Cabernet Sauvignon and Syrah. While pursuing her wine-making degree, St. Clair also studied brewing; a few of her light-, medium-, and full-bodied brews are always on tap. You can taste the wines or beers by the glass or flight or enjoy them paired with appetizers that might include pork rillette with pickled tomatoes from the garden or addictive almonds roasted with rosemary, lemon zest, and lemon olive oil. Tuesday and Wednesday visits are by appointment only. ✉ *816 Vallejo St. ✛ Off Soscol Ave.* ☎ *707/255-5591* ⊕ *www.stclairbrown.com* 🍷 *Tastings from $12 flights, from $4 by the glass.*

★ Studio by Feast it Forward

WINERY/DISTILLERY | Fans of the online Feast it Forward lifestyle network flock to its brick-and-mortar location in downtown Napa to experience food, wine, and entertainment with a philanthropic component—at least 5% of the proceeds goes to charity. On any given day, tastings of impressive boutique wines might be taking place downstairs, a sommelier-taught class upstairs, and a musician or other performer mesmerizing millennials in the covered, open-air performance space out back. The upbeat vibe, good intentions, high-quality food and kitchenware products, and well-curated events make this Oxbow District space worth investigating. ⊠ 1031 McKinstry St. ✛ Near 1st St. ☎ 707/819-2403 ⊕ www.feastitforward.com ☜ Tastings from $20.

★ Trefethen Family Vineyards

WINERY/DISTILLERY | Superior estate Chardonnay, Dry Riesling, Cabernet Sauvignon, Merlot, Pinot Noir, and the Malbec-heavy Dragon's Tooth blend are the trademarks of this family-run winery founded in 1968. To find out how well Trefethen wines age, book a reserve tasting, which includes pours of limited-release wines and one or two older vintages. The terra-cotta-color historic winery on-site, built in 1886, was designed with a gravity-flow system, with the third story for crushing, the second for fermenting the resulting juice, and the first for aging. The wooden building suffered severe damage in the 2014 Napa earthquake. After extensive renovations, it reopened in 2017 as the main tasting room. Reserve and elevated tastings take place at the early-1900s Arts and Crafts–style Villa, situated amid gardens. Reservations, preferred for all tastings, are required for some. ⊠ 1160 Oak Knoll Ave. ✛ Off Hwy. 29 ☎ 866/895-7696 ⊕ www.trefethen.com ☜ Tastings from $25, tour $45.

Truchard Vineyards

WINERY/DISTILLERY | Diversity is the name of the game at this family-owned winery on prime acreage amid the Carneros District's rolling hills. High-profile Napa Valley wineries purchase most of the grapes grown here, but some of the best are held back for estate-only wines—the Chardonnays and Pinot Noirs the region is known for, along with Roussanne, Zinfandel, Merlot, Syrah, Cabernet Sauvignon, and a few others. You must call ahead to taste either current releases or a few of them and two older wines, but if you do, you'll be rewarded with a casual experience tailored to your interests. The included tour takes in the vineyards and the wine cave. ■ TIP➔ Climb the small hill near the winery for a photo-op view of the pond and the pen of Angora goats over the ridge. ⊠ 3234 Old Sonoma Rd. ✛ Off Hwy. 121 ☎ 707/253-7153 ⊕ www.truchardvineyards.com ☜ Tasting from $40.

★ Whetstone Wine Cellars

WINERY/DISTILLERY | Pinot Noir, Syrah, and Viognier are the specialties of this boutique appointment only winery with a tasting room inside a 19th-century French-style château. Hamden McIntyre, whose other Napa Valley wineries include the majestic Inglenook in Rutherford and Greystone (now the Culinary Institute of America) in St. Helena, designed this less showy yet still princely 1885 stone structure. The tree-shaded front lawn is a civilized spot in good weather to enjoy a full tasting or a glass of wine ($20). The influence of winemaker Jamey Whetstone's mentor Larry Turley, known for velvety Zinfandels, is most evident in the Pinot and the Syrah, but their élan is Whetstone's alone. ⊠ 1075 Atlas Peak Rd. ✛ Off Monticello Rd. ☎ 707/254-0600 ⊕ www.whetstonewinecellars.com ☜ Tastings from $45.

4

Napa Valley NAPA

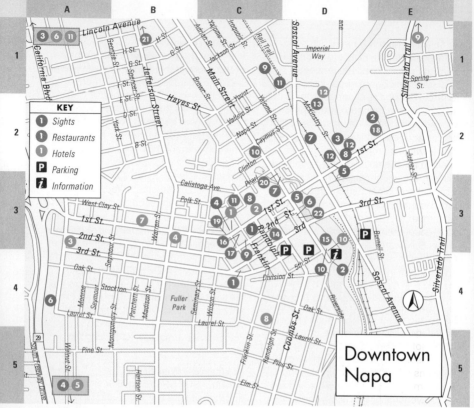

Downtown Napa

Sights ▼

1 Acumen Wine Gallery... **C3**
2 CIA at Copia **E2**
3 Cru @ The Annex....... **D2**
4 John Anthony Vineyards Tasting Room............. **C3**
5 Mark Herold Wines..... **D2**
6 Napa Valley Distillery .. **A4**
7 Napa Valley Wine Train..................... **D2**
8 Oxbow Public Market.. **D2**
9 RAD Napa **C1**
10 RiverHouse by Bespoke Collection................ **D3**
11 St. Clair Brown Winery & Brewery.............. **C1**
12 Studio by Feast it Forward................ **D2**

Restaurants ▼

1 Alexis Baking Company and Café **C4**
2 Angèle **D4**
3 Bistro Don Giovanni **A1**
4 The Boon Fly Café **A5**
5 Bounty Hunter Wine Bar & Smokin' BBQ......... **D3**
6 Carpe Diem Wine Bar.. **D3**
7 Cole's Chop House...... **D3**
8 Compline................. **C3**
9 Grace's Table............. **C3**
10 Gran Eléctrica............ **C2**
11 Kenzo..................... **C3**
12 Kitchen Door **D2**
13 La Toque **D2**
14 Miminashi **D3**
15 Morimoto Napa **D3**
16 Norman Rose Tavern.... **C3**
17 Oenotri **C3**
18 Restaurant at CIA Copia **E2**
19 Tarla Mediterranean Grill **C3**
20 Torc....................... **C2**
21 Yak & Yeti **B1**
22 ZuZu **D3**

Hotels ▼

1 Andaz Napa **C3**
2 Archer Hotel Napa **C3**
3 Best Western Plus Elm House Inn........... **A3**
4 Blackbird Inn............ **B3**
5 Carneros Resort & Spa.................... **A5**
6 Cottages of Napa Valley................... **A1**
7 The Inn on First **B3**
8 Inn on Randolph **C4**
9 Milliken Creek Inn **E1**
10 Napa River Inn **D3**
11 Senza Hotel.............. **A1**
12 Westin Verasa Napa ... **D1**

🍴 Restaurants

★ Alexis Baking Company and Café

$ | **AMERICAN** | Visitors instantly take to this endearing spot for coffee and pastries, full breakfasts (served all day), and lunches with sandwiches served on homemade potato buns. The namesake owner, who opened her bakery in 1985, sets the tone—the scones, blueberry muffins, lemon-ricotta pancakes, egg sandwiches, and other menu items are prepared with care and offered in bonhomie. **Known for:** homemade soups; homespun vibe; breakfast until 3 daily except Sunday (until 2). [$] *Average main: $11* ✉ *1517 3rd St.* ☎ *707/258–1827* 🌐 *www.abcnapa.com.*

Angèle

$$$$ | **FRENCH** | A vaulted wood-beamed ceiling and paper-topped tables spaced close together set the scene for romance at this softly lit French bistro inside an 1890s boathouse. Look for clever variations on classic dishes such as croque monsieur (grilled Parisian ham and Gruyère) and Niçoise salad for lunch, steamed mussels with white wine–and–saffron broth for dinner, and, sometimes, crispy veal sweetbreads at both. **Known for:** classic bistro cuisine; romantic setting; outdoor seating in good weather under bright-yellow umbrellas. [$] *Average main: $34* ✉ *540 Main St.* ↔ *At 5th St.* ☎ *707/252–8115* 🌐 *www.angelerestaurant.com.*

Bistro Don Giovanni

$$$ | **ITALIAN** | The chefs at this boisterous bistro with a roadhouse feel prepare inventive, comforting Cal-Italian food. Regulars, some since the restaurant's mid-1990s debut, favor the fritto misto (lightly battered deep-fried calamari, onions, fennel, and rock shrimp), spinach ravioli with lemon-cream or tomato sauce, slow-braised lamb shank with Tuscan-bean ragout, and wood-fired prosciutto pizza. **Known for:** robust cuisine; patio and lawn dining in good weather; specialty cocktails and varied wines by the glass. [$] *Average main: $27* ✉ *4110 Howard La.* ↔ *Off Hwy. 29* ☎ *707/224–3300* 🌐 *www.bistrodongiovanni.com.*

The Boon Fly Cafe

$$ | **MODERN AMERICAN** | This small spot that melds rural charm with industrial chic serves updated American classics such as fried chicken (free-range in this case), burgers (with Kobe beef), and pork chops (with lush tomato fondue). The flatbreads, including a smoked salmon one made with fromage blanc, Parmesan, lemon crème fraîche, and capers, are worth a try. **Known for:** open all day; signature doughnuts for breakfast; cocktail selection and wines by the glass. [$] *Average main: $22* ✉ *Carneros Resort and Spa, 4048 Sonoma Hwy.* ☎ *707/299–4870* 🌐 *www.boonflycafe.com* ☞ *Reservations for dinner only.*

Bounty Hunter Wine Bar & Smokin' BBQ

$$ | **AMERICAN** | Every dish on the small menu at this wine store, wine bar, and restaurant is a standout, including the pulled-pork and beef brisket sandwiches served with three types of barbecue sauce, the meltingly tender St. Louis–style ribs, and the signature beer-can chicken (only Tecate will do). The space is whimsically rustic, with stuffed-game trophies mounted on the wall and leather saddles standing in for seats at a couple of tables. **Known for:** lively atmosphere; combo plates; good sides and sauces. [$] *Average main: $18* ✉ *975 1st St.* ↔ *Near Main St.* ☎ *707/226–3976* 🌐 *www.bountyhunterwinebar.com.*

Carpe Diem Wine Bar

$$$ | **MODERN AMERICAN** | Patrons at this restaurant's sociable happy hour wash down nibbles such as truffle popcorn, tacos, and harissa-spiced house fries with draft-beer and weekly wine specials. Those who remain for dinner graze on steak tartare, house-made burrata, brick-oven flatbreads topped with roasted wild mushrooms and other ingredients, and larger plates that include an ostrich

burger smothered in triple-cream Brie. **Known for:** small plates; artisanal cheeses and charcuterie; wines and draft beers. Ⓢ *Average main: $27* ⊠ *1001 2nd St.* ✢ *At Brown St.* ☎ *707/224–0800* ⊕ *www. carpediemwinebar.com* ⊘ *Closed Sun. No lunch.*

Cole's Chop House

$$$$ | **STEAKHOUSE** | When only a thick, flawlessly cooked New York or porterhouse (dry-aged by the eminent Allen Brothers of Chicago) will do, this steak house inside an 1886 stone building is just the ticket. New Zealand lamb chops are the nonbeef favorite, with oysters Rockefeller, creamed spinach, grilled asparagus with hollandaise, all prepared with finesse, among the options for starters and sides. **Known for:** excellent meat sources; borderline-epic wine list; whiskey flights. Ⓢ *Average main: $46* ⊠ *1122 Main St.* ✢ *At Pearl St.* ☎ *707/224–6328* ⊕ *www.coleschophouse.com* ⊘ *No lunch.*

★ Compline

$$$ | **MODERN AMERICAN** | The full name of the three-in-one enterprise masterminded by master sommelier Matt Stamp and restaurant wine vet Ryan Stetins is Compline Wine Bar, Restaurant, and Merchant, and indeed you can just sip wine or purchase it here. The place evolved into a hot spot, though, for its youthful vibe and chef Yancy Windsperger's eclectic small and large plates that might include poached egg and polenta or gnocchi vegetable Bolognese. **Known for:** youthful vibe; by-the-glass wines; knowledgeable staff. Ⓢ *Average main: $25* ⊠ *1300 1st St., Suite 312* ☎ *707/492–8150* ⊕ *complinewine.com* ⊘ *Closed Tues.*

Grace's Table

$$$ | **ECLECTIC** | A dependable, varied, three-squares-a-day menu makes this modest corner restaurant occupying a brick-and-glass storefront many Napans' go-to choice for a simple meal. Iron-skillet corn bread with lavender honey and

butter shows up at all hours, with chilaquiles scrambled eggs a breakfast favorite, savory fish tacos a lunchtime staple, and cassoulet and roasted young chicken popular for dinner. **Known for:** congenial staffers; good beers on tap; eclectic menu focusing on France, Italy, and the Americas. Ⓢ *Average main: $24* ⊠ *1400 2nd St.* ✢ *At Franklin St.* ☎ *707/226–6200* ⊕ *www.gracestable.net.*

Gran Eléctrica

$$ | **MEXICAN** | A neon sign toward the back of Gran Eléctrica translates to "badass bar," but the same goes for the restaurant and its piquant lineup of *botanas* (snacks), tacos, tostadas, quesadillas, entrées, and sides. Ceviche tostadas, fish and carnitas tacos, the chile relleno, and duck-confit mole are among the year-round favorites, with dishes like grilled street-style corn with chipotle mayo appearing in-season. **Known for:** zippy decor; outdoor patio; tequila and mescal flights, specialty cocktails. Ⓢ *Average main: $19* ⊠ *1313 Main St.* ✢ *Near Clinton St.* ☎ *707/258–1313* ⊕ *www.granelectrica.com/about-napa* ⊘ *No lunch Mon.–Sat.*

Kenzo

$$$$ | **JAPANESE** | From the limestone floor to the cedar walls and cypress tabletops, most of the materials used to build this downtown Napa restaurant specializing in seasonally changing multicourse *kaiseki* meals were imported from Japan, as was the ceramic dinnerware. Delicate preparations such as straw-smoked grilled sea bass, broiled eel, and slow-roasted Wagyu tenderloin are typical of the offerings on the prix-fixe menu, which also includes impeccably fresh, artistically presented sashimi and sushi courses. **Known for:** beautiful, spare aesthetic; delicate preparations; wine and sake selection. Ⓢ *Average main: $225* ⊠ *1339 Pearl St., at Franklin St.* ☎ *707/294–2049* ⊕ *kenzonapa.com* ⊘ *Closed Mon. No lunch.*

Kitchen Door

$$ | **ECLECTIC** | Todd Humphries has overseen swank Manhattan, San Francisco, and Napa Valley kitchens, but for his casual Oxbow Public Market restaurant he set more modest goals, focusing on multicultural comfort cuisine. The signature dishes include a silky cream of mushroom soup whose triumph lies in its magical stock and soupçon of marsala, with pizzas and flatbreads, chicken pho, rice bowls, Niman Ranch burgers, and duck banh mi sandwiches (voluptuous duck jus) among the other customer favorites. **Known for:** multicultural comfort cuisine; communal atmosphere; river-view patio. [$] *Average main: $18* ✉ *Oxbow Public Market, 610 1st St.* ✥ *At McKinstry St.* ☎ *707/226–1560* 🌐 *www.kitchendoornapa.com.*

★ **La Toque**

$$$$ | **MODERN AMERICAN** | Chef Ken Frank's La Toque is the complete package: his imaginative French cuisine, served in a formal brown-hued dining space, is complemented by a wine lineup that earned the restaurant a coveted *Wine Spectator* Grand Award. Signature dishes that might appear on the prix-fixe four- or five-course tasting menu include rösti potato with Kaluga caviar, Angus beef tenderloin with grilled king trumpet mushrooms, and New York strip loin with Fiscalini cheddar pearl tapioca and Rutherford red-wine sauce. **Known for:** chef's table menu for entire party; astute wine pairings; vegetarian tasting menu. [$] *Average main: $110* ✉ *Westin Verasa Napa, 1314 McKinstry St.* ✥ *Off Soscol Ave.* ☎ *707/257–5157* 🌐 *www.latoque.com* ⏲ *No lunch.*

★ **Miminashi**

$$$ | **JAPANESE** | Japanese *izakaya*—gastropubs that serve appetizers downed with sake or cocktails—inspired chef Curtis Di Fede's buzz-worthy downtown Napa restaurant, where two peaks in the slatted poplar ceiling echo Shinto and Buddhist temple designs. Ramen, fried rice, and yakitori anchor the menu, whose highlights include wok-fried edamame and the ooh-inspiring *okonomiyaki* pancake with bacon, cabbage, and dried fermented tuna flakes; wines and sakes selected by Jessica Pinzon, formerly of Thomas Keller's Yountville restaurants Bouchon and Ad Hoc, further elevate Di Fede's dishes. **Known for:** distinctive design; wine and sake selection; soft-serve ice cream for dessert and from to-go window. [$] *Average main: $29* ✉ *821 Coombs St.* ✥ *Near 3rd St.* ☎ *707/254–9464* 🌐 *miminashi.com* ⏲ *No lunch.*

Morimoto Napa

$$$$ | **JAPANESE** | *Iron Chef* star Masaharu Morimoto is the big name behind this downtown Napa restaurant where everything is delightfully overdone, right down to the desserts. Organic materials such as twisting grapevines above the bar and rough-hewn wooden tables seem simultaneously earthy and modern, creating a fitting setting for the gorgeously plated Japanese fare, from sashimi served with grated fresh wasabi to elaborate concoctions that include sea-urchin carbonara made with Inaniwa udon noodles. **Known for:** elaborate concoctions; gorgeous plating; chef's choice omakase menu (from $130). [$] *Average main: $37* ✉ *610 Main St.* ✥ *At 5th St.* ☎ *707/252–1600* 🌐 *www.morimotonapa.com.*

Norman Rose Tavern

$$ | **AMERICAN** | **FAMILY** | If downtown Napa had its own version of the casual, something-for-everyone bar in the TV show *Cheers,* it would be "The Rose." Salads, burgers, chili, and sandwiches—all a cut above what you might expect from a tavern—are on the menu, with beer-batter fish-and-chips, pan-roasted half chicken, and meat loaf with a barbecue glaze among the larger plates. **Known for:** top-quality meat and fish purveyors; truffle-and-Parmesan fries; gourmet hot dogs, creative sandwiches. [$] *Average main: $18* ✉ *1401 1st St.* ✥ *At Franklin*

St. ☎ 707/258–1516 ⊕ www.norman-rosenapa.com.

Oenotri

$$$ | ITALIAN | Often spotted at local farmers' markets and his restaurant's gardens, Oenotri's ebullient chef-owner and Napa native Tyler Rodde is ever on the lookout for fresh produce to incorporate into his rustic southern-Italian cuisine. His restaurant, a brick-walled contemporary space with tall windows and wooden tables, is a lively spot to sample house-made salumi and pastas, thin-crust pizzas, and entrées that might include roasted squab, Atlantic salmon, or pork sausage. **Known for:** fresh ingredients; Margherita pizza with San Marzano tomatoes; lively atmosphere. Ⓢ *Average main: $27* ✉ *1425 1st St.* ✛ *At Franklin St.* ☎ *707/252–1022* ⊕ *www.oenotri.com.*

Restaurant at CIA Copia

$$$ | MODERN AMERICAN | The chefs at CIA Copia toil in a gleaming open kitchen (watching them at work is both educational and entertaining) bordering a cheery dining room that neatly splits the difference between fancy restaurant and upscale cafeteria. The menu changes seasonally based in part on what's in the culinary garden out front but might include steak Diane, shrimp tagliatelle with a pesto of garden herbs, and bacon-wrapped pork tenderloin with mascarpone polenta. **Known for:** wine, beer, craft cocktails; outdoor patio and olive grove seating; counter dining to watch chefs at work. Ⓢ *Average main: $27* ✉ *500 1st St.* ✛ *Near McKinstry St.* ☎ *707/967–2555* ⊕ *www.ciarestaurantgroup.com/the-restaurant-at-cia-copia.*

Tarla Mediterranean Grill

$$$ | MEDITERRANEAN | You can build a meal at Tarla by combining traditional Mediterranean mezes (small plates)—stuffed grape leaves with fresh tzatziki, perhaps, and spanakopita—with contemporary creations such as lentil and kale salad with Granny Smith apples. Entrées include updates of moussaka and other Turkish and Greek standards, along with fancifully modern items like beef short ribs braised with a pomegranate-wine sauce. **Known for:** sidewalk seating; no corkage on Tuesday; updates of Turkish and Greek standards. Ⓢ *Average main: $26* ✉ *Andaz Napa, 1480 1st St.* ✛ *At School St.* ☎ *707/255–5599* ⊕ *www.tarlagrill.com.*

★ Torc

$$$$ | MODERN AMERICAN | *Torc* means "wild boar" in an early Celtic dialect, and owner-chef Sean O'Toole, who formerly helmed kitchens at top Manhattan, San Francisco, and Yountville establishments, occasionally incorporates the restaurant's namesake beast into his eclectic offerings. A recent menu featured sea urchin with Persian melon carpaccio, Maine-lobster risotto, and veal sweetbreads with sweet and sour tomatoes, all prepared by O'Toole and his team with style and precision. **Known for:** gracious service; specialty cocktails; Bengali sweet-potato pakora and deviled-egg appetizers. Ⓢ *Average main: $36* ✉ *1140 Main St.* ✛ *At Pearl St.* ☎ *707/252–3292* ⊕ *www.torcnapa.com* ☾ *Closed Tues. No lunch weekdays.*

Yak & Yeti

$$ | NEPALESE | The strip-mall location next to a pizza-chain franchise couldn't be more modest, but the chef—a Himalayan Sherpa—at this restaurant serving Nepalese, Tibetan, and Indian cuisine is a charmer, and his dishes are flavor revelations. *Pakoras* (fritters), samosas, daal soup, and steamed dumplings all make excellent starters, with meat and vegetable curries, kabobs, and sizzling tandoori platters among the mains. **Known for:** many vegetarian options; good choice for lunch; reasonable food, beer, and wine prices. Ⓢ *Average main: $17* ✉ *3150B Jefferson St.* ✛ *At Sheridan Dr., 2 miles north of downtown* ☎ *707/666–2475* ⊕ *yakandyetinapa.com.*

At di Rosa the art treasures can be found indoors and out.

★ ZuZu

$$$ | **SPANISH** | At festive ZuZu the focus is on cold and hot tapas, paella, and other Spanish favorites often downed with cava or sangria. Regulars revere the paella, made with Spanish *bomba* rice, and small plates that might include grilled octopus, garlic shrimp, jamón Ibérico, and white anchovies with sliced egg and rémoulade on grilled bread. **Known for:** singular flavors and spicing; Latin jazz on the stereo; sister restaurant La Taberna three doors south for beer, wine, and bar bites. $ *Average main: $30* ✉ *829 Main St.* ✛ *Near 3rd St.* ☎ *707/224–8555* ⊕ *www.zuzunapa.com* ☾ *No lunch weekends.*

Hotels

★ Andaz Napa

$$$ | **HOTEL** | Part of the Hyatt family, this boutique hotel with an urban-hip vibe has spacious, luxurious rooms with flat-screen TVs, laptop-size safes, and white-marble bathrooms stocked with high-quality bath products. **Pros:** proximity to downtown restaurants, theaters, and tasting rooms; access to modern fitness center; complimentary beverage upon arrival; complimentary snacks and nonalcoholic beverages in rooms. **Cons:** parking can be a challenge on weekends; unremarkable views from some rooms; expensive on weekends in high season. $ *Rooms from: $306* ✉ *1450 1st St.* ☎ *707/687–1234* ⊕ *andaznapa.com* ⊅ *141 rooms* ⊺⊙⊺ *No meals.*

★ Archer Hotel Napa

$$$ | **HOTEL** | A hybrid of New York City and Las Vegas glamour infused downtown Napa with the 2018 completion of this five-story hotel ideal for travelers seeking design pizzazz, a see-and-be-seen atmosphere, and a slate of first-class amenities. **Pros:** restaurants and room service by chef Charlie Palmer; Sky & Vine rooftop bar; views from upper-floor rooms (especially south and west). **Cons:** not particularly rustic; expensive in high season; occasional service, hospitality lapses. $ *Rooms from: $374* ✉ *1230 1st St.* ☎ *707/690–9800, 855/437–9100*

🌐 *archerhotel.com/napa* 🛏 *183 rooms* 🍴 *No meals.*

Best Western Plus Elm House Inn
$$ | **HOTEL** | In a region known for over-the-top architecture and amenities (and prices to match), this inn delivers style and even a touch of class at affordable rates. **Pros:** polite staff; generous continental breakfasts; quiet garden rooms away from street noise. **Cons:** hot tub but no pool; about a mile from downtown; road-construction noise from nearby project into 2021. [$] *Rooms from: $249* ✉ *800 California Blvd.* ☎ *707/255–1831* 🌐 *bestwesternelmhouseinn.com* 🛏 *22 rooms* 🍴 *Breakfast.*

Blackbird Inn
$$ | **B&B/INN** | Arts and Crafts style infuses this home from the turn of the last century, from the lobby's enormous fieldstone fireplace to the lamps that cast a warm glow over the impressive wooden staircase to the guest rooms' period-accurate, locally crafted oak beds, matching night tables, and other furniture. **Pros:** gorgeous architecture and period furnishings; convenient to downtown Napa; free afternoon wine service. **Cons:** must be booked well in advance; some rooms are on the small side; street noise in rooms on inn's west side. [$] *Rooms from: $229* ✉ *1755 1st St.* ☎ *707/226–2450* 🌐 *www.blackbirdinnnapa.com* 🛏 *8 rooms* 🍴 *Breakfast.*

★ **Carneros Resort & Spa**
$$$$ | **RESORT** | Freestanding board-and-batten cottages with rocking chairs on each porch are simultaneously rustic and chic at this luxurious property made even more so by a $6.5 million makeover. **Pros:** cottages have lots of privacy; beautiful views from hilltop pool and hot tub; heaters on private patios. **Cons:** long drive to upvalley destinations; least expensive accommodations pick up highway noise; pricey pretty much year-round. [$] *Rooms from: $600* ✉ *4048 Sonoma Hwy./Hwy. 121* ☎ *707/299–4900, 888/400–9000* 🌐 *www.carnerosresort.com* 🛏 *100 rooms* 🍴 *No meals.*

Cottages of Napa Valley
$$$ | **B&B/INN** | Although most of the accommodations here date from the 1920s—when they rented for $5 *a month* (imagine that)—contemporary design touches and amenities, plush new furnishings, up-to-date bathrooms, and attentive service ensure a cozy, 21st-century experience. **Pros:** private porches and patios; basket of Bouchon pastries each morning; kitchen with utensils in each cottage. **Cons:** hum of highway traffic; per innkeeper "not appropriate" for children under age 12; weekend minimum-stay requirement. [$] *Rooms from: $395* ✉ *1012 Darms La.* ☎ *707/252–7810* 🌐 *www.napacottages.com* 🛏 *9 cottages* 🍴 *Breakfast.*

★ **The Inn on First**
$$ | **B&B/INN** | Guests gush over the hospitality at this inn whose painstakingly restored 1905 mansion facing 1st Street contains five rooms, with five additional accommodations, all suites, in a building behind a secluded patio and garden. **Pros:** full gourmet breakfast by hosts-with-the-most owners; gas fireplaces and whirlpool tubs in all rooms; away from downtown but not too far. **Cons:** no TVs; owners "respectfully request no children"; lacks pool, fitness center, and other amenities of larger properties. [$] *Rooms from: $220* ✉ *1938 1st St.* ☎ *707/253–1331* 🌐 *www.theinnonfirst.com* 🛏 *10 rooms* 🍴 *Breakfast.*

★ **Inn on Randolph**
$$ | **B&B/INN** | A few calm blocks from the downtown action on a nearly 1-acre lot with landscaped gardens, the Inn on Randolph—with a Gothic Revival–style main house and its five guest rooms plus five historic cottages out back—is a sophisticated haven celebrated for its gourmet gluten-free breakfasts and snacks. **Pros:** quiet residential neighborhood; spa tubs in cottages and two main-house rooms; romantic setting. **Cons:** a bit of a walk

from downtown; expensive in-season; weekend minimum-stay requirement. $ *Rooms from: $299* ✉ *411 Randolph St.* ☎ *707/257–2886* ⊕ *www.innonrandolph. com* ⌐ *10 rooms* ❑ *Breakfast.*

Milliken Creek Inn

$$$$ | B&B/INN | Early-evening wine-and-cheese receptions set a romantic mood at this hotel where the chic rooms take a page from the stylebook of British-colonial Asia, and the intimate lobby's terrace overlooks a lush lawn and the Napa River. **Pros:** countryside feeling but 1 mile from Oxbow Public Market area; serene spa; breakfast delivered to your room or elsewhere on the beautiful grounds. **Cons:** expensive in-season; road noise audible in outdoor areas; no pool, fitness center, or bar. $ *Rooms from: $449* ✉ *1815 Silverado Trail* ☎ *707/255–1197* ⊕ *www. millikencreekinn.com* ⌐ *14 rooms* ❑ *Breakfast.*

Napa River Inn

$$ | B&B/INN | Part of a complex of restaurants, shops, a nightclub, and a spa, this well-appointed if not showy waterfront inn is within walking distance of downtown hot spots. **Pros:** wide range of room sizes and prices; near downtown action; no parking or resort fees. **Cons:** river views could be more scenic; some rooms get noise from nearby restaurants; dated decor in some rooms. $ *Rooms from: $249* ✉ *500 Main St.* ☎ *707/251–8500, 877/251–8500* ⊕ *www.napariverinn.com* ⌐ *66 rooms* ❑ *Breakfast.*

Senza Hotel

$$$ | HOTEL | Exterior fountains, gallery-quality outdoor sculptures, and decorative rows of grapevines signal the Wine Country–chic aspirations of this boutique hotel operated by the owners of Hall Wines. **Pros:** high-style fixtures; fireplaces in all rooms; elegant atmosphere. **Cons:** just off highway; 5-mile drive to downtown Napa or Yountville; some bathrooms have no tub. $ *Rooms from: $399* ✉ *4066 Howard La.* ☎ *707/253–0337*

⊕ *www.senzahotel.com* ⌐ *41 rooms* ❑ *Breakfast.*

Westin Verasa Napa

$$$ | HOTEL | Near the Napa Valley Wine Train depot and Oxbow Public Market, this spacious mostly suites resort is soothing and sophisticated, particularly in the guest quarters, where pristine white bedding plays well off the warm earth tones of the other contemporary furnishings. **Pros:** heated saline pool and hot tub; most rooms have well-equipped kitchenettes (some have full kitchens); destination La Toque restaurant. **Cons:** amenities fee added to room rate; slightly corporate feel; expensive in high season. $ *Rooms from: $379* ✉ *1314 McKinstry St.* ☎ *707/257–1800, 888/627–7169* ⊕ *www.westinnapa.com* ⌐ *180 rooms* ❑ *No meals.*

Nightlife

Blue Note Napa

MUSIC CLUBS | The famed New York jazz room's West Coast club hosts national headliners such as Brian McKnight, Dee Dee Bridgewater, and Coco Montoya, along with local talents such as Lavay Smith & Her Red Hot Skillet Lickers. There's a full bar, and you can order a meal or small bites from the kitchen. ✉ *Napa Valley Opera House, 1030 Main St.* ⊹ *At 1st St.* ☎ *707/880–2300* ⊕ *www. bluenotenapa.com.*

Cadet Wine + Beer Bar

WINE BARS—NIGHTLIFE | Cadet plays things urban-style cool with a long bar, high-top tables, an all-vinyl soundtrack, and a low-lit, generally loungelike feel. When they opened their bar, the two owners described their outlook as "unabashedly pro-California," but their wine-and-beer lineup circles the globe. The crowd here is youngish, the vibe festive. ✉ *930 Franklin St.* ⊹ *At end of pedestrian alley between 1st and 2nd Sts.* ☎ *707/224–4400* ⊕ *www.cadetbeerandwinebar.com.*

JaM Cellars

WINE BARS—NIGHTLIFE | Although it opens at 10 am daily for wine tasting, evening is the best time to visit this fun tasting room, especially during live-music events, mostly pop, rock, and soul. JaM Chardonnay, Cabernet, rosé, and sparkling wine are the pours here. ⊠ *1460 1st St.* ⊹ *Near School St.* ☎ *707/265–7577* ⊕ *www.jamcellars.com.*

 Performing Arts

Uptown Theatre

MUSIC | At 860 seats, this art deco former movie house attracts Ziggy Marley, Lyle Lovett, Roseanne Cash, Napa Valley resident Boz Scaggs, and other performers. ⊠ *1350 3rd St.* ⊹ *At Franklin St.* ☎ *707/259–0123* ⊕ *www.uptowntheatrenapa.com.*

Shopping

Copperfield's Books

BOOKS/STATIONERY | Check the Napa page on this indie chain's website for readings or signings by local authors while you're in town. ⊠ *Bel Aire Plaza, 3740 Bel Aire Plaza* ⊹ *Off Trancas St., near Jefferson St.* ☎ *707/252–8002* ⊕ *www.copperfieldsbooks.com/napa.*

Ivy, Twig & Twine

GIFTS/SOUVENIRS | Napa Valley native Michael Holmes expresses his creativity as a floral and interior designer, a painter and sculptor, and the curator of this gift and home-decor boutique. It's fun to pop in and see what has caught his eye, especially during Halloween and Christmas, when he goes way over the top. Look up to see the chandeliers made of wine barrel staves and hoops. ⊠ *606 Main St.* ⊹ *At 5th St.* ☎ *707/226–3655* ⊕ *www.michaelholmesdesigns.com/ivy-twig-twine.*

Makers Market

CERAMICS/GLASSWARE | Wine Country and San Francisco Bay Area artisans are well represented at this downtown store that sells jewelry, home-decor, apothecary, and many other hand-crafted items revealing "the soul or the mark of a proud maker." ⊠ *First Street Napa, 1300 1st St., Suite 301* ☎ *707/637–4637* ⊕ *makersmarket.us.*

Mecox

HOUSEHOLD ITEMS/FURNITURE | Art, antiques, housewares, and midcentury modern–inspired furniture are on display at the Napa location of this minichain whose first store opened in Southampton, Long Island, in 1996. ⊠ *1214 1st St.* ⊹ *Near Coombs St.* ☎ *707/225–7507* ⊕ *mecox.com* ⊙ *Closed Mon. and Tues.*

Napa Bookmine

BOOKS/STATIONERY | An indie shop with a second location in the Oxbow Public Market, Napa Bookmine sells current magazines and new and used books and hosts author events. Specialties include children's and teen titles, travel books, and works by local writers. ⊠ *964 Pearl St.* ⊹ *Near Main St.* ☎ *707/265–8131* ⊕ *www.napabookmine.com.*

Shackford's Kitchen Store

HOUSEHOLD ITEMS/FURNITURE | This shop that opened in 1975 looks more like a hardware store than the low-key celebration of the art of cooking it is, but if you need kitchenware, accessories, or hard-to-find replacement items, you'll likely find what you're looking for. In late 2018 new owners acquired the shop from founder John Shackford, saying they planned to keep it essentially the same but add a culinary center and install an executive chef. ⊠ *1350 Main St., at Caymus St.* ☎ *707/226–2132.*

The Spa at Napa River Inn

SPA/BEAUTY | All stress will be under arrest after a massage, facial, or other treatment at this spa inside Napa's vaguely late-deco former police station. You can opt for therapeutic massages that might incorporate Swedish or other familiar techniques, or go more exotic

Musical performances and other events take place at CIA at Copia's outdoor amphitheater.

with Adjust Your Ki, which involves Reiki, an ancient Japanese relaxation technique. The four-hour Royal Treatment pulls out all the stops with a full-body massage, foot rehab, exfoliation, a body wrap, and an antioxidant facial. ■ TIP➜ If you're traveling with a dog in need of TLC, the spa will pamper your pet with a walk, a treat, and a minimassage while you're indulging yourself. ✉ 500 Main St. ✛ At 5th St. ☎ 707/265–7537 ⊕ www. napariverinn.com/the-spa ✉ Treatments from $25.

Store at CIA Copia
FOOD/CANDY | Nearly every piece of kitchenware is a work of art at this Culinary Institute of America shop that has the feel of a museum store. Cookbooks, oils, and specialty food items are in the mix, too. ✉ 500 1st St. ✛ Near McKinstry St. ☎ 707/967–2545 ⊕ shop.ciaatcopia.com.

Activities

Balloons Above the Valley
TOUR—SIGHT | This company's personable and professional pilots make outings a delight. Participants meet up with the flight escorts at the Oxbow Public Market and conclude with a champagne brunch there. You can extend the pleasure with packages that include a picnic lunch and winery tours. ✉ Napa ☎ 707/253–2222, 800/464–6824 ⊕ www.balloonrides.com ✉ From $189.

Enjoy Napa Valley
KAYAKING | Napa native Justin Perkins leads a history-oriented Napa River kayak tour that passes by downtown sights. On the easy paddle, Perkins points out the wildlife and regales participants with amusingly salacious tales of Napa's river-town past. Enjoy Napa Valley also rents paddleboards. ✉ Main Street Boat Dock, 680 Main St. ✛ Riverfront Promenade south of 3rd St. Bridge ☎ 707/227–7364 ⊕ enjoy-napa-valley.com ✉ $71.

Few experiences are as exhilarating yet serene as an early-morning balloon ride above the vineyards.

Gondola Servizio

TOUR—SPORTS | Rides in authentic gondolas that seat up to six depart from downtown Napa's municipal dock along the Riverfront Promenade. You'll never mistake the Napa River for the Grand Canal, but on a sunny day this is a pleasant excursion. ⊠ *Main Street Boat Dock, 680 Main St.* ✛ *Riverfront Promenade south of 3rd St. Bridge* ☎ *707/373–2100* ⊕ *gondolaservizio.com* ☞ *From $60 (30 mins for 2 passengers).*

Yountville

9 miles north of downtown Napa; 9 miles south of St. Helena.

These days Yountville (population about 3,000) is something like Disneyland for food lovers. It all started with Thomas Keller's The French Laundry, one of the best restaurants in the United States. Keller is also behind a few other Yountville enterprises—a French bistro, a bakery, American and Oaxacan restaurants, and a food-oriented boutique. And that's only the tip of the iceberg: you could stay here for a week and not exhaust all the options in this tiny town with an outsize culinary reputation.

Yountville is full of small inns and luxurious hotels catering to those who prefer to be able to walk rather than drive to their lodgings after dinner. Although visitors use Yountville as a home base, touring Napa Valley wineries by day and returning to dine, you could easily while away a few hours downtown, wandering through the shops on or just off Washington Street, or visiting the many tasting rooms. The Yountville Chamber of Commerce, on the southern end of town across from Hotel Villagio, has maps with wine-tasting and history walks.

The town is named for George C. Yount, who in 1836 received the first of several large Napa Valley land grants from the Mexican government. Yount is credited with planting the valley's first vinifera grapevines in 1838. The vines are long gone, but wisps of Yountville's

19th-century past bleed through, most notably along Washington Street, where a burger and ice-cream joint at 6525 Washington occupies the former train depot, and V Marketplace's shops and restaurants east of it inhabit the former Groezinger Winery.

GETTING HERE AND AROUND

If you're traveling north from Napa on Highway 29, take the Yountville/Veterans Home exit, make a right on California Drive and a left onto Washington Street. Traveling south on Highway 29, turn left onto Madison Street and right onto Washington Street. Nearly all of Yountville's businesses and restaurants are clustered along a 1-mile stretch of Washington Street. Yountville Cross Road connects downtown Yountville to the Silverado Trail, where you'll find several wineries. VINE buses serve Yountville. The Yountville Trolley circles the downtown area and hits a few spots beyond.

CONTACT Yountville Trolley. ☎ *707/312–1509 (or download the Ride the Vine smartphone app)* ⊕ *www.ridethevine.com/yountville-trolley.*

VISITOR INFORMATION

CONTACT Yountville Chamber Of Commerce. ✉ *6484 Washington St.* ✛ *At Oak Circle* ☎ *707/944–0904* ⊕ *yountville.com.*

 Sights

★ **Cliff Lede Vineyards**
WINERY/DISTILLERY | Inspired by his passion for classic rock, owner and construction magnate Cliff Lede named the blocks in his Stags Leap District vineyard after hits by the Grateful Dead and other bands. The vibe at his efficient, high-tech winery is anything but laid-back, however. Cutting-edge agricultural and enological science informs the vineyard management and wine making here. Architect Howard Backen designed the winery and its tasting room, where Lede's Sauvignon Blanc, Cabernet Sauvignons, and other wines, along with

some from sister winery FEL, which produces much-lauded Anderson Valley Pinot Noirs, are poured. ■**TIP➔ Walk-ins are welcome at the tasting bar, but appointments are required for the veranda outside and a nearby gallery that displays rock-related art.** ✉ *1473 Yountville Cross Rd.* ✛ *Off Silverado Trail* ☎ *707/944–8642* ⊕ *cliffledevineyards.com* ⊠ *Tastings from $35.*

Domaine Chandon

WINERY/DISTILLERY | On a knoll shaded by ancient oak trees, this French-owned maker of sparkling wines claims one of Yountville's prime pieces of real estate. Chandon is best known for bubbles, but the still wines—among them Cabernet Sauvignon, Chardonnay, and Pinot Noir—are also worth a try. You can sip by the flight or by the glass at the bar, or begin there and sit at tables in the lounge and return to the bar as needed; in good weather, tables are set up outside. Bottle service is also available. ✉ *1 California Dr.* ✛ *Off Hwy. 29* ☎ *707/204–7530, 888/242–6366* ⊕ *www.chandon.com* ⊠ *Tastings from $10.*

Goosecross Cellars

WINERY/DISTILLERY | When Christi Coors Ficeli purchased this boutique winery in 2013 and commissioned a new barnlike tasting space, she and her architect had one major goal: bring the outside in. Large retractable west-facing windows open up behind the tasting bar to idyllic views of Cabernet vines—in fine weather, guests on the outdoor deck can practically touch them. Goosecross makes Chardonnay and Pinot Noir from Carneros grapes, but the soul of this cordial operation is its 12-acre estate vineyard, its 10 planted acres mostly Cabernet Sauvignon and Merlot with some Cabernet Franc and Petit Verdot. The Cab and Merlot are the stars, along with the Aeros Bordeaux-style blend of the best estate grapes. Aeros isn't usually poured, but a Howell Mountain Petite Sirah with expressive tannins (there's also a Howell

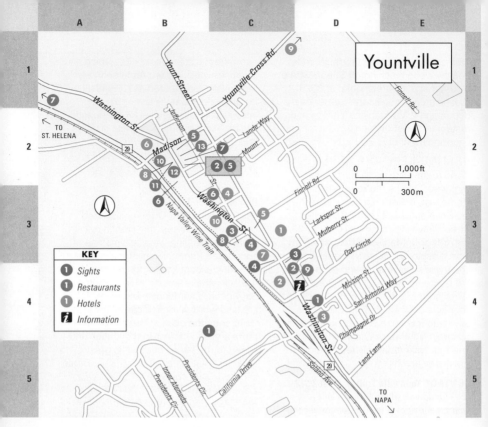

Yountville

KEY

- 1 Sights
- 1 Restaurants
- 1 Hotels
- *i* Information

Sights ▼	Restaurants ▼	Hotels ▼
1 Domaine Chandon...... **B4**	1 Ad Hoc **C4**	1 Bardessono **C3**
2 Handwritten Wines..... **B2**	2 Bistro Jeanty............ **C4**	2 Hotel Villagio **C4**
3 Hill Family Estate........ **D3**	3 Bottega **C3**	3 Hotel Yountville......... **D4**
4 JCB Tasting Salon **C3**	4 Bouchon Bistro **C3**	4 Lavender Inn **C3**
5 Jessup Cellars **B2**	5 Ciccio **B2**	5 Maison Fleurie **C3**
6 RH Yountville **B2**	6 The French	6 Napa Valley Lodge...... **B2**
7 Stewart Cellars **B2**	Laundry **C3**	7 Napa Valley
	7 Mustards Grill........... **A1**	Railway Inn............... **C3**
	8 Ottimo **C3**	8 North Block
	9 Protéa	Hotel...................... **B2**
	Restaurant............... **C4**	9 Poetry Inn................ **D1**
	10 R+D Kitchen **B2**	10 Vintage House **C3**
	11 Redd Wood.............. **B2**	
	12 RH Yountville **B2**	
	13 Southside Yountville at	
	Stewart Cellars **B2**	

Mountain Cabernet) often is. Visits to Goosecross are by appointment only. ✉ *1119 State La.* ✛ *Off Yountville Cross Rd.* ☎ *707/944-1986* ⊕ *www.goosecross.com* 🍷 *Tastings from $40.*

Handwritten Wines

WINERY/DISTILLERY | Handcrafted, 100% Cabernet Sauvignons from hillside and mountain vineyards 2 acres or smaller are the emphasis of this boutique sister winery to Jessup Cellars. The lineup also includes Sauvignon Blanc and Chardonnay, along with a Pinot Noir from Santa Barbara County's Sta. Rita Hills AVA. Until a southern Yountville space opens in late 2019, appointment-only seated tastings take place in a pert 325-square-foot cottage across from RH Yountville. ■TIP➜ **Handwritten offers a one-of-a-kind culinary experience at a secluded hillside farmhouse in St. Helena; call or check the website for details.** ✉ *6720 Washington St.* ✛ *At Pedroni St.* ☎ *707/944-8524* ⊕ *www.handwrittenwines.com* 🍷 *Tasting $40.*

Hill Family Estate

WINERY/DISTILLERY | For years Doug Hill produced grapes for prominent Napa Valley wineries, but at the urging of his son, Ryan, the family established its own line of Merlot, Cabernet Sauvignon, and other wines. Crafted by Alison Green-Doran, a protégé of the late Napa winemaker André Tchelistcheff, these are refined wines you can sample in the family's downtown tasting salon, whose decor includes an autographed major-league baseball bat, a surfboard, and other memorabilia—even a classic Fender guitar—ingeniously stained in Hill red wine. In summer and early fall, entertaining "secret garden" tours (by appointment, weather permitting) are conducted of Jacobsen Orchards, a small nearby farm that grows produce for The French Laundry and other top restaurants. ✉ *6512 Washington St.* ✛ *At Mulberry St.* ☎ *707/944-9580* ⊕ *www.hillfamilyestate.*

com 🍷 *Tastings from $35, tours from $55 (includes tasting).*

JCB Tasting Salon

WINERY/DISTILLERY | Mirrors and gleaming surfaces abound in this eye-catching ode to indulgence named for its French owner, Jean-Charles Boisset (JCB). The JCB label first made its mark with sparkling wine, Chardonnay, and Pinot Noir, with Cabernet Sauvignon a more recent strong suit. In addition to providing a plush setting for sampling his wines, Boisset's downtown Yountville tasting space is also a showcase for home decor items from the likes of Lalique and Baccarat. Preserved roses hang from the ceiling of JCB Salon Privé, decked in white marble and white feathered chairs and used for more intimate private tastings. The adjacent Atelier Fine Foods sells cheeses, charcuterie, and other gourmet foods, all quite good if in some cases *très cher* (very expensive). You can purchase them separately or assembled as a picnic tray. ✉ *6505 Washington St.* ✛ *At Mulberry St.* ☎ *707/934-8237* ⊕ *jcbcollection.com/visit* 🍷 *Tastings from $30.*

Jessup Cellars

WINERY/DISTILLERY | This winery's downtown Yountville tasting room attracts a loyal following for its upbeat vibe, smartly curated art gallery, and the lush red wines of its The Art of the Blend Series. Three of the series' wines—Table for Four, Juel, and Manny's Blend, with, respectively, Cabernet Sauvignon, Merlot, and Zinfandel as the lead grape—are among Jessup's most popular offerings. Their success spawned two additional blends, Graziella (Cabernet and Sangiovese) and Rougette (Grenache). Winemaker Rob Lloyd also crafts Chardonnay, Merlot, and Pinot Noir from southern Napa Valley vineyards with maritime climates, sourcing Zinfandel and Petite Sirah from hotter northern locales and Cabernet from both. ■TIP➜ **Jessup's gallery often hosts evening events, including art openings, live music, and film**

A Scenic Southern Napa Drive

Wine, art, sweeping vistas, shopping, and more wine await on a scenic drive from the town of Napa up Mt. Veeder and down the Oakville Grade into Oakville, with a final stop in Yountville.

Art and Wine in Napa

Head north from downtown Napa on Highway 29 to the Trancas Street/Redwood Road exit and turn west (left) onto Trancas Street. After you cross over Highway 29, the road's name changes to Redwood. Continue west, bearing left at the fork when Redwood narrows from four lanes to two. From here, two signs point the way to the **Hess Collection.** Allow an hour or so to taste the wines and browse the modern art collection.

Making the (Oakville) Grade

From Hess, backtrack on Redwood about 1¼ miles to Mt. Veeder Road and turn left. After a little more than 8 miles, turn right (east) onto Dry Creek Road. After ½ mile this road is signed as the Oakville Grade. The views east as you twist your way downhill to Highway 29 can be stunning, especially when a low-lying fog shrouds the valley floor. (If anyone in your party is prone to carsickness, take Redwood back to Highway 29 and turn north.) From the Oakville Grade, turn left (north) onto Highway 29 and right (east) in about ¼ mile onto Oakville Cross Road.

Amazing Cabernets

Head east on Oakville Cross, visiting either **Silver Oak** or, if you've reserved a tour and wine and food pairing ahead of time, **B Cellars.** Both wineries have enviable grape sources and highly skilled winemakers who blend astounding Cabernets.

Yountville Temptations

After your Oakville tasting, continue east on Oakville Cross, turning right (south) on the Silverado Trail and right again (west) onto Yountville Cross Road. Turn left at Yount Street, which leads into downtown **Yountville,** whose bakeries and boutiques tempt body and bank account. Washington Street, one block west of Yount, holds most of the action. To taste more wine, slip into the glam **JCB Tasting Salon** or **The Wine Vault at the Historic Ma(i)sonry Building.** Or drop by **Southside Yountville at Stewart Cellars,** where (until 3) you can have a light meal (and, until 6, a tasting). **Kollar Chocolates** in V Marketplace is another sweet option. Remain in Yountville for dinner, or return to Napa.

---

screenings, many of which sell out well in advance. ☒ *6740 Washington St. ⊹ At Pedroni St.* ☎ *707/944–8523* ⊕ *jessupcellars.com* ☒ *Tastings from $15.*

RH Yountville

MUSEUM | Gargantuan crystal chandeliers, century-old olive trees, and strategically placed water features provide visual and aural continuity at Restoration Hardware's quadruple-threat food, wine, art, and design compound. An all-day café fronts two steel, glass, and concrete home-furnishings galleries, with a bluestone walkway connecting them to a reboot of the Ma(i)sonry wine salon. Inside a two-story 1904 manor house constructed from Napa River stone and rechristened The Wine Vault at the Historic Ma(i)sonry Building, it remains an excellent tasting choice. Classic and Connoisseur flights focus on small-lot Napa and Sonoma bottlings; hosts at Collector tastings pour Napa Valley wines by elite winemakers like Heidi Barrett and Philippe Melka. In good weather, some tastings take place in outdoor living rooms where patrons can also enjoy coffee, tea, or wine by the glass or bottle. Walk-ins are welcome, but reservations are recommended (and wise on weekends in-season). ✉ *6725 Washington St.* ✣ *At Pedroni St.* ☎ *707/339–4654* 🌐 *www.restorationhardware.com* 🎫 *Tasting from $50.*

★ Robert Sinskey Vineyards

WINERY/DISTILLERY | Although the winery produces a well-regarded Stags Leap Cabernet Sauvignon, two Bordeaux-style red blends (Marcien and POV), and white wines, Sinskey is best known for its intense, brambly Carneros District Pinot Noirs. All the grapes are grown in organic, certified biodynamic vineyards. The influence of Robert's wife, Maria Helm Sinskey—a chef and cookbook author and the winery's culinary director—is evident during the tastings, which are accompanied by a few bites of food with each wine. **■ TIP→ The Perfect Circle Tour, offered daily, takes in the winery's gardens and ends with a seated pairing of food and wine. Even more elaborate, also by appointment, is the five-course Chef's Table pairing of seasonal dishes with current and older wines.** ✉ *6320 Silverado Trail, Napa* ✣ *At Yountville Cross Rd.* ☎ *707/944–9090* 🌐 *www.robertsinskey.com* 🎫 *Tastings from $40, tours (with tastings) from $95.*

★ Stewart Cellars

WINERY/DISTILLERY | Three stone structures meant to mimic Scottish ruins coaxed into modernity form this complex that includes public and private tasting spaces, a bright outdoor patio, and a hip, independently run café. The attention to detail in the ensemble's design mirrors that of the wines, whose grapes come from coveted vineyards, most notably all six of the Beckstoffer Heritage Vineyards, among the Napa Valley's most historic sites. Although Cabernet is the focus, winemaker Blair Guthrie, with input from consulting winemaker Paul Hobbs, also makes Sauvignon Blanc, Chardonnay, Pinot Noir, and Merlot. **■ TIP→ On sunny days this is a good stop around lunchtime, when you can order a meal from the café and a glass of wine from the tasting room—for permit reasons this must be done separately—and enjoy them on the patio.** ✉ *6752 Washington St.* ✣ *Near Pedroni St.* ☎ *707/963–9160* 🌐 *www.stewartcellars.com* 🎫 *Tastings from $30.*

🍴 Restaurants

★ Ad Hoc

$$$$ | **MODERN AMERICAN** | At this low-key dining room with zinc-top tables and wine served in tumblers, superstar chef Thomas Keller offers a single, fixed-price, nightly menu that might include smoked beef short ribs with creamy herb rice and charred broccolini or sesame chicken with radish kimchi and fried rice. Ad Hoc also serves a small but decadent Sunday brunch, and Keller's Addendum annex, in a separate small building behind the restaurant, sells boxed lunches to go (beyond moist buttermilk fried chicken) from Thursday to Saturday except in winter. **Known for:** casual cuisine at great prices for a Thomas Keller restaurant; don't-miss buttermilk-fried-chicken night; streetside outdoor seating. [$] *Average main: $55* ✉ *6476 Washington St.* ✣ *At Oak Circle* ☎ *707/944–2487* 🌐 *www.adhocrestaurant.com* ⏲ *No lunch Mon.–Sat.; no dinner Tues. and Wed.* ☞ *Call day ahead to find out next day's menu.*

★ Bistro Jeanty

$$$ | **FRENCH** | Escargots, cassoulet, *daube de boeuf* (beef stewed in red wine), and other French classics are prepared with the utmost precision at this country bistro whose lamb tongue and other obscure delicacies delight daring diners. Regulars often start with the rich tomato soup in a flaky puff pastry before proceeding to sole meunière or coq

Domaine Chandon claims a prime piece of real estate.

au vin, completing the French sojourn with a lemon meringue tart or other authentic desserts. **Known for:** traditional preparations; oh-so-French atmosphere; European wines. $ *Average main: $29* ✉ *6510 Washington St.* ✥ *At Mulberry St.* ☎ *707/944–0103* 🌐 *www.bistrojeanty.com.*

Bottega

$$$ | **ITALIAN** | At his softly lit, exposed-redbrick downtown trattoria, which occupies sections of a 19th-century winery, chef Michael Chiarello transforms local ingredients into regional Italian dishes. Ricotta gnocchi with old-hen tomato sauce, wood oven–baked zucchini and potato lasagna, and grilled acorn-fed pork shoulder with pork jus and apple *mostarda* (candied apples in a mustard-laced syrup) show the chef at his most rustic yet sophisticated. **Known for:** rustic yet sophisticated cuisine; many gluten-free items; Italian and California wines. $ *Average main: $25* ✉ *6525 Washington St.* ✥ *Near Mulberry St.* ☎ *707/945–1050* 🌐 *www.bottegnapavalley.com* 🕒 *No lunch Mon.*

★ Bouchon Bistro

$$$$ | **FRENCH** | The team that created The French Laundry is also behind this place, where everything—the lively and crowded zinc-topped bar, the elbow-to-elbow seating, the traditional French onion soup—could have come straight from a Parisian bistro. Pan-seared rib eye with béarnaise and mussels steamed with white wine, saffron, and Dijon mustard—both served with crispy, addictive fries—are among the perfectly executed entrées. **Known for:** bistro classics; raw bar; Bouchon Bakery next door. $ *Average main: $32* ✉ *6534 Washington St.* ✥ *Near Humboldt St.* ☎ *707/944–8037* 🌐 *www.bouchonbistro.com.*

Ciccio

$$ | **MODERN ITALIAN** | The ranch of Ciccio's owners, Frank and Karen Altamura, supplies some of the vegetables and herbs for the modern Italian cuisine prepared in the open kitchen of this remodeled former grocery store. Seasonal growing

Hit the (Vine) Trail

The Napa Valley Vine Trail is a planned 47-mile scenic path that backers hope will eventually run the length of the valley. As 2019 dawned, about 13 miles had been completed, including a mostly flat 9-mile paved stretch between northern Yountville and Napa's Oxbow Commons.

Follow the Tracks—and the Art

For most of the way this section of the path follows the same route as the Napa Valley Wine Train. In Yountville pick up the trail near the traffic light at Madison Street and Highway 29, just west of R+D Kitchen restaurant. This portion ends in Napa at Vallejo Street west of Soscol Avenue near St. Clair Brown Winery's greenhouse, though after a short break in the trail you can continue south 3 more miles.

(Head east across Soscol and immediately south on McKinstry Street at the Westin hotel.) Many of the murals commissioned by RAD Napa (Rail Arts District Napa) grace formerly unsightly warehouse walls and utility boxes around St. Clair Brown.

Markers, Stations

Markers along the trail let riders, walkers, and joggers know where they are, and interpretive signs convey a bit of history. Bike stations—there's one at 1046 McKinstry Street outside the Oxbow Public Market's Cru @ The Annex tasting room—have bike racks, pumps, and tools for minor repairs. Get more information and rent bikes and helmets at Napa Valley Bike Tours, at 6500 Washington Street in Yountville. The Vine Trail's website (⊕ vinetrail.org) has a downloadable map.

cycles dictate the menu, with fried-seafood appetizers (calamari, perhaps, or softshell crabs), a few pasta dishes, bavette steak with red-wine jus, and pancetta pizzas among the frequent offerings. **Known for:** Negroni bar; prix-fixe chef's dinner; mostly Napa Valley wines, some from owners' winery. $ *Average main: $19* ⊠ *6770 Washington St.* ✢ *At Madison St.* ☎ *707/945–1000* ⊕ *www.ciccionapavalley.com* ✆ *Closed Mon. and Tues. No lunch* ✆ *No reservations, except for prix-fixe chef's dinner (required; for 2–10 guests).*

★ The French Laundry

$$$$ | AMERICAN | An old stone building laced with ivy houses chef Thomas Keller's destination restaurant. Some courses on the two prix-fixe menus, one of which highlights vegetables, rely on luxe ingredients such as *calotte* (cap of the rib eye) while other courses take humble elements like carrots or fava beans and elevate them to art; many courses offer "supplements"—sea urchin, for instance, or black truffles. **Known for:** signature starter "oysters and pearls"; intricate flavors; superior wine list. $ *Average main: $325* ⊠ *6640 Washington St.* ✢ *At Creek St.* ☎ *707/944–2380* ⊕ *www.frenchlaundry.com* ✆ *No lunch Mon.–Thurs.* ᐧ *Jacket required* ✆ *Reservations essential wks ahead.*

Mustards Grill

$$$ | AMERICAN | Cindy Pawlcyn's Mustards Grill fills day and night with fans of her hearty cuisine, equal parts updated renditions of traditional American dishes—what Pawlcyn dubs "deluxe truck stop classics"—and fanciful contemporary fare. Barbecued baby back pork ribs and a lemon-lime tart piled high with brown-sugar meringue fall squarely in the first category, with sweet corn

tamales with tomatillo-avocado salsa and wild mushrooms representing the latter. **Known for:** roadhouse setting; convivial mood; hoppin' bar. [$] *Average main: $28* ✉ *7399 St. Helena Hwy./Hwy. 29, Napa* ✥ *1 mile north of Yountville* ☎ *707/944–2424* 🌐 *www.mustardsgrill.com.*

Ottimo

$ | **ITALIAN** | Chef Michael Chiarello opened this casual "multifaceted culinary experience" (*ottimo* is Italian for "optimal") across from his flagship restaurant, Bottega. The stations include a bakery, a *birreria* (craft brewery some of whose beers are made from grapes and rice), a *mozzeria* (fresh mozzarella stand) and pizzeria, a wine bar, and a tasting bar for preserves, pickled products, and oils and vinegars. **Known for:** pizzas and pastries; gelati and desserts; patio dining. [$] *Average main: $11* ✉ *V Marketplace, 6525 Washington St.* ✥ *Across from Bottega entrance* ☎ *707/944–0102* 🌐 *ottimo-nv.com* 🕒 *No dinner.*

★ Protéa Restaurant

$$ | **LATIN AMERICAN** | A meal at Yountville's The French Laundry motivated Puerto Rico–born Anita Cartagena to pursue a career as a chef, which she did for several years at nearby Ciccio and elsewhere before opening this perky storefront serving Latin-inspired multiculti fast-food cuisine. What's in season and the chef's whims determine the order-at-the-counter fare, but Puerto Rican rice bowls (often with pork), empanadas, and sweet-and-sour ramen stir-fries make regular appearances. **Known for:** patio and rooftop seating; beer and wine lineup; eager-to-please staff. [$] *Average main: $16* ✉ *6488 Washington St.* ✥ *At Oak Circle* ☎ *707/415–5035* 🌐 *www.proteayv.com* 🕒 *Closed Wed.*

R+D Kitchen

$$$ | **ECLECTIC** | As the name suggests, the chefs here are willing to experiment, starting with sushi plates that include hiramasa rolls topped with rainbow-trout caviar. Among the items served at both lunch and dinner are the Greek-style rotisserie chicken in egg-lemon sauce, the buttermilk fried-chicken sandwich topped with Swiss, and a slow-roasted pork sandwich with avocado and slaw. **Known for:** good value; cheerful service; Dip Duo (guacamole and pimento cheese with chips) patio appetizer with wine or specialty cocktails. [$] *Average main: $24* ✉ *6795 Washington St.* ✥ *At Madison St.* ☎ *707/945–0920* 🌐 *rd-kitchen.com/locations/yountville.*

Redd Wood

$$ | **ITALIAN** | Chef Richard Reddington's casual restaurant specializes in thin-crust wood-fired pizzas and contemporary variations on Italian classics. With potato–and–green garlic soup, pizzas such as the sausage with a blend of goat cheese and mozzarella, and the pork chop entrée enlivened in fall by persimmon, Redd Wood does for Italian comfort food what nearby Mustards Grill does for the American version: it spruces it up but retains its innate pleasures. **Known for:** industrial decor; easygoing service; lunch through late-night menu. [$] *Average main: $22* ✉ *North Block Hotel, 6755 Washington St.* ✥ *At Madison St.* ☎ *707/299–5030* 🌐 *www.redd-wood.com.*

RH Yountville

$$$ | **MODERN AMERICAN** | Crystal chandeliers and fountains worthy of a French château supply the pizzazz at Restoration Hardware's streetside café, and the all-day menu's boards (charcuterie, cheeses, and other starters), greens (salads), mains (from a burger modeled on one from Chicago's Au Cheval restaurant to delicate Atlantic sole in brown butter) easily live up to it. The prosciutto's flown in from Parma (the burrata from Puglia), the greens are ever-so-fresh, and the plating impresses. **Known for:** streetside patio; shaved rib-eye sandwich; banana split, chocolate-chip cookies. [$] *Average main: $26* ✉ *6725 Washington St.* ✥ *At Pedroni St.* ☎ *707/339–4654* 🌐 *www.restorationhardware.com.*

Southside Yountville at Stewart Cellars

$ | MODERN AMERICAN | Comfort food for breakfast and lunch never looked as pretty as it does at the Yountville outpost of local-fave Southside Napa. The Lat-in-tinged California cuisine changes with the season but might include stone-fruit and ricotta toast for breakfast and shrimp ceviche tostadas for lunch. **Known for:** buttermilk biscuits and chorizo-sausage gravy; wine available (separately) from tasting room; healthful items like "super-food" and protein bowls. $ Average main: $9 ⊠ 6752 Washington St. ✛ Near Pedroni St. ☎ 707/947–7120 ⊕ www.southsidenapa.com/southside-yountville ⊘ No dinner.

 Hotels

★ **Bardessono**

$$$$ | RESORT | Tranquillity and luxury with a low carbon footprint are among the goals of this ultragreen wood, steel, and glass resortlike property in downtown Yountville, but there's nothing spartan about its accommodations, arranged around four landscaped courtyards. **Pros:** large rooftop lap pool; in-room spa treatments; smooth service. **Cons:** expensive; limited view from some rooms; a bit of street traffic on hotel's west side. $ Rooms from: $700 ⊠ 6526 Yount St. ☎ 707/204–6000 ⊕ www.bardessono.com ⟳ 62 rooms ⎧⊘⎫ No meals.

Hotel Villagio

$$$ | RESORT | At this slick yet inviting downtown haven of tranquillity, the streamlined furnishings, subdued color schemes, and high ceilings create a sense of spaciousness in the rooms and suites, each of which has a wood-burning fireplace and a balcony or patio. **Pros:** central location; steps from restaurants and tasting rooms; 13,000-square-foot spa. **Cons:** sometimes bustling with large groups; highway noise audible from some rooms on property's west side; expensive on weekends in high season. $ Rooms from: $355 ⊠ 6481 Washington St. ☎ 707/944–8877, 800/351–1133 ⊕ www.villagio.com ⟳ 112 rooms ⎧⊘⎫ Breakfast.

Hotel Yountville

$$$$ | HOTEL | The landscaped woodsy setting, resortlike pool area, glorious spa, and exclusive yet casual ambience of the Hotel Yountville attract travelers wanting to get away from it all yet still be close—but not too close—to fine dining and tasting rooms. **Pros:** chic rooms; close to Yountville fine dining; glorious spa. **Cons:** occasional service lapses unusual at this price point; expensive in high season; minimum-stay requirement some weekends. $ Rooms from: $550 ⊠ 6462 Washington St. ☎ 707/967–7900, 888/944–2885 for reservations ⊕ www.hotelyountville.com ⟳ 80 rooms ⎧⊘⎫ No meals.

★ **Lavender Inn**

$$$ | B&B/INN | Travelers looking for per-sonalized service from innkeepers who take the trouble to learn guests' names and preferences will enjoy this intimate inn just off Yountville's main drag. **Pros:** on-site free bike rental; use of pool at nearby sister property; personalized ser-vice. **Cons:** hard to book in high season; lacks amenities of larger properties; not sceney enough for some guests. $ Rooms from: $320 ⊠ 2020 Webber St. ☎ 707/944–1388 ⊕ www.lavendernapa.com ⟳ 9 rooms ⎧⊘⎫ Breakfast.

Maison Fleurie

$$ | B&B/INN | A stay at this comfortable, reasonably priced inn, said to be the oldest hotel in the Napa Valley, places you within walking distance of Yountville's fine restaurants. **Pros:** smallest rooms a bargain; outdoor hot tub and pool; free bike rental. **Cons:** breakfast room can be crowded at peak times; some rooms pick up noise from nearby Bouchon Bakery; hard to book in high season. $ Rooms from: $229 ⊠ 6529 Yount St. ☎ 707/944–2056 ⊕ www.maisonfleurienapa.com ⟳ 13 rooms ⎧⊘⎫ Breakfast.

Napa Valley Lodge

$$ | **HOTEL** | Clean rooms in a convenient motel-style setting draw travelers willing to pay more than at comparable lodgings in the city of Napa to be within walking distance of Yountville's tasting rooms, restaurants, and shops. **Pros:** clean rooms; filling continental breakfast; large pool area. **Cons:** no elevator; lacks amenities of other Yountville properties; pricey on weekends in high season. [$] *Rooms from: $280* ✉ *2230 Madison St.* ☎ *707/944–2468, 888/944–3545* 🌐 *www.napavalleylodge.com* 🛏 *55 rooms* 🍴 *Breakfast.*

Napa Valley Railway Inn

$$ | **HOTEL** | Budget-minded travelers and those with kids appreciate these basic accommodations—inside actual railcars—just steps away from Yountville's best restaurants. **Pros:** central location; quaint appeal; semi-reasonable rates. **Cons:** office is sometimes unstaffed; west-side rooms pick up some Highway 29 noise; lacks pool, fitness center, and other amenities. [$] *Rooms from: $225* ✉ *6523 Washington St.* ☎ *707/944–2000* 🌐 *www.napavalleyrailwayinn.com* 🛏 *9 rooms* 🍴 *No meals.*

★ North Block Hotel

$$$$ | **HOTEL** | A two-story boutique property near downtown Yountville's northern edge, the North Block attracts sophisticated travelers who appreciate its clever but unpretentious style and offhand luxury. **Pros:** extremely comfortable beds; attentive service; room service by Redd Wood restaurant. **Cons:** outdoor areas get some traffic noise; weekend minimum-stay requirement; rates soar on high-season weekends. [$] *Rooms from: $425* ✉ *6757 Washington St.* ☎ *707/944–8080* 🌐 *northblockhotel.com* 🛏 *20 rooms* 🍴 *No meals.*

★ Poetry Inn

$$$$ | **B&B/INN** | All the rooms at this splurge-worthy hillside retreat have full vistas of the lower Napa Valley from their westward-facing balconies; indoors, the polished service, comfortably chic decor, and amenities that include a private spa and a fully stocked wine cellar only add to the exquisite pleasure of a stay here. **Pros:** valley views; discreet, polished service; gourmet breakfasts. **Cons:** expensive pretty much year-round; party types might find atmosphere too low-key; shops and restaurants 3 miles away. [$] *Rooms from: $1025* ✉ *6380 Silverado Trail* ☎ *707/944–0646* 🌐 *poetryinn.com* 🛏 *5 rooms* 🍴 *Breakfast.*

Vintage House

$$$ | **RESORT** | Part of the 22-acre Estate Yountville complex—other sections include sister lodging Hotel Villagio and the shops and restaurants of V Marketplace—this downtown hotel consists of two-story brick buildings along verdant landscaped paths shaded by mature trees. **Pros:** aesthetically pleasing accommodations; private patios and balconies; secluded feeling yet near shops, tasting rooms, and restaurants. **Cons:** highway noise audible in some exterior rooms; very expensive on summer and fall weekends; weekend minimum-stay requirement. [$] *Rooms from: $355* ✉ *6541 Washington St.* ☎ *707/944–1112* 🌐 *www.vintagehouse.com* 🛏 *80 rooms* 🍴 *Breakfast.*

Shopping

B Spa Therapy Center

SPA/BEAUTY | Many of this spa's patrons are Bardessono Hotel guests who take their treatments in their rooms' large, customized bathrooms—all of them equipped with concealed massage tables—but the main facility is open to guests and nonguests. An in-room treatment popular with couples starts with massages in front of the fireplace and ends with a tea bath and a split of sparkling wine. The two-hour Yountville Signature treatment, which can be enjoyed in-room or at the spa, begins with a shea-butter-enriched sugar scrub, followed by a Chardonnay grape-seed oil

Oakville's Nickel & Nickel pairs horse-country flair with single-vineyard Cabernets.

massage and a hydrating hair-and-scalp treatment. The spa engages massage therapists skilled in Swedish, Thai, and several other techniques. In addition to massages, the services include facials and other skin-care treatments. ✉ *Bardessono Hotel, 6526 Yount St. ✛ At Mulberry St.* ☎ *707/204–6050* ⊕ *www.bardessono.com/spa* ✉ *Treatments from $165.*

Finesse, the Store

FOOD/CANDY | This small store sells chef Thomas Keller logo items such as The French Laundry hats and aprons, Ad Hoc wine tumblers, and Bouchon Bakery milk bottles, all displayed with high style. You can also buy chocolates, cookbooks, cookware sets, and mixes. ✉ *6540 Washington St. ✛ Near Humboldt St.* ☎ *707/363–9552* ⊕ *store.tkrg.com.*

Hunter Gatherer

CLOTHING | A Napa Valley play on the classic general store, Colby Hallen's high-end lifestyle shop sells women's clothing and accessories from designers such as Frēda Salvador and Emerson Fry.

She carries some men's items, too, along with everything from ceramic flasks and small gifts and cards to artisanal honey and Vintner's Daughter Active Botanical Serum face oil. ✉ *6795 Washington St., Bldg. B ✛ At Madison St.* ⊕ *www.huntergatherernapavalley.com.*

Kelly's Filling Station and Wine Shop

CONVENIENCE/GENERAL STORES | The fuel is more than petrol at this gas station–convenience store whose design recalls the heyday of Route 66 travel. The shop inside sells top-rated wines, hot dogs, fresh scones from nearby R+D Kitchen, gourmet chocolates, and ice cream. Gas up, grab some picnic items, order coffee, espresso, or a cool drink to go, and be ever-so-merrily on your way. ✉ *6795 Washington St. ✛ At Madison St.* ☎ *707/944–8165.*

Kollar Chocolates

FOOD/CANDY | The aromas alone will lure you into this shop whose not-too-sweet, European-style chocolates are made on-site with imaginative ingredients. The artisanal truffles, many incorporating local ingredients, include lavender milk chocolate, chai milk chocolate, and chili dark chocolate. ⊠ *V Marketplace, 6525 Washington St.* ☎ *707/738–6750* ⊕ *www. kollarchocolates.com.*

North Block Spa

SPA/BEAUTY | Well-trained massage therapists soothe patrons in the North Block Hotel's softly lit basement spa. Popular treatments include the Un-Corked, a foot and back exfoliation followed by a massage. For the full-body Signature Scrub, a blend of walnut-shell powder, sweet almond, and blood orange is applied prior to a massage that incorporates pink grapefruit. A session for hotel guests only called "Playful Passion" involves couples exfoliating each other, receiving dual massages, and playing a sensual game after relaxation sets in. Facials, skin regimens, and "Stiletto Blues" therapy for ladies betrayed by tall pointy heels are among the other treatments. ⊠ *North Block Hotel, 6757 Washington St.* ✛ *Near Madison St.* ☎ *707/944–8080* ⊕ *northblockhotel.com/spa* ⊠ *Treatments from $150.*

The Spa at The Estate

SPA/BEAUTY | Formerly known as Spa Villagio, the joint 13,000-square-foot facility of the Vintage House and the Hotel Villagio is a five-minute walk from the former's lobby and half that from the latter's. Private spa suites have long been popular with couples, who enjoy the separate relaxation areas, indoor and outdoor fireplaces, steam showers, saunas, and extra-large tubs. The signature treatments involve the experiences and products of the internationally respected skin-care company ESPA. The spa's director has developed exclusive therapies involving the use of an O2CHAIR designed to optimize breathing and promote relaxation. Facials and massages are among the à la carte services. ⊠ *6481 Washington St.* ✛ *At Oak Circle* ☎ *707/948–5050, 800/351–1133* ⊕ *www.*

villagio.com/spavillagio ⊠ *Treatments from $85.*

V Marketplace

SHOPPING CENTERS/MALLS | This two-story redbrick market, which once housed a winery, a livery stable, and a brandy distillery, now contains clothing boutiques, art galleries, a chocolatier, and food, wine, and gift shops. Celebrity chef Michael Chiarello operates a restaurant (Bottega), a tasting room for his wines, and Ottimo, with pizza, fresh mozzarella, and other stands plus retail items. Show some love to the shops upstairs, especially Knickers and Pearls (lingerie and loungewear) and Lemondrops (kids' clothing and toys). ⊠ *6525 Washington St.* ✛ *Near Mulberry St.* ☎ *707/944–2451* ⊕ *www.vmarketplace.com.*

Activities

Napa Valley Aloft

BALLOONING | Between 8 and 12 passengers soar over the Napa Valley in balloons that launch from downtown Yountville. Rates include preflight refreshments and a huge breakfast. ⊠ *V Marketplace, 6525 Washington St.* ✛ *Near Mulberry St.* ☎ *707/944–4400, 855/944–4408* ⊕ *www. nvaloft.com* ⊠ *From $200.*

Napa Valley Bike Tours

BICYCLING | With dozens of wineries within 5 miles, this shop makes a fine starting point for guided and self-guided vineyard and wine-tasting excursions. The outfit also rents bikes. ⊠ *6500 Washington St.* ✛ *At Mulberry St.* ☎ *707/944–2953* ⊕ *www.napavalleybiketours.com* ⊠ *From $124 (½-day guided tour).*

Napa Valley Balloons

BALLOONING | The valley's oldest balloon company offers trips that are elegant from start to finish. Full-day packages combine a balloon tour and bicycle tours, wine tours, or both. ⊠ *Domaine Chandon, 1 California Dr.* ✛ *At Solano Ave., west of Hwy. 29* ☎ *707/944–0228, 800/253–2224* ⊕ *www.*

napavalleyballoons.com ✉ *$239 per person.*

Oakville

2 miles northwest of Yountville.

Barely a blip on the landscape as you drive north on Highway 29, Oakville is marked only by its grocery store. The town's small size belies the big mark it makes in the wine-making world. Slightly warmer than Yountville and Carneros to the south, but a few degrees cooler than Rutherford and St. Helena to the north, the Oakville area benefits from gravelly, well-drained soil. This allows roots to go deep—sometimes more than 100 feet—so that the vines produce intensely flavored fruit. Cabernet Sauvignon from the most famous vineyard here, To Kalon, at the base of the Mayacamas range, goes into many top-rated wines from winemakers throughout the valley. Big-name wineries within this appellation include Silver Oak, Far Niente, and Robert Mondavi.

GETTING HERE AND AROUND

If you're driving along Highway 29, you'll know you've reached Oakville when you see the Oakville Grocery on the east side of the road. Here the Oakville Cross Road provides access to the Silverado Trail (head east). Oakville wineries are scattered along Highway 29, Oakville Cross Road, and the Silverado Trail in roughly equal measure.

You can reach Oakville from the town of Glen Ellen in Sonoma County by heading east on Trinity Road from Highway 12. The twisting route, along the mountain range that divides Napa and Sonoma counties, eventually becomes the Oakville Grade. The views of both valleys on this drive are breathtaking, though the continual curves make it unsuitable for those who suffer from motion sickness. VINE buses serve Oakville.

 Sights

B Cellars

WINERY/DISTILLERY | The chefs take center stage in the open-hearth kitchen of this boutique winery's hospitality house, and with good reason: creating food-friendly wines is B Cellars's raison d'être. Visits to the Oakville facility—all steel beams, corrugated metal, and plate glass yet remarkably cozy—begin with a tour of the winery's culinary garden and in some cases also the caves. Most guests return to the house to sample wines paired with small bites, with some visitors remaining in the caves for exclusive tastings of Cabernet Sauvignons from several historic vineyards of Andy Beckstoffer, a prominent grower. Kirk Venge, whose fruit-forward style well suits the winery's food-oriented approach, crafts these and other wines, among them red and white blends and single-vineyard Cabernets from other noteworthy vineyards. All visits here are strictly by appointment. ✉ *703 Oakville Cross Rd.* ✛ *West of Silverado Trail* ☎ *707/709–8787* ⊕ *www. bcellars.com* ✉ *Tastings from $65.*

Far Niente

WINERY/DISTILLERY | Hamden McIntyre, a prominent winery architect of his era also responsible for Inglenook and what's now the Culinary Institute of America at Greystone, designed the centerpiece 1885 stone winery here. Abandoned in the wake of Prohibition and only revived beginning in 1979, Far Niente now ranks as one of the Napa Valley's most beautiful properties. Guests participating in the main tour and tasting learn some of this history while strolling the winery and its aging caves. The trip completed, hosts pour the flagship wines, a Chardonnay and a Cabernet Sauvignon blend. The tasting session concludes with Dolce, a late-harvest Sémillon and Sauvignon Blanc wine. Two shorter tastings, one highlighting older vintages, the other showcasing the output of affiliated wineries, dispense with the tour. ■TIP➔ **Aged**

4

Napa Valley OAKVILLE

and rare Cabernets from the Far Niente wine library are served at Cave Collection tastings. ⊠ *1350 Acacia Dr.* ⊹ *Off Oakville Grade Rd.* ☎ *707/944–2861* ⊕ *www. farniente.com* ✉ *Tastings from $80; tour and tasting $80.*

★ Nickel & Nickel

WINERY/DISTILLERY | A corral out front and a farm-style windmill add horse-country flair to this winery, which makes smooth, almost sensual, single-vineyard Cabernet Sauvignons. Some of Nickel & Nickel's best derive from the home-base Oakville AVA—in particular the John C. Sullenger Vineyard, which surrounds the property—with impressive Cabernets from other Napa Valley appellations supplying the contrast. Tastings, all by appointment, begin with Chardonnay in the immaculate 1884 Sullenger House, followed by a tour of a rebuilt 18th-century barn and underground aging caves. Tasting of more wines resumes back at the house. You can also reserve a private tasting, minus the tour, adding an artisanal cheese and charcuterie plate if you wish. ■ TIP→ **Cabernet lovers won't want to miss this sister winery to elegant Far Niente.** ⊠ *8164 St. Helena Hwy./Hwy. 129* ⊹ *North of Oakville Cross Rd.* ☎ *707/967–9600* ⊕ *www.nickelandnickel.com* ✉ *Tastings from $80; tour and tasting $80.*

PlumpJack Winery

WINERY/DISTILLERY | With its metal chandelier and wall hangings, the tasting room at this casual appointment-only winery looks like a stage set for a modern Shakespearean production. (The name "PlumpJack" is a nod to Shakespeare's Falstaff.) A youngish crowd assembles here to sample vintages that include the citrusy reserve Chardonnay and a Merlot that's blended like a Cab, providing sufficient tannins to ensure ageability. PlumpJack also makes Syrah and a lusty Cabernet. Hosts pour the wines of the affiliated Cade Estate and Odette Estate along with PlumpJack wines at seated tastings on a vineyard-view patio or in a garden courtyard. ■ TIP→ **The Hilltop Tasting takes in the cellar and grounds and ends with a seated tasting overlooking the vineyards. Limited to six guests, it books up quickly in summer.** ⊠ *620 Oakville Cross Rd.* ⊹ *Off Silverado Trail* ☎ *707/945–1220* ⊕ *www.plumpjackwinery.com* ✉ *Tastings from $40.*

Robert Mondavi Winery

WINERY/DISTILLERY | The graceful arch at the center of the winery's mission-style building frames the lawn and the vineyard behind, inviting a stroll under the arcades. You can head for one of the walk-in tasting rooms, but if you've not toured a winery before, the 75-minute Signature Tour and Tasting is a good way to learn about enology and the late Robert Mondavi's role in California wine making. Those new to tasting should consider the 45-minute Wine Tasting Basics experience. Serious wine lovers can opt for the Exclusive Cellar tasting, during which a server pours and explains limited-production, reserve, and older vintages. The three-course Harvest of Joy Lunch and wine pairing starts with a tour. All visits except walk-in tastings require reservations. ■ TIP→ **Well-attended concerts take place in summer on the lawn.** ⊠ *7801 St. Helena Hwy./Hwy. 29* ☎ *888/766–6328* ⊕ *www.robertmondaviwinery.com* ✉ *Tastings and tours from $25.*

★ Silver Oak

WINERY/DISTILLERY | The first review of this winery's Napa Valley Cabernet Sauvignon declared the debut 1972 vintage not all that good and, at $6 a bottle, overpriced. Oops. The celebrated Bordeaux-style Cabernet blend, still the only Napa Valley wine bearing its winery's label each year, evolved into a cult favorite, and Silver Oak founders Ray Duncan and Justin Meyer received worldwide recognition for their signature use of exclusively American oak to age the wines. At the Oakville tasting room, constructed out of reclaimed stone and other materials from

Far Niente ages its Cabernets and Chardonnays in 40,000 square feet of caves.

a 19th-century Kansas flour mill, you can sip the current Napa Valley vintage, its counterpart from Silver Oak's Alexander Valley operation, and a library wine without an appointment. One is required for tours, private tastings, and food–wine pairings. ✉ *915 Oakville Cross Rd.* ✥ *Off Hwy. 29* ☎ *707/942–7022* 🌐 *www.silveroak.com* 🎫 *Tastings from $30, tours from $40 (includes tasting).*

🍴 Restaurants

Oakville Grocery
$ | **DELI** | Built in 1881 as a general store, Oakville Grocery carries high-end groceries and prepared foods. On summer weekends the place is often packed with customers stocking up on picnic provisions—meats, cheeses, breads, and gourmet sandwiches—but during the week it serves as a mellow pit stop to sip an espresso out front, have a picnic out back, or taste wines next door. **Known for:** breakfast burritos, scones, muffins; gourmet sandwiches and salads; picnic items and well-made coffee drinks. [$] *Average main: $12* ✉ *7856 St. Helena Hwy./Hwy. 29* ✥ *At Oakville Cross Rd.* ☎ *707/944–8802* 🌐 *www.oakvillegrocery.com.*

Rutherford

2 miles northwest of Oakville.

The spot where Highway 29 meets Rutherford Road in the tiny community of Rutherford may well be the most significant wine-related intersection in the United States. With its singular microclimate and soil, Rutherford is an important viticultural center, with more big-name wineries than you can shake a corkscrew at, including Beaulieu, Inglenook, Mumm Napa, and St. Supéry.

Cabernet Sauvignon is king here. The soil is ideal for those vines, and since this part of the valley gets plenty of sun, the grapes develop intense flavors. Legendary winemaker André Tchelistcheff's famous claim that "it takes Rutherford dust to grow great Cabernet" is quoted by just about every winery in the area that produces the stuff. That "Rutherford dust" varies from one part of the region to another, but the soils here are primarily gravel, sand, and loam, a well-drained home for Cabernet Sauvignon grapes, which don't like to get their feet wet.

GETTING HERE AND AROUND

Wineries around Rutherford are dotted along Highway 29 and the parallel Silverado Trail just north and south of Rutherford Road/Conn Creek Road, which connects these two major thoroughfares. VINE buses serve Rutherford.

VISITOR INFORMATION

CONTACT Rutherford Dust Society.
☎ 707/987–9821 ⊕ www.rutherforddust.org.

 # Sights

Beaulieu Vineyard

WINERY/DISTILLERY | The influential André Tchelistcheff (1901–1994), who helped define the California style of wine making, worked his magic here for many years. BV, founded in 1900 by Georges de Latour and his wife, Fernande, makes several widely distributed wines, but others are produced in small lots and are available only at the winery. The most famous of these is the Georges de Latour Private Reserve Cabernet Sauvignon, first crafted in the late 1930s. Reservations are required for some tastings here. ■ TIP→ **Book a Cabernet Collector tasting to sample current and older Cabernet Sauvignons and the most recent Georges de Latour vintage.** ⊠ 1960 St. Helena Hwy./Hwy. 29 ✛ At Hwy. 128 ☎ 800/373–5896 ⊕ www.bvwines.com ⌲ Tastings from $30.

Cakebread Cellars

WINERY/DISTILLERY | Jack and Dolores Cakebread were among the wave of early-1970s vintners whose efforts not only raised the Napa Valley's wine-making profile but also initiated what became known as the Wine Country lifestyle. Guests at current-release tastings sample Chardonnay and Cabernet Sauvignon, which helped establish the company, along with Merlot, Pinot Noir, Syrah, or other wines. At any tasting you'll learn about the winery's history—Jack was a photographer whose mentors included Ansel Adams—but book a tour for deeper insight. Cakebread, now run by the second generation, works with so many different varietals that you can opt for an all-red or all-white tasting or one focusing on estate-grown wines. New tasting spaces are part of a renovation and expansion project scheduled for completion in 2019. All visits are by appointment. ⊠ 8300 St. Helena Hwy./Hwy. 29 ☎ 707/963–5222 for info, 800/588–0298 for reservations ⊕ www.cakebread.com ⌲ Tastings from $25, tour $35.

Caymus Vineyards

WINERY/DISTILLERY | This winery's Special Selection Cabernet Sauvignon twice won Wine Spectator wine of the year. In good weather you can sample the latest vintage and a few other wines outdoors in a landscaped area in front of the tasting room. Chuck Wagner started making wine on this property in 1972 and still oversees Caymus production. His children craft wines for other brands within the Wagner Family of Wines portfolio. Son Charlie Wagner is the owner-winemaker of Mer Soleil, known for oaked and unoaked Chardonnays, a Pinot Noir, and a Malbec; daughter Jenny Wagner makes Sauvignon and Merlot for Emmolo, established by her mother. Especially on weekends, it's wise to make an appointment to taste here. ⊠ 8700 Conn Creek Rd. ✛ Off Rutherford Rd. ☎ 707/967–3010 ⊕ www.caymus. com ⌲ Tasting $50.

Elizabeth Spencer Winery

WINERY/DISTILLERY | Although its first vintage (1998) debuted long after those of neighbors Inglenook and Beaulieu, this winery owned by wife and husband Elizabeth Pressler and Spencer Graham lays claim to a slice of Rutherford history: guests gain entry to the courtyard tasting area, open most of the year, via the town's 1872 redbrick former post office. Varietal and geographical variety is a primary goal, with Cabernet Sauvignon, Grenache, Merlot, Pinot Noir, and Syrah among the reds winemaker Sarah Vandenriessche crafts from Napa, Sonoma, and Mendocino county grapes. Whites include Chardonnay, Pinot Blanc, and Sauvignon Blanc. Tastings, all seated, require an appointment. In winter, they take place in a warehouse space on-site made slightly snug by its fireplace. ☒ 1165 Rutherford Rd. ⊹ At Hwy. 29 ☎ 707/963–6067 ⊕ www.elizabethspencerwines.com ☜ Tastings from $25.

★ Frog's Leap

WINERY/DISTILLERY | FAMILY | It you're a novice, the tour at Frog's Leap is a fun way to begin your education. You'll taste wines that might include Zinfandel, Merlot, Chardonnay, Sauvignon Blanc, and an estate-grown Cabernet Sauvignon. The winery includes a barn built in 1884, 5 acres of organic gardens, an eco-friendly visitor center, and a frog pond topped with lily pads. Reservations are required for all visits here. ■TIP➜ **The tour is recommended, but you can also just sample wines either inside or on a porch overlooking the garden.** ☒ 8815 Conn Creek Rd. ☎ 707/963–4704, 800/959–4704 ⊕ www.frogsleap.com ☜ Tastings from $25, tour $35.

Honig Vineyard & Winery

WINERY/DISTILLERY | FAMILY | Sustainable farming is the big story at this family-run winery. The Eco Tour, offered seasonally, focuses on the Honig family's environmentally friendly farming and production methods, which include using biodiesel to fuel the tractors, monitoring water use in the vineyard and winery, and generating power for the winery with solar panels. The family produces only Sauvignon Blanc and Cabernet Sauvignon. By appointment, you can taste whites and reds at a standard tasting; the reserve tasting pairs single-vineyard Cabernets

with small bites. ☒ 850 Rutherford Rd. ⊹ Near Conn Creek Rd. ☎ 800/929–2217 ⊕ www.honigwine.com ☜ Tastings from $30, tour $45.

★ Inglenook

WINERY/DISTILLERY | Filmmaker Francis Ford Coppola began his wine-making career in 1975, when he bought part of the historic Inglenook estate. Over the decades he reunited the original property acquired by Inglenook founder Gustave Niebaum, remodeled Niebaum's ivy-covered 1880s château, and purchased the rights to the Inglenook name. The Inglenook Experience, an escorted tour of the château, vineyards, and caves, ends with a seated tasting of wines paired with artisanal cheeses. Among the topics discussed are the winery's history and the evolution of Coppola's signature wine, Rubicon, a Cabernet Sauvignon–based blend. The Heritage Tasting, which also includes a Rubicon pour, is held in the opulent Pennino Salon. Reservations are required for some tastings and tours, and are recommended for all. ■TIP➜ **Walk-ins can sip wines by the glass or bottle at The Bistro, a wine bar with a picturesque courtyard.** ☒ 1991 St. Helena Hwy./ Hwy. 29 ⊹ At Hwy. 128 ☎ 707/968–1100 ⊕ www.inglenook.com ☜ Tastings from $45, private experiences from $75.

Mumm Napa

WINERY/DISTILLERY | In Mumm's light-filled tasting room or adjacent outdoor patio you can enjoy bubbly by the flight, but the sophisticated sparkling wines, elegant setting, and vineyard views aren't the only reasons to visit. An excellent gallery displays original Ansel Adams prints and presents temporary exhibitions by premier photographers. Winery tours cover the major steps in making sparklers. For a leisurely tasting of several vintages of the top-of-the-line DVX wines, book an Oak Terrace tasting. Reservations are required for this tasting and the tour; they're recommended for tastings inside or on the patio. ☒ 8445 Silverado Trail

4

Napa Valley RUTHERFORD

⚓ *1 mile south of Rutherford Cross Rd.* ☎ *707/967–7700, 800/783–5826* ⊕ *www. mummnapa.com* ✉ *Tastings from $25, tour $40 (includes tasting).*

Piña Napa Valley

WINERY/DISTILLERY | The Piña family, whose Napa Valley heritage dates from the 1850s, is known locally as much for its first-rate vineyard-management company as its modest winery that specializes in single-vineyard, 100% Cabernet Sauvignon wines. Winemaker Anna Monticelli crafts robust Cabs from mostly hillside fruit, all estate grown. Though she doesn't blend in other varietals, commonly done to soften Cabernet, Piña doesn't release its wines until age has mellowed them. If he's not busy elsewhere, Larry Piña, the winery's genial managing partner and among his family's seventh generation involved in the wine business, often drops by the no-frills barrel-room tasting area. Appointments aren't necessary, but it's good to call 30 minutes ahead to make sure there's space. ■**TIP**➜ **A short hillside path behind the barrel room leads to a picnic platform with views west to Rutherford.** ✉ *8060 Silverado Trail* ⚓ *0.2 miles north of Skellenger La.* ☎ *707/738–9328* ⊕ *pinanapavalley. com* ✉ *Tasting $25.*

Provenance Vineyards

WINERY/DISTILLERY | Far northwest in the Rutherford appellation, Provenance makes first-rate Bordeaux-style wines from estate grapes and others sourced from top Napa Valley vineyards. Because the Cabernets poured in the Reserve Tasting hail from different subappellations, sampling them provides the opportunity to learn what makes a valley-floor Oakville or Rutherford Cab different, for instance, from a Howell or Diamond Mountain one. Provenance also produces the single annual bottling of the separately labeled and highly praised Hewitt Vineyard Cabernet Sauvignon from grapes grown nearby. Seated indoor tastings of several Hewitt vintages require

a reservation, but walk-ins are welcome to taste the Provenance wines, either indoors or on the merry patio out front. ✉ *1695 St. Helena Hwy./Hwy. 29* ⚓ *Near Mee La.* ☎ *707/968–3633* ⊕ *provenancevineyards.com* ✉ *Provenance tastings from $25, Hewitt tasting $75.*

Round Pond Estate

FARM/RANCH | Sophisticated wines come from Round Pond, but the estate also produces premium olive oils, most from olives grown and crushed on the property. Guests participating in the Vino & Olio experience pass through the high-tech olive mill and taste the aromatic oils, both alone and with housemade red-wine vinegars, before heading across the street to the winery to sample Round Pond's well-rounded red and other wines. The flagship Estate Cabernet Sauvignon has the structure and heft of the classic 1970s Rutherford Cabs but acknowledges 21st-century palates with smoother, if still sturdy, tannins. Tastings, some of which involve food, and tours are by appointment only (24–48 hours in advance). ■**TIP**➜ **The full Il Pranzo lunch incorporates products made and produce grown on-site, as does the well-attended Sunday brunch.** ✉ *875 Rutherford Rd.* ⚓ *Near Conn Creek Rd.* ☎ *707/302–2575, 888/302–2575* ⊕ *www.roundpond.com* ✉ *Tastings from $40.*

Sequoia Grove

WINERY/DISTILLERY | A stand of sequoias shades the outdoor areas and woodsy tasting room of this Cabernet Sauvignon producer. A current-release tasting includes the Napa Valley Cabernet—a blend with grapes from several vineyards—along with wines that might include Sauvignon Blanc, Chardonnay, Merlot, or Syrah. You can also request a tasting of single-vineyard Cabernets (price varies depending on what's being poured). A Taste for Cabernet, a thoughtful seminar focused on the output of five vineyards, provides surprising insights into which tastes—sweet, sour, bitter,

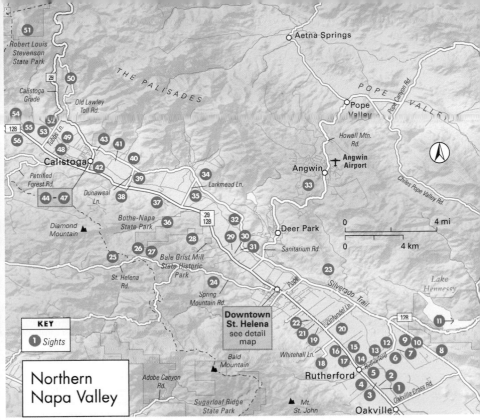

Northern Napa Valley

KEY

1️⃣ Sights

Barnett Vineyards **26**

Beaulieu Vineyard **14**

Bennett Lane Winery **55**

Brian Arden Wines **41**

Ca' Toga Galleria d'Arte ...**44**

Cade Estate Winery **33**

Cakebread Cellars **1**

Castello di Amorosa **37**

Caymus Vineyards **7**

Chateau Montelena **52**

Corison Winery **19**

Davis Estates **34**

Duckhorn Vineyards **31**

Ehlers Estate **29**

Elizabeth Spencer
Winery **5**

Frank Family Vineyards **35**

Frog's Leap **12**

Hall St. Helena **21**

Honig Vineyard
& Winery **13**

Inglenook **4**

Jericho Canyon
Vineyard **50**

Joseph Phelps Vineyards ..**23**

Mumm Napa **9**

Nichelini Family Winery ...**11**

Pestoni Family
Estate Winery **16**

Piña Napa Valley **8**

Prager Winery &
Port Works **22**

Pride Mountain
Vineyards **25**

The Prisoner Wine
Company **15**

Provenance Vineyards **17**

Raymond Vineyards **20**

Robert Louis
Stevenson State Park **51**

Rombauer Vineyards **32**

Romeo Vineyards
& Cellars **45**

Round Pond Estate **6**

St. Supéry Estate
Vineyards & Winery **3**

Schramsberg **36**

Sequoia Grove **2**

Sharpsteen Museum of
Calistoga History **46**

Smith-Madrone
Vineyards & Winery **27**

Spring Mountain
Vineyard **24**

Sterling Vineyards **39**

Stony Hill Vineyard **28**

Storybook Mountain
Vineyards **56**

T-Vine Winery **42**

Tamber Bey Vineyards **53**

Tedeschi Family Winery ...**48**

Tom Eddy Winery **54**

Tres Sabores Winery **18**

Trinchero Napa Valley **30**

Twomey Cellars **38**

Venge Vineyards **40**

Vermeil Wines **47**

Vincent Arroyo Winery **49**

Von Strasser
Family of Wines **43**

ZD Wines **10**

Round Pond Estate makes sophisticated wines and extra-virgin olive oils.

salty, and umami—best complement Cabernet Sauvignon. ✉ 8338 St. Helena Hwy./Hwy. 29 ✛ Near Bella Oaks La. ☎ 707/944–2945, 800/851–7841 ⊕ www.sequoiagrove.com ✉ Tastings from $30.

St. Supéry Estate Vineyards & Winery

WINERY/DISTILLERY | The French fashion company Chanel purchased St. Supéry in late 2015, adding further glamour to this winery whose Rutherford vineyards surround its immaculate hospitality center and production facility. St. Supéry makes two widely distributed wines, a Sauvignon Blanc and a Cabernet Sauvignon, but tastings here focus on limited-production efforts from the Rutherford property and the 1,500-acre Dollarhide Ranch on Howell Mountain. Reservations are preferred for the Featured Wine Flight, which includes whites and reds; you can also opt for an all-Cabernet tasting. Among the specialized experiences (all requiring a reservation), the popular Aromatherapy with a Corkscrew involves blind sniffing and tasting to learn how to identify citrus, tropical, and other aromas in wines. ■ TIP→ **In fine weather, sipping Sauvignon Blanc outside and playing pétanque (like boccie), feels like a mini-excursion to the old country.** ✉ 8440 St. Helena Hwy./Hwy. 29 ✛ Near Manley La. ☎ 707/963–4507 ⊕ www.stsupery.com ✉ Tastings from $35.

ZD Wines

WINERY/DISTILLERY | Founded in 1969 by Norman and Rosa Lee deLeuze and run these days by their family's second and third generations, this winery respected for its organic practices and local philanthropy specializes in Chardonnay and Pinot Noir from its Carneros estate and Cabernet Sauvignon from its Rutherford estate, where the wines are made and presented to the public. Most tastings take place in a second-floor space with broad vineyard views west across the Napa Valley to the Mayacamas Mountains. Walk-ins are welcome to sip current-release wines, but an appointment is required for three other tastings that include a vineyard or cellar tour or in one case both. ■ TIP→ **The Abacus solera-style**

Prohibition and Depression

The National Prohibition Act, which passed in 1919 under the popular name of the Volstead Act, had far-reaching effects on California wineries. Prohibition forced many to shut down altogether, but some, particularly Napa operations such as Beaulieu Vineyard, Beringer, and (on the St. Helena site now occupied by the Culinary Institute of America) the Christian Brothers, stayed in business by making sacramental wines. Others took advantage of the exception permitting home wine making and sold grapes and in some cases do-it-yourself kits with "warnings" about the steps that would result in grape juice turning into wine. A few wineries kept their inventories in bond, storing their wine in warehouses certified by the Department of Internal Revenue and guaranteed secure by bonding agencies. Magically, wine flowed out the back doors of the bonded warehouses into barrels and jugs brought by customers, and just as magically it seemed to replenish itself. Now and then a revenuer would crack down, but enforcement seems to have been lax at best.

Struggle and Survival

Prohibition, which ended in 1933, did less damage in the Napa Valley, where grapes thrive but fruit trees grow poorly on the rocky and gravelly slopes, benchlands, and alluvial fans, than it did in Sonoma County, where plum, walnut, and other orchards had replaced many vineyards. Fewer Napa growers had been able to convert to other crops, and more had been able to survive with sacramental wine, so more vineyards could be brought back to fine-wine production after repeal. Several major wineries survived Prohibition, including Inglenook and Charles Krug (acquired in the 1940s by the Cesare Mondavi family), which made very good wines during this period. Nevertheless, the wine industry struggled well into the 1960s to regain its customer base.

blend—complex from a logistical standpoint and in its mouthfeel—contains wine from every vintage of ZD Reserve Cabernet Sauvignon since 1992. ✉ *8383 Silverado Trail* ☎ *800/487–7757* 🌐 *www.zdwines.com* 🎫 *Tastings $40, tours (with tastings) from $85.*

🍴 Restaurants

★ Restaurant at Auberge du Soleil

$$$$ | **MODERN AMERICAN** | Possibly the most romantic roost for dinner in all the Wine Country is a terrace seat at the Auberge du Soleil resort's illustrious restaurant, and the Mediterranean-inflected cuisine more than matches the dramatic vineyard views. The prix-fixe dinner menu, which relies mainly on local produce, might include crispy veal sweetbreads and chanterelles or prime beef pavé with hearts of palm, arugula pesto, and tomato confit. **Known for:** polished service; comprehensive wine list; over-the-top weekend brunch. [$] *Average main: $120* ✉ *Auberge du Soleil, 180 Rutherford Hill Rd.* ✣ *Off Silverado Trail* ☎ *707/963–1211, 800/348–5406* 🌐 *www.aubergedusoleil.com.*

★ Rutherford Grill

$$$ | **AMERICAN** | Dark-wood walls, subdued lighting, and red-leather banquettes make for a perpetually clubby mood at this Rutherford hangout whose patio, popular for its bar, fireplace, and rocking chairs, is open for full meal service

or drinks and appetizers when the weather's right. Many entrées—steaks, burgers, fish, rotisserie chicken, and barbecued pork ribs—emerge from an oak-fired grill operated by master technicians. **Known for:** signature French dip sandwich and grilled jumbo artichokes; reasonably priced wine list with rarities; patio's bar, fireplace, and rocking chairs. $ *Average main: $30* ⊠ *1180 Rutherford Rd.* ⊹ *At Hwy. 29* ☎ *707/963–1792* ⊕ *www.rutherfordgrill.com.*

Hotels

★ Auberge du Soleil

$$$$ | **RESORT** | Taking a cue from the olive-tree-studded landscape, this hotel with a renowned restaurant and spa cultivates a luxurious look that blends French and California style. **Pros:** stunning views over the valley; spectacular pool and spa areas; the most expensive suites are fit for a superstar. **Cons:** stratospheric prices; least expensive rooms get some noise from the bar and restaurant; weekend minimum-stay requirement. $ *Rooms from: $950* ⊠ *180 Rutherford Hill Rd.* ☎ *707/963–1211, 800/348–5406* ⊕ *www.aubergedusoleil.com* ➷ *52 rooms* ⧆ *Breakfast.*

St. Helena

2 miles northwest of Rutherford.

Downtown St. Helena is the very picture of good living in the Wine Country: sycamore trees arch over Main Street (Highway 29), where visitors flit between boutiques, cafés, and storefront tasting rooms housed in sun-faded redbrick buildings. The genteel district pulls in rafts of tourists during the day, though like most Wine Country towns St. Helena more or less rolls up the sidewalks after dark.

The Napa Valley floor narrows between the Mayacamas and Vaca mountains around St. Helena. The slopes reflect heat onto the vineyards below, and since there's less fog and wind, things get pretty toasty. This is one of the valley's hottest AVAs, with midsummer temperatures often reaching the mid-90s. Bordeaux varietals are the most popular grapes grown here—especially Cabernet Sauvignon but also Merlot, Cabernet Franc, and Sauvignon Blanc. High-profile wineries bearing a St. Helena address abound, with Beringer, Charles Krug, and Ehlers Estate among the ones whose stories begin in the 19th century. The successes of relatively more recent arrivals such as Stony Hill, Rombauer, Duckhorn, Hall, Phelps, and a few dozen others have only added to the town's enological cachet.

GETTING HERE AND AROUND
The stretch of Highway 29 that passes through St. Helena is called Main Street, and many of the town's shops and restaurants are clustered on two pedestrian-friendly blocks between Pope and Adams Streets. Wineries are found both north and south of downtown along Highway 29 and the Silverado Trail, but some of the less touristy and more scenic spots are on the eastern and western slopes of Spring Mountain. VINE buses stop along Main Street.

VISITOR INFORMATION
CONTACT St. Helena Chamber of Commerce. ⊠ *1320A Main St.* ⊹ *Near Hunt Ave.* ☎ *707/963–4456* ⊕ *www.sthelena.com.*

Sights

Barnett Vineyards
WINERY/DISTILLERY | Scenic Spring Mountain Road winds past oaks and madrones and, in the springtime, sprays of wildflowers to this winery's lofty east-facing hillside setting. Arrive a little early to give yourself more time to bask in perspectives on the northern Napa Valley rivaling those from a balloon. When the weather's fine, tastings are held

St. Helena History

Unlike many other parts of the Napa Valley, where milling grain was the primary industry until the late 1800s, St. Helena took to vines almost instantly. The town got its start in 1854, when Henry Still built a store. Still wanted company, so he donated land lots on his townsite to anyone who wanted to erect a business. Soon he was joined by a wagon shop, a shoe shop, hotels, and churches. Dr. George Crane planted a vineyard in 1858 and was the first to produce wine in commercially viable quantities. Charles Krug followed suit a couple of years later, and other wineries soon followed.

In the late 1800s, phylloxera began to destroy France's vineyards, and Napa Valley wines caught the world's attention. The increased demand for Napa wines spawned a building frenzy in St. Helena. Many of the mansions still gracing the town's residential neighborhoods were built around this time. During the same period, some entrepreneurs attempted to turn St. Helena into an industrial center to supply specialized machinery to local viticulturists. Several stone warehouses were built near the railroad tracks downtown. Other weathered stone buildings on Main Street, mostly between Adams and Spring Streets and along Railroad Avenue, date from the same era. Modern facades sometimes camouflage these old-timers, but you can study the old structures by strolling the back alleys.

4

Napa Valley ST. HELENA

outside to take advantage of the views across the valley to Howell Mountain and beyond; if not, they're held in the atmospheric wine-aging cave. Barnett's winemaker, David Tate, makes restrained, beautifully balanced wines: Chardonnay and Pinot Noir, with fruit sourced from prestigious vineyards, and Cabernet Franc, Cabernet Sauvignon, and Merlot from the steeply terraced mountain estate. Quietly dazzling, they'll draw your attention from those vistas. Tastings are by appointment. ⊠ *4070 Spring Mountain Rd.* ✛ *At Napa–Sonoma county line* ☎ *707/963–7075* ⊕ *www.barnettvineyards.com* ▣ *Tasting $75.*

Beringer Vineyards
WINERY/DISTILLERY | Brothers Frederick and Jacob Beringer opened the winery that still bears their name in 1876. One of California's earliest bonded wineries, it is the oldest one in the Napa Valley never to have missed a vintage—no mean feat, given Prohibition. Frederick's grand Rhine House Mansion, built in 1884, serves as the reserve tasting room. Here, surrounded by Belgian art-nouveau hand-carved oak and walnut furniture and stained-glass windows, you can sample wines that include a limited-release Chardonnay, a few big Cabernets, and a Sauterne-style dessert wine. A less expensive tasting takes place in the original stone winery. Reservations are required for some tastings and recommended for tours. ■TIP➜ **The one-hour Taste of Beringer tour of the property and sensory gardens surveys the winery's history and wine making and concludes with a seated wine-and-food pairing.** ⊠ *2000 Main St./Hwy. 29* ✛ *Near Pratt Ave.* ☎ *707/963–8989* ⊕ *www.beringer.com* ▣ *Tastings from $25, tours from $30.*

Cade Estate Winery
WINERY/DISTILLERY | The staff and owners of this Howell Mountain winery specializing in collector-worthy Cabernets pride themselves on their eco-friendly farming,

winery, and hospitality practices. Polished, well-informed hosts pour arriving guests Sauvignon Blanc before embarking on a tour of the production facility and its 30,000-square-foot cave. Upon returning to the hospitality center—or in good weather the gravel patio out front, complete with infinity waterfall and robinia shade trees—a tasting commences of estate-grown Cabernet Sauvignon. Winemaker Danielle Cyrot's attention to detail begins in the vineyard and continues in the cellar, where she uses five dozen barrel types from two dozen coopers to bring out the best in the frisky (as in highly tannic) mountain fruit. All visits are by appointment. ■ TIP→ On a clear day the gasp-inducing views south down the valley stretch all the way to the Carneros. ⊠ 360 Howell Mountain Rd. S ✛ From Silverado Trail, head northeast on Deer Park Rd. ☎ 707/965–2746 ⊕ www.cadewinery. com ⌖ Tasting $80.

Charles Krug Winery

WINERY/DISTILLERY | A historically sensitive renovation of its 1874 Redwood Cellar Building transformed the former production facility of the Napa Valley's oldest winery into an epic hospitality center. Charles Krug, a Prussian immigrant, established the winery in 1861 and ran it until his death in 1892. Italian immigrants Cesare Mondavi and his wife, Rosa, purchased Charles Krug in 1943, and operated it with their sons Peter and Robert (who later opened his own winery). The winery, still run by Peter's family, specializes in small-lot Yountville and Howell Mountain Cabernet Sauvignons and makes Chardonnay, Merlot, Pinot Noir, Sauvignon Blanc, Zinfandel, and a Zinfandel port. The tour is by appointment only. ⊠ 2800 Main St./Hwy. 29 ✛ Across from the Culinary Institute of America ☎ 707/967–2229 ⊕ www. charleskrug.com ⌖ Tasting $45, tour $75 (includes tasting).

Clif Family Tasting Room

WINERY/DISTILLERY | Cyclists swarm to the tasting room of Gary Erickson and Kit Crawford, best known for the Clif energy bar, a staple of many a pedaling adventure. Cycling trips through Italian wine country inspired the couple to establish a Howell Mountain winery and organic farm whose bounty they share at this merry hangout. The King of the Mountain Tasting of estate Cabernets shows winemaker Laura Barrett at her most nuanced, but she crafts whites and reds for all palates. If hungry, you can pair the wines with soups, salads, and *bruschette* (open-face grilled-bread sandwiches) from the Bruschetteria food truck parked outside. ■ TIP→ The Tour de St. Helena Bike Rental with Tasting begins with an espresso and a Clif Bar, followed by biking, window shopping, and finally a well-earned wine tasting. ⊠ 709 Main St./ Hwy. 29 ✛ At Vidovich La. ☎ 707/968–0625 ⊕ www.cliffamily.com ⌖ Tastings from $30.

★ Corison Winery

WINERY/DISTILLERY | Respected for three 100% Cabernet Sauvignons, Corison Winery harks back to simpler days, with tastings amid oak barrels inside an unadorned, barnlike facility. The straightforward approach suits the style of Cathy Corison, one of the Napa Valley's first women owner-winemakers, who eschews blending because she believes her sunny St. Helena AVA vineyards (and other selected sites) can ripen Cabernet better than anywhere else in the world. Critics tend to agree, often waxing ecstatic about these classic wines. Library tastings start with a tour of the winery and the estate's Kronos Vineyard. They include both recent releases and older vintages, which together illustrate Corison's consistency as a winemaker and how gracefully her wines mature. Tastings are by appointment. ⊠ 987 St. Helena Hwy. ✛ At Stice La. ☎ 707/963–0826 ⊕ www.corison.com ⌖ Tastings from $55.

Crocker & Starr

WINERY/DISTILLERY | Wines that express "power and elegance" and "a deep sense of place"—in the latter case well-draining valley floor St. Helena AVA vineyards west of the Napa River—are the goals of this winery jointly owned by Charlie Crocker and winemaker Pam Starr. Cabernet Sauvignon is the main event, but Starr also crafts Sauvignon Blanc, Cabernet Franc, and Malbec, along with the Bridesmaid series Sauvignon Blanc and Cabernet Franc–dominant red blend. You can have a quick tasting on the porch of a century-old farmhouse, but to learn more about Crocker & Starr and its historic property, farmed prior to Prohibition by the Dowdell family, consider the experience that includes a brief foray into the vineyards and a peek at the winery, or with one those activities plus a wine-and-food pairing. ⊠ 700 Dowdell La. ⊹ ¼-mile east of Hwy. 29 ☎ 707/967–9111 ⊕ www.crockerstarr. com ⊠ Tastings from $35.

Culinary Institute of America at Greystone

COLLEGE | The West Coast headquarters of the country's leading school for chefs is in the 1889 Greystone Cellars, an imposing building once the world's largest stone winery. On the ground floor you can check out the quirky Corkscrew Museum and browse the Spice Islands Marketplace store, stocked with gleaming gadgets and many cookbooks. The Bakery Café by illy serves soups, salads, sandwiches, and baked goods. One-day and multiday cooking and beverage classes often take place. Students run the Gatehouse Restaurant, which serves dinner except during semester breaks. ⊠ 2555 Main St./Hwy. 29 ☎ 707/967–1100 ⊕ www.ciachef.edu/california ⊠ Museum free, tour $10; class prices vary.

Duckhorn Vineyards

WINERY/DISTILLERY | Merlot's moment in the spotlight might have passed, but you wouldn't know it at Duckhorn, whose Three Palms Merlot was crowned wine of the year by *Wine Spectator* magazine in 2017. You can taste Cabernet Sauvignon, Merlot, Chardonnay, Sauvignon Blanc, and other wines in the airy, high-ceilinged tasting room; you'll be seated at a table and served by staffers who make the rounds to pour. In good weather, you might do your sipping on a fetching wraparound porch overlooking carefully tended vines. "Elevated" experiences include a tasting of estate and single-vineyard wines offered twice daily, as well as a once-a-day (except Saturday) private hosted tasting. All tastings are by appointment. ⊠ 1000 Lodi La. ⊹ At Silverado Trail N ☎ 707/963–7108 ⊕ www. duckhorn.com ⊠ Tastings from $40.

Ehlers Estate

WINERY/DISTILLERY | New and old blend seamlessly at this winery whose 1886 tasting room's contemporary furnishings and changing artworks benefit from the gravitas and sense of history the original stone walls and exposed redwood beams impart. The wine-making team crafts complex Cabernet Sauvignon and other Bordeaux-style wines from 100% organically and biodynamically farmed estate grapes. Seated, appointment-only tastings focus on the growing practices and the winery's fascinating history, including Prohibition hijinks and the property's late-20th-century revival by a dynamic French couple. ■ TIP➔ **Croissants are served at the Start Your Day tasting, which commences at 9:30 am.** ⊠ 3222 Ehlers La. ⊹ At Hwy. 29 ☎ 707/963–5972 ⊕ www. ehlersestate.com ⊠ Tastings from $35.

Hall St. Helena

WINERY/DISTILLERY | The Cabernet Sauvignons produced here are works of art and the latest in organic-farming science and wine-making technology. A glass-walled tasting room allows guests to see in action some of the high-tech equipment winemaker Steve Leveque employs to craft wines that also include Merlot, Cabernet Franc, and Sauvignon Blanc.

4

Napa Valley ST. HELENA

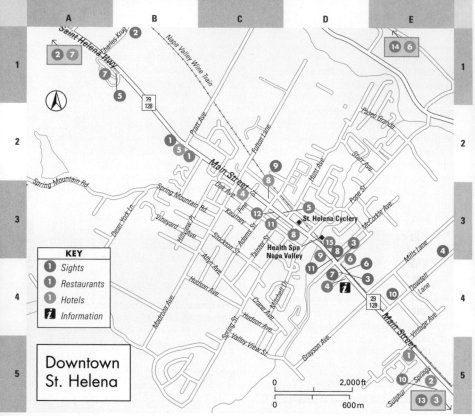

Downtown St. Helena

KEY
- ① Sights
- ① Restaurants
- ① Hotels
- 🛈 Information

Sights ▼
1 Beringer Vineyards..... **B2**
2 Charles Krug Winery ... **B1**
3 Clif Family Tasting Room **D4**
4 Crocker & Starr **E3**
5 Culinary Institute of America at Greystone................ **B1**
6 Long Meadow Ranch and Cafe **D4**
7 Mad Fritz Brewing Co. **D4**
8 Merryvale Vineyards ... **D3**
9 Robert Louis Stevenson Museum **C2**
10 VGS Chateau Potelle **E4**
11 Yao Family Wines **D3**

Restaurants ▼
1 Acacia House by Chris Cosentino **B2**
2 Brasswood Bar + Bakery + Kitchen **A1**
3 Charter Oak.............. **D3**
4 Clif Family Bruschetteria Food Truck............... **D4**
5 Cook St. Helena.......... **C3**
6 Farmstead at Long Meadow Ranch......... **D3**
7 Gatehouse Restaurant............... **A1**
8 Goose & Gander **D3**
9 Gott's Roadside **D3**
10 Harvest Table **E5**
11 Market **C3**
12 Model Bakery............. **C3**
13 Press **E5**
14 The Restaurant at Meadowood.............. **E1**
15 Tra Vigne Pizzeria and Restaurant.......... **D3**

Hotels ▼
1 El Bonita Motel........... **E5**
2 Harvest Inn by Charlie Palmer **E5**
3 Ink House **E5**
4 Inn St. Helena **C3**
5 Las Alcobas Napa Valley.............. **B2**
6 Meadowood Napa Valley.............. **E1**
7 Wine Country Inn **A1**
8 Wydown Hotel **C3**

Westward from the second-floor tasting area, rows of neatly spaced Cabernet vines capture the eye, and beyond them the tree-studded Mayacamas Mountains. The main guided tour takes in the facility, the grounds, and a restored 19th-century winery, passing artworks by John Baldessari, Jaume Plensa, and other contemporary talents. On Friday and weekends, tastings of limited-production Baca label Zinfandels take place. ■TIP→ **Hall Rutherford, an appointment-only sister winery, provides an exclusive, elegant wine-and-food pairing atop a Rutherford hillside.** ⊠ *401 St. Helena Hwy./Hwy. 29 ⊹ Near White La.* ☎ *707/967–2626* ⊕ *www.hallwines.com* ⊠ *Tastings from $30, tours from $40.*

★ **Joseph Phelps Vineyards**

WINERY/DISTILLERY | An appointment is required for tastings at the winery started by the late Joseph Phelps, but it's well worth the effort—all the more so after an inspired renovation of the main redwood structure, a classic of 1970s Northern California architecture. Known for wines crafted with grace and precision, Phelps does produce fine whites, but the blockbusters are red, particularly the Cabernet Sauvignon and the luscious-yet-subtle Bordeaux-style blend called Insignia. In good weather, one-hour seated tastings take place on a terrace overlooking vineyards and oaks. At 90-minute tastings as thoughtfully conceived as the wines, guests explore such topics as wine-and-cheese pairing, wine blending, and the role oak barrels play in wine making. Participants in the blending seminar mix the various varietals that go into the Insignia blend. ⊠ *200 Taplin Rd. ⊹ Off Silverado Trail* ☎ *707/963–2745, 800/707–5789* ⊕ *www.josephphelps.com* ⊠ *Tastings and seminars from $75.*

Long Meadow Ranch General Store & Cafe

WINERY/DISTILLERY | The first floor of the circa-1875 Logan-Ives House, named for two of several owners over the years, bustles throughout the day with patrons dropping by for wine, whiskey, and olive-oil tastings or shopping for food products and soft goods. A massive blue spruce shades the open-air café, a quick stop for breakfast or, later on, a pulled-chicken or other sandwich. The wines, among them Sauvignon Blanc, Chardonnay, Pinot Noir, Merlot, and Cabernet Sauvignon, come from the ranch's two Napa Valley estates plus a third in Mendocino's Anderson Valley. Olive trees on the Mayacamas Estate that date from the 1870s are thought to be the Napa Valley's oldest. Olives from them and newer trees are milled on-site. ■TIP→ **For captivating midvalley views and wine tasting in a cave, book a tour of the Mayacamas Estate, high up a hillside a hair west of the Rutherford appellation.** ⊠ *738 Main St. ⊹ At Charter Oak Ave.* ☎ *707/963–4555* ⊕ *www.longmeadow-ranch.com.*

★ **Mad Fritz Brewing Co.**

WINERY/DISTILLERY | #Beerpassion reigns at this St. Helena tap room where enthusiastic fans and palate-cleansing wine tourists stop to quaff small-lot lagers and ales crafted with a winemaker's sensibility. The goal of founder and master brewer Nile Zacherle, who, when he's not at the brewery, works at a Pritchard Hill winery, isn't merely to make great beers. He and his wife, Whitney Fisher, succeed at that, but they also create what they call "origin specific beers," with each label listing where the couple sourced every ingredient from hops to barley to water. The beers' label art and names, among them The Wind and the Sun and The Donkey and the Thistle, derive from a centuries-old *Aesop's Fables* edition. Along with the label's ingredients list is a summary of the bottling's fable and, in boldface, its moral. ⊠ *1282B Vidovich Ave. ⊹ At Hwy. 29* ☎ *707/968–5097* ⊕ *www.madfritz.com* ⊠ *Tastings from $3 per pour.*

Merryvale Vineyards

WINERY/DISTILLERY | Chardonnay and Cabernet Sauvignon are this winery's

Long Meadow Ranch's St. Helena compound includes a tasting room, a general store, a café, and a restaurant.

claims to fame, with Merlot and small-lot Cabernet Franc and Malbec among the other wines made. The winery has been in existence as Merryvale since 1991, but the building it occupies, the former Sunny St. Helena Winery, dates from just after Prohibition. No reservations are needed for the Signature Flight ($30) of current releases or the Reserve Tasting ($50) of winery and wine-club exclusive bottlings. They're required a day ahead, though, for the wine-and-artisanal-cheese pairing and for private tastings of Profile, a Cabernet Sauvignon–heavy Bordeaux-style blend of each vintage's best grapes. ⊠ 1000 Main St. ✛ At Charter Oak Ave. ☎ 707/963–7777 ⊕ www.merryvale.com 🍷 Tastings from $35.

Nichelini Family Winery

WINERY/DISTILLERY | A scenic drive east of the Silverado Trail winds past Lake Hennessey to Nichelini, the Napa Valley's oldest continuously operated family-owned winery. Erected in the late 1800s by Anton Nichelini, an Italian-Swiss immigrant, the old winery buildings, still in use, cling to a steep embankment where the road skirts a cliff. Anton's great-great-granddaughter Aimée Sunseri makes the wines, which include Cabernet Sauvignon and old-vine Muscadelle. ■TIP→ **The winery is open for walk-in tastings from Friday through Sunday, the rest of the week by appointment.** ⊠ 2950 Sage Canyon Rd./Hwy. 128 ✛ 8 miles east of Silverado Trail ☎ 707/963–0717 ⊕ www.nicheliniwinery.com 🍷 Tasting $20; tour with tasting $25.

Pestoni Family Estate Winery

WINERY/DISTILLERY | A 19th-century wine-bottling contraption, a Prohibition-era safe with tales to tell, and photos and documents spanning five generations enhance a visit to this winery run by the descendants of Albino Pestoni, their Swiss-Italian forebear. Pourers share the Pestoni story while dispensing wines made from grapes grown in choice vineyards the family has acquired over the decades. The Howell Mountain Merlots and Cabernet Sauvignons at Legacy tastings always stand out. Estate tastings often include Sauvignon Blanc, Sangiovese, and Cabernet grown on the Pestonis' Rutherford Bench property. The 1892 Field Blend from Lake County heirloom grapes—Zinfandel, Cabernet, and Petite Sirah—commemorates the year Albino entered the wine business. ■ TIP→ After a tasting flight, guests are welcome to picnic in the winery's tree-shaded pavilion. ☒ 1673 St. Helena Hwy. S/Hwy. 29 ⊹ Near Galleron Rd. ☎ 707/963–0544 ⊕ www.pestonifamily.com ⊠ Tastings from $25.

Prager Winery & Port Works

WINERY/DISTILLERY | "If door is locked, ring bell," reads a sign outside the weathered-redwood tasting shack at this family-run winery known for red, white, and tawny ports. The sign, the bell, and the thousands of dollar bills tacked to the walls and ceilings inside are your first indications that you're drifting back in time with the old-school Pragers, who have been making regular and fortified wines in St. Helena since the late 1970s. Five members of the second generation, along with two spouses, run this homespun operation founded by Jim and Imogene Prager. In addition to ports the winery makes Petite Sirah and Sweet Claire, a late-harvest Riesling dessert wine. ☒ 1281 Lewelling La. ⊹ Off Hwy. 29 ☎ 707/963–7678 ⊕ www.pragerport.com ⊠ Tasting $30 (includes glass).

Pride Mountain Vineyards

WINERY/DISTILLERY | This winery 2,200 feet up Spring Mountain straddles Napa and Sonoma counties, confusing enough for visitors but even more complicated for the wine-making staff: government regulations require separate wineries and paperwork for each side of the property. It's one of several amusing Pride Mountain quirks, but winemaker Sally Johnson's "big red wines," including a Cabernet Sauvignon that earned 100-point scores from a major wine critic two years in a row, are serious business. At tastings and on tours you can learn

about the farming and cellar strategies behind Pride's acclaimed Cabs (the winery also produces Syrah, a Cab-like Merlot, Viognier, and Chardonnay among others). The tour, which takes in vineyards and caves, also includes tastings of wine still in barrel. ■ TIP→ The views here are knock-your-socks-off gorgeous. ☒ 4026 Spring Mountain Rd. ⊹ Off St. Helena Rd. (extension of Spring Mountain Rd. in Sonoma County) ☎ 707/963–4949 ⊕ www.pridewines.com ⊠ Tastings from $30 ⊘ Closed Tues.

The Prisoner Wine Company

WINERY/DISTILLERY | The iconoclastic brand opened an industrial-chic space with interiors by the wildly original Napa-based designer Richard Von Saal to showcase its flagship The Prisoner red blend. "Getting the varietals to play together" is winemaker Chrissy Wittmann's goal with that wine (Zinfandel, Cabernet Sauvignon, Petite Sirah, Syrah, Charbono) and siblings like the Blindfold white (Viognier, Roussanne, Chenin Blanc, Vermentino). Walk-in patrons can sip these and other selections in the Tasting Lounge, more hip hotel bar than traditional tasting room, or outside in the casual open-air The Yard. Southward in The Makery, private appointment-only experiences unfold, some involving boldly flavored plates the winery kitchen turns out. Several alcoves within The Makery contain products for sale inspired by the Wine Country. The Prisoner's tasting space is quite the party, for most of which a reservation is required. ☒ 1178 Galleron Rd. ⊹ At Hwy. 29 ☎ 707/967–3823, 877/283–5934 ⊕ www.theprisonerwine-company.com ⊠ Tastings from $45.

Raymond Vineyards

WINERY/DISTILLERY | All the world's a stage to Jean-Charles Boisset, Raymond's charismatic owner—even his vineyards, where his five-act Theater of Nature includes a series of gardens and displays that explain biodynamic agriculture. The theatrics continue indoors in the

4

Napa Valley ST. HELENA

Tastings in Raymond's atmospheric Barrel Cellar include wines that are still aging.

disco-dazzling Crystal Cellar tasting room (chandeliers and other accoutrements by Baccarat), along with several additional spaces, some sedate and others equally expressive. Despite goosing up the glamour—gal pals out for a fun afternoon love this place—Boisset and winemaker Stephanie Putnam have continued the winery's tradition of producing reasonably priced premium wines. The Cabernet Sauvignons and Merlots often surprise. Some tours and tastings are by appointment only. ■TIP➜ **Concerned about dogs being left in hot cars during tastings, Boisset established the on-site Frenchie Winery, where canines lounge in comfort while their guardians sip wine.** ✉ *849 Zinfandel La.* ✛ *Off Hwy. 29* ☎ *707/963-3141* ⊕ *www.raymondvineyards.com* ✉ *Tastings from $25, tour and tasting $55.*

Robert Louis Stevenson Museum

MUSEUM | The rare manuscripts, first editions, photographs, childhood toys, and other artifacts at this small museum document the life and literary career of Robert Louis Stevenson (*Treasure Island, Kidnapped*). One exhibit examines the months Stevenson, at the time impoverished, spent in an abandoned miners' bunkhouse north of Calistoga. The interlude later became the inspiration for the author's book *The Silverado Squatters.* ✉ *1490 Library La.* ✛ *At Adams St.* ☎ *707/963-3757* ⊕ *www. stevensonmuseum.org* ✉ *Free* ☉ *Closed Sun. and Mon.*

Rombauer Vineyards

WINERY/DISTILLERY | The great-aunt of winery founder the late Korner Rombauer defined generations of American home cuisine with her best-selling book *The Joy of Cooking*, but he laid claim to a similar triumph. "Iconic" is an adjective often associated with Rombauer Chardonnays, particularly the flagship Carneros bottling. Although often described simply as "buttery," at their best the wines express equal parts ripeness, acidity, and creaminess, with vanilla accents courtesy of skillful oak aging. You can enjoy these famous Chards in the tasting room or over a glass sipped on the vineyard-view porch or while strolling the landscaped grounds. Rombauer, which requires reservations for all visits, also makes Sauvignon Blanc, Zinfandel, Cabernet Sauvignon, Merlot, and dessert wines. On tours of a portion of the caves, which extend more than a mile, the wines poured are mostly reds. ■TIP➜ Picnicking is permitted on a first-come, first-served basis (bring your own provisions). ⊠ 3522 Silverado Trail N ✛ ¾ mile north of Glass Mountain Rd. ☎ 800/622–2206 ⊕ rombauer.com ⌦ Tastings from $12, cave tour and tasting $100.

★ Smith-Madrone Vineyards & Winery

WINERY/DISTILLERY | For a glimpse of the Napa Valley before things got precious, head up Spring Mountain to the vineyard Stu Smith purchased in 1970 and still farms. His low-tech winery is a family affair: brother Charlie has made Smith-Madrone's critically acclaimed wines for more than four decades, and son Sam is Charlie's assistant. Blissfully informal tastings of Chardonnay, Cabernet Sauvignon, and Riesling take place by appointment four days a week in a weather-worn no-frills redwood barn. Charlie mostly lets the grapes do the talking, but profound wisdom underlies his restraint: these food-friendly wines are marvels of acidity, minerality, but most of all flavor. ■TIP➜ Before departing, walk or drive to the lawn east of the barn and bask in the views across the valley to Howell Mountain. ⊠ 4022 Spring Mountain Rd. ✛ Near Napa/Sonoma county line ☎ 707/ 963–2283 ⊕ www.smithmadrone.com ⌦ Tasting $25 ⊘ Closed Sun., Tues., Thurs.

Spring Mountain Vineyard

WINERY/DISTILLERY | Hidden off a winding road behind a security gate, the family-owned Spring Mountain Vineyard has the feeling of a private country estate, even though it's only a few miles from downtown St. Helena. The winery produces Chardonnay and Sauvignon Blanc, and Pinot Noir in limited quantities, but the calling card here is bold, robust Cabernet Sauvignon reflecting its mountain origin. A tasting of current releases reveals the wines' charms. The estate tasting includes a meander through the elegant property, from the 19th-century caves to the beautifully preserved 1885 mansion. Other tastings explore library vintages of Cabernet Sauvignon and the signature Bordeaux blend, Elivette. All visits require an appointment. ⊠ 2805 Spring Mountain Rd. ✛ Off Madrona Ave. ☎ 707/967–4188 ⊕ www.springmountainvineyard.com ⌦ Tastings from $40.

★ Stony Hill Vineyard

WINERY/DISTILLERY | Few wineries embrace low-tech more than Stony Hill, an ageless wonder known for Old World–style Chardonnays that sommeliers love. The magic takes place in a *Hobbit*-like cellar, itself worth the steep drive up Spring Mountain's eastern slope. Crammed with barrels—many a half-century old—it's a reminder that savvy and restraint are as crucial to wine making as fancy gadgets. Private tours (reservations required) begin at the home of the late Fred and Eleanor McCrea, whose first Chardonnay debuted in 1952. (Gewürztraminer, White Riesling, and a lean Cabernet are among the other wines made.) After walking the grounds and touring the winery, guests taste a few wines, often ending with Semillon du Soleil, a dessert one made from grapes dried in the sun after harvesting. In 2018 the founding family, the McCreas, sold the winery to the family that owns Long Meadow Ranch, but most of the longtime team remains involved. ⊠ 3331 St. Helena Hwy. N ✛ Near Bale Grist Mill ☎ 707/963–2636 ⊕ stonyhillvineyard.com ⌦ Tour $45 (includes tasting).

★ Tres Sabores Winery

WINERY/DISTILLERY | A long, narrow lane with two sharp bends leads to splendidly workaday Tres Sabores, where the sight of sheep, golden retrievers, guinea hens, pomegranate and other trees and plants, a slew of birds and bees, and a heaping compost pile help reinforce a simple point: despite the Napa Valley's penchant for glamour this is, first and foremost, farm country. Owner-winemaker Julie Johnson specializes in single-vineyard wines that include Cabernet Sauvignon and Zinfandel from estate-grown certified-organic Rutherford bench vines. She also excels with Petite Sirah from dry-farmed Calistoga fruit, Sauvignon Blanc, and the zippy ¿Por Qué No? (Why not?) red blend. *Tres sabores* is Spanish for "three flavors," which to Johnson represents the land, her vines, and, as she puts it, "the spirit of the company around the table." Tastings by appointment only are informal and often held outside. ⊠ *1620 S. Whitehall La.* ✛ *West of Hwy. 29* ☎ *707/967–8027* ⊕ *www.tressabores. com* ☕ *Tasting $50.*

Trinchero Napa Valley

WINERY/DISTILLERY | Sipping this winery's Malbec or Forté red Bordeaux blend, it seems inconceivable that last century's White Zinfandel craze made possible these willfully tannic wines. Over the years, the Trinchero family, owners of Sutter Home, which invented White Zin and stills sells 2 million–plus bottles annually, assembled a quality portfolio of estate vineyards from which winemaker Mario Monticelli crafts wines that truly live up to the term "terroir-driven." The wowsers include the Single Vineyard Collection reds—four Cabs, two Petit Verdots, two Malbecs, and Merlot, Cabernet Franc, and Petite Sirah—most from the Napa Valley's Atlas Peak, Calistoga, Mt. Veeder, and St. Helena subappellations. All are served in an elegant, exuberant tasting room designed by St. Helena's internationally acclaimed Erin Martin. Some tastings require reservations. ⊠ *3070 St. Helena Hwy. N* ✛ *Near Ehlers La.* ☎ *707/963–1160* ⊕ *www.trincheronapavalley.com* ☕ *Tastings from $35.*

★ VGS Chateau Potelle

WINERY/DISTILLERY | Sophisticated whimsy is on full display at the Chateau Potelle tasting room. Jean-Noel Fourmeaux, its bon vivant owner, fashioned this jewel of a space out of a nondescript 1950s bungalow south of downtown St. Helena. Decorated with contemporary art, some of it wine-themed, the residence is now the scene of leisurely paced sit-down tastings accompanied by gourmet bites from Napa's La Toque restaurant. Fourmeaux prefers fruit grown at higher elevations because he believes the relatively lengthy time grapes take to ripen in a cooler environment produces more complex and flavorful wines. His Cabernet Sauvignon, Syrah, and other reds support this thesis. The Chardonnay stars among the whites. Tastings are by appointment only. ■TIP➜ **Be sure to ask what "VGS" stands for.** ⊠ *1200 Dowdell La.* ✛ *At Hwy. 29* ☎ *707/255–9440* ⊕ *www.vgschateaupotelle.com* ☕ *Tasting $60.*

Yao Family Wines

WINERY/DISTILLERY | While playing for the NBA's Houston Rockets, the team's superstar center and future Hall of Famer Yao Ming became captivated by high-end Cabernets sipped at fine-dining spots after games. Before retiring from basketball, the Shanghai-born player was introduced to winemaker Tom Hinde, who helped him develop two upscale Cabernets, Yao Ming Napa Valley and Yao Ming Family Reserve. These wines and the Sauvignon Blanc and Bordeaux-style red blend of the more moderately priced Napa Crest line can be tasted at Yao's contempo-chic storefront space near Gott's Restaurant. Memorabilia on display sheds light on Yao's sports career and his philanthropic work in support of endangered species, clean drinking water, and other causes. ⊠ *929 Main St.* ✛ *At Charter Oak Ave.* ☎ *707/968–5874* ⊕ *www.yaofamilywines.com* ☕ *Tastings from $25.*

🍴 Restaurants

★ Acacia House by Chris Cosentino

$$$$ | MODERN AMERICAN | San Francisco restaurateur and celebrity chef Chris Cosentino, a *Top Chef Masters* winner, masterminds all the cuisine at Las Alcobas Napa Valley resort. The PBLT (pork belly, lettuce, and tomato) sandwich for lunch and 30-day dry-aged striploin au poivre for dinner are two of the farm-to-table mainstays, but noncarnivores won't feel left out: beet tarte tatin with smoked mascarpone and rigatoni with kale pesto graced a recent menu. **Known for:** impeccable presentation; specialty cocktails; extensive wine list. $ *Average main: $33* ⊠ *Las Alcobas Napa Valley, 1915 Main St. ⊕ At Pratt Ave.* ☎ *707/963–9004.*

Brasswood Bar + Bakery + Kitchen

$$$$ | ITALIAN | After Napa Valley fixture Tra Vigne lost its lease, many staffers regrouped a few miles north at the restaurant (the titular Kitchen) of the Brasswood complex, which also includes a bakery, shops, and a wine-tasting room. Along with dishes developed for the new location, chef David Nuno incorporates Tra Vigne favorites such as *arancini* (mozzarella-stuffed risotto balls) into his Mediterranean-leaning menu. **Known for:** top-tier mostly Napa-Sonoma wine list; no corkage on first bottle; Tra Vigne favorites. $ *Average main: $33* ⊠ *3111 St. Helena Hwy. N ⊕ Near Ehlers La.* ☎ *707/968–5434* ⊕ *www.brasswood. com.*

Charter Oak

$$$ | MODERN AMERICAN | Executive chef Christopher Kostow prepares ornate swoonworthy haute cuisine at The Restaurant at Meadowood, but he and chef Katianna Hong take a simpler approach (fewer ingredients chosen for maximum effect) at this high-ceilinged, brown-brick downtown restaurant. On a recent menu the strategy translated into dishes like hearth-roasted ham with horseradish, black cod grilled in corn leaves, and cauliflower with raisins and brown butter. **Known for:** exceedingly fresh produce; patio dining in brick courtyard; new chicken-wings appetizer recipe from high-profile restaurant each month. $ *Average main: $29* ⊠ *1050 Charter Oak Ave., at Hwy. 29* ☎ *707/302–6996* ⊕ *www.thecharteroak.com* ⊗ *No lunch Mon.–Thurs.*

Clif Family Bruschetteria Food Truck

$ | ITALIAN | Although it does venture out for special events, this walk-up spot for Italian-inflected fast food has a steady gig outside the Clif Family Tasting Room. Order a tomato, mushroom, pork, or other bruschetta, then enjoy it on the back patio or indoors, purchasing a glass or flight of wine, an espresso, or other beverage separately. **Known for:** canny flavor combos; soups and salads; many organic ingredients. $ *Average main: $12* ⊠ *Clif Family Tasting Room, 709 Main St./Hwy. 29 ⊕ At Vidovich La.* ☎ *707/968–0625 for tasting room* ⊗ *Closed Mon. No dinner Thurs.–Tues.* ⌗ *Truck hrs Thurs.–Tues. 11–4:30, Wed. 11–7:30.*

★ Cook St. Helena

$$$ | ITALIAN | A curved marble bar spotlit by contemporary art-glass pendants adds a touch of style to this downtown restaurant whose Northern Italian cuisine pleases with similarly understated sophistication. Mussels with house-made sausage in a spicy tomato broth, chopped salad with pancetta and pecorino, and the daily changing risotto are among the dishes regulars revere. **Known for:** top-quality ingredients; reasonably priced local and international wines; Cook Tavern two doors down for pizza and small plates. $ *Average main: $23* ⊠ *1310 Main St. ⊕ Near Hunt Ave.* ☎ *707/963–7088* ⊕ *www.cooksthelena.com.*

★ Farmstead at Long Meadow Ranch

$$$ | MODERN AMERICAN | Housed in a high-ceilinged former barn, Farmstead revolves around an open kitchen where executive chef Stephen Barber's team prepares meals with grass-fed beef and lamb, fruits and vegetables, and eggs, olive oil, wine, honey, and other ingredients from Long Meadow Ranch. Entrées might include wood-grilled trout with fennel, mushroom, onion and a bacon-mustard vinaigrette; Yukon potato gnocchi with wild mushrooms; or a wood-grilled heritage pork chop with jalapeño grits and chutney. **Known for:** Tuesday fried-chicken night; house-made charcuterie; seasonal cocktails. $ Average main: $29 ⊠ 738 Main St. ⚜ At Charter Oak Ave. ☎ 707/963–4555 ⊕ www.longmeadowranch.com/eat-drink/restaurant.

Gatehouse Restaurant

$$$$ | **MODERN AMERICAN** | Gung-ho Culinary Institute of America students in their final semester run this restaurant in a historic stone structure. A solid value, the three- or four-course prix-fixe meals—oft-changing, nicely plated dishes such as zucchini cumin cream soup (with Greek spiced meatballs and crème fraîche), phyllo-wrapped cod, and seared squab breast—emphasize local ingredients, some so local they're grown on-site or across the street at the CIA's student-tended garden at Charles Krug Winery. **Known for:** passionate service; many repeat customers; patio seating in good weather. $ Average main: $45 ⊠ 2555 Main St. ⚜ Near Deer Park Rd. ☎ 707/967–2300 ⊕ www.ciagatehouserestaurant.com ☉ Closed Sun. and Mon. and during semester breaks (check website or call for updates). No lunch.

Goose & Gander

$$$ | **MODERN AMERICAN** | The pairing of food and drink at G&G is as likely to involve cool cocktails as wine. Main courses such as koji-poached sea bass, heritage-pork porterhouse, and dry-aged New York steak with black-lime and pink-peppercorn butter work well with starters that might include blistered shishito peppers and grilled Spanish octopus. **Known for:** intimate main dining room with fireplace; alfresco dining

on patio in good weather; basement bar among Napa's best drinking spots. $ Average main: $26 ⊠ 1245 Spring St. ⚜ At Oak St. ☎ 707/967–8779 ⊕ www.goosegander.com.

Gott's Roadside

$ | **AMERICAN** | A 1950s-style outdoor hamburger stand goes upscale at this spot whose customers brave long lines to order breakfast sandwiches, juicy burgers, root-beer floats, and garlic fries. Choices not available a half century ago include the ahi tuna burger and the Vietnamese chicken salad. **Known for:** tasty (if pricey) 21st-century diner cuisine; shaded picnic tables (arrive early or late for lunch to get one); second branch at Napa's Oxbow Public Market. $ Average main: $13 ⊠ 933 Main St./Hwy. 29 ☎ 707/963–3486 ⊕ www.gotts.com ☞ Reservations not accepted.

Harvest Table

$$$ | **MODERN AMERICAN** | Several culinary gardens at the Harvest Inn by Charlie Palmer supply produce and herbs for its restaurant's seasonal cuisine, which might include starter plates such as beef tartare and smoked hamachi flatbread and mains like crispy duck-egg risotto and herb-roasted king salmon accompanied by fennel salad. With few exceptions, the wines hail from the Napa Valley, and the bartenders use spirits from local craft distillers for some of the artisanal cocktails. **Known for:** cozy dining room with large stone fireplace; outdoor dining in summer; truffle chicken for two. $ Average main: $29 ⊠ 1 Main St. ⚜ Near Sulphur Springs Ave. ☎ 707/967–4695 ⊕ www.harvesttablenapa.com ☉ No lunch Thurs. No dinner Mon.

Market

$$$ | **AMERICAN** | Ernesto Martinez, this understated eatery's Mexico City–born chef-owner, often puts a clever Latin spin on farm-to-table American classics. Although he plays things straight with the Caesar salad, fish-and-chips, and braised short ribs, the fried chicken

comes with cheddar-jalapeño corn bread, and the fried calamari owes its piquancy to the accompanying peppers, nopales cactus, chipotle aioli, and avocado tomatillo sauce. **Known for:** free corkage; full bar's Pomtinis and other specialty cocktails; Sunday brunch. [$] *Average main: $27* ✉ *1347 Main St.* ✥ *Near Hunt Ave.* ☎ *707/963–3799* 🌐 *marketsthelena.com.*

Model Bakery

$ | **BAKERY** | Thanks to plugs by Oprah, each day's batch of doughnutlike English muffins here sells out quickly, but the scones, croissants, breads, and other baked goods also inspire. Breakfast brings pastries and sandwiches with scrambled eggs, bacon, and Canadian ham; the lunch menu expands to include soups, salads, pizzas, and more sandwiches—turkey panini, Italian hoagies, muffalettas, and Cubanos among them. **Known for:** signature English muffins; people-watching at outdoor tables; second Oxbow market location. [$] *Average main: $11* ✉ *1357 Main St.* ✥ *Near Adams Ave.* ☎ *707/963–8192* 🌐 *www.themodelbakery.com* ⏲ *No dinner.*

★ **Press**

$$$$ | **MODERN AMERICAN** | Few taste sensations surpass the combination of a sizzling steak and a Napa Valley red, a union the chef and sommeliers at Press celebrate with a reverence bordering on obsession. Grass-fed beef from celebrated California purveyor Bryan Flannery cooked on the cherry-and-almond-wood-fired grill is the star—especially the 38-ounce Porterhouse and the *côte de boeuf* bone-in rib eye, both dry-aged—but the cooks also prepare pork chops, free-range chicken, and fish. **Known for:** extensive wine cellar; impressive cocktails; casual-chic ambience. [$] *Average main: $59* ✉ *587 St. Helena Hwy./Hwy. 29* ✥ *At White La.* ☎ *707/967–0550* 🌐 *www.pressnapavalley.com* ⏲ *Closed Tues. No lunch.*

★ **The Restaurant at Meadowood**

$$$$ | **MODERN AMERICAN** | Chef Christopher Kostow has garnered rave reviews—and three Michelin stars for several years running—for creating a unique dining experience. Patrons choosing the Tasting Menu option ($285 per person) enjoy their meals in the dining room, its beautiful finishes aglow with warm lighting, but up to four guests can select the Counter Menu ($500 per person) for the chance to sit in the kitchen and watch Kostow's team prepare the food ("the height of our vacation," said four recent guests). **Known for:** complex cuisine; first-class service; romantic setting. [$] *Average main: $275* ✉ *900 Meadowood La.* ✥ *Off Silverado Trail N* ☎ *707/967–1205, 800/458–8080* 🌐 *www.therestaurantatmeadowood.com* ⏲ *Closed Sun. and Mon. No lunch* ☞ *Jacket suggested but not required.*

Tra Vigne Pizzeria and Restaurant

$ | **PIZZA** | Crisp, thin-crust Neapolitan-style pizzas—among them the unusual Positano, with sautéed shrimp, crescenza cheese, and fried lemons—are the specialties of this family-friendly offshoot of the famous, now departed, Tra Vigne restaurant. Hand-pulled mozzarella, bucatini carbonara, and a few other beloved Tra Vigne dishes are on the menu, along with salads, pizzas, and pastas. **Known for:** oysters (good price) at happy hour (4–6); relaxed atmosphere; create-your-own-pizza option. [$] *Average main: $15* ✉ *1016 Main St.* ✥ *At Charter Oak Ave.* ☎ *707/967–9999* 🌐 *www.travignerestaurant.com.*

Hotels

El Bonita Motel

$ | **HOTEL** | A classic 1950s-style neon sign marks the driveway to this well-run roadside motel that—when it isn't sold out—offers great value to budget-minded travelers. **Pros:** cheerful rooms; hot tub; microwaves and mini-refrigerators. **Cons:** road noise a problem in some rooms;

noise in ground-floor rooms from second floor; lacks amenities of fancier properties. $ *Rooms from: $149* ⌂ *195 Main St./Hwy. 29* ☎ *707/963–3216, 800/541–3284* ⊕ *www.elbonita.com* ⏎ *52 rooms* ⏃ *Breakfast.*

Harvest Inn by Charlie Palmer

$$$ | HOTEL | Although this inn sits just off Highway 29, its patrons remain mostly above the fray, strolling 8 acres of gardens, enjoying views of the vineyards adjoining the property, partaking in spa services, and drifting to sleep in beds adorned with fancy linens and down pillows. **Pros:** garden setting; spacious rooms; near choice wineries, dining spots, and shops. **Cons:** some lower-price rooms lack elegance; high weekend rates; occasional service lapses. $ *Rooms from: $354* ⌂ *1 Main St.* ☎ *707/963–9463, 800/950–8466* ⊕ *www.harvestinn.com* ⏎ *78 rooms* ⏃ *Breakfast.*

Ink House

$$$$ | B&B/INN | The goal of the Castellucci family, which lavishly refurbished an 1885 Italianate along Highway 29, is to provide "a curated luxury experience" in impeccably styled rooms with 11-foot ceilings and vineyard views out tall windows. **Pros:** panoramic views from the cupola; attention to detail; Elvis Presley slept here (but it wasn't this stylish). **Cons:** extremely pricey; lacks on-site pool, fitness center, spa; two bathrooms have showers only (albeit nice ones). $ *Rooms from: $500* ⌂ *1575 St. Helena Hwy.* ☎ *707/968–9686* ⊕ *www.inkhousenapavalley.com/inn* ⏎ *4 rooms* ⏃ *Free Breakfast.*

Inn St. Helena

$$ | B&B/INN | A large room at this spiffed-up downtown St. Helena inn is named for author Ambrose Bierce *(The Devil's Dictionary)*, who lived in the main Victorian structure in the early 1900s, but sensitive hospitality and modern amenities are what make a stay worth writing home about. **Pros:** filling breakfast; outdoor porch and swing; convenient to shops, tasting rooms, restaurants. **Cons:** no pool, gym, room service, or other hotel amenities; two-night minimum on weekends (three with Monday holiday); per website "children 16 and older are welcome." $ *Rooms from: $279* ⌂ *1515 Main St.* ☎ *707/963–3003* ⊕ *www.innsthelena. com* ⏎ *8 rooms* ⏃ *Breakfast.*

Las Alcobas Napa Valley

$$$$ | HOTEL | Upscale-casual luxury is the goal of this hillside beauty—part of the Starwood chain's Luxury Collection—next to Beringer Vineyards and six blocks north of Main Street shopping and dining. **Pros:** pool, spa, and fitness center; vineyard views from most rooms; chef Chris Cosentino's Acacia House restaurant. **Cons:** pricey; per website no children under age 17 permitted; no self-parking. $ *Rooms from: $638* ⌂ *1915 Main St.* ☎ *707/963–7000* ⊕ *www.lasalcobasnapavalley.com* ⏎ *68 rooms* ⏃ *Breakfast.*

★ Meadowood Napa Valley

$$$$ | RESORT | Founded in 1964 as a country club, Meadowood evolved into an elite resort, a gathering place for Napa's wine-making community, and a celebrated dining destination. **Pros:** superb restaurant; all-organic spa; gracious service. **Cons:** very expensive; far from downtown St. Helena; weekend minimum-stay requirement. $ *Rooms from: $650* ⌂ *900 Meadowood La.* ☎ *707/963–3646, 800/458–8080* ⊕ *www.meadowood.com* ⏎ *85 rooms* ⏃ *No meals.*

Wine Country Inn

$$$ | B&B/INN | Vineyards flank the three buildings, containing 24 rooms, and five cottages of this pastoral retreat, where blue oaks, maytens, and olive trees provide shade, and gardens feature lantana (small butterflies love it) and lavender. **Pros:** staff excels at anticipating guests' needs; good-size swimming pool; vineyard views from most rooms. **Cons:** some rooms let in noise from neighbors; expensive in high season; weekend minimum-stay requirement. $ *Rooms from:*

$349 ✉ *1152 Lodi La.* ⊕ *East of Hwy. 29* ☎ *707/963–7077, 888/465–4608* 🌐 *www.winecountryinn.com* 🛏 *29 rooms* 🍴 *Breakfast.*

★ Wydown Hotel

$$$ | HOTEL | This smart boutique hotel near downtown shopping and dining delivers comfort with a heavy dose of style: the storefront lobby's high ceiling and earth tones, punctuated by rich-hued splashes of color, hint at the relaxed grandeur owner-hotelier Mark Hoffmeister and his design team achieved in the rooms upstairs. **Pros:** well run; eclectic decor; downtown location. **Cons:** lacks the amenities of larger properties; large corner rooms pick up some street noise; two-night minimum on weekends. [$] *Rooms from: $329* ✉ *1424 Main St.* ☎ *707/963–5100* 🌐 *www.wydownhotel.com* 🛏 *12 rooms* 🍴 *No meals.*

Nightlife

Cameo Cinema

FILM | The art nouveau Cameo Cinema, built in 1913 and now beautifully restored, screens first-run and art-house movies, and occasionally hosts live performances. ✉ *1340 Main St.* ⊕ *Near Hunt Ave.* ☎ *707/963–9779* 🌐 *www.cameocinema.com.*

The Saint

WINE BARS—NIGHTLIFE | This high-ceilinged downtown wine bar benefits from the grandeur and gravitas of its setting inside a stone-walled late-19th-century former bank. Lit by chandeliers and decked out in contemporary style with plush sofas and chairs and Lucite stools at the bar, it's a classy, loungelike space to expand your enological horizons comparing the many small-lot Napa Valley wines on offer with their counterparts in France and beyond. There's live or DJ music some nights. ✉ *1351 Main St.* ⊕ *Near Adams St.* ☎ *707/302–5130* 🌐 *www.thesaintnapavalley.com.*

Shopping

Acres Home and Garden

HOUSEHOLD ITEMS/FURNITURE | Part general store, part gift shop, Acres sells bulbs, gardening implements, and home decor items "for the well-tended life." ✉ *1219 Main St.* ⊕ *Near Spring St.* ☎ *707/967–1142* 🌐 *www.acreshomeandgarden.com.*

Aerena Galleries & Gardens

ART GALLERIES | This airy gallery exhibits abstract and contemporary realist paintings, works on paper, and sculpture. ✉ *1354 Main St.* ⊕ *Near Adams St.* ☎ *707/603–8787* 🌐 *www.aerenagalleries.com.*

Caldwell Snyder

ART GALLERIES | Inside the handsome Star Building (1900), this gallery exhibits contemporary American, European, and Latin American paintings and sculptures. ✉ *1328 Main St.* ⊕ *Near Hunt Ave.* ☎ *707/200–5050* 🌐 *www.caldwellsnyder.com.*

Dean & Deluca

FOOD/CANDY | The specialty grocery chain's Napa Valley branch sells kitchenware and has a large wine selection, but most visitors come for the produce, prepared foods, and deli items to picnic in style. ✉ *607 St. Helena Hwy./Hwy. 29* ⊕ *At White La.* ☎ *707/967–9980* 🌐 *www.deandeluca.com.*

Health Spa Napa Valley

SPA/BEAUTY | The focus at this local favorite is on health, wellness, and fitness, so there are personal trainers offering advice and an outdoor lap pool in addition to the extensive regimen of massages and body treatments. The Harvest Mud Wrap, for which clients are slathered with grape-seed mud and French clay, is a more indulgent, less messy alternative to a traditional mud bath. Afterward you can take advantage of the sauna, hot tub, and eucalyptus steam rooms. ■ **TIP→ Longtime patrons book treatments before noon to take advantage of**

the all-day access. ⊠ *1030 Main St.* ✛ *At Pope St.* ☎ *707/967–8800* ⊕ *www.napav-alleyspa.com* 🎫 *Treatments from $20.*

Jan de Luz
HOUSEHOLD ITEMS/FURNITURE | Fine French table linens and high-quality items for home and garden fill this shop where you can also pick up dish towels too pretty to actually use and monogrammed seer-sucker pajamas and other items indispen-sable to a life properly lived. ⊠ *1219 Main St.* ✛ *At Spring St.* ☎ *707/963–1550* ⊕ *www.jandeluzlinens.com.*

Napa Valley Olive Oil Manufacturing Company
$ | |**FOOD/CANDY** | "There's a crazy little shack beyond the tracks," the song goes, but in this case the barnlike building east of the railroad tracks sells tickle-your-taste-buds olive oils and vinegars, along with cheeses, meats, breads, and other delectables to take on the road or enjoy at picnic tables right outside. This is old Napa—no frills, cash only—with a shout-out to old Italy. ⊠ *835 Charter Oak Ave.* ✛ *Off Main St.* ☎ *707/963–4173* ⊕ *oliveoilsainthelena.com.*

★ Pearl Wonderful Clothing
CLOTHING | Sweet Pearl carries the latest in women's fashions in a space that makes dramatic use of the section of the historic stone building the shop occupies. Celebs find bags, shoes, jewelry, and out-fits here—and you might, too. ⊠ *1219C Main St.* ☎ *707/963–3236* ⊕ *pearlwon-derfulclothing.com.*

Woodhouse Chocolate
FOOD/CANDY | Elaborate confections made on the premises are displayed like miniature works of art at this shop that resembles an 18th-century Parisian salon. ⊠ *1367 Main St.* ✛ *At Adams St.* ☎ *707/963–8413, 800/966–3468* ⊕ *www.woodhousechocolate.com.*

 Activities

St. Helena Cyclery
SPORTS—SIGHT | Rent hybrid and road bikes by the hour or day at this shop that has a useful "Where to Ride" page on its website (see the About tab). ⊠ *1156 Main St.* ✛ *At Spring St.* ☎ *707/963–7736* ⊕ *www.sthelenacyclery.com* 🎫 *From $15 per hr, $45 per day.*

Calistoga

3 miles northwest of St. Helena.

The false-fronted shops, 19th-century buildings, and unpretentious cafés lining the main drag of Lincoln Avenue give Calistoga a slightly rough-and-tumble feel that's unique in the Napa Valley. With Mt. St. Helena rising to the north and visible from downtown, Calistoga looks a bit like a cattle town tucked into a remote mountain valley.

In 1859 Sam Brannan—Mormon mission-ary, entrepreneur, and vineyard develop-er—learned about a place in the upper Napa Valley, called Agua Caliente by set-tlers, that was peppered with hot springs and even had its own "Old Faithful" gey-ser. He snapped up 2,000 acres of prime property and laid out a resort. Planning a place that would rival New York's famous Saratoga Hot Springs, he built an elegant hotel, bathhouses, cottages, stables, an observatory, and a distillery (the last a questionable choice for a Mormon mis-sionary). Brannan's gamble didn't pay off as he'd hoped, but Californians kept com-ing to "take the waters," supporting small hotels and bathhouses built wherever a hot spring bubbled to the surface. In the 21st century Calistoga began to get back to its roots, with new luxury properties springing up and old standbys getting a sprucing up. At the Brannan Cottage Inn *(see Hotels, below)*, you can spend a night in part of the only Sam Brannan cottage still on its original site.

The astounding Castello di Amorosa has 107 rooms.

GETTING HERE AND AROUND

To get here from St. Helena or anywhere else farther south, take Highway 29 north and then turn right on Lincoln Avenue. Alternatively, you can head north on Silverado Trail and turn left on Lincoln. VINE buses serve Calistoga.

VISITOR INFORMATION

CONTACT Calistoga Chamber of Commerce. ⊠ *1133 Washington St.* ✛ *Near Lincoln Ave.* ☎ *707/942–6333* ⊕ *www.visitcalistoga.com.*

 Sights

Bennett Lane Winery

WINERY/DISTILLERY | The stated goal of Rob Hunter, Bennett Lane's consulting winemaker, is "to create the greatest Cabernet Sauvignon in the world." At this appointment-only winery's tastefully casual salon in the far northern Napa Valley you can find out how close he and the team come. Although known for Cabernet, Bennett Lane also produces other reds, a sparkling wine, Chardonnay, and the Maximus White Feasting Wine,

a blend of Sauvignon Blanc, Chardonnay, and Muscat. Signature flight tastings survey the winery's white and red wines. There's also a Cab-focused reserve tasting. ■**TIP**→ **Given the quality of their grapes, the Napa Valley Cabernet and Cab-heavy Maximus Red Feasting Wine are relative bargains.** ⊠ *3340 Hwy. 128* ✛ *3 miles north of downtown* ☎ *877/629–6272* ⊕ *www.bennettlane.com* 🝢 *Tastings from $20.*

Brian Arden Wines

WINERY/DISTILLERY | This winery with a contemporary stone, glass, and metal facility a quarter mile south of the Solage resort takes its name from its son (Brian Harlan) and father (Arden Harlan) vintners. Brian, who makes the wines, has early memories of a 19th-century Lake County Zinfandel vineyard his family still farms, but his passion for the grape grew out of wine-related work in the restaurant industry. In addition to the expected Cabernet Sauvignon, in this case an exemplary one from a labor-intensive vineyard up Howell Mountain, Brian also makes

Cabernet Franc, Sangiovese, Zinfandel from the family ranch, Sauvignon Blanc, and a blend called B.A. Red that changes each vintage. These wines and a few others are poured in the tasting room or on an outdoor patio with Calistoga Palisades views. ⊠ *331 Silverado Trail* ✢ *Near Rosedale Rd.* ☎ *707/942–4767* ⊕ *www. brianardenwines.com* ⊠ *Tastings from $30* ⊗ *Closed Wed.*

Castello di Amorosa

WINERY/DISTILLERY | An astounding medieval structure complete with drawbridge and moat, chapel, stables, and secret passageways, the Castello commands Diamond Mountain's lower eastern slope. Some of the 107 rooms contain artist Fabio Sanzogni's replicas of 13th-century frescoes (cheekily signed with his website address), and the dungeon has an iron maiden from Nuremberg, Germany. You must pay for a tour to see most of Dario Sattui's extensive eight-level property, though with a basic tasting you'll have access to part of the complex. Bottlings of note include several Italian-style wines, including La Castellana, a robust "super Tuscan" blend of Cabernet Sauvignon, Sangiovese, and Merlot; and Il Barone, a deliberately big Cab primarily of Rutherford grapes. ■TIP➜ **The 2½-hour Royal Food & Wine Pairing Tour by sommelier Mary Davidek (by appointment only) is among the Wine Country's best.** ⊠ *4045 N. St. Helena Hwy./Hwy. 29* ✢ *Near Maple La.* ☎ *707/967–6272* ⊕ *www.castellodiamorosa.com* ⊠ *Tastings from $30, tours from $40 (include tastings).*

Ca' Toga Galleria d'Arte

MUSEUM | The boundless wit, whimsy, and creativity of the Venetian-born Carlo Marchiori, this gallery's owner-artist, finds expression in paintings, watercolors, ceramics, sculptures, and other artworks. Marchiori often draws on mythology and folktales for his inspiration. A stop at this magical gallery might inspire you to tour Villa Ca' Toga, the artist's fanciful Palladian home, a tromp-l'oeil tour de

force open for tours from May through October on Saturday morning only, by appointment. ⊠ *1206 Cedar St.* ✢ *Near Lincoln Ave.* ☎ *707/942–3900* ⊕ *www. catoga.com* ⊗ *Closed Tues. and Wed.*

Chateau Montelena

WINERY/DISTILLERY | Set amid a bucolic northern Calistoga landscape, this winery helped establish the Napa Valley's reputation for high-quality wine making. At the pivotal Paris tasting of 1976, the Chateau Montelena 1973 Chardonnay took first place, beating out four white Burgundies from France and five other California Chardonnays, an event immortalized in the 2008 movie *Bottle Shock*. A 21st-century Napa Valley Chardonnay is always part of a Current Release Tasting—the winery also makes Sauvignon Blanc, Riesling, a fine estate Zinfandel, and Cabernet Sauvignon—or you can opt for a Limited Release Tasting focusing more on Cabernets. The walking Estate Tour takes in the grounds and covers the history of this stately property whose stone winery building was erected in 1888. Guests board a vehicle for the seasonal Vineyard Tour. Tours and some tastings require a reservation. ⊠ *1429 Tubbs La.* ✢ *Off Hwy. 29* ☎ *707/942–5105* ⊕ *www. montelena.com* ⊠ *Tastings from $30, tours from $50.*

Davis Estates

WINERY/DISTILLERY | Owners Mike and Sandy Davis transformed a ramshackle property into a plush winery whose predominantly Bordeaux-style wines live up to the magnificent setting. In fashioning the couple's haute-rustic appointment-only hospitality center, the celebrated Wine Country architect Howard Backen incorporated cedar, walnut, and other woods. In fine weather, many guests sit on the open-air terrace's huge swinging sofas, enjoying broad valley views while tasting wines by Cary Gott. The winemaker, who counts Ram's Gate and Round Pond among previous clients, makes Sauvignon Blanc, Viognier, and Chardonnay whites, with Pinot Noir, Merlot, and Cabernet-heavy blends among the reds. The wines can be paired with small bites by Mark Caldwell, the executive chef. Tastings are by appointment only. ■ TIP→ **Philippe Melka, an elite wine consultant, crafts two collector-quality wines labeled Phase V, a Cabernet and a Petite Sirah.** ⊠ *4060 Silverado Trail N ⊕ At Larkmead La.* ☎ *707/942-0700* ⊕ *www. davisestates.com* ◴ *Tastings from $60.*

Frank Family Vineyards

WINERY/DISTILLERY | As a former Disney film and television executive, Rich Frank knows a thing or two about entertainment, and it shows in the chipper atmosphere that prevails in the winery's bright-yellow Craftsman-style tasting room. The site's wine-making history dates from the 19th century, and portions of an original 1884 structure, reclad in stone in 1906, remain standing today. From 1952 until 1990, Hanns Kornell made sparkling wines on this site. Frank Family makes sparklers itself, but the high-profile wines are the Cabernet Sauvignons, particularly the Rutherford Reserve and the Winston Hill red blend. Tastings are mostly sit-down affairs, indoors, on the popular back veranda, or at picnic tables under 100-year-old elms. Reservations are required from Friday through Sunday; they're wise on other days, too. ⊠ *1091 Larkmead La. ⊕ Off Hwy. 29* ☎ *707/942-0859* ⊕ *www. frankfamilyvineyards.com* ◴ *Tastings from $40.*

Jericho Canyon Vineyard

WINERY/DISTILLERY | The grapes at family-owned Jericho Canyon grow on hillsides that slope as much as 55 degrees. The rocky, volcanic soils of this former cattle ranch yield intensely flavored berries that winemaker Nicholas Bleecher, the son of the founders, transforms in consultation with blending specialist Michel Rolland into the flagship Jericho Canyon Cabernet Sauvignon and other wines. The nuances of sustainable farming in this challenging environment are among the topics covered during tastings that usually take place in the wine-aging cave after, weather permitting, a brief vineyard tour. All visits, customized based on guests' interests, are by appointment only. ⊠ *3322 Old Lawley Toll Rd. ⊕ Off Hwy. 29* ☎ *707/331-9076* ⊕ *jerichocanyonvineyard.com* ◴ *Tastings from $75.*

Robert Louis Stevenson State Park

NATIONAL/STATE PARK | Encompassing the summit of Mt. St. Helena, this mostly undeveloped park is where Stevenson and his bride, Fanny Osbourne, spent their honeymoon in an abandoned bunkhouse of the Silverado Mine. This stay in 1880 inspired the writer's travel memoir *The Silverado Squatters*, and Spyglass Hill in *Treasure Island* is thought to be a portrait of Mt. St. Helena. A marble memorial marks the site of the bunkhouse. The 10-mile trail is steep and lacks shade in spots, but the summit is often cool and breezy. ■ TIP→ **Bring plenty of water, and dress in layers.** ⊠ *Hwy. 29 ⊕ 7 miles north of town* ☎ *707/942-4575* ⊕ *www.parks.ca.gov/?page_id=472* ◴ *Free.*

Romeo Vineyards & Cellars

WINERY/DISTILLERY | Redwoods and cedars tower over the jolly downtown Calistoga garden patio and carriage-house tasting room of this under-the-radar producer of Bordeaux-varietal wines. Alison Green-Doran, whose first wine-making gig was working as a harvest intern in the 1970s for André Tchelistcheff, the premier California winemaker of his era, extracts intensely rich flavors from grapes grown a few miles away in Romeo's half-century-old southern Calistoga vineyard. The Napa Valley Cabernet is a bona fide bargain for the quality; the Malbec and Petit Verdot are also strong suits, as are the Sauvignon Blanc and Petit Verdot rosé. ■ TIP→ **The outdoor Perfect Pizza Pairings (7-inch gourmet pizza plus a glass of wine) keep things hopping on summer Friday and**

Saturday afternoons. ⊠ *1224 Lincoln Ave.* ✦ *At Cedar St.* ☎ *707/942–8239* ⊕ *www. romeovineyards.com.*

★ **Schramsberg**

WINERY/DISTILLERY | On a Diamond Mountain site first planted to grapes in the early 1860s, Schramsberg produces sparkling wines using the *méthode traditionnelle* (aka *méthode champenoise*). A fascinating tour covering Schramberg's history and wine-making techniques precedes the tasting. In addition to glimpsing the winery's historic architecture you'll visit caves, some dug in the 1870s by Chinese laborers, where 2 million–plus bottles are stacked in gravity-defying configurations. Tastings include pours of very different bubblies. To learn more about them, consider attending the session at which the wines are paired with cheeses; not held every day, this tasting focuses on the ways wine influences our experience of food and vice versa. All visits here are by appointment. ⊠ *1400 Schramsberg Rd.* ✦ *Off Hwy. 29* ☎ *707/942–4558, 800/877–3623* ⊕ *www. schramsberg.com* ⌖ *Tastings from $70.*

Sharpsteen Museum of Calistoga History

MUSEUM | Walt Disney animator Ben Sharpsteen, who retired to Calistoga, founded this museum whose centerpiece is an intricate diorama depicting the Calistoga Hot Springs Resort during its 19th-century heyday. A restored cottage from the resort, moved to this site, sits next door to the museum. One of the permanent exhibits focuses on Sharpsteen's career as an animator. ⊠ *1311 Washington St.* ✦ *At 1st St.* ☎ *707/942–5911* ⊕ *www.sharpsteenmuseum.org* ⌖ *$3.*

Sterling Vineyards

WINERY/DISTILLERY | **FAMILY** | An aerial tram whisks guests to this hillside winery with sweeping Napa Valley views. Free self-guided tours included in all visits take in the production facility, whose 2017 overhaul saw the installation of state-of-the-art equipment like optical sorters that select only the best grapes at harvesttime. On the hospitality side, the indoor tasting spaces and umbrella-shaded terraces received upgrades, too, with the various experiences showcasing Sterling's Diamond Mountain, sparkling, single-vineyard, and top-tier Platinum Merlot and Cabernet wines. A few tastings involve food-and-wine pairings overseen by executive chef Spencer Wolf, whose previous stops include the Culinary Institute of America at Greystone and Harvest Inn by Charlie Palmer. ⊠ *1111 Dunaweal La.* ✦ *Off Hwy. 29* ☎ *707/942–3300, 800/726–6136* ⊕ *www.sterlingvineyards. com* ⌖ *Tastings from $35 (includes tram ride, self-guided tour).*

Storybook Mountain Vineyards

WINERY/DISTILLERY | Tucked into a rock face in the Mayacamas range, this winery established in 1976 occupies a picture-perfect site with rows of vines rising steeply in dramatic tiers. Zinfandel is king—there's even a Zin Gris, a dry rosé of Zinfandel grapes. Tastings, all by appointment, are preceded by a low-key tour that includes a short walk up the hillside and a visit to the atmospheric tunnels, parts of which have the same rough-hewn look as they did when Chinese laborers dug them by hand around 1888. Jerry Seps, who started Storybook with his wife, Sigrid, continues to make the wines, these days with their daughter, Colleen. ⊠ *3835 Hwy. 128* ✦ *4 miles northwest of town* ☎ *707/942–5310* ⊕ *www.storybookwines.com* ⌖ *Tasting and tour $35* ⊙ *Closed Sun.*

T-Vine Winery

WINERY/DISTILLERY | Robust reds reflecting "a sense of place" are the draws at this winery that provides a break from Cabernet with Zinfandels, a Grenache, and wines from less common varietals like Carignane and Charbono. Winemaker Bertus van Zyl gooses up the Grenache with a year in 50% new French oak, producing a more tannic wine than one usually expects of this grape. T-Vine hadn't made a white wine since 2000 until van Zyl fashioned the Homegrown blend of old-vine Gewürstraminer and Grüner Veltliner in 2017. Although many of the wines derive from Northern California legacy vineyards, they're poured in a barn-moderne tasting room whose tall plateglass windows and outdoor patio have views east to the Calistoga Palisades. ⊠ *810 Foothill Blvd./Hwy. 29 ✛ Near Lincoln Ave.* ☎ *707/942–1543* ⊕ *www.tvinewinery.com* ▱ *Tasting $25.*

Tamber Bey Vineyards

WINERY/DISTILLERY | Endurance riders Barry and Jennifer Waitte share their passion for horses and wine at their glam-rustic winery north of Calistoga. Their 22-acre Sundance Ranch remains a working equestrian facility, but the site has been revamped to include a state-of-the-art winery with separate fermenting tanks for grapes from Tamber Bey's vineyards in Yountville, Oakville, and elsewhere. The winemakers produce three Chardonnays and a Sauvignon Blanc, but the stars are several subtly powerful reds, including the flagship Oakville Cabernet Sauvignon and a Yountville Merlot. The top-selling wine, Rabicano, is a Cabernet Sauvignon-heavy blend that in a recent vintage contained the four other main Bordeaux red grapes: Malbec, Merlot, Petit Verdot, and Cabernet Franc. Visits here require an appointment. ⊠ *1251 Tubbs La. ✛ At Myrtledale Rd.* ☎ *707/942–2100* ⊕ *www.tamberbey.com* ▱ *Tastings from $45.*

Tedeschi Family Winery

WINERY/DISTILLERY | Time-travel back to the days when the Napa Valley "lifestyle" revolved around a family rolling up its collective sleeves to grow grapes, make wines, and pour them at a slab of wood held up by used oak barrels. The first Tedeschi arrived in the valley in 1919 from Pisa, Italy, and the grandparents of the current winemaker, Mario, and general manager, his amiable brother Emilio, purchased the Calistoga property, then an orchard, in the 1950s. The Estate Cabernet, among Mario's best, is made from an acre of grapes grown on-site, with fruit for Sauvignon Blanc, Merlot, Petite Sirah, and other wines coming from Napa Valley and Sonoma County sources. ■ **TIP➔ An appointment to taste is required, but it's possible to make one same-day (just call ahead).** ⊠ *2779 Grant St., Napa ✛ At Greenwood Ave.* ☎ *707/337–6835* ⊕ *www.tedeschifamilywinery.com* ▱ *Tastings from $25.*

Tom Eddy Winery

WINERY/DISTILLERY | If you miss the driveway to Tom and Kerry Eddy's hillside slice of paradise, you'll soon find yourself in Sonoma County—their tree-studded 22-acre property, home to deer, wild turkeys, and a red-shouldered hawk, is that far north. Tom, the winemaker, and Kerry, a sommelier and talented sculptor (look for her works in the wine-aging cave), pour their wines by appointment only. Except for the estate Kerry's Vineyard Cabernet Sauvignon, they're made from grapes sourced from as near as Calistoga and, in the case of the Sauvignon Blanc, as far away as New Zealand. A past president of the Calistoga Winegrowers Association and a winery and wine-making consultant, Tom also makes other Cabernets, Chardonnay, Petit Verdot, Petite Sirah, Pinot Noir, and Syrah. A visit here is enchanting. ⊠ *3870 Hwy. 128 ✛ 4¼ miles north of downtown* ☎ *707/942–4267* ⊕ *tomeddywinery.com* ▱ *Tastings from $75.*

Twomey Cellars

WINERY/DISTILLERY | A fortuitous acquisition led to the creation of this winery and its flagship Merlot. Parent company Silver Oak purchased Soda Canyon Ranch Vineyard as a primary fruit source for its flagship Napa Valley Cabernet. Then-winemaker Daniel Baron soon realized that a few blocks of Merlot clones were among the world's finest and proposed a stand-alone wine. Silver Oak only makes Cabernet, so the Twomey label was launched to explore new varietals and vineyards. Since 2012 Jean Claude Berrouet, responsible for decades of vintages at France's Château Petrus, has consulted on the Merlot, which is made at Twomey's Calistoga location. Tastings of Sauvignon Blanc and Pinot Noirs made by Erin Miller at the company's Healdsburg winery precede the Merlot. ✉ *1183 Dunaweal La.* ✛ *Off Hwy. 29* ☎ *707/942-7026* ⊕ *www.twomey.com* ▭ *Tasting $15.*

★ **Venge Vineyards**

WINERY/DISTILLERY | As the son of Nils Venge, the first winemaker to earn a 100-point score from the wine critic Robert Parker, Kirk Venge had a hard act to follow. Now a consultant to exclusive wineries himself, Kirk is an acknowledged master of balanced, fruit-forward Bordeaux-style blends. At his casual ranch-house tasting room you can sip wines that might include the estate Bone Ash Cabernet Sauvignon, an Oakville Merlot, and the Silencieux Cabernet, a blend of grapes from several appellations. With its views of the well-manicured Bone Ash Vineyard and, west across the valley, Diamond Mountain, the ranch house's porch would make for a magical perch even if Venge's wines weren't works of art in themselves. Tastings are by appointment only. ✉ *4708 Silverado Trail* ✛ *1½ miles south of downtown, near Dunaweal La.* ☎ *707/942-9100* ⊕ *www.vengevineyards.com* ▭ *Tasting $45* ⊙ *Reservations recommended 3–4 wks in advance for weekend visits.*

Vermeil Wines

WINERY/DISTILLERY | Sports memorabilia fills the tasting room of Dick Vermeil, the former football broadcaster and Super Bowl–winning NFL coach. Unlike many sports figures who jump into the wine business with no previous connection, Vermeil, a Calistoga native, has roots going back four generations, when his ancestors owned part of what's now the Frediani Vineyard northeast of downtown. Winemaker Andy Jones and consulting winemaker Thomas Rivers Brown, a major Napa Valley talent, produce a lineup that focuses on Cabernet Sauvignon and other Bordeaux varietals. The Jean Louis Vermeil Cabernet Sauvignon and the Frediani Vineyard Cabernet Franc are two to watch out for, along with the Charbono, a red varietal rarely planted in California. ✉ *1255 Lincoln Ave.* ✛ *At Cedar St.* ☎ *707/341-3054* ⊕ *www.vermeilwines.com* ▭ *Tastings from $25.*

Vincent Arroyo Winery

WINERY/DISTILLERY | Fans of this down-home winery's flagship Petite Sirah snap it up so quickly that visitors to the plywood-paneled tasting room have to buy "futures" of wines still aging in barrels. The same holds true of the other small-lot wines. The namesake original owner and winemaker quit his mechanical engineering career in the 1970s to become a farmer, replacing a prune orchard with plantings of Petite Sirah and Cabernet Sauvignon, these days with Zinfandel the winery's top sellers. Later came more acreage and other varietals, including Merlot, Tempranillo, Sangiovese, and Chardonnay—all dry-farmed. These days Vince's daughter, Adrian, and her husband (and current winemaker), Matthew Moye, own and run the winery. The presentation here, experienced by appointment only, is charmingly old-school, with Arroyo, his daughter, and Moye often on hand. ✉ *2361 Greenwood Ave.* ✛ *Off Hwy. 29* ☎ *707/942-6995* ⊕ *www.vincentarroyo.com* ▭ *Tasting $10.*

Von Strasser Family of Wines

WINERY/DISTILLERY | Winemaker Rudy von Strasser's namesake single-vineyard Diamond Mountain Cabernet Sauvignons earned decades of acclaim and high-90s wine scores, so to some insiders it seemed an odd match when he acquired Lava Vine Winery, a valley-floor establishment known for its partylike atmosphere and eclectic wine roster. Von Strasser, though, welcomed the opportunity to extend his range: for Lava Vine he produces Sauvignon Blanc, Grüner Veltliner, Grenache, Charbono, Petite Sirah, and anything else that captures his fancy. Tastings take place in a barnlike space (walk-ins okay most weekdays, but make a reservation on weekends) whose hip-rustic touches include slatted bucket chandeliers that throw off spiffy light patterns. ■ TIP➜ The winery offers glass and bottle service in its outdoor picnic area. ✉ 965 Silverado Trail N ✛ Near Brannan St. ☎ 707/942–9500 ⊕ vonstrasser.com ⊠ Tastings from $25.

🍴 Restaurants

All Seasons Bistro
$$$ | AMERICAN | Flowers top the tables at this downtown restaurant that opened in 1983 and, to regulars' delight, in 2018 lured back a chef from its glory days to revamp the menu. Tuna carpaccio, a ham and Brie crepe, and a little gem salad with blue cheese are typical starters, with grilled sustainable salmon and morels and rib-eye steak with Bordelaise and chanterelles among likely entrées. Known for: wine list with 1970s and 1980s gems; warm dark chocolate torte, vanilla-bean crème brûlée for dessert; French-bistro atmosphere. $ Average main: $28 ✉ 1400 Lincoln Ave. ✛ At Washington St. ☎ 707/942–9111 ⊕ allseasonsnapavalley.com ⊗ Closed Tues.

Buster's Southern BarBeQue & Bakery
$ | BARBECUE | A roadside stand at the west end of Calistoga's downtown, Buster's lives up to its name with barbecue basics, sweet-potato pies, and corn bread muffins. Local-fave sandwiches at lunch include the tri-tip, spicy hot links, and pulled pork, with tri-tip and pork or beef ribs the hits at dinner. Known for: mild and searing hot sauces; slaw, baked beans, and other sides; down-home dining area. $ Average main: $13 ✉ 1207 Foothill Blvd./Hwy. 29 ✛ At Lincoln Ave. ☎ 707/942–5605 ⊕ www.busterssouthernbbq.com ☞ Closes in early evening (6 or 7 in winter, 7 or 8 in summer).

Calistoga Inn Restaurant & Brewery
$$$ | AMERICAN | When the weather's nice, the inn's outdoor patio and beer garden edging the Napa River are swell places to hang out and sip some microbrews. Among the beer-friendly dishes, the garlic-crusted calamari appetizer and the country paella entrée stand out, along with the Reuben with ale-braised corned beef, the pizzas, and the burger topped with Tillamook cheddar and applewood-smoked bacon. Known for: pleasing decor; kid-friendly patio; wine and beer flights. $ Average main: $24 ✉ 1250 Lincoln Ave. ✛ At Cedar St. ☎ 707/942–4101 ⊕ www.calistogainn.com.

★ Evangeline
$$$ | MODERN AMERICAN | The gas-lamp-style lighting fixtures, charcoal-black hues, and bistro cuisine at Evangeline evoke old New Orleans with a California twist. Executive chef Gustavo Rios, whose previous stops include Calistoga's Solbar and Yountville's Bouchon Bistro, puts a jaunty spin on dishes that might include shrimp étouffée, duck confit, or steak frites; the elaborate weekend brunch, with everything from avocado toast to buttermilk biscuits and sausage gravy, is an upvalley favorite. Known for: outdoor courtyard; palate-cleansing Sazeracs; addictive fried pickles. $ Average main: $27 ✉ 1226 Washington St. ✛ Near Lincoln Ave. ☎ 707/341–3131 ⊕ www.evangelinenapa.com ⊗ No lunch weekdays.

Johnny's Restaurant & Bar
$$ | MODERN AMERICAN | Across the lobby from the Mount View Hotel's fine-dining restaurant, whose executive chef also developed the menu here, casual Johnny's serves comfort cuisine a cut well above typical tavern fare. Fried-chicken sliders with buttermilk slaw, brioche croques madame, and Wagyu hamburgers make this a good stop for a low-key dinner or to catch sports events on any of several large TVs. Known for: comfort cuisine; happy hour (4–6:30); brunch Friday

and weekends. $ *Average main: $22* *Mount View Hotel & Spa, 1457 Lincoln Ave.* *Near Fair Way* 707/942–5938 *www.johnnyscalistoga.com* *No lunch Mon.–Thurs.*

★ Lovina

$$$$ | **MODERN AMERICAN** | A vintage-style neon sign outside this bungalow restaurant announces "Great Food," and the chefs deliver with imaginative, well-plated dishes served in three intimate rooms or on a streetside patio that in good weather is especially festive during weekend brunch. Staples on the seasonally changing menu include Chef Jenna's Chicken Tiki Yum-Yum, served with jasmine rice and crispy lentil chips, with heirloom tomato gazpacho a summer refresher and chicken-dumpling soup its warming winter counterpart. **Known for:** imaginative cuisine; weekend brunch scene; no corkage Thursdays. $ *Average main: $31* *1107 Cedar St.* *At Lincoln Ave.* 707/942–6500 *www.lovinacalistoga.com* *Closed Tues. and Wed.*

Sam's Social Club

$$$ | **MODERN AMERICAN** | Tourists, locals, and spa guests—some of the latter in bathrobes after treatments—assemble at this resort restaurant for breakfast, lunch, bar snacks, or dinner. Lunch options include pizzas, sandwiches, an aged-cheddar burger, and entrées such as chicken paillard, with the burger reappearing for dinner along with pan-seared Alaskan halibut, rib-eye steak frites, and similar fare, perhaps preceded by oysters and other cocktail-friendly starters. **Known for:** casual atmosphere; active patio scene; thin-crust lunch pizzas. $ *Average main: $28* *Indian Springs Resort and Spa, 1712 Lincoln Ave.* *At Wappo Ave.* 707/942–4969 *www.samssocialclub.com.*

★ Solbar

$$$$ | **MODERN AMERICAN** | As befits a restaurant at a spa resort, the sophisticated menu at Solbar is divided into "healthy, lighter dishes" and "hearty cuisine," with the stellar wine list's many half-bottle selections encouraging moderation, too. On the lighter side, seared black cod served with bok choy, ginger endive, and carrots, with heartier options recently including hibachi-grilled Wagyu rib eye with new potatoes. **Known for:** stylish dining room; festive outdoor patio; Sunday brunch. $ *Average main: $35* *Solage Calistoga, 755 Silverado Trail* *At Rosedale Rd.* 866/942–7442 *solage.aubergeresorts.com/dine.*

Sushi Mambo

$$ | **JAPANESE** | Preparations are traditional and unconventional at this sushi and country-Japanese restaurant whose owner vows diners will not leave hungry. They don't lack for choice either, and though the menu's diversity might daunt you into sticking to the familiar, consider ordering offbeat items like the Fungus Among Us (tempura mushrooms stuffed with spicy tuna), Batman Roll (eel and cream cheese), and Hottie (panko deep-fried shrimp with spicy tuna). **Known for:** upbeat vibe and offbeat items; vegetarian options; dessert mochi. $ *Average main: $20* *1631 Lincoln Ave.* *At Wappo Ave.* 707/942–4699 *www.napasushi.com.*

Veraison

$$$ | **FRENCH** | Chef James Richmond aims to prepare "good, tasty, contemporary but not too complicated French food," served in a softly lit space off the Mount View Hotel's lobby. The menu, which changes with the seasons, might include steak tartare, porcini risotto, seared short-rib steak, Alaskan halibut, and pan-roasted half chicken with creamy polenta, dishes that pair well with the mostly French and California wines from the carefully selected list. **Known for:** oysters on the half shell; house-made charcuterie; daily-changing chef's menu. $ *Average main: $28* *Mount View Hotel & Spa, 1457 Lincoln Ave.* *Near Fair Way* 707/942–5938 *www.veraisoncalistoga.com* *No lunch.*

Almost half the lodgings at the posh Calistoga Ranch have private hot tubs.

 Hotels

Best Western Plus Stevenson Manor

$ | HOTEL | Budget travelers get what they pay for—and a little bit more—at this motel a few blocks from Calistoga's downtown. **Pros:** great price for region, especially midweek and off-season; nice pool area; complimentary full breakfast. **Cons:** weekends pricey in high season; guest rooms have a budget-chain feel; some downstairs rooms feel a tad dark. $ Rooms from: $175 ⊠ 1830 Lincoln Ave. ☎ 707/942–1112, 800/780–7234 ⊕ www. stevensonmanor.com ↪ 34 rooms ⦿ Breakfast.

Brannan Cottage Inn

$$ | B&B/INN | Recent renovations injected glamour and vintage-yet-modern style into this small inn whose centerpiece is an 1860s cottage from Calistoga's original spa era. **Pros:** short walk from downtown; plush mattresses; helpful staff. **Cons:** noise from neighbors can be heard in some rooms; showers but no bathtubs in some rooms; lacks pool and other amenities of larger properties. $ Rooms from: $297 ⊠ 109 Wappo Ave. ✛ At Lincoln Ave. ☎ 707/942–4200 ⊕ www.brannancottageinn.com ↪ 6 rooms ⦿ Breakfast.

Bungalows of Calistoga

$$$ | B&B/INN | The owners of these spacious (584–889 square foot), contemporary bungalows aim to provide guests an upscale up-to-date home away from home, with fireplaces, outdoor patios and dining areas, wireless and streaming-service connectivity, fully stocked kitchens (complete with utensils plus dishwashers, refrigerators, and microwaves), and washers and dryers. **Pros:** contemporary style; five-minute walk to downtown Calistoga; rates include up to four guests. **Cons:** lacks room service and other hotel amenities; no pool or fitness center; two-night minimum. $ Rooms from: $375 ⊠ 207 Wappo Ave. ☎ 707/341–6544 ⊕ thebungalowsatcalistoga.com ↪ 3 bungalows ⦿ No meals.

Calistoga Motor Lodge

$$ | HOTEL | A 1947 roadside motel renovated in midcentury-modern style, the family-friendly, dog-friendly Calistoga Motor Lodge recalls the past while simultaneously escorting its guests into a pleasant and reasonably affordable present. **Pros:** 10-minute walk to downtown shops and restaurants; on-site full-service MoonAcre Spa and Baths; complimentary room beverages replenished daily. **Cons:** streetside rooms pick up traffic noise (ask for a room in back); rooms have showers with rain heads but no tubs; pool area feels crowded when motel is full up. ⑤ *Rooms from: $249* ⊠ *1880 Lincoln Ave.* ☎ *707/942–0991* ⊕ *www.calistogamotorlodgeandspa.com* ⊷ *50 rooms* ⑩ *No meals.*

Calistoga Ranch

$$$$ | RESORT | Spacious cedar-shingle lodges throughout this posh wooded Auberge Resorts property have outdoor living areas—even the restaurant, spa, and reception space have outdoor seating and fireplaces. **Pros:** many lodges have private hot tubs on the deck; hiking trails on property; guests have reciprocal facility privileges at Auberge du Soleil and Solage Calistoga. **Cons:** indoor-outdoor concept works better in fine weather than in rain or cold; no self-parking; expensive. ⑤ *Rooms from: $895* ⊠ *580 Lommel Rd.* ☎ *707/254–2800, 855/942–4220* ⊕ *www.calistogaranch.com* ⊷ *52 lodges* ⑩ *No meals.*

Cottage Grove Inn

$$$ | B&B/INN | A long driveway lined with freestanding, elm-shaded cottages with rocking chairs on their porches looks a bit like Main Street USA, but inside each skylighted building you'll find all the perks necessary for a romantic weekend getaway. **Pros:** early evening wine and cheese; plenty of privacy; huge bathtubs. **Cons:** no pool; some rooms pick up street noise; weekend minimum-stay requirement. ⑤ *Rooms from: $369* ⊠ *1711 Lincoln Ave.* ☎ *707/942–8400,*

800/799–2284 ⊕ *www.cottagegrove.com* ⊷ *16 cottages* ⑩ *Breakfast.*

★ Embrace Calistoga

$$$ | B&B/INN | Extravagant hospitality defines the Napa Valley's luxury properties, but Embrace Calistoga takes the prize in the "small lodging" category. **Pros:** attentive owners; marvelous breakfasts; restaurants, tasting rooms, and shopping within walking distance. **Cons:** light hum of street traffic; no pool or spa; two-night minimum some weekends. ⑤ *Rooms from: $309* ⊠ *1139 Lincoln Ave.* ☎ *707/942–9797* ⊕ *embracecalistoga.com* ⊷ *5 rooms* ⑩ *Breakfast.*

★ Francis House

$$$$ | B&B/INN | Built in 1886 of locally quarried tufa, abandoned for half a century but gloriously restored, the Second Empire–style Francis House opened in 2018 as a five-room luxury inn. **Pros:** ultrachic style evokes the past but feels utterly contemporary; full gourmet breakfast outdoors or in light-filled dining area; pool and lawn area in back. **Cons:** pricey for Calistoga (but less costly than the plushest resorts); more for romantic getaways than family adventures; weekend minimum-stay requirement. ⑤ *Rooms from: $495* ⊠ *1403 Myrtle St.* ☎ *707/341–3536* ⊕ *thefrancishouse.com* ⊷ *5 rooms* ⑩ *Free Breakfast.*

Indian Springs Resort and Spa

$$ | RESORT | Palm-studded Indian Springs—operating as a spa since 1862—ably splits the difference between laid-back and chic in accommodations that include lodge rooms, suites, 14 historic cottages, three stand-alone bungalows, and two houses. **Pros:** palm-studded grounds with outdoor seating areas; on-site Sam's Social Club restaurant; enormous mineral pool. **Cons:** lodge rooms are small; many rooms have showers but no tubs; two-night minimum on weekends (three with Monday holiday). ⑤ *Rooms from: $279* ⊠ *1712 Lincoln Ave.* ☎ *707/942–4913* ⊕ *www.*

indianspringscalistoga.com 🛏 113 rooms 🍴 No meals.

★ **Meadowlark Country House**

$$ | B&B/INN | Two charming European gents run this laid-back but sophisticated inn on 20 wooded acres just north of downtown. **Pros:** charming innkeepers; tasty sit-down breakfasts; welcoming vibe that attracts diverse guests. **Cons:** clothing-optional pool policy isn't for everyone; one room has a shower but no tub; maximum occupancy in most rooms is two. [$] *Rooms from: $285* ✉ *601 Petrified Forest Rd.* ☎ *707/942–5651* 🌐 *www.meadowlarkinn.com* 🛏 *10 rooms* 🍴 *Breakfast.*

Mount View Hotel & Spa

$$ | B&B/INN | Although it's in a 1919 building that's been designated a National Historic Landmark, the Mount View skews modern, with a cheery lobby and a boutique, slightly Euro feel. **Pros:** full-service spa; spacious suites and cottages. **Cons:** outside noise can be heard in some rooms; ground-floor rooms are dark; some standard rooms are small and have two twin beds. [$] *Rooms from: $219* ✉ *1457 Lincoln Ave.* ☎ *707/942–6877, 800/816–6877* 🌐 *www.mountviewhotel.com* 🛏 *31 rooms* 🍴 *No meals.*

★ **Solage Calistoga**

$$$$ | RESORT | The aesthetic at this 22-acre property, where health and wellness are priorities, is Napa Valley barn meets San Francisco loft: guest rooms have high ceilings, polished concrete floors, recycled walnut furniture, and all-natural fabrics in soothingly muted colors. **Pros:** great service; complimentary bikes; separate pools for kids and adults. **Cons:** vibe might not suit everyone; longish walk from some lodgings to spa and fitness center; expensive in-season. [$] *Rooms from: $481* ✉ *755 Silverado Trail* ☎ *866/942–7442, 707/226–0800* 🌐 *www.solagecalistoga.com* 🛏 *89 rooms* 🍴 *No meals.*

🍸 Nightlife

Hydro Bar & Grill

BARS/PUBS | Open until midnight on Friday and Saturday with live music, this might well be Calistoga's premier all-purpose nightspot. That's not saying much, but the vibe is festive. Except for the burger, a local fave, it's best to dine elsewhere. ✉ *1403 Lincoln Ave.* ✣ *At Washington St.* ☎ *707/942–9777.*

Susie's Bar

BARS/PUBS | Calistoga's entrant in the dive-bar sweepstakes is on the demure side, but it's a good place to toss back a top-shelf cocktail or a local brew at well below resort prices and after other nightspots have thrown in the bar towel. ✉ *1365 Lincoln Ave.* ✣ *At Washington St.* ☎ *707/942–6710* 🌐 *susiescalistoga.com.*

🛍 Shopping

Baths at Roman Spa

SPA/BEAUTY | Dispensing with high design and highfalutin treatments, this down-to-earth spa delivers the basics at reasonable prices. The decor—utilitarian in spots—is generally soothing, and the staff members seem eager to provide an experience that transforms. The signature Deluxe Spa Combination consists of mud and mineral baths followed by a full-body massage of 85 or 110 minutes. You can have all these treatments à la carte, and aromatherapy and Reiki sessions are also an option. ■ **TIP→ Not all Calistoga spas have rooms for couples, but this one does.** ✉ *Roman Spa Hot Springs Resort, 1300 Washington St.* ✣ *At 1st St.* ☎ *707/942–2122, 800/404–4772* 🌐 *bathsromanspa.com* 🎟 *Treatments $85–$199.*

Calistoga Pottery

CERAMICS/GLASSWARE | You might recognize the dinnerware and other pottery sold by owners Jeff and Sally Manfredi—their biggest customers are the area's inns, restaurants, and wineries. ✉ *1001 Foothill Blvd./Hwy. 29* ✣ *500 feet south*

of Lincoln Ave. ☏ 707/942–0216 ⊕ www.
calistogapottery.com ⊙ Closed Sun.

Dr. Wilkinson's Hot Springs Resort
SPA—SIGHT | Newer, fancier establishments might have eclipsed Dr. Wilkinson's, but loyal fans appreciate its reasonable prices and unpretentious vibe. The mud baths here are a mix of volcanic ash and Canadian peat, warmed by the spa's own hot springs. Fun fact: back in 1952, "The Works"—a mud bath, steam room, blanket wrap, and a massage—cost $3.50; the charge now is $149. ✉ 1507 Lincoln Ave. ✛ At Fair Way ☏ 707/942–4102 ⊕ www.drwilkinson. com ▱ Treatments from $77.

Enoteca Wine Shop
WINE/SPIRITS | The extensive tasting notes posted alongside nearly all of the wines sold here—among them some hard-to-find bottles from Napa, Sonoma, and around the world—help you make a wise choice. ✉ 1348-B Lincoln Ave. ☏ 707/942–1117 ⊕ www.enotecawine-shop.com.

Indian Springs Spa
SPA/BEAUTY | Even before Sam Brannan constructed a spa on this site in the 1860s, the Wappo Indians were building sweat lodges over its thermal geysers. Treatments include a Calistoga-classic, pure volcanic-ash mud bath followed by a mineral bath, after which clients are wrapped in a flannel blanket for a 15-minute cool-down session or until called for a massage if they've booked one. Intraceuticals oxygen-infusion facials are another specialty. Spa clients have access to the Olympic-size mineral-water pool, kept at 92°F in summer and a toasty 102°F in winter. ✉ 1712 Lincoln Ave. ✛ At Wappo Ave. ☏ 707/942–4913 ⊕ www.indianspringscalistoga.com/spa ▱ Treatments from $95.

Mad Mod Shop
CLOTHING | Find the new polka-dotted, patent-leathered you at this quirky stop for vintage-inspired dresses, skirts, tops, and accessories in all sizes. ✉ 1410 Lincoln Ave. ✛ At Washington St. ☏ 707/942–1059 ⊕ madmodshop.com ⊙ Closed Tues.

★ Spa Solage
This eco-conscious spa reinvented the traditional Calistoga mud-and-mineral-water regimen with the hour-long "Mudslide." The three-part treatment includes a mud body mask self-applied in a heated lounge, a soak in a thermal bath, and a power nap in a sound-vibration chair. The mud here, less gloppy than at other resorts, is a mix of clay, volcanic ash, and essential oils. Traditional spa services—combination Shiatsu-Swedish and other massages, full-body exfoliations, facials, and waxes—are available, as are yoga and wellness sessions. ✉ 755 Silverado Trail ✛ At Rosedale Rd. ☏ 707/226–0825 ⊕ solage.aubergeresorts.com/spa ▱ Treatments from $110.

⚡ Activities

Calistoga Balloons
TOUR—SIGHT | You'll gaze down on the valley's northern vineyards on this company's balloon rides. With an add-on in collaboration with Calistoga Bikeshop, you can tour wineries by bicycle in the afternoon. ✉ 1458 Lincoln Ave. ☏ 707/942–5758 ⊕ calistogaballoons. com ▱ From $239.

Calistoga Bikeshop
BICYCLING | Options here include regular and fancy bikes that rent for $28 and up for two hours, and there's a self-guided Cool Wine Tour ($110) that includes tastings at three or four small wineries. ✉ 1318 Lincoln Ave. ✛ Near Washington St. ☏ 707/942–9687 ⊕ www.calistoga-bikeshop.net.

SONOMA VALLEY AND PETALUMA

👁 Sights	🍴 Restaurants	🛏 Hotels	🛍 Shopping	🍸 Nightlife
★★★★★	★★★★☆	★★★★☆	★★★☆☆	★★★☆☆

WELCOME TO SONOMA VALLEY AND PETALUMA

TOP REASONS TO GO

★ **California and wine history:** Sonoma's mission and nearby sites shine a light into California's history; at Buena Vista you can explore the wine industry's roots.

★ **Literary trails:** Work off the wine and fine cuisine—and just enjoy the scenery—while hiking the trails of Jack London State Park, which contains the ruins of London's Wolf House.

★ **Peaceful Glen Ellen:** As writers from Jack London to M.F.K. Fisher discovered, peaceful Glen Ellen is a good place to decompress and tap into one's creativity. (Hunter S. Thompson found it too sedate.)

★ **Seated Pinot Noir tastings:** Patz & Hall, Sojourn, the Donum Estate, and other wineries host seated tastings focusing on high-quality Pinots from Los Carneros and beyond.

★ **Wineries with a view:** The views from the outdoor tasting spaces at McEvoy Ranch, Ram's Gate, and Kunde encourage lingering over a glass of your favorite varietal.

1 Sonoma. The Wine Country's oldest town has it all: fine dining, historical sites, and wineries from down-home to high style. Much of the activity takes place around Sonoma Plaza, where in 1846 some American settlers declared independence from Mexico and established the California Republic. The republic only lasted a month, but during the next decade, Count Agoston Haraszthy laid the foundation for modern California wine making.

2 Glen Ellen. Sonoma Creek snakes through Glen Ellen's tiny "downtown." The lodgings here are small, and the town, home to Jack London State Park, has retained its rural character.

3 Kenwood. St. Francis and a few other name wineries straddle Highway 12 in Kenwood, whose vague center lies about 5 miles north of Glen Ellen. At Kunde Family Estate you can survey the whole Kenwood scene during a Mountain Top Tasting.

4 Petaluma. This southern Sonoma County town's agricultural roots stretch back to the mid-1830s; the 2018 approval of the Petaluma Gap AVA recognized the area's potential for grape growing, especially Pinot Noir and Chardonnay.

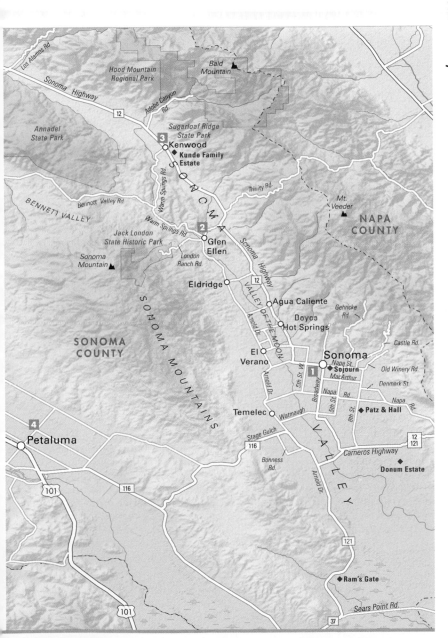

Los Alamos Rd.

Sonoma Highway

Hood Mountain
Regional Park

Bald
Mountain

Adobe Canyon Rd.

Sugarloaf Ridge
State Park

12

Annadel
State Park

3 Kenwood
◆ Kunde Family
Estate

Trinity Rd.

Mt.
Veeder

NAPA
COUNTY

Bennett Valley Rd.

BENNETT VALLEY

Warm Springs Rd.

Warm Springs Rd.

SONOMA

2

Jack London
State Historic Park

Glen
Ellen

Sonoma
Mountain

London
Ranch Rd.

Sonoma Highway

Eldridge

12

VALLEY OF THE MOON

Agua Caliente

Gehricke
Rd.

SONOMA
COUNTY

SONOMA MOUNTAINS

Boyes
Hot Springs

El
Verano

Arnold Dr.

5th St. W.

Sonoma

Napa St.

1 ◆ Sojourn
MacArthur

Castle Rd.

Old Winery Rd.

Denmark St.

4

Petaluma

Temelec

Watmaugh

Arnold Dr.

Brazil

Napa Rd.

5th St.

8th St.

Napa Rd.

◆ Patz & Hall

Stage Gulch

116

Bonness
Rd.

Carneros Highway

12
121

Donum Estate

101

116

Arnold Dr.

VALLEY

121

◆ Ram's Gate

101

Sears Point Rd.

37

The birthplace of modern California wine making, the Sonoma Valley seduces with its unpretentious attitude and pastoral landscape. Tasting rooms, restaurants, and historical sites abound near Sonoma Plaza, but beyond downtown Sonoma the wineries and attractions are spread out along gently winding roads.

Sonoma County's half of the Carneros District lies within Sonoma Valley, whose other towns of note include Glen Ellen and Kenwood. To Sonoma Valley's west, bustling Petaluma has in recent years come into its own as a Wine Country destination. A walkable downtown, a burgeoning dining scene, and relatively inexpensive lodgings all add to its allure.

Sonoma Valley tasting rooms are often less crowded than those in Napa or northern Sonoma County, especially midweek, and the vibe here, though sophisticated, is definitely less sceney. That's not to suggest that the Sonoma Valley is undiscovered territory. On the contrary, along Highway 12, the main corridor through the Sonoma Valley, you'll spot classy inns, restaurants, and spas in addition to wineries. In high season Glen Ellen and Kenwood are filled with well-heeled wine buffs, and the best restaurants can be crowded.

The historic Sonoma Valley towns offer glimpses of the past. Sonoma, with its tree-filled central plaza, is rich with 19th-century buildings. Two names pop up on many plaques affixed to them: General Mariano Guadalupe Vallejo, who

in the 1830s and 1840s was Mexico's highest-ranking military officer in these parts, and Count Agoston Haraszthy, who opened Buena Vista Winery in 1857. Glen Ellen, meanwhile, has a special connection with the author Jack London. Kenwood claims a more recent distinction: in 1999 its Chateau St. Jean winery was the first in Sonoma County to earn a wine of the year award from *Wine Spectator* magazine, one of several signs that Sonoma Valley wine making had come of age.

Bounded by the Mayacamas Mountains on the east and Sonoma Mountain on the west, this scenic valley extends north from San Pablo Bay nearly 20 miles to the eastern outskirts of Santa Rosa. The varied terrain, soils, and climate—cooler in the south because of the bay influence and hotter toward the north—allow grape growers to raise cool-weather varietals such as Chardonnay and Pinot Noir as well as Cabernet Sauvignon and other heat-seeking grapes.

In 1836 General Vallejo established the Rancho de Petaluma as an agricultural concern. The oldest surviving structure, the Petaluma Adobe, is now a state park.

Much of the surrounding land is still used for farming, some of it grapes.

MAJOR REGIONS

The Sonoma Valley lies just north of San Pablo Bay, itself an extension of the larger San Francisco Bay. The largest town, Sonoma, about 41 miles north of San Francisco's Golden Gate Bridge, is bisected by Highway 12, which continues north to Glen Ellen and Kenwood. About 11,000 people live in Sonoma proper, with another 22,000 within its orbit; Glen Ellen has about 800 residents, Kenwood a little more than 1,000. West of the Sonoma Valley in southern Sonoma County—a straight shot north from the Golden Gate Bridge—U.S. 101 bisects Petaluma, with just under 60,000 residents the county's second-largest city after Santa Rosa.

Planning

When to Go

The best time to visit the Sonoma Valley is between late spring and early fall, when the weather is warm and wineries bustle with activity. September and October, when grape harvesting and crushing are in full swing, are the busiest months. At this time—and on all summer weekends—lodging prices tend to be at their highest. Tasting rooms throughout the Sonoma Valley are generally not too crowded during the week, even in high season, except perhaps on holiday Mondays.

Getting Here and Around

BUS TRAVEL

Sonoma Transit buses provide service within Sonoma and Petaluma and to Glen Ellen and Kenwood. *For more information about arriving by bus, see Bus Travel in the Travel Smart chapter. For more* *information about local bus service, see the Bus Travel sections for the individual towns in this chapter.*

CAR TRAVEL

Traveling by car is the easiest way to tour the Sonoma Valley. Highway 12, also called the Sonoma Highway, is the main thoroughfare through the valley, running north–south through Sonoma, Glen Ellen, and Kenwood into Santa Rosa. Arnold Drive heads north from Highway 121 in southern Sonoma to Glen Ellen. On the north side of town it reconnects with (and dead-ends at) Highway 12. A turn left (north) leads to Kenwood. Access Petaluma, which lies southwest of Sonoma, off U.S. 101.

From San Francisco: To get to the Sonoma Valley from San Francisco, travel north on U.S. 101 to the Highway 37 turnoff (Exit 460A), driving east for about 7 miles to Highway 121, the main route through the Carneros District. Highway 12 leads north from Highway 121 into the town of Sonoma. For Petaluma, continue on U.S. 101 to Kastania Road (Exit 472A), turn right and then quickly left, and follow signs on Petaluma Boulevard South to downtown.

From the Napa Valley: To reach the Sonoma Valley from Napa, turn west off Highway 29 onto Highway 121/12 and drive north on Highway 12 when it splits off from Highway 121. For Petaluma, turn west off Highway 12 onto Watmaugh Road 2 miles before Sonoma Plaza and follow Highway 116 west; for Sonoma, continue north on Highway 12, by this time signed as Broadway. A more adventurous route (not for the carsick) leads west over the Mayacamas range on highly scenic—but slow and winding—Oakville Grade Road, which turns into Trinity Road before it reaches Highway 12 in Glen Ellen. If coming to the Sonoma Valley from Calistoga, travel north a few miles on Highway 128 and then west on Petrified Forest Road and later Calistoga Road to reach Highway 12 in Santa Rosa. From there, head south into the valley.

Avoiding confusion: In the Carneros District, Highway 121 is often signposted as the Carneros Highway, the Sonoma Highway (the parts that coincide with Highway 12), or Arnold Drive. It's all the same road.

Restaurants

Fine dining in the Sonoma Valley is generally low-key. Cafe La Haye, the Girl and the Fig, and Harvest Moon Cafe, all in Sonoma, turn out thoughtful, complex cuisine that emphasizes locally produced meat, fish, cheese, vegetables, and fruit. Manuel Azevedo serves winning Portuguese-influenced dishes at LaSalette and the tavernlike Tasca Tasca, separate spots near Sonoma Plaza. Glen Ellen Star is its town's must-do, but you can't go wrong at any of the fine-dining restaurants here, among them the Fig Cafe for Cal-French comfort food and Yeti for Indian and Himalayan cuisine. El Molino Central—as with Yeti, modern in its use of organic ingredients but traditional in its preparations—is the top stop in Sonoma for Mexican.

Hotels

Sonoma has the valley's most varied accommodations, with motels and small inns, vacation condos, and boutique hotels all in the mix. Small inns are the norm in Glen Ellen and Kenwood. Spa lovers have two high-end choices at either end of the valley: the large and splashy Fairmont Sonoma Mission Inn & Spa in Sonoma and the Mediterranean-style Kenwood Inn and Spa, in Kenwood. Chain motels predominate in Petaluma, though the Hampton Inn here is inside a former silk mill.

For weekend stays it's wise to book a month or more ahead from late May through October. Most small lodgings require a two-night minimum stay on weekends at this time, three if Monday is a holiday.

What it Costs			
$	$$	$$$	$$$$
RESTAURANTS			
under $16	$16–$22	$23–$30	over $30
HOTELS			
under $201	$201–$300	$301–$400	over $400

Planning Your Time

You can hit Sonoma Valley's highlights in a day or two—a half or a full day exploring western Carneros District wineries and some in Sonoma proper, and the same amount of time to check out Glen Ellen and Kenwood. Most visitors stay in Sonoma. Traffic usually isn't an issue, except on Highway 12 north of Sonoma Plaza (though a recent road-widening has mitigated congestion during most of the day) and the intersection of Highways 116 and 121 during the morning and afternoon commutes. It takes at least half a day to get to know Petaluma.

Several star wineries—Patz & Hall, Scribe, and the Donum Estate among them—accept visitors by appointment only. On weekdays you may be able to reserve a space on short notice, but for weekend visits, especially during the summer and early fall, booking ahead is essential even when food pairings (which wineries need time to plan for) are not involved. A good strategy year-round is to book appointment-only wineries in the morning; this gives you more flexibility in the afternoon should lunch or other stops take longer than expected.

Visitor Information

CONTACTS Sonoma Valley Visitors Bureau.
✉ *Sonoma Plaza, 453 1st St. F, Sonoma*
☎ *707/996–1090* ⊕ *www.sonomavalley.com.*

Appellations

Although Sonoma *County* is a vast growing region that encompasses several different appellations, the much smaller Sonoma *Valley,* at the southern end of Sonoma County, is comparatively compact and consists mostly of the **Sonoma Valley AVA,** which stretches northwest from San Pablo Bay toward Santa Rosa. The weather and soils here are unusually diverse. Pinot Noir and Chardonnay vineyards are most likely to be found in the AVA's southernmost parts, the sections cooled by fog from San Pablo Bay. (This part of the Sonoma Valley AVA overlaps with the Sonoma County portions of **Los Carneros AVA.**) Zinfandel, Cabernet Sauvignon, and Sauvignon Blanc grapes are more plentiful farther north, near Glen Ellen and Kenwood, both of which tend to be a few degrees warmer than the southern Sonoma Valley.

The **Sonoma Mountain AVA** rises to the west of Glen Ellen on the western border of the Sonoma Valley AVA. Benefiting from a sunny location and rocky soil, the vineyards here produce deep-rooted vines and intensely flavored grapes that are made into complex red wines, primarily Cabernet Sauvignon. Opposite Sonoma Mountain southeast across the Sonoma Valley lies the **Moon Mountain District Sonoma County AVA.** This mountainside sliver, on the western slopes of the Mayacamas Mountains (just west of the Napa Valley's Mt. Veeder subappellation), contains some of California's oldest Zinfandel and Cabernet Sauvignon vines. Vines on the heavily sloped, rocky soils here produce smaller berries than their counterparts on the valley floor, and the higher skin-to-juice ratio yields intense flavor.

Portions of the **Sonoma Coast AVA** overlap Los Carneros and the Sonoma Valley. The tiny **Bennett Valley AVA,** also part of the Sonoma Valley AVA, falls within the city of Santa Rosa *(see Chapter 6).* West of the Sonoma Valley AVA and approved in 2018 is the **Petaluma Gap AVA,** whose name references a break in the Coast Range that permits cooling Pacific Ocean fog and wind to flow through. Except for a wee bit that edges into Marin County, the rest of this subappellation lies within the Sonoma Coast AVA.

Sonoma

14 miles west of Napa; 45 miles north east of San Francisco.

One of the few towns in the valley with multiple attractions not related to food and wine, Sonoma has plenty to keep you busy for a couple of hours before you head out to the wineries. And you needn't leave town to taste wine: about three dozen tasting rooms do business on or near Sonoma Plaza, a few of them pouring wines from more than one winery.

The valley's cultural center, Sonoma, founded in 1835 when California was still part of Mexico, is built around tree-filled Sonoma Plaza. If you arrive from the south, on Broadway (Highway 12), you'll be retracing the last stretch of what long ago was California's most important road—El Camino Real, or "the royal road," the only overland route through the state. During California's Spanish and Mexican periods, it ran past all of the state's 21 missions, beginning at San Diego de Alcalá (1769) and ending at Mission San Francisco Solano (1823). This last mission still sits in the center of Sonoma.

GETTING HERE AND AROUND
Highway 12 from the south (San Francisco) or north (Santa Rosa) is the main route into the town of Sonoma. For

Top Tastings and Tours

Tastings

McEvoy Ranch, Petaluma. The bucolic ranch's At Our Table Tasting of wines, oils, seasonal edibles from the organic gardens, and artisanal cheeses unfolds on a pond's-edge flagstone patio.

Scribe, Sonoma. The 1915 mission revival–style hacienda here overlooks vineyards with Riesling, Sylvaner, and other grapes German immigrants planted in Sonoma a century and a half ago.

Tours

Benziger Family Winery, Glen Ellen. On this winery's tram tour, you'll learn about Benziger's unique microclimates and deep commitment to biodynamic farming principles.

Buena Vista Winery, Sonoma. Tours of this winery founded in 1857 pass through caves dug by Chinese laborers, and there's a high-tech museum of wine-making tools.

Setting

The Donum Estate, Sonoma. Known for Pinot Noirs displaying both power and elegance, Donum pours its wines in a hilltop tasting room whose views include museum-quality outdoor sculptures.

Kunde Estate Winery & Vineyards, Kenwood. The Mountain Top Tastings passenger-van tour here winds 1,400 feet above the valley floor. On a shaded deck you'll enjoy memorable vistas while sipping reserve wines.

Food Pairing

Patz & Hall, Sonoma. The gourmet bites at this respected winery's Salon Tastings show just how food-friendly its Chardonnays and Pinot Noirs are.

St. Francis Winery, Kenwood. The five petite plates of this famous winery's executive chef pair well with its Zins, Cabs, and other wines.

several blocks south of Sonoma Plaza, the street's name changes to Broadway. There are two- and three-hour unmetered parking spaces around the plaza, and free all-day parking can be found off 1st Street East a third of a block north of the plaza. Once you've parked, a pleasant stroll takes you past many of the town's restaurants, shops, and tasting rooms. High-profile and boutique wineries can be found a mile or so east; arrow-shape signs on East Spain Street and East Napa Street will direct you.

Sonoma Transit buses connect Sonoma with other Sonoma County towns.

 Sights

Abbot's Passage Supply Co
WINERY/DISTILLERY | Past and present merge gracefully at this tasting room inside a restored 19th-century barn. Sixth-generation vintner Katie Bundschu, who's also involved in her family's historic Gundlach Bundschu winery, focuses on wines made from organic grapes grown in other family-owned, mostly Sonoma County vineyards. Most of the wines are old-style field blends in which different types of grapes from the same vineyard are fermented and aged together rather than separately, as is more common these days. A white, a rosé, and a few distinctive reds, the well-crafted wines all impress with their

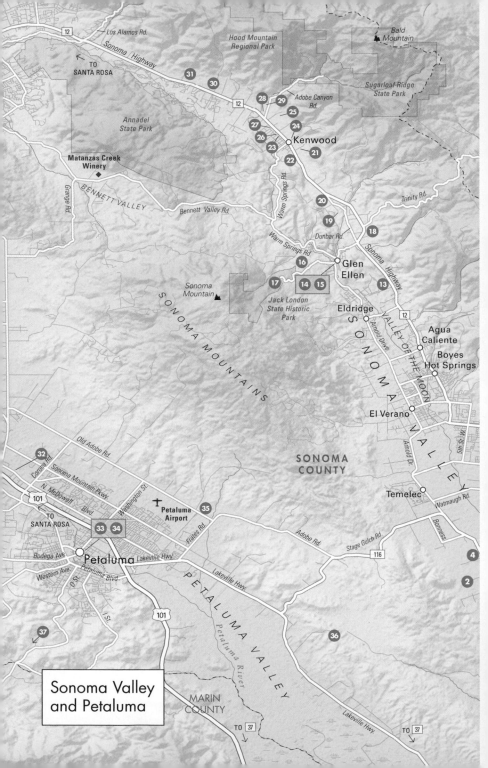

Sonoma Valley
and Petaluma

Adobe Road Winery 33
Anaba Wines 4
Benziger Family Winery 16
B.R. Cohn 13
Buena Vista Winery 11
D Wine Vineyards Tasting Lounge ... 26
Chateau St. Jean 25
Cornerstone Sonoma 3
Deerfield Ranch Winery 22
The Donum Estate 6
Gloria Ferrer Caves and Vineyards 2
Gundlach Bundschu 8
Hanson of Sonoma Organic Vodka 5
Jack London State Historic Park 17
Keller Estate 36
Kenwood Vineyards 24
Kivelstadt Cellars 14
Kunde Estate Winery & Vineyards ... 21
Landmark Vineyards 28
La Rochelle Winery 29
Lagunitas Brewing Company 32
Lasseter Family Winery 19
Laurel Glen Vineyard 15
Ledson Winery & Vineyards 31
Loxton Cellars 20
McEvoy Ranch 37
Paradise Ridge Kenwood
Tasting Room 27
Patz & Hall 9
Petaluma Adobe State
Historic Park 35
Quarryhill Botanical Garden 18
Ram's Gate Winery 1
Ravenswood Winery 12
St. Francis Winery 30
Scribe 7
Sonoma Portworks 34
Sonoma TrainTown Railroad 10
VJB Cellars 23

Sonoma Valley and Petaluma SONOMA

5

balance, approachability, and rich flavors. ■TIP→ **Down alleys off Napa Street and Broadway (the latter route's the shortest), Abbot's Passage can be tricky to find but is worth seeking out.** ✉ *27 E. Napa St.* ✛ *Off 1st alley on east side of Broadway south of Sonoma Plaza* ☎ *707/939–3024* ⊕ *www.abbotspassage.com* ☕ *Tastings from $25.*

Anaba Wines

WINERY/DISTILLERY | Reprising the greatest hits of Burgundy (Chardonnay, Pinot Noir) and the Rhône (Grenache, Mourvèdre, Syrah, Viognier), Anaba tries to be all things to most wine drinkers and succeeds. Pinot Noirs from Wildcat Mountain Vineyard, one of the highest-elevation vineyards in the Carneros District, and Soberanes Vineyard in Monterey County's Santa Lucia Highlands AVA are among the standouts, but all the wines, made by Ross Cobb and Katy Wilson, both Pinot Noir pros, are thoughtfully crafted. A new tasting room in the board-and-batten style, set back from the intersection of Highways 121 and 116, should be open by mid-2019. ✉ *60 Bonneau Rd.* ✛ *At intersection of Hwys. 116 and 121* ☎ *707/996–4188* ⊕ *www.anabawines. com* ☕ *Tastings from $20; tour included in tasting fee* ⊙ *No tour Tues.–Thurs.*

Bedrock Wine Co.

WINERY/DISTILLERY | Wines, notably Zinfandel, celebrating Sonoma County's heritage vineyards are the focus of Bedrock, whose backstory involves several historical figures. Tastings take place in a home just east of Sonoma Plaza owned in the 1850s by General Joseph Hooker. By coincidence, Hooker planted grapes at what's now the estate Bedrock Vineyard a few miles away. General William Tecumseh Sherman was his partner in the vineyard (a spat over it affected their Civil War interactions), which newspaper magnate William Randolph Hearst's father, George, replanted in the late 1880s. Some Hearst vines still produce grapes. Current owner-winemaker

Morgan Twain-Peterson learned about Zinfandel from his dad, Joel Peterson, who started Ravenswood Winery. ■TIP→ **The shaded patio out back faces the circa-1840 Blue Wing Inn, where Hooker often partied.** ✉ *General Joseph Hooker House, 414 1st St. E* ☎ *707/343–1478* ⊕ *www.bedrockwineco.com* ☕ *Tasting $30* ⊙ *Closed Tues.*

Buena Vista Winery

WINERY/DISTILLERY | The birthplace of modern California wine making has been transformed into an entertaining homage to the accomplishments of the 19th-century wine pioneer Count Agoston Haraszthy. Tours pass through the original aging caves dug deep into the hillside by Chinese laborers, and banners, photos, and artifacts inside and out convey the history made on this site. The rehabilitated former press house (used for pressing grapes into wine), which dates to 1862, hosts the standard tastings. Chardonnay, Pinot Noir, several red blends, and a vibrant Petit Verdot are the strong suits here. ■TIP→ **The high-tech Historic Wine Tool Museum displays implements, some decidedly low-tech, used to make wine over the years.** ✉ *18000 Old Winery Rd.* ✛ *Off E. Napa St.* ☎ *800/926–1266* ⊕ *www. buenavistawinery.com* ☕ *Tastings from $20; tours from $25.*

Cornerstone Sonoma

GARDEN | The ¼-acre Sunset Test Gardens are the big draw at this collection of tasting rooms and design, housewares, and gift shops. Sunset divides its section into five "rooms"—Farm Garden, Gathering Space, Backyard Orchard, Flower Room, and Cocktail Garden—intended to expand visitors' agri-lifestyle horizons. The remaining handful of landscape installations from the pre-Sunset era make artistic and political statements that inspire on levels beyond the agrarian. Chateau Sonoma, Artefact Design & Salvage, and Nomad Chic are three shops worth checking out. ■TIP→ **The Poseidon Vineyard & Obsidian Ridge tasting room is**

among the wine stops here, with Prohibition Spirits pouring gin, brandy, and specialty products. ⊠ *23570 Arnold Dr./Hwy. 121* ⊹ *Across from Gloria Ferrer winery* ☎ *707/933-3010* ⊕ *www.cornerstonesonoma.com* ⊠ *Free.*

★ The Donum Estate

WINERY/DISTILLERY | Anne Moller-Racke, the founder of this prominent Chardonnay and Pinot Noir producer, calls herself a winegrower in the French *vigneron* tradition that emphasizes agriculture—selecting vineyards with the right soils, microclimates, and varietals, then farming with precision—over wine-making wizardry. The Donum Estate, whose white board-and-batten tasting room affords guests hilltop views of Los Carneros, San Pablo Bay, and beyond, farms two vineyards surrounding the structure, along with one in the Russian River Valley and another in Mendocino County's Anderson Valley. All the wines exhibit the "power yet elegance" that sealed the winery's fame in the 2000s. Tastings are by appointment only. ■ **TIP→ Large museum-quality outdoor sculptures by Anselm Kiefer, Lynda Benglis, Ai Weiwei, and three dozen other contemporary talents add a touch of high culture to a visit here.** ⊠ *24500 Ramal Rd.* ⊹ *Off Hwy. 121/12* ☎ *707/732-2200* ⊕ *www.thedonumestate.com* ⊠ *Tasting $80.*

Gloria Ferrer Caves and Vineyards

WINERY/DISTILLERY | A tasting at Gloria Ferrer is an exercise in elegance: at tables inside the Spanish hacienda–style winery or outside on the terrace (no standing at the bar at Gloria Ferrer), you can take in vistas of gently rolling Carneros hills while sipping sparkling and still wines. The Chardonnay and Pinot Noir grapes from the surrounding vineyards are the product of old-world wine-making knowledge—the same family started the sparkling-wine maker Freixenet in 16th-century Spain—and contemporary soil management techniques and clonal research. The daily tour covers *méthode*

traditionelle wine making, the Ferrer family's history, and the winery's vineyard sustainability practices. ⊠ *23555 Carneros Hwy./Hwy. 121* ☎ *707/933-1917* ⊕ *www.gloriaferrer.com* ⊠ *Tastings from $9, tour with tasting $25.*

Gundlach Bundschu

WINERY/DISTILLERY | The Bundschu family, which has owned most of this property since 1858, makes reds that include Cabernet Franc, Cabernet Sauvignon, Merlot, and a Bordeaux-style blend of each vintage's best grapes. Gewürztraminer, Chardonnay, and two rosés are also in the mix. Parts of the 1870 stone winery where standard tastings unfold are still used for wine making. For a more comprehensive experience, book a cave tour, a Pinzgauer vehicle vineyard tour, or a Heritage Reserve pairing of limited-release wines with small gourmet bites. Some tastings and all tours are by appointment only. "Gun lock bun shoe" gets you close to pronouncing this winery's name correctly, though everyone here shortens it to Gun Bun. ⊠ *2000 Denmark St.* ⊹ *At Bundschu Rd., off 8th St. E, 3 miles southeast of Sonoma Plaza* ☎ *707/938-5277* ⊕ *www.gunbun.com* ⊠ *Tastings from $20, tours $45 (includes tastings).*

Hanson of Sonoma Organic Vodka

WINERY/DISTILLERY | The Hanson family makes grape-based organic vodkas, one of them straightforward and four others infused with cucumbers, ginger, mandarin oranges, and habanero and other chili peppers. To produce these vodkas and a few seasonal offerings, white wine is made from three grape types and then distilled. The family pours its vodkas, which have racked up some impressive awards, in an industrial-looking tasting room heavy on the steel, with wood reclaimed from Deep South smokehouses adding a rustic note. Because you're in a tasting room rather than a bar, there's a limit to the amount poured, but it's sufficient to get to know the product.

Wine-Making Pioneer

Count Agoston Haraszthy arrived in Sonoma in 1857 and set out to make fine wine commercially. He planted European vinifera varietals rather than mission grapes (varietals brought to the Americas by Spanish missionaries) and founded Buena Vista Winery the year he arrived.

Two Breakthroughs

Haraszthy deserves credit for two breakthroughs. At Buena Vista he grew grapes on dry hillsides instead of in the wetter lowlands as had been customary in the mission and rancho periods. His success demonstrated that Sonoma's climate was moist enough to sustain grapes without irrigation. The innovative count was also the first to try aging his wine in redwood barrels, which were much less expensive than oak ones. More affordable barrels made it feasible to ratchet up wine production. For almost 100 years, redwood barrels would be the California wine industry's most popular storage method, even though redwood can impart an odd flavor.

Adaptable Zinfandel

Despite producing inferior wines, the prolific mission grapes were preferred by California growers over better varieties of French, German, and Italian vinifera grapes through the 1860s and into the 1870s. But Haraszthy's success had begun to make an impression. A new red-wine grape, Zinfandel, was becoming popular, both because it made excellent Claret (as good red wine was then called) and because it had adapted to the area's climate.

Balance Lost

By this time, however, Haraszthy had disappeared, literally, from the scene. After a business setback during the 1860s, the count lost control of Buena Vista and ventured to Nicaragua to restore his fortune in the sugar and rum industries. While crossing a stream infested with alligators, the count lost his balance and plunged into the water below. The body of modern California wine making's first promoter and pioneer was never recovered.

Book distillery tours through Hanson's website. ■ TIP→ **A popular tasting involves three vodka sips and a well-mixed cocktail.** ✉ *22985 Burndale Rd.* ✛ *Off Carneros Hwy. (Hwy. 121)* ☎ *707/343–1805* ⊕ *hansonofsonoma.com* ⏻ *Tastings from $15; tours from $25 (includes tasting).*

Pangloss Cellars Tasting Lounge

WINERY/DISTILLERY | The high-ceilinged tasting room of this winery named for the optimistic doctor from Voltaire's satire *Candide* occupies a restored 1902 stone building across from Sonoma Plaza. Originally a general store, it's a striking setting to enjoy wines by Erich Bradley, also the winemaker at nearby Sojourn Cellars.

The Pangloss roster—white and red blends plus Sauvignon Blanc, Chardonnay, Pinot Noir, Zinfandel, and Cabernet Sauvignon—aims to represent the range of Sonoma County's viticultural portfolio. Without a reservation you can sip wines by the flight or glass in the lounge area, or taste at the bar, but you'll need one for a private Cellar tasting of wines and local cheeses and charcuterie. ■ TIP→ **Bradley also makes the collector-worthy wines of the affiliated Texture winery; they're poured in a dedicated room in the back of the Pangloss building.** ✉ *35 E. Napa St.* ✛ *At 1st St. E* ☎ *707/933–8565* ⊕ *www.panglosscellars.com* ⏻ *Tastings from $25.*

★ Patz & Hall

WINERY/DISTILLERY | Sophisticated single-vineyard Chardonnays and Pinot Noirs are the trademark of this respected winery whose tastings take place in a fashionable single-story residence 3 miles southeast of Sonoma Plaza. It's a Wine Country adage that great wines are made in the vineyard—the all-star fields represented here include Hyde, Durell, and Gap's Crown—but winemaker James Hall routinely surpasses peers with access to the same fruit, proof that discernment and expertise (Hall is a master at oak aging) play a role, too. You can sample wines at the bar and on some days on the vineyard-view terrace beyond it, but to learn how food-friendly these wines are, consider the Salon Tasting, at which they're paired with gourmet bites. Tastings are by appointment only. ✉ 21200 8th St. E ✚ Near Peru Rd. ☎ 707/265–7700 ⊕ www.patzhall.com ✉ Tastings from $35.

Ram's Gate Winery

WINERY/DISTILLERY | Stunning views, ultra-chic architecture, and wines made from grapes grown by acclaimed producers make a visit to Ram's Gate an event. The welcoming interior spaces—think Restoration Hardware with a dash of high-style whimsy—open up to the entire western Carneros. In fine weather you'll experience the cooling breezes that sweep through the area while sipping sophisticated wines, mostly Pinot Noirs and Chardonnays but also Pinot Blanc, Syrah, and the estate Vent de Colline blend of Syrah, Grenache, and Grenache Blanc. With grapes sourced from Sangiacomo, Hudson, and other illustrious vineyards, the wine-making team focuses on creating balanced wines that express what occurred in nature that year. Appointments are recommended for all visits. ■ TIP→ **You can sip current releases at the tasting bar, take a tour and taste single-vineyard wines, or enjoy wines paired with food.** ✉ 28700 Arnold Dr./Hwy. 121 ☎ 707/721–8700 ⊕ www.

ramsgatewinery.com ✉ Tastings from $40, tour $65 (includes tasting) ⊘ Closed Tues. and Wed.

Ravenswood Winery

WINERY/DISTILLERY | "No wimpy wines" is the punchy motto of this producer, famous for big, bold Zinfandels. Ravenswood also makes Petite Sirah and Bordeaux-style red blends; the whites include Chardonnay, Gewürztraminer, and lightly sparkling Moscato. You can taste flights of small-lot Zinfandels and Cabernets, some available only at the winery, without an appointment at the bar or, when the weather permits, outdoors on the terrace. Reservations are required for the daily tour. Focusing on viticultural practices, it includes a barrel tasting of wines in the cellar. To learn even more about the wine-making process, make an appointment for one of the wine-blending sessions. ✉ 18701 Gehricke Rd. ✚ Off E. Spain St. ☎ 707/933–2332 ⊕ www.ravenswoodwinery.com ✉ Tastings from $25, tour $30, blending session $75.

Rhône Room

WINERY/DISTILLERY | Sondra Bernstein, a local champion of Rhône varietals, opened this roadside tasting room in front of the Girl and the Fig Farm, where she grows herbs, fruit, and vegetables for her same-named Sonoma Plaza restaurant and other enterprises. The lineup includes Viognier, Grenache, and Syrah (plus, in summer, a light-and-dry Grenache rosé) from Bernstein's own label, along with selections "curated from friends" in California, France, and elsewhere. Guest winemakers sometimes pour their wines on the weekends. The decor of the bungalowlike tasting room is country farmhouse; in good weather you can taste on the outside patio that adjoins the garden. ✉ 20816 Broadway ✚ 1½ miles south of Sonoma Plaza ☎ 707/933–3000 ⊕ www.therhoneroom.com ✉ Tastings from $10 ⊘ Closed Mon.

★ Scribe

WINERY/DISTILLERY | Andrew and Adam Mariani established Scribe in 2007 on land first planted to grapes in 1858 by Emil Dresel, a German immigrant. Dresel's claims to fame include cultivating Sonoma's first Riesling and Sylvaner, an achievement the brothers honor by growing both varietals on land he once farmed. Using natural wine-making techniques, they craft bright, terroir-driven wines from those grapes, along with Chardonnay, Pinot Noir, Syrah, and Cabernet Sauvignon. In restoring their property's 1915 mission revival–style hacienda, the brothers preserved various layers of history—original molding and light fixtures, for instance, but also fragments of floral-print wallpaper and 1950s newspapers. Now a tasting space, the hacienda served during Prohibition as a bootleggers' hideout, and its basement harbored a speakeasy. Tastings, which include meze plates whose ingredients come from Scribe's farm, are by appointment only. ⌧ 2100 Denmark St. ✛ Off Napa Rd. ☎ 707/939–1858 ⊕ scribewinery.com ⊠ Tastings from $60.

★ Sojourn Cellars

WINERY/DISTILLERY | Superior fruit sources and a winemaker with a wisely light touch have earned Sojourn Cellars high ratings from major wine critics for its Chardonnay, Pinot Noir, and Cabernet Sauvignon wines. The initial releases of this winery founded in 2001 were Cabernets, but it's best known these days for ten well-balanced Pinot Noirs from the Sonoma Coast and Russian River Valley appellations. The five Chardonnays all hail from the Sonoma Coast, with the grapes for the five Cabernets from the Napa and Sonoma valleys. In part because winemaker Erich Bradley uses oak in such a consistent way, the informative tastings (by appointment only) at Sojourn's bungalow just east of Sonoma Plaza focus on the subtle variations caused by climate, terrain, and clone type depending on the grape sources. ⌧ 141 E. Napa St. ✛ ½ block east of Sonoma Plaza ☎ 707/938–7212 ⊕ www.sojourncellars. com ⊠ Tasting $35.

Sonoma Mission

RELIGIOUS SITE | The northernmost of the 21 missions established by Franciscan friars in California, Sonoma Mission was founded in 1823 as Mission San Francisco Solano. These days it serves as the centerpiece of **Sonoma State Historic Park,** which includes several other sites in Sonoma and nearby Petaluma. Some early mission structures were destroyed, but all or part of several remaining buildings date to the era of Mexican rule over California. Worth a look are the **Sonoma Barracks,** a half block west of the mission at 20 East Spain Street, which housed troops under the command of General Mariano Guadalupe Vallejo, who controlled vast tracts of land in the region. **General Vallejo's Home,** a Victorian-era structure, is a few blocks west. ⌧ 114 E. Spain St. ✛ At 1st St. E ☎ 707/938–9560 ⊕ www.parks.ca.gov ⊠ $3, includes same-day admission to other historic sites.

Sonoma Plaza

PLAZA | Dating to the mission era, Sonoma Plaza is surrounded by 19th-century adobes, atmospheric hotels, and the swooping marquee of the Depression-era Sebastiani Theatre. A statue on the plaza's northeastern side marks the spot where California proclaimed its independence from Mexico on June 14, 1846. Despite its historical roots, the plaza is not a museum piece. On summer days it's a hive of activity, with children blowing off steam in the playground, couples enjoying picnics from gourmet shops, and groups listening to live music at the small amphitheater. The stone **city hall** is also here. If you're wondering why the 1906 structure looks the same from all angles, here's why: its four sides were purposely made identical so that none of the plaza's merchants would feel that city hall had turned its back to them. ⌧ North

Sonoma Mission was the last of California's 21 missions.

end of Broadway/Hwy. 12 ✛ Bordered by E. Napa St., 1st St. E, E. Spain St., and 1st St. W.

Sonoma TrainTown Railroad

AMUSEMENT PARK/WATER PARK | FAMILY | A quarter-scale train at this fun, well-run attraction geared to kids under 10 chugs for 4 miles through tunnels and past a lake, a waterfall, and a miniature town with a petting zoo. Back near the entrance are a turntable and a round-house, amusement rides, and a com-bination snack bar and souvenir stand. ✉ 20264 Broadway ✛ Near Napa Rd. ☎ 707/938–3912 ⊕ www.traintown.com ⬛ Free to main park area, $8 for train ride; additional fee for amusement rides ⊘ Closed rainy days and Mon.–Thurs. Sept.–May.

★ Three Sticks Wines

WINERY/DISTILLERY | Pinot Noir artiste Bob Cabral makes Pinots and Chardonnays from prized estate vineyards, including Durell and Gap's Crown, of Bill Price, the owner of Three Sticks Wines. Cabral also crafts Rhône-style wines that bear the Casteñeda label in honor of the restored 1842 Vallejo-Casteñeda Adobe, where the Three Sticks wines are poured. San Francisco–based designer Ken Fulk transformed the structure, Sonoma's longest-occupied residence, into a showcase both lavish and refined. Seated private tastings unfold at a long elm table inside the Adobe or, weather permitting, at a cast-stone table under a willow-cov-ered arbor. In either setting a tasting here (by appointment only) feels like a special occasion. ✉ 143 W. Spain St. ✛ At 1st St. W ☎ 707/996–3328 ⊕ www.threes-tickswines.com ⬛ Tastings from $40.

Walt Wines

WINERY/DISTILLERY | This sister winery to Hall St. Helena specializes in Pinot Noir from Sonoma County, Mendocino County, California's Central Coast, and Oregon's Willamette Valley and also pro-duces Chardonnay. Walk-ins are welcome to sample current releases inside a mid-1930s Tudor-inspired home or, weather permitting, at backyard tables beneath a tall, double-trunk redwood tree. To see

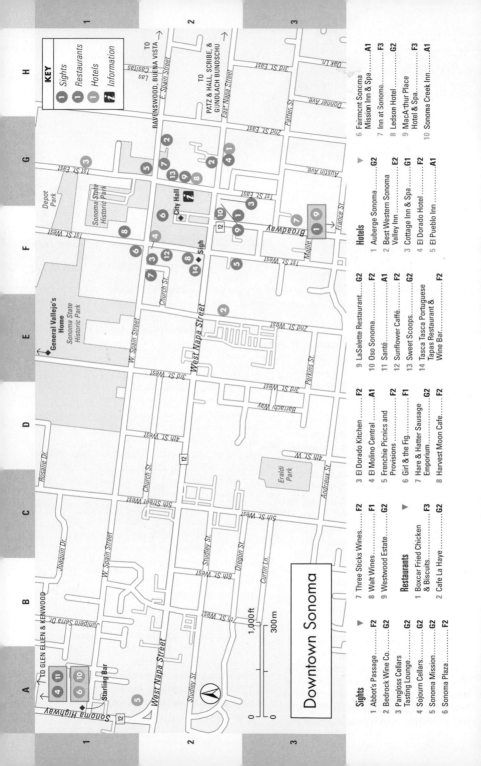

Downtown Sonoma

Sights
7 Three Sticks Wines........**F2**
8 Walt Wines........**F1**
9 Westwood Estate........**G2**

1 Abbot's Passage........**F2**
2 Bedrock Wine Co........**G2**
3 Pangloss Cellars
Tasting Lounge........**G2**
4 Sojourn Cellars........**G2**
5 Sonoma Mission........**G2**
6 Sonoma Plaza........**F2**

Restaurants
1 Boxcar Fried Chicken
& Biscuits........**F3**
2 Cafe La Haye........**G2**
3 El Dorado Kitchen........**F2**
4 El Molino Central........**A1**
5 Frenchie Picnics and
Provisions........**F2**
6 Girl & the Fig........**F1**
7 Hare & Hatter Sausage
Emporium........**G2**
8 Harvest Moon Cafe........**F2**

9 LaSalette Restaurant........**G2**
10 Oso Sonoma........**F2**
11 Santé........**A1**
12 Sunflower Caffé........**F2**
13 Sweet Scoops........**G2**
14 Tasca Tasca Portuguese
Tapas Restaurant &
Wine Bar........**F2**

Hotels
1 Auberge Sonoma........**G2**
2 Best Western Sonoma
Valley Inn........**E2**
3 Cottage Inn & Spa........**G1**
4 El Dorado Hotel........**F2**
5 El Pueblo Inn........**A1**

6 Fairmont Sonoma
Mission Inn & Spa........**A1**
7 Inn at Sonoma........**F3**
8 Ledson Hotel........**G2**
9 MacA'thur Place
Hotel & Spa........**F3**
10 Sonoma Creek Inn........**A1**

KEY
1 Sights
1 Restaurants
1 Hotels
ℹ Information

how the wines pair with food—in this case small bites from the Girl & the Fig across the street—make a reservation for the Root 101: A Single Vineyard Exploration. The Portfolio Tasting includes Walt wines, Hall Cabernets, and a Zinfandel of a third label, Zaca. ✉ 380 1st St. W ✛ At W. Spain St. ☎ 707/933–4440 ⊕ www. waltwines.com ✇ Tastings from $30.

★ Westwood Estate
WINERY/DISTILLERY | This winery's 23 acres of vineyards in the Annadel Gap of the northern Sonoma Valley occupy a zone hospitable to cool-climate grapes such as Pinot Noir, along with Syrah and other Rhône varietals. Consulting winemaker Philippe Melka fashions the remarkable fruit grown here into exciting, thought-provoking wines. Because the estate ones all come from the same vineyard, the focus is on which Pinot Noir or Rhône clones they derive from and how Melka and his team bring out the best in each. Appointments aren't necessary at Westwood's small tasting room, just south of Sonoma Plaza, but it's a good idea to call ahead, especially on weekends. ✉ Vine Alley Complex, 11 E. Napa St., No. 3 ✛ At Broadway ☎ 707/933–7837 ⊕ www.westwood-wine.com ✇ Tastings from $30 ✇ Closed Tues. and Wed.

🍽 Restaurants

Boxcar Fried Chicken & Biscuits
$$ | SOUTHERN | The owners of the retro-yet-au-courant Fremont Diner abruptly closed the roadhouse restaurant in June 2018, then just as suddenly reopened it three months later with a stripped-down menu of Southern favorites. As the new name suggests, fried chicken remains a focus, with a 21st-century variation on a po'boy, a few salads, and sides that include deviled eggs, hush puppies, and chicken biscuits with pepper jelly. **Known for:** down-home Southern cuisine with modern twists; small-batch brews; vineyard-view outdoor seating. $ Average

main: $16 ✉ 2698 Fremont Dr. ✛ At Hwy. 121/12 ☎ 707/938–7370 ⊕ boxcar-fried-chicken.com ✇ Closed Sun. No dinner Mon.–Wed. (subject to change).

★ Cafe La Haye
$$$ | AMERICAN | In a postage-stamp-size open kitchen (the dining room, its white walls adorned with contemporary art, is nearly as compact), chef Jeffrey Lloyd turns out understated, sophisticated fare emphasizing seasonably available local ingredients. Chicken, beef, pasta, and fish get deluxe treatment without fuss or fanfare—the daily risotto special is always good. **Known for:** Napa-Sonoma wine list with French complements; signature butterscotch pudding dessert; owner Saul Gropman on hand to greet diners. $ Average main: $24 ✉ 140 E. Napa St. ✛ Just off Sonoma Plaza ☎ 707/935–5994 ⊕ www.cafelahaye.com ✇ Closed Sun. and Mon. No lunch.

El Dorado Kitchen
$$$ | MODERN AMERICAN | This restaurant owes its visual appeal to its clean lines and handsome decor, but the eye inevitably drifts westward to the open kitchen, where the chefs craft dishes full of subtle surprises. The menu might include ahi tuna tartare with wasabi tobiko caviar as a starter, with paella awash with seafood and dry-cured Spanish chorizo sausage among the entrées. **Known for:** subtle tastes and textures; truffle-oil fries with Parmesan; pot de crème and other desserts. $ Average main: $27 ✉ El Dorado Hotel, 405 1st St. W ✛ At W. Spain St. ☎ 707/996–3030 ⊕ eldoradokitchen.com.

★ El Molino Central
$ | MEXICAN | Fans purchase Karen Waikiki's tortillas and tamales—handmade from stone-ground heritage corn and other organic ingredients—at Bay Area stores and farmers' markets. At her roadside restaurant, which has more tables outside than in, you can pick from the full lineup, with choices including the star tamales (chicken mole and Niman Ranch pork), tacos filled with beer-battered fish

or crispy beef, and enchiladas and burritos. **Known for:** high-quality ingredients; authentic techniques; breakfast chilaquiles Merida, with soft-scrambled eggs and spicy roasted tomato. $ *Average main: $12* ⊠ *11 Central Ave., Boyes Hot Springs* ✛ *At Hwy. 12* ☎ *707/939–1010* ⊕ *www. elmolinocentral.com.*

Frenchie Picnics and Provisions

$ | **MODERN AMERICAN** | From gourmet grab-and-go vittles and quirky beverages to picnic baskets and Frisbees, the two owners of this shop steps south of Sonoma Plaza supply everything necessary for a memorable outdoor meal. For those unclear on the picnicking concept, the duo provides step-by-step advice ("pick 2–3 cheeses, 1–2 cured meats …") on what to select from a seasonally changing menu that might include Vietnamese shrimp salad, ham and Brie on a baguette, chicken salad, and edamame guacamole. **Known for:** salads, sandwiches, chips, dips; kids' items; beer and wine (both okay to consume in Sonoma Plaza). $ *Average main: $13* ⊠ *521b Broadway* ☎ *707/343–7559* ⊕ *www. frenchiesonoma.com* ⊗ *Closed Wed.*

★ Girl & the Fig

$$$ | **FRENCH** | At this hot spot for inventive French cooking inside the historic Sonoma Hotel bar, you can always find a dish with owner Sondra Bernstein's signature figs on the menu, whether it's a fig-and-arugula salad or an aperitif blending sparkling wine with fig liqueur. Also look for duck confit, a burger with matchstick fries, and wild flounder meunière. **Known for:** Rhône-wines emphasis; artisanal cheese platters; croque monsieur and eggs Benedict at Sunday brunch. $ *Average main: $28* ⊠ *Sonoma Hotel, 110 W. Spain St.* ✛ *At 1st St. W* ☎ *707/938–3634* ⊕ *www. thegirlandthefig.com.*

Hare & Hatter Sausage Emporium

$ | **AMERICAN** | There's an artisanal angle to everything made at this casual stop for gourmet sausage sandwiches, breakfast all day, freshly baked pastries, and beer, wine, sodas, and juices. Sausage choices include pork andouille, spicy chicken with kimchi, German bratwurst, and traditional (more or less) hot dogs, all on buns baked locally. **Known for:** sausage sandwiches that regularly win local awards; artisanal fair-trade organic coffee; flat-bread pizza of the day. $ *Average main: $9* ⊠ *El Paseo Courtyard, 414 1st St. E* ✛ *At E. Spain St.* ☎ *707/934–8637* ⊕ *harehatter.com* ⊗ *Closed Tues. No dinner.*

★ Harvest Moon Cafe

$$$ | **AMERICAN** | Everything at this little restaurant with an odd, zigzagging layout is so perfectly executed and the vibe is so genuinely warm that a visit here is deeply satisfying. The ever-changing menu might include homey dishes such as hand-cut tagliatelle with sautéed mushrooms or panfried swordfish with herbed quinoa pilaf. **Known for:** friendly service; patio dining area; husband-and-wife chefs Nick and Jen Demarest. $ *Average main: $28* ⊠ *487 1st St. W* ✛ *At W. Napa St.* ☎ *707/933–8160* ⊕ *www. harvestmooncafesonoma.com* ⊗ *Closed Tues. No lunch.*

★ LaSalette Restaurant

$$$ | **PORTUGUESE** | Born in the Azores and raised in Sonoma, chef-owner Manuel Azevedo serves cuisine inspired by his native Portugal in this warmly decorated spot. The wood-oven-roasted fish is always worth trying, and there are usually boldly flavored lamb and pork dishes, along with stews, salted cod, and other hearty fare. **Known for:** authentic Portuguese cuisine; sophisticated spicing; olive-oil cake with queijo fresco (fresh cheese) ice cream. $ *Average main: $28* ⊠ *452 1st St. E* ✛ *Near E. Spain St.* ☎ *707/938–1927* ⊕ *www.lasalette-restaurant.com.*

Oso Sonoma

$$$ | **MODERN AMERICAN** | Chef David Bush, who achieved national recognition for his food pairings at St. Francis Winery,

El Dorado Kitchen's chefs craft flavorful dishes full of subtle surprises.

owns this barlike small-plates restaurant whose menu evolves throughout the day. Lunch might see mole-braised pork-shoulder tacos or an achiote chicken sandwich, with dinner fare perhaps of steamed mussels, miso-glazed salmon, or poutine, all of it served in an 1890s structure, erected as a livery stable, that incorporates materials reclaimed from the building's prior incarnations. **Known for:** bar menu between lunch and dinner; smart beer and wine selections; Sonoma Plaza location. [$] *Average main: $29* ✉ *9 E. Napa St.* ✣ *At Broadway* ☎ *707/931–6926* 🌐 *www.ososonoma.com* 🕓 *No lunch Mon.–Wed.*

Santé

$$$$ | AMERICAN | Elegant Santé is the Fairmont resort's restaurant for haute cuisine focusing on seasonal local ingredients. You can dine à la carte, but the intricate dishes on the chef's tasting menu make it worth trading up. **Known for:** chef's tasting menu; excellent wines; elegant setting. [$] *Average main: $45* ✉ *Fairmont Sonoma Mission Inn & Spa, 100 Boyes Blvd./Hwy. 12* ✣ *2½ miles north of Sonoma Plaza* ☎ *707/938–9000* 🌐 *www.santediningroom.com* 🕓 *No lunch.*

Sunflower Caffé

$ | AMERICAN | Whimsical art and brightly painted walls set a jolly tone at this casual eatery whose assets include sidewalk seating with Sonoma Plaza views and the verdant patio out back. Omelets and waffles are the hits at breakfast, with the smoked duck *banh mi,* served on a toasted baguette with Sriracha aioli, a favorite for lunch. **Known for:** combination café, gallery, and wine bar; local cheeses and hearty soups; free Wi-Fi. [$] *Average main: $14* ✉ *421 1st St. W* ✣ *At W. Spain St.* ☎ *707/996–6645* 🌐 *www.sonomasunflower.com* 🕓 *No dinner.*

Sweet Scoops

$ | AMERICAN | The scent of waffle cones baking in back draws patrons into this family-run parlor serving artisanal ice cream made fresh daily. Butter brickle, Mexican chocolate, and salted caramel ice cream are among the 180 alternating flavors that include sorbets, sometimes sherbets, and always a vegan option. **Known for:** shakes, floats, and sundaes; peppy decor and staffers; husband and wife owners (he makes the ice cream, and she runs the business). [$] *Average main: $5* ✉ *408 1st St. E* ✣ *Near E. Spain St.* ☎ *707/721–1187* 🌐 *www.sweetscoopsicecream.com.*

Tasca Tasca Portuguese Tapas Restaurant & Wine Bar
$ | **PORTUGUESE** | Late-night Sonoma dining—or nibbling, given the portion sizes—received a boost when Azores-born chef Manuel Azevedo opened this retro-contempo tavern dedicated to Portuguese small bites. Dividing his menu into five parts—Cheese, Garden, Sea, Land, Sweet—Azevedo, who also owns the nearby restaurant LaSalette, serves everything from hearty *caldo verde* stew, foie gras, and salted codfish cakes to São Jorge cheese topped with marmalade. **Known for:** Portuguese wines; dessert mousses and sorbets; good for lunch, open late. [$] *Average main: $15* ✉ *122 W. Napa St.* ✣ *Near 1st St. W* ☎ *707/996–8272* 🌐 *www.tascatasca.com.*

Hotels

Auberge Sonoma
$$$ | **RENTAL** | If you are traveling in a group of three or four, or just prefer lodgings that feel more like home, consider the two-bedroom suites at this charmer just off Sonoma Plaza. **Pros:** good value for couples traveling together; close to Sonoma Plaza shops, restaurants, and tasting rooms; owners operate similar nearby lodgings if these are full. **Cons:** two-night minimum (three on summer weekends); lacks pool and other amenities; more or less self-serve. [$] *Rooms from: $360* ✉ *151 E. Napa St.* ☎ *707/939–5670 voice mail* 🌐 *www.aubergesonoma.com* 🛏 *3 suites* 🍴 *No meals.*

Best Western Sonoma Valley Inn
$$ | **HOTEL** | A low(er)-budget option just off Sonoma Plaza, this motel serves buffet breakfasts that surpass expectations and is accessible to a Whole Foods Market, bakeries, and similar businesses shrewd travelers frequent to stretch their dollars. **Pros:** wine-tasting coupons; front desk staffed 24/7; within walking distance of tasting rooms, shops, and restaurants. **Cons:** smallest rooms short on bathroom counter space; public areas nicer than the rooms; convention facilities and rooms in front can be noisy. [$] *Rooms from: $249* ✉ *550 2nd St. W* ☎ *707/938–9200, 800/334–5784* 🌐 *www.sonomavalleyinn.com* 🛏 *80 rooms* 🍴 *Breakfast.*

★ Cottage Inn & Spa
$$ | **B&B/INN** | Delivering romance, relaxation, and Zen-like tranquillity is the innkeepers' goal at this courtyard complex 1½ blocks north of Sonoma Plaza. **Pros:** convenient yet quiet location; winery passes; four suites with double Jacuzzi tubs. **Cons:** books up far ahead from late spring to early fall; some bathrooms only have a shower; lacks amenities such as room service, restaurant, pool, or gym. [$] *Rooms from: $250* ✉ *310 1st St. E* ☎ *707/996–0719* 🌐 *www.cottageinnandspa.com* 🛏 *9 rooms* 🍴 *Breakfast.*

El Dorado Hotel
$$ | **HOTEL** | Guest rooms in this remodeled 1843 building strike a rustic-contemporary pose with their Restoration Hardware furnishings, but the Mexican-tile floors hint at Sonoma's mission-era past. **Pros:** stylish for the price; on-site El Dorado Kitchen restaurant; central location. **Cons:** rooms are small, though patios and balconies keep them from feeling claustrophobic; street noise audible in some rooms; parking can be problematic. [$] *Rooms from: $275* ✉ *405 1st St. W* ☎ *707/996–3030* 🌐 *www.eldoradosonoma.com* 🛏 *27 rooms* 🍴 *No meals.*

El Pueblo Inn

$$ | HOTEL | A giant pepper tree and a few palms tower over the garden courtyard of this updated motel run by the third generation of the family that opened it in 1959. **Pros:** festive pool area; expanded continental breakfast buffet; winery passes. **Cons:** rates can spike in high season; street noise an issue in some rooms; several blocks west of Sonoma Plaza. ⓢ *Rooms from: $249* ✉ *896 W. Napa St.* ✛ *Off Hwy. 12 near Riverside Dr.* ☎ *707/996–3651* ⊕ *www.elpuebloinn. com* ⇆ *54 rooms* ⦅〇⦆ *Breakfast.*

Fairmont Sonoma Mission Inn & Spa

$$$ | RESORT | The real draw at this mission-style resort is the extensive spa with its array of massages and treatments, some designed for couples. **Pros:** full-service hotel; enormous spa and other wellness services; in-the-know concierges. **Cons:** smallish standard rooms; lacks the intimacy of similarly priced options; hefty resort fee, though it does include many perks. ⓢ *Rooms from: $399* ✉ *100 Boyes Blvd./Hwy. 12* ✛ *2½ miles north of Sonoma Plaza* ☎ *707/938–9000* ⊕ *www. fairmont.com/sonoma* ⇆ *226 rooms* ⦅〇⦆ *No meals.*

Inn at Sonoma

$$ | B&B/INN | Little luxuries delight at this well-run inn ¼-mile south of Sonoma Plaza: wine and hors d'oeuvres are served every evening in the lobby, where a jar brims with cookies from noon to 8 pm and free beverages are always available. **Pros:** last-minute specials are a great deal; comfortable beds; good soundproofing blocks out Broadway street noise. **Cons:** on a busy street rather than right on the plaza; pet-friendly rooms book up quickly; some rooms on the small side. ⓢ *Rooms from: $249* ✉ *630 Broadway* ☎ *707/939–1340* ⊕ *www.innatsonoma. com* ⇆ *27 rooms* ⦅〇⦆ *Breakfast.*

★ Ledson Hotel

$$$ | B&B/INN | With just six rooms the Ledson feels intimate, and the furnishings and amenities—down beds, mood lighting, gas fireplaces, whirlpool tubs, and balconies for enjoying breakfast or a glass of wine—stack up well against Wine Country rooms costing more, especially in high season. **Pros:** convenient Sonoma Plaza location; spacious, individually decorated rooms with whirlpool tubs; complimentary tasting at ground-floor Zina Lounge wine bar. **Cons:** maximum occupancy in all rooms is two people; children must be at least 12 years old; front rooms have plaza views but pick up some street noise. ⓢ *Rooms from: $350* ✉ *480 1st St. E* ☎ *707/996–9779* ⊕ *www.ledsonhotel.com* ⇆ *6 rooms* ⦅〇⦆ *Free Breakfast.*

★ MacArthur Place Hotel & Spa

$$$ | HOTEL | Guests at this 7-acre boutique property five blocks south of Sonoma Plaza bask in ritzy seclusion in plush accommodations set amid landscaped gardens. **Pros:** verdant garden setting; tranquil spa; great for a romantic getaway. **Cons:** a bit of a walk from the plaza; some traffic noise audible in street-side rooms; pricey in high season. ⓢ *Rooms from: $359* ✉ *29 E. MacArthur St.* ☎ *707/938–2929, 800/722–1866* ⊕ *www. macarthurplace.com* ⇆ *64 rooms* ⦅〇⦆ *No meals.*

Sonoma Creek Inn

$ | B&B/INN |FAMILY | The exterior of this property between Sonoma and Glen Ellen says "motel," but the design sensibility and customer service are more quaint country inn, with the rates splitting the difference between the two. **Pros:** clean, well-lighted bathrooms; lots of charm for the price; popular with bicyclists. **Cons:** office not staffed 24 hours; 10-minute drive from Sonoma Plaza; a few rooms cramped. ⓢ *Rooms from: $165* ✉ *239 Boyes Blvd.* ✛ *Off Hwy. 12* ☎ *707/939–9463, 888/712–1289* ⊕ *www. sonomacreekinn.com* ⇆ *16 rooms* ⦅〇⦆ *No meals.*

Nightlife

Sigh

WINE BARS—NIGHTLIFE | From the oval bar and walls the color of a fine Blanc de Blancs to retro chandeliers that mimic champagne bubbles, everything about this sparkling-wine bar's frothy space screams "have a good time." That owner Jayme Powers and her posse are trained in the fine art of *sabrage* (opening a sparkler with a saber) only adds to the festivity. ■**TIP**→ **Sigh opens at noon, so it's a good daytime stop, too.** ⊠ *120 W. Napa St.* ✢ *At 1st St. W* ☎ *707/996–2444* ⊕ *www.sighsonoma.com.*

Starling Bar Sonoma

BARS/PUBS | Chat up the locals at this neighborhood hangout with a welcoming vibe and bartenders slinging the classics and craft cocktails, some of whose ingredients are grown out back. Signature drinks include the Starling Mule, with ginger beer made in-house, vodka, lime, and whiskey bitters. The bar hosts live music and other events on some nights. ⊠ *19380 Hwy. 12* ✢ *At W. Spain St.* ☎ *707/938–7442* ⊕ *www.starlingsonoma. com.*

Swiss Hotel

BARS/PUBS | Old-timers head to the hotel's old-timey bar for a blast of Glariffee, a cold and potent cousin to Irish coffee that loosens the tongue. ⊠ *18 W. Spain St.* ✢ *At 1st St. W* ☎ *707/938–2884* ⊕ *www.swisshotelsonoma.com.*

Valley of the Moon Certified Farmers' Market

GATHERING PLACES | With live music, food vendors, and wine and beers poured, Tuesday night on Sonoma Plaza (from 5:30 to sunset, May through September) is as much a block party as a chance to buy produce. It's a good place to chat up the locals. ⊠ *Sonoma Plaza, 453 1st St. E* ✢ *At E. Napa St.* ☎ *707/694–3611* ⊕ *www.sonomaplazamarket.org* ☕ *Free.*

 Performing Arts

Sebastiani Theatre

FILM | This theater, built on Sonoma Plaza in 1934 by Italian immigrant and entrepreneur Samuele Sebastiani, schedules first-run films, as well as occasional musical and theatrical performances. ⊠ *476 1st St. E* ✢ *Near W. Spain St.* ☎ *707/996– 2020* ⊕ *www.sebastianitheatre.com.*

Shopping

Chateau Sonoma

HOUSEHOLD ITEMS/FURNITURE | The fancy furniture, lighting fixtures, and objets d'art at this upscale shop make it a dangerous place to enter: after just a few minutes you may find yourself reconsidering your entire home's aesthetic. The owner's keen eye for French style makes a visit here a pleasure. ⊠ *Cornerstone Sonoma, 23588 Arnold Dr.* ✢ *Across from Gloria Ferrer* ☎ *707/935–8553* ⊕ *www.chateausonoma.com.*

Fat Pilgrim & Harvest Home

HOUSEHOLD ITEMS/FURNITURE | This combination "contemporary general store" (Fat Pilgrim) and home-furnishings emporium (Harvest Home) carries many locally made gift items and food and beauty products, along with furniture and home accessories, some of them also from Sonoma or Napa. The tone in the huge outdoor section, which abuts the Girl & the Fig restaurant's garden, is decidedly whimsical, with colorful metal sculptures of chickens, pigs, and other animals. Stopping at the compound provides a break from wine tasting, though you can do that, too, at the Rhône Room bungalow, also on-site. ⊠ *20820 Broadway* ✢ *At Fisher La.* ☎ *707/933–9044* ⊕ *www. fatpilgrim.com.*

G's General Store

CERAMICS/GLASSWARE | The inventory of this "modern general store" runs the gamut from cute bunny LED nightlights and Euro-suave kitchen utensils to bright-print shirts and fancy ceramic ware. The owner used to buy for Smith & Hawken and Williams-Sonoma, so expect upscale merchandise presented with style. ⊠ *19 W. Napa St.* ✛ *Near Broadway* ☎ *707/933–8082* ⊕ *www.ggeneralstore. com.*

★ Sonoma Valley Certified Farmers Market

OUTDOOR/FLEA/GREEN MARKETS | To discover just how bountiful the Sonoma landscape is—and how talented its farmers and food artisans are—head to Depot Park, just north of the Sonoma Plaza, on Friday morning. This market is considered Sonoma County's best. ⊠ *Depot Park, 1st St. W* ✛ *At Sonoma Bike Path* ☎ *707/538–7023* ⊕ *www.svcfm.org.*

Vella Cheese Company

FOOD/CANDY | North and east of Sonoma Plaza, this Italian cheese shop has been making superb cheeses, including raw-milk cheddars and several varieties of jack, since 1931. A bonus: plenty of free samples. ⊠ *315 2nd St. E* ✛ *½ block north of E. Spain St.* ☎ *707/938–3232, 800/848–0505* ⊕ *vellacheese.com* ☾ *Closed Sun.*

Willow Stream Spa at Fairmont Sonoma Mission Inn & Spa

SPA/BEAUTY | By far the Wine Country's largest spa, the Fairmont resort's 40,000-square-foot facility provides every amenity you could possibly want, including pools and hot tubs fed by local thermal springs. The signature 2½-hour Sonoma Organic Lavender Kur and Facial includes a botanical body wrap, a full-body massage, and a facial. Couples seeking romance often request the treatment room with the two-person copper bathtub. ⊠ *100 Boyes Blvd./Hwy. 12* ✛ *2½ miles north of Sonoma Plaza* ☎ *707/938–9000* ⊕ *www.fairmont.com/ sonoma/willow-stream* ☱ *Treatments $79–$539.*

Activities

Sonoma Valley Bike Tours

BICYCLING | A mile south of Sonoma Plaza, this Napa Valley Bike Tours offshoot rents bikes and conducts guided bicycle tours of wineries. ⊠ *1254 Broadway* ✛ *At Woolworth La.* ☎ *707/251–8687* ⊕ *sonomavalleybiketours.com* ☱ *Bike rentals from $29 for 2 hrs; guided winery tours from $124.*

Wine Country Cyclery

BICYCLING | You can rent comfort/hybrid, tandem, and road bikes by the hour or the day at this shop west of the plaza. ⊠ *262 W. Napa St.* ✛ *At 3rd St. W* ☎ *707/996–6800* ⊕ *winecountrycyclery. com* ☱ *From $10 per hr, $30 per day.*

Glen Ellen

7 miles north of Sonoma.

Craggy Glen Ellen epitomizes the difference between the Napa and Sonoma valleys. Whereas small Napa towns like St. Helena get their charm from upscale boutiques and restaurants lined up along well-groomed sidewalks, Glen Ellen's crooked streets are shaded with stands of old oak trees and occasionally bisected by the Sonoma and Calabazas creeks. Tucked among the trees of a narrow canyon, where Sonoma Mountain and the Mayacamas pinch in the valley floor, Glen Ellen looks more like a town of the Sierra foothills gold country than a Wine Country village.

Wine has been part of Glen Ellen since the 1840s, when a French immigrant, Joshua Chauvet, planted grapes and later built a winery and the valley's first distillery. Machinery at the winery was powered by steam, and boilers were fueled with wood from local oaks. Other valley farmers followed Chauvet's example, and grape growing took off, although Prohibition took its toll on most of these operations. Today dozens of wineries in

Benziger tram tours take to the fields to show biodynamic farming techniques in action.

the area beg to be visited, but sometimes it's hard not to succumb to Glen Ellen's slow pace and lounge poolside at your lodging or linger over a leisurely picnic. The renowned cook and food writer M.F.K. Fisher, who lived and worked in Glen Ellen for 22 years until her death in 1992, would surely have approved. Hunter S. Thompson, who lived here for a spell before he became famous, might not: he found the place too sedate. Glen Ellen's most famous resident, however, was Jack London, who epitomized the town's rugged spirit.

GETTING HERE AND AROUND

To get to Glen Ellen from Sonoma, drive west on Spain Street. After about a mile, take Highway 12 north for 7 miles to Arnold Drive, which deposits you in the middle of town. Many of Glen Ellen's restaurants and inns are along a half-mile stretch of Arnold Drive. Sonoma Transit Bus 30 and Bus 38 serve Glen Ellen from Sonoma and Kenwood.

 Sights

Benziger Family Winery

WINERY/DISTILLERY | One of the best-known Sonoma County wineries sits on a sprawling estate in a bowl with 360-degree sun exposure, the benefits of which are explored on tram tours that depart several times daily. Guides explain Benziger's biodynamic farming practices and provide a glimpse of the extensive cave system. Choose from a regular tram tour or a more in-depth excursion that concludes with a seated tasting. Known for Chardonnay, Cabernet Sauvignon, Merlot, Pinot Noir, and Sauvignon Blanc, the winery is a beautiful spot for a picnic. ■TIP➜ **Reserve a seat on the tram tour through the winery's website or arrive early in the day on summer weekends and during harvest season.** ⌧ *1883 London Ranch Rd. ✛ Off Arnold Dr. ☎ 888/490–2739, ⊕ www.benziger.com ✉ Tastings from $20, tours from $30 (includes tastings).*

B.R. Cohn

WINERY/DISTILLERY | Classic-rock fans acknowledge this Glen Ellen winery's musical chops—Bruce Cohn, the long-time manager of the Doobie Brothers, founded it in 1984—but the enological pedigree is equally noteworthy: the first winemaker was the now-famous consultant Helen Turley, and Pinot Noir specialist Merry Edwards followed her. The wines, still crafted in Turley's fruit-forward style, include Sauvignon Blanc, Chardonnay, and Pinot Gris whites, and Cabernet Sauvignon, Malbec, and Zinfandel reds. A 1920s residence was expanded to create the tasting room, which bustles on most weekend afternoons. ■TIP→ A gourmet shop near the patio outside the tasting room sells olive oil from the property's 19th-century olive trees, along with vinegars and other food items. ⊠ 15000 Sonoma Hwy./Hwy. 12 ✛ ½ mile north of Madrone Rd. ☎ 707/938–4064 ⊕ brcohn.com ⌂ Tastings from $25.

★ Jack London State Historic Park

NATIONAL/STATE PARK | The pleasures are pastoral and intellectual at author Jack London's beloved Beauty Ranch, where you could easily spend the afternoon hiking some of the 30-plus miles of trails that loop through meadows and stands of oaks, redwoods, and other trees. Manuscripts and personal artifacts depicting London's travels are on view at the House of Happy Walls Museum, which provides an overview of the writer's life, literary passions, humanitarian and conservation efforts, and promotion of organic farming. A short hike away lie the ruins of Wolf House, which burned down just before London was to move in. Also open to visitors are a few outbuildings and the restored wood-framed cottage where London penned many of his later works. He's buried on the property. ■TIP→ Well-known performers headline the park's Broadway Under the Stars series, a hot ticket in summer. ⊠ 2400 London Ranch Rd. ✛ Off Arnold Dr. ☎ 707/938–5216 ⊕ www.jacklondonpark. com ⌂ Parking $10 ($5 walk-in or bike), includes admission to museum; cottage $4.

Kivelstadt Cellars

WINERY/DISTILLERY | Adventuresome sorts gravitate to Kivelstadt Cellars, described by a staff member as "three wineries trapped in one body." Founder Jordan Kivelstadt, an engineer by training and the son of two grape growers, likes to experiment, getting his full geek on with the fanciful KC Labs bottlings, among them a sprightly Mendocino County Zinfandel the hosts serve not at room temperature but chilled. Two standouts are the estate Pinot Noir and a Syrah called The Inheritance that winemaker Sam Baron crafts with old-world restraint, light on the oak. Other wines have more fruit-forward leanings. With this broad range of styles, something will appeal to most palates. The amusingly offhand crew pours the wines in a downtown Glen Ellen tasting room whose hip-rustic decor emphasizes new and reclaimed wood. ⊠ 13750 Arnold Dr. ✛ At London Ranch Rd. ☎ 707/938–7001 ⊕ www.kivelstadtcellars.com ⌂ Tastings from $15 ⊙ Closed Tues. and Wed.

★ Lasseter Family Winery

WINERY/DISTILLERY | Immaculately groomed grapevines dazzle the eye at John and Nancy Lasseter's secluded winery, and it's no accident: Phil Coturri, Sonoma Valley's premier organic vineyard manager, tends them. Even the landscaping, which includes an insectary to attract beneficial bugs, is meticulously maintained. Come harvesttime, the wine-making team oversees gentle processes that transform the fruit into wines of purity and grace: a Sémillon–Sauvignon Blanc blend, two rosés, and Bordeaux and Rhône reds. Evocative labels illustrate the tale behind each wine. These stories are well told on tours that precede some tastings of wines, paired with local artisanal cheeses, in an elegant room whose east-facing window frames vineyard and

Mayacamas Mountains views. Tastings, by the glass or flight, also take place on the winery's outdoor patio. All visits are by appointment only. ✉ *1 Vintage La.* ✥ *Off Dunbar Rd.* ☎ *707/933–2814* 🌐 *www.lasseterfamilywinery.com* 🎟 *Tastings (some including tours) from $30.*

★ Laurel Glen Vineyard

WINERY/DISTILLERY | As a longtime wine-industry marketing director, Bettina Sichel knew the potential pitfalls of winery ownership, but when she discovered a uniquely situated volcanic-soiled Sonoma Mountain vineyard for sale, she plunged in enthusiastically. Because her 14 acres of Cabernet Sauvignon vines face east, the mountain shelters the grapes from the hot late-afternoon sun and excessively cool Pacific influences. Sichel's impressive wine-making team includes Phil Coturri, an organic farming expert *Wine Spectator* magazine calls the "Wizard of Green," and winemaker Randall Watkins. By appointment at Sichel's industrial-chic tasting room in downtown Glen Ellen, you can taste the impressive estate Cabernet, along with another Cabernet, a rosé from the vineyard's oldest vines, and a Russian River Valley Sauvignon Blanc. ✉ *969 Carquinez Ave.* ✥ *East of Arnold Dr.* ☎ *707/933–9877* 🌐 *www.laurelglen.com* 🎟 *Tastings from $25.*

Loxton Cellars

WINERY/DISTILLERY | Back in the day when tasting rooms were low-tech and the winemaker often poured the wines, the winery experience unfolded pretty much the way it does at Loxton Cellars today. The personable Australia-born owner, Chris Loxton, who's on hand many days, crafts Zinfandels, Syrahs, a Pinot Noir, and a Cabernet Sauvignon, all quite good, and some regulars swear by the seductively smooth Syrah Port. You can sample a few current releases without an appointment, but one is needed to taste library- and limited-release wines. **■ TIP→ To learn more about Loxton's wine-making philosophy and practices, book a Walkabout tour (weekends only) of the vineyard and winery that's followed by a seated tasting.** ✉ *11466 Dunbar Rd.* ✥ *At Hwy. 12* ☎ *707/935–7221* 🌐 *www.loxtonwines.com* 🎟 *Tastings from $15, tour $40.*

Quarryhill Botanical Garden

GARDEN | Rare East Asian trees and plants thrive in this 25-acre woodland garden a little over a mile north of downtown Glen Ellen. There's also a heritage rose garden near the entrance. The colors at Quarryhill are most vibrant in spring, but year-round a visit here makes for a pleasant break from wine touring. ✉ *12841 Hwy. 12* ✥ *¼ mile north of Arnold Dr.* ☎ *707/996–3166* 🌐 *www.quarryhillbg.org* 🎟 *$12.*

🍴 Restaurants

Fig Cafe

$$ | **FRENCH** | The compact menu at this cheerful bistro focuses on California and French comfort food—pot roast and duck confit, for instance, as well as thin-crust pizza. Steamed mussels are served with crispy fries, which also accompany the Chef's Burger (top sirloin with Gruyère), two of the many dependable dishes that have made this restaurant a downtown Glen Ellen fixture. **Known for:** daily three-course prix-fixe specials; no corkage fee; local winemakers pouring wines on Wednesday evening. [$] *Average main: $19* ✉ *13690 Arnold Dr.* ✥ *At O'Donnell La.* ☎ *707/938–2130* 🌐 *www.thefigcafe.com* ⏲ *No lunch.*

★ Glen Ellen Star

$$$ | **ECLECTIC** | Chef Ari Weiswasser honed his craft at The French Laundry, Daniel, and other bastions of culinary finesse, but at his Wine Country outpost he prepares haute-rustic cuisine, much of it emerging from a wood-fired oven that burns a steady 600°F. Crisp-crusted, richly sauced Margherita and other pizzas thrive in the torrid heat, as do tender whole fish entrées and vegetables

Jack London Country

The rugged, rakish author and adventurer Jack London is perhaps best known for his travels to Alaska and his exploits in the Pacific, which he immortalized in tales such as *The Call of the Wild*, *White Fang*, and *South Sea Tales*. But he loved no place so well as the hills of eastern Sonoma County, where he spent most of his thirties and where he died in 1916 at the age of 40.

Between 1905 and 1916 London bought seven parcels of land totaling 1,400 acres, which he dubbed Beauty Ranch. When he wasn't off traveling, he dedicated most of his time to cultivating the land and raising livestock. He also maintained a few acres of wine grapes for his personal use.

Dreams and Mysteries

In 1913 London rhapsodized about his beloved ranch near Glen Ellen, writing, "The grapes on a score of rolling hills are red with autumn flame. Across Sonoma Mountain wisps of sea fog are stealing. The afternoon sun smolders in the drowsy sky. I have everything to make me glad I am alive. I am filled with dreams and mysteries."

Much of Beauty Ranch is now preserved as **Jack London State** Historic Park, worth visiting not only for its museum and other glimpses into London's life but also for the trails that skirt vineyards and meander through a forest of Douglas fir, coastal redwoods, oak, and madrones. London and his wife spent two years here constructing their dream home, Wolf House, before it burned down one hot August night in 1913, days before they were scheduled to move in. A look at the remaining stone walls and fireplaces gives you a sense of the building's grand scale. Within, a fireproof basement vault was to hold London's manuscripts. Elsewhere in the park stands the unusually posh pigsty that London's neighbors called the Pig Palace.

Legacy Vineyards

Parts of Beauty Ranch are still owned by London's descendants, from whom Kenwood Vineyards leases and farms legacy vineyards producing Cabernet Sauvignon, Merlot, Syrah, and Zinfandel. The wines from Beauty Ranch are among the winery's best.

roasted in small iron skillets. **Known for:** kitchen-view counter for watching chefs cook; prix-fixe Wednesday "neighborhood night" menu with free corkage; Weiswasser's sauces, emulsions, and spices. [$] *Average main: $28* ✉ *13648 Arnold Dr.* ✥ *At Warm Springs Rd.* ☎ *707/343–1384* 🌐 *glenellenstar.com* 🕒 *No lunch.*

Yeti Restaurant

$$$ | INDIAN | Glen Ellen's finer restaurants emphasize seasonal local produce, but instead of riffs on French, Italian, or California styles, the farm-to-table creations at this casual space (open kitchen, paper lanterns, wooden tables and chairs) fuse Indian and Himalayan cuisine. Start with samosas or tomato-based Himalayan pepper pot soup from Nepal—so warming on a chilly day—then proceed to curries, sizzling tandooris, or chicken, prawn, or vegetable biryanis upon ethereally aromatic saffron basmati rice. **Known for:** deck overlooking Sonoma Creek; international beer selection; smart wine choices at all price points. [$] *Average main: $25* ✉ *Jack London Village, 14301 Arnold Dr.* ✥ *¾ mile south of downtown* ☎ *707/996–9930* 🌐 *www.yetirestaurant.com.*

Hotels

Beltane Ranch

$$ | **B&B/INN** | On a slope of the Mayacamas range with gorgeous Sonoma Valley views, this working ranch, vineyard, and winery contains charmingly old-fashioned rooms. **Pros:** bountiful breakfasts; timeless feel; ranch setting. **Cons:** downstairs rooms get some noise from upstairs rooms; ceiling fans instead of air-conditioning; may feel too remote or low-key for some guests. $ *Rooms from: $240* ⊠ *11775 Sonoma Hwy./Hwy. 12* ☎ *707/833–4233* ⊕ *www.beltaneranch. com* ⊷ *6 rooms* ⦿ *Breakfast.*

★ Gaige House + Ryokan

$$$ | **B&B/INN** | There's no other place in Sonoma or Napa quite like the Gaige House + Ryokan, which blends the best elements of a traditional country inn, a boutique hotel, and a longtime expat's classy Asian hideaway. **Pros:** short walk to Glen Ellen restaurants, shops, and tasting rooms; bottomless jar of cookies in the common area; full breakfasts, afternoon wine and appetizers. **Cons:** sound carries in the main house; the least expensive rooms are on the small side; oriented more toward couples than families with children. $ *Rooms from: $358* ⊠ *13540 Arnold Dr.* ☎ *707/935–0237, 800/935–0237* ⊕ *www.gaige.com* ⊷ *23 rooms* ⦿ *Breakfast.*

★ Olea Hotel

$$$ | **B&B/INN** | The husband-and-wife team of Ashish and Sia Patel operate this boutique lodging that's at once sophisticated and down-home country casual, and the attention to detail impresses most visitors almost instantly, from the exterior landscaping, pool, and hot tub to the colors and surfaces in the guest rooms and public spaces. **Pros:** beautiful style; complimentary wine; chef-prepared breakfasts. **Cons:** minor road noise in some rooms; fills up quickly on weekends; weekend minimum-stay requirement. $ *Rooms from: $308* ⊠ *5131*

Warm Springs Rd. ✛ *West off Arnold Dr.* ☎ *707/996–5131* ⊕ *www.oleahotel.com* ⊷ *15 rooms* ⦿ *Breakfast.*

Kenwood

4 miles north of Glen Ellen.

Tiny Kenwood consists of little more than a few restaurants, shops, tasting rooms, and a historic train depot, now used for private events. But hidden in this pretty landscape of meadows and woods at the north end of Sonoma Valley are several good wineries, most just off the Sonoma Highway. Varietals grown here at the foot of the Sugarloaf Mountains include Sauvignon Blanc, Chardonnay, Zinfandel, and Cabernet Sauvignon.

GETTING HERE AND AROUND

To get to Kenwood from Glen Ellen, head northeast on Arnold Drive and north on Highway 12. Sonoma Transit Bus 30 and Bus 38 serve Kenwood from Glen Ellen and Sonoma.

Sights

B Wise Vineyards Tasting Lounge

WINERY/DISTILLERY | The stylish roadside tasting room (walk-ins welcome) of this producer of small-lot reds sits on the valley floor, but B Wise's winery and vineyards occupy prime acreage high in the Moon Mountain District AVA. The winery made its name crafting big, bold Cabernets, including one from owner Brion Wise's estate, but in recent years has also focused on Pinot Noirs from Sonoma County and Oregon's Willamette Valley. Among the other stars in the uniformly excellent lineup is the Cabernet-heavy blend Trios, whose grapes, all from Wise's estate, include Merlot, Petit Verdot, Syrah, and Tannat. The winery also makes Chardonnay and a rosé of Pinot Noir that quickly sells out. A tasting here may whet your appetite for a visit to the estate, done by appointment only.

✉ *9077 Sonoma Hwy.* ✛ *At Shaw Ave.* ☎ *707/282-9169* ⊕ *www.bwisevineyards. com* ✉ *Tasting $20.*

Chateau St. Jean

WINERY/DISTILLERY | At the foot of the Mayacamas Mountains stretch the impeccably groomed grounds of Chateau St. Jean, an old-country estate. After a spin around the gardens, whose layout harmonizes with the sprawling, Mediterranean-style villa, step inside for a tasting of Chardonnay, Fumé Blanc, Pinot Gris, and other whites, along with reds that include Pinot Noir, Cabernet Sauvignon, Merlot, and Syrah. Some tastings are by appointment. ✉ *8555 Sonoma Hwy./ Hwy. 12* ☎ *707/257-5784* ⊕ *www.chateaustjean.com* ✉ *Tastings from $15.*

Deerfield Ranch Winery

WINERY/DISTILLERY | The focus at Deerfield is on producing "clean wines"—low in histamines and sulfites—the better to eliminate the headaches and allergic reactions some red-wine drinkers experience. Winemaker Robert Rex accomplishes this goal with no loss of flavor or complexity: Deerfield wines are bold and fruit-forward, with a long finish. To sip wines that include several Bordeaux-style reds, Pinot Noir, Chardonnay, and a blend of four white grapes, you walk deep into a 23,000-square-foot cave for a seated tasting in a relaxed, loungelike space. ✉ *10200 Sonoma Hwy./Hwy. 12* ☎ *707/833-5215* ⊕ *www.deerfieldranch. com* ✉ *Tastings from $20, library tour and tasting $45.*

Kenwood Vineyards

WINERY/DISTILLERY | The best of the Kenwood wines—Cabernet Sauvignons, Zinfandels, Syrahs, and Merlots—are made from Sonoma Mountain AVA grapes the winery farms on the author Jack London's old vineyard. Kenwood, established in 1970, is best known for these wines, its widely distributed Sauvignon Blanc, and the Artist Series Cabernet Sauvignon, named for the artworks commissioned for the labels. Collectively the Kenwood wines represent a survey of notable Sonoma County appellations and vineyards. A new tasting room is planned for a knoll with views across the estate; until its completion, tastings will take place in a redwood barn in which the property's original vintners began making wine in 1906. ✉ *9592 Sonoma Hwy./Hwy. 12* ☎ *707/282-4228* ⊕ *www.kenwoodvineyards.com* ✉ *Tastings from $15.*

Kunde Estate Winery & Vineyards

WINERY/DISTILLERY | On your way into Kunde you pass a terrace flanked by fountains, virtually coaxing you to stay for a picnic with views over the vineyard. Family owned for more than a century, Kunde prides itself on producing 100% estate wines from its 1,850-acre property, which rises 1,400 feet from the valley floor. Kunde's whites include several Chardonnays and a Sauvignon Blanc, with Cabernet Sauvignon, Merlot, and a Zinfandel from 1880s vines among the reds. ■**TIP**➔ **Make a reservation for the Mountain Top Tasting, a tour by luxury van that ends with a sampling of reserve wines.** ✉ *9825 Sonoma Hwy./Hwy. 12* ☎ *707/833-5501* ⊕ *www.kunde.com* ✉ *Tastings from $15, grounds and cave tour free.*

Landmark Vineyards

WINERY/DISTILLERY | High-quality Chardonnays have always been Landmark's claim to fame, led by the flagship Overlook blend of grapes from multiple vineyards. The winery also makes single-vineyard Chardonnays, including ones from Rodgers Creek (Sonoma Coast) and Lorenzo Vineyard (Russian River Valley). Landmark's other specialty is Pinot Noir. As with the Chardonnays, there's an Overlook Pinot Noir using grapes from multiple sources, and winemaker Greg Stach crafts single-vineyard wines, among them the highly praised Sonoma Coast Grand Detour Pinot Noir. Stop here to sip a spell, relax in the landscaped picnic area, and play boccie ball with the craggy Mayacamas Mountains and

Sugarloaf Ridge forming the backdrop. The estate tour and tasting is by appointment only. ■TIP→ **Free vineyard tours in a horse-drawn carriage take place on Saturday afternoon from midspring to early fall.** ⊠ *101 Adobe Canyon Rd.* ⊹ *At Hwy. 12* ☎ *707/833–0053* ⊕ *www.landmarkwine. com* ⊠ *Tastings from $20, estate tour and tasting from $30, carriage tour free.*

★ La Rochelle Winery

WINERY/DISTILLERY | Chuck Easley, a wine-industry veteran who worked for Mirassou, J. Lohr, and other well-known brands, runs this boutique producer of Pinot Noir that traces its roots back to the first person to bring clippings of the varietal to California. Most tastings of La Rochelle Pinots, crafted from grapes grown in 10 appellations from Mendocino County to the state's Central Coast, take place on a patio with views of walnut trees, a koi pond, and estate Chardonnay vines. The premier vineyard sources include Donum Estate (Carneros), Tondre Grapefield (Santa Lucia Highlands), Ferrington (Anderson Valley), and Bacigalupi (Russian River Valley). ■TIP→ **Book a reserve tasting to sample single-vineyard Pinots and discover what occurs in the vineyard and winery to produce them.** ⊠ *233 Adobe Canyon Rd.* ⊹ *Off Hwy. 12 (Sonoma Hwy.)* ☎ *707/302–8000* ⊕ *www.lrwine.com* ⊠ *Tastings from $20.*

Ledson Winery & Vineyards

WINERY/DISTILLERY | The Normandy-style castle visible from the highway was intended as winery owner Steve Ledson's family home when construction began in 1989, but this 16,000-square-foot space has always been a production facility and hospitality center. Pourers stationed amid a warren of tasting rooms introduce guests to the several dozen mostly single-varietal wines Ledson makes, everything from Zinfandel and Cabernet Sauvignon to Rhône varietals such as Syrah and Mourvèdre. ■TIP→ **The on-site Marketplace sells salads, sandwiches, artisanal cheeses, and other edibles you** can enjoy on the picnic grounds (no outside food, though). ⊠ *7335 Sonoma Hwy./Hwy. 12* ☎ *707/537–3810* ⊕ *www.ledson.com* ⊠ *Tastings from $20.*

Paradise Ridge Kenwood Tasting Room

WINERY/DISTILLERY | Its winery one of only a handful destroyed during the Wine Country's October 2017 wildfires, Paradise Ridge began 2019 still in rebuilding mode at its 156-acre Santa Rosa hillside estate, but its Kenwood tasting room continues to host guests. Wines to seek out include the Convict Zinfandel and Elevation Cabernet Sauvignon, from Rockpile AVA grapes grown at elevations of 1,800 feet and 2,000 feet respectively. From spring to fall the tasting room manager conducts a Wine Sensory Experience based on herbs grown in the garden outside. ⊠ *8860 Sonoma Hwy.* ⊹ *At Greene St.* ☎ *707/282–9020* ⊕ *pr-winery.com* ⊠ *Tastings from $20.*

St. Francis Winery

WINERY/DISTILLERY | Nestled at the foot of Mt. Hood, St. Francis has earned national acclaim for its wine-and-food pairings. With its red-tile roof and bell tower and views of the Mayacamas Mountains just to the east, the winery's California mission–style visitors center occupies one of Sonoma County's most scenic locations. The charm of the surroundings is matched by the mostly red wines, including rich, earthy Zinfandels from the Dry Creek, Russian River, and Sonoma valleys. Five-course pairings with small bites and wine—chicken medallions with Chardonnay, for instance, or a grilled lamb chop with Cabernet Franc—are offered from Thursday through Monday; pairings with cheeses and charcuterie are available daily. ⊠ *100 Pythian Rd.* ⊹ *Off Hwy. 12* ☎ *707/538–9463, 888/675–9463* ⊕ *www.stfranciswinery.com* ⊠ *Tastings from $15.*

VJB Cellars

WINERY/DISTILLERY | This Tuscan-inspired courtyard marketplace with tasting spaces and food shops is a fine spot to sip

A Great Day in Sonoma Valley

The drive through the Sonoma Valley from Sonoma in the south to Kenwood in the north takes half an hour, but you can easily fill a day touring the wineries and historic sites along the way.

Breakfast and Buena Vista

To hit the highlights, start in the town of Sonoma. Have breakfast at **Sunflower Caffé** or the **Hare & Hatter Sausage Emporium,** on opposite sides of Sonoma Plaza. From your breakfast spot, head east on East Napa Street and north on Old Winery Road to reach **Buena Vista Winery,** the birthplace of modern California wine making. (Alternatively, for sophisticated Chardonnays and Pinot Noirs, book a tasting at **Patz & Hall;** to reach its hospitality center, turn south from East Napa Street onto 8th Street East.)

Wine, Food, and Wine

Enjoy your tasting, then backtrack to East Napa Street and head west. The road eventually becomes Highway 12, which you'll take west and north to photogenic **St. Francis Winery** for the 1 pm wine and food pairing (reserve a few days ahead). If you arrive early, ask about the self-guided vineyard tour, which ends at the culinary garden that supplies ingredients for the pairing. From St. Francis, head back south 2 miles on Highway 12 to **B Wise Vineyards Tasting Lounge** (look for it on the right). Stop at this rustic-chic roadside tasting room for Cabernet, Pinot, and Chardonnay.

Literary Stroll

From B Wise, continue south on Highway 12 and take Arnold Drive into the picturesque town of Glen Ellen. Turn right on London Ranch Road and wind your way uphill for a few minutes to reach **Jack London State Historic Park.** Take a short stroll through the grounds and observe the historic buildings near the parking area before the park closes at 5 pm. Backtrack down London Ranch road for an early dinner at **Glen Ellen Star** or return to Sonoma on Highway 12.

wines, enjoy a pizza or a deli sandwich, and just relax. Mostly from Italian varietals, some rare in these parts, the wines are, like the complex, less rustic than in the old country and clearly adapted for contemporary American tastes. This isn't always a bad thing, and the best wines—the Barbera, the Sangiovese, and the Montepulciano—are lively and clean on the palate. Reservations are required for seated tastings. **■ TIP→ For gourmet dolci, check out Wine Truffle Boutique, which sells chocolates, Italian gelato, and wine-infused sorbets.** ✉ *60 Shaw Ave.* ✣ *Off Hwy. 12* ☎ *707/833–2300* 🌐 *www.vjbcellars.com* 🍷 *Tastings from $15.*

🍴 Restaurants

Café Citti

$ | ITALIAN | Classical music in the background, a friendly staff, and a roaring fire when it's cold outside keep this roadside café from feeling too spartan. Stand in line to order dishes such as roast chicken, pasta prepared with the sauce of your choice, and slabs of tiramisu for dessert, and someone will deliver your meal to a table indoors or on an outdoor patio. **Known for:** welcoming atmosphere; prepared salads and sandwiches; to-go winery picnics. [$] *Average main: $14* ✉ *9049 Sonoma Hwy./Hwy. 12* ☎ *707/833–2690* 🌐 *www.cafecitti.com.*

Palooza Gastropub & Wine Bar
$$ | **AMERICAN** | Palooza pleases with 16 beers on tap, jazzed-up pub grub, casual decor, and an often-packed covered outdoor patio. Pulled-pork sandwiches, falafel wraps, pan-seared salmon, fish and fries, blue-cheese-and-bacon burgers, and Chicago-style hot dogs are among the popular items, with fish tacos and shredded-kale and apple-spinach salads for those seeking lighter fare. **Known for:** many local brews; Sonoma Valley wines only; beer-battered fried pickles, mozzarella-ball appetizers. [$] *Average main: $16* ✉ *8910 Sonoma Hwy./Hwy. 12* ☎ *707/833–4000* 🌐 *www.paloozafresh.com.*

★ **Salt & Stone**
$$$ | **MODERN AMERICAN** | The menu at this upscale roadhouse with a sloping wood-beamed ceiling focuses on seafood (salt) and beef, lamb, chicken, duck, and other meats (stone), with many dishes in both categories grilled. Start with the classics, perhaps a martini and oysters Rockefeller, before moving on to well-plated contemporary entrées that might include crispy-skin salmon or duck breast, fish stew, or grilled rib-eye. **Known for:** suave cocktails including signature New York Sour; mountain-view outdoor seating area; Monday–Wednesday "Bistro Nights" three-course dinners. [$] *Average main: $25* ✉ *9900 Sonoma Hwy.* ✥ *At Kunde Winery Rd.* ☎ *707/833–6326* 🌐 *www.saltstonekenwood.com* 🕒 *No lunch Tues. and Wed.*

Tips Roadside
$$ | **AMERICAN** | The owners of a local-fave tri-tip food trolley seen at many events opened this comfort-food restaurant in a 90-year-old building that was originally a gas station and later an inn. In addition to tri-tip, the New Orleans–inspired menu consists of small bites like crispy oysters and barbecued shrimp and larger bites that include smoke-braised short ribs, fried chicken, and grits with white cheddar and smoked mushrooms. **Known for:** open-air dining with mountain views; beer, wine, and cocktails; beignets with Meyer lemon sauce. [$] *Average main: $19* ✉ *8445 Sonoma Hwy.* ✥ *At Adobe Rd.* ☎ *707/509–0078* 🌐 *www.tipsroadside.com* 🕒 *Closed Tues.*

🛏 Hotels

Kenwood Inn and Spa
$$$$ | **B&B/INN** | Fluffy feather beds, custom Italian furnishings, and French doors in most cases opening onto terraces or balconies lend this inn's uncommonly spacious guest rooms a romantic air. **Pros:** large rooms; lavish furnishings; romantic setting. **Cons:** road or lobby noise in some rooms; expensive in high season; geared more to couples than families with children. [$] *Rooms from: $489* ✉ *10400 Sonoma Hwy./Hwy. 12* ☎ *707/833–1293, 800/353–6966* 🌐 *www.kenwoodinn.com* 🛏 *29 rooms* 🍴 *Breakfast.*

🛍 Shopping

★ **Spa at Kenwood Inn**
SPA/BEAUTY | A pretty setting, expert practitioners, and rejuvenating therapies using products from iS Clinical, Intraceuticals, and the French line Caudalíe make a visit to this spa, completely remodeled in 2018, an ethereal experience. The delicious-sounding Honey Wine Wrap, one of the signature treatments, involves a warming, full-body slathering of wine yeast and honey. The Crushed Cabernet Scrub raises the sweetness ante by adding brown sugar to the honey, along with crushed grape seeds and grape-seed oil. The spa's other services include massages and facials. A terrace treatment area for couples has its own tub and shower. ✉ *10400 Sonoma Hwy./Hwy. 12* ☎ *707/833–1293, 800/353–6966* 🌐 *www.kenwoodinn.com/spa* 🎟 *Treatments from $149.*

Activities

Sugarloaf Ridge State Park

BICYCLING | On a clear day you can see all the way to San Francisco and sometimes east to the Sierras at this hilltop park on the Napa–Sonoma border. The easiest hiking trail follows Sonoma Creek for a mile from the visitors center; the hardest (8.2 miles) heads over Bald Mountain for those superlative views. Wildflower viewing is a major pastime from spring to early summer. You can mountain bike year-round. ⊠ *2605 Adobe Canyon Rd.* ✛ *Off Hwy. 12* ☎ *707/833–5712* ⊕ *www. sugarloafpark.org* ⌛ *$8.*

Petaluma

14 miles west of Sonoma; 39 miles north of San Francisco.

The first thing you should know about Petaluma is that this is a farm town—with more than 60,000 residents, a large one—and the residents are proud of it. Recent years have seen an uptick in the quality of Petaluma cuisine, fueled in part by the proliferation of local organic and artisanal farms and boutique wine production. With the 2018 approval of the Petaluma Gap AVA, the town even has its name on a wine appellation.

Petaluma's agricultural history reaches back to the mid-1800s, when General Mariano Vallejo established Rancho de Petaluma as the headquarters of his vast agrarian empire. From the late 1800s into the 1960s Petaluma marketed itself as the "Egg Capital of the World," and with production totals that peaked at 612 million eggs in 1946, the point was hard to dispute. Although a poultry processor remains Petaluma's second-largest employer, the town has diversified. The adobe, an interesting historical stop, was once the area's *only* employer, but these days its visitation figures are dwarfed by Lagunitas Brewing Company, whose free

tour is a hoot. At McEvoy Ranch, which started out producing gourmet olive oil and now also makes wine, you can taste both products and tour parts of the farm.

GETTING HERE AND AROUND

Petaluma lies west of Sonoma and southwest of Glen Ellen and Kenwood. From Highway 12 or Arnold Drive, take Watmaugh Road west to Highway 116 west. Sonoma Transit buses (Nos. 30, 40, and 53) serve Petaluma from the Sonoma Valley. From San Francisco take U.S. 101 (or Golden Gate Transit Bus 101) north.

VISITOR INFORMATION

CONTACTS Visit Petaluma. ⊠ *210 Lakeville St.* ☎ *707/769–0429* ⊕ *visitpetaluma.com.*

◉ Sights

Adobe Road Winery

WINERY/DISTILLERY | An upbeat atmosphere prevails in the downtown Petaluma tasting room of this winery founded by former race-car driver Kevin Buckler and his wife, Debra. To produce its portfolio of mostly small-lot wines, Adobe Road sources grapes from top-tier growers, among them Beckstoffer for Cabernet Sauvignon and Malbec, and Sangiacomo for Chardonnay, Pinot Noir, and Syrah from the Petaluma Gap AVA. The Cabernet and Malbec shine, as does a red blend of both. ■TIP➔ **The Bucklers are developing a combination tasting room, winery, and car museum along the waterfront near the current space; the new facility, at C and 1st Streets, is scheduled to open in 2020.** ⊠ *6 Petaluma Blvd. N* ✛ *At B St.* ☎ *707/774–6699* ⊕ *www.adoberoadwines.com* ⌛ *Tastings from $20.*

Keller Estate

WINERY/DISTILLERY | This boutique winery's guests discover why "wind to wine" is the Petaluma Gap AVA's slogan. The steady Pacific Ocean and San Pablo Bay breezes that mitigate the midday heat give the grapes thick "sailor's skin," heightening their tannins and flavor, says Ana Keller, whose parents planted vineyards three decades ago on former dairy fields. Keller Estate concentrates on Chardonnay, Pinot Noir, and Syrah. In good weather, tastings take place on a stone terrace shaded by umbrellas and flowering pear trees. Book a walking tour to see the property's cave, winery, vineyards, and olive trees, or go farther afield touring in a 1956 Mercedes van. ■ **TIP→ The winery requires reservations for all tastings and tours, but same-day visits are usually possible if you call ahead.** *✉ 5875 Lakeville Hwy. ✥ At Cannon La. ☎ 707/765–2117 🌐 www.kellerestate.com 🎫 Tasting $25, tours (with tastings) from $35 ⏲ Closed Tues. and Wed.*

★ Lagunitas Brewing Company

WINERY/DISTILLERY | These days owned by Heineken International, Lagunitas began as a craft brewery in Marin County in 1993 before moving to Petaluma in 1994. In addition to its large facility, the company operates a taproom, the Schwag Shop, and an outdoor beer garden that in good weather bustles even at midday. Guides leading the free weekday Tasting/Walking Tour, which starts with a flight of four beers, provide an irreverent version of the company's rise to international acclaim. An engaging tale involves the state alcohol board's sting operation commemorated by Undercover Investigation Shut-down Ale, one of several small-batch brews made here. ■ **TIP→ The taproom closes on Monday and Tuesday, but tours take place and the gift shop stays open.** *✉ 1280 N. McDowell Blvd. ✥ ½ mile north of Corona Rd. ☎ 707/769–4495 🌐 lagunitas.com/taproom/petaluma 🎫 Tour free ⏲ Taproom closed Mon. and Tues.*

★ McEvoy Ranch

WINERY/DISTILLERY | The pastoral retirement project of the late Nan McEvoy after departing as board chair of the *San Francisco Chronicle,* the ranch produces organic extra virgin olive oil and Pinot Noir and other wines, the estate ones from the Petaluma Gap AVA. Some guests sip a few selections at the bar inside, but far better is to reserve an At Our Table Tasting of wines, oils, seasonal edibles from the organic gardens, and artisanal cheeses. In good weather these relaxing sessions unfold on a pond's-edge flagstone patio with views of alternating rows of Syrah grapes and mature olive trees. Walkabout Ranch Tours of four guests or more take in vineyards, gardens, a Chinese pavilion, and other sites. All visits require an appointment. *✉ 5935 Red Hill Rd. ✥ 6½ miles south of downtown ☎ 866/617–6779 🌐 www.mcevoyranch.com 🎫 Tastings from $20, tour and tasting $95 ⏲ Closed Mon. and Tues. No tour Sun.*

Petaluma Adobe State Historic Park

NATIONAL/STATE PARK | A 10-foot cactus fence lines the blacktop path from the parking lot to the Petaluma Adobe, the largest extant 19th-century residential adobe in the United States. History buffs won't want to miss this landmark, from 1836 to 1846 the headquarters of General Mariano Vallejo's vast (66,000 acres at its peak) agricultural domain. Exhibits and docent programs focus on Vallejo's role as Mexico's head honcho before California joined the United States; life at what the general called Rancho de Petaluma for native peoples and Spanish and Mexican settlers; and the hide and tallow trade that kept the enterprise financially afloat. *✉ 3325 Adobe Rd. ✥ Near Casa Grande Rd. ☎ 707/762–4871 🌐 www.parks.ca.gov 🎫 $3, includes same-day admission to Sonoma Mission and other historical sites.*

Sonoma Portworks

WINERY/DISTILLERY | More than two decades ago Bill Reading got the bright idea to create the world's first chocolate wine. The concept went nowhere, but a later experiment adding dark-chocolate essences to port proved a winner—and became the first Sonoma Portworks product, Deco Port, these days made from Zinfandel and Petite Sirah. Reading followed this up by adding hazelnut essences to what's now called Duet Sherry. Individual ports made from Petite Sirah, Petit Verdot, and Norton, the last of which dates back to early-19th-century Virginia, are among the additional offerings. Reading and his upbeat crew pour these crowd-pleasing wines in a warehouselike space on downtown's southern edge. ✉ *613 2nd St.* ✥ *Near H St.* ☎ *707/769–5203* 🌐 *portworks.com* 🎟 *Tastings free–$15* 🕑 *Closed Tues. and Wed.*

🍴 Restaurants

Brewsters Beer Garden
$$ | **AMERICAN** |**FAMILY** | Succulent fried chicken and barbecued ribs whose meat glides off the bone are among the hits at this open-air, partially covered restaurant where diners at sturdy oak picnic or high-top communal tables choose from two dozen mostly craft beers on tap. Although the Southern-born chef draws on his heritage, many of the ingredients come from top artisanal protein and produce purveyors. **Known for:** easygoing atmosphere; full bar, good wine selection; kids playground and adult boccie court. [$] *Average main: $21* ✉ *229 Water St. N* ✥ *Near E. Washington St.* ☎ *707/981–8330* 🌐 *brewstersbeergarden.com.*

★ Central Market
$$$ | **MODERN AMERICAN** | A participant in the Slow Food movement, Central Market serves creative, upscale Cal-Mediterranean dishes—many of whose ingredients come from the restaurant's organic farm—in a century-old building with exposed brick walls and an open kitchen. The menu, which changes daily depending on chef Tony Najiola's inspiration and what's ripe and ready, might include tortilla soup or a buttermilk-fried halibut-cheeks starter, a slow-roasted-beets salad, pizzas and stews, and wood-grilled fish and meat. **Known for:** chef's tasting menus; superior wine list; historic setting. [$] *Average main: $25* ✉ *42 Petaluma Blvd. N* ✥ *Near Western Ave.* ☎ *707/778–9900* 🌐 *www.centralmarketpetaluma.com* 🕑 *Closed Wed. No lunch.*

Crocodile French Cuisine
$$ | **FRENCH** | Chef Michael Dotson aims to convey a sense of place—Sonoma County—through a French lens with seasonally changing dishes that might include escargot and steak frites but also ahi tuna confit à la Niçoise or a green-curry lentil galette. Dotson's sommelier-wife, Moira Beveridge, selects "fun and quirky" beers, ales, ciders, and wines and oversees their tall-ceilinged corner storefront, whose wooden tables and bar provide a rustic counterpoint to the otherwise industrial look. **Known for:** pot de crème, soufflés; good happy-hour eats; beverage pairings. [$] *Average main: $22* ✉ *140 2nd St., Suite 100* ☎ *707/981–8159* 🌐 *www.crocodilepetaluma.com.*

★ Pearl
$$ | **MEDITERRANEAN** | Regulars of this southern Petaluma "daytime café" with indoor and outdoor seating rave about its Eastern Mediterranean–inflected cuisine—then immediately downplay their enthusiasm lest this 2018 arrival become more popular. The menu, divided into "smaller," "bigger," and "sweeter" options, changes often, but mainstays include buckwheat polenta, a lamb burger dripping with tzatziki (pickled fennel and yogurt sauce), and *shakshuka* (tomato-based stew with chickpeas, fava beans, and baked egg). **Known for:** weekend brunch; zippy beverage lineup; menu prices include gratuity. [$] *Average main: $18* ✉ *500 1st St.* ✥ *At G St.* ☎ *707/559–5187* 🌐 *pearlpetaluma.com* 🕑 *Closed Tues. No dinner.*

🛏 Hotels

Hampton Inn Petaluma
$ | **HOTEL** | The former Carlson-Currier Silk Mill, its oldest section dating to 1892, houses this atypical Hampton, some of

whose guest rooms have 14-foot ceilings and exposed-brick walls. **Pros:** original architectural details in some rooms; classy breakfast area; reasonable rates. **Cons:** traffic noise (ask for a historic room away from the road); some standard rooms are small; no pool, nondescript neighborhood. [$] *Rooms from: $179* ✉ *450 Jefferson St.* ☎ *707/397–0000* 🌐 *www.hampton.com* 🛏 *75 rooms* 🍴 *Free Breakfast.*

Hotel Petaluma

$ | **HOTEL** | Reasonable rates and vintage allure make this 1923 art-deco property, the recipient of a top-to-bottom renovation completed in 2018, a smart choice for budget travelers seeking a convenient downtown location and a touch of style. **Pros:** solid value in downtown location; chipper staff; excellent restaurant. **Cons:** public spaces grander than the mostly small rooms; hallway sound carries into rooms; lacks parking lot, fitness center, and other amenities. [$] *Rooms from: $160* ✉ *205 Kentucky St.* ☎ *707/559–3393* 🌐 *www.hotelpetaluma.com* 🛏 *57 rooms* 🍴 *No meals.*

Nightlife

The Big Easy

MUSIC CLUBS | The music club of the Speakeasy Bistro presents live music—rock, big band, jazz, country, folk, and several other genres. A good strategy for getting a seat is to order dinner from the Speakeasy for delivery to your Big Easy table. The club serves well-selected wines and craft beers. ✉ *128 American Alley* ✣ *Behind Putnam Park, off Petaluma Blvd. N* ☎ *707/ 776–4631* 🌐 *www.bigeasypetaluma.com.*

★ Ernie's Tin Bar

BARS/PUBS | Ramshackle Ernie's shares a corrugated tin building with a frozen-in-time roadside garage, with part of the bar actually in the garage. Mounted stag heads and a toothy wild boar watch over this rural-neighborhood hangout with a long, narrow bar, a patio outside, and Pliny the Elder and another 20 or so brews on tap. Signs everywhere ban cellphone use, though patrons and even staffers occasionally flout them. ✉ *5100 Lakeville Hwy.* ✣ *At Stage Gulch Rd. (Hwy. 116)* ☎ *707/762–2075.*

Incavo Wine Lounge & Collective

WINE BARS—NIGHTLIFE | A smart-casual wine bar with a heated outdoor patio, Incavo pours selections by the glass, flight, or bottle from a dozen-plus boutique wineries. Winemakers of renown are represented but also low-profile producers. **■ TIP→ If you get hungry, you can order off the menu at nearby (and often crowded) Central Market restaurant for delivery to your table at Incavo.** ✉ *100 Petaluma Blvd. N* ✣ *At Water St.* ☎ *707/789–0505* 🌐 *www.incavowine.com.*

Performing Arts

Mystic Theatre & Music Hall

CONCERTS | In keeping with its roots as a vaudeville house, the Mystic, which opened in 1911, books all sorts of acts and events, from indie bands and comedians to folk and alternative singer-songwriter Amanda Shires and rockers like the Zombies and the English Beat. For live performances, the space holds about 500 people. ✉ *23 Petaluma Blvd. N* ✣ *Near Western Ave.* ☎ *707/775–6048* 🌐 *www.mystictheatre.com.*

Chapter 6

NORTHERN SONOMA, RUSSIAN RIVER, AND WEST COUNTY

👁 Sights	🍴 Restaurants	🛏 Hotels	👜 Shopping	🍸 Nightlife
★★★★★	★★★★★	★★★★☆	★★★★☆	★★★☆☆

WELCOME TO NORTHERN SONOMA, RUSSIAN RIVER, AND WEST COUNTY

TOP REASONS TO GO

★ **Back-roads biking:** The region's ultrascenic back roads include gentle hills and challenging terrain you can traverse with a guide or on your own.

★ **Diverse dining:** Area chefs tickle diners' palates with diverse offerings—everything from haute-French and Peruvian cuisine to playful variations on American standards.

★ **Hillside Cabs and old-vine Zins:** Alexander Valley hillside Cabernet Sauvignon and Dry Creek Valley old-vine Zinfandel grapes—as far as the eye can see in spots—thrive in the high heat here.

★ **Hip Healdsburg shopping:** Healdsburg wins the shopping wars fair and square, with more captivating galleries, design-oriented shops, and clothing stores than anywhere in the Wine Country.

★ **Pinot aplenty and Chardonnay, too:** Russian River Valley and Sonoma Coast wineries large and small produce some of California's most celebrated Pinot Noirs and Chardonnays.

1 **Healdsburg.** With its many wineries and downtown hotels, restaurants, and shops, this town off U.S. 101 is a tourist hub.

2 **Geyserville.** North of Healdsburg off U.S. 101, mostly rural Geyserville has a fun small downtown.

3 **Forestville.** West of Healdsburg along River Road and Highway 116, Forestville nestles among Russian River redwoods.

4 **Guerneville.** Lively Guerneville has been a vacation retreat for a century-plus.

5 **Jenner.** The cliffs of Jenner, at Highways 116 and 1, overlook the estuary where the Russian River empties into the Pacific.

6 **Bodega Bay.** Harbor seals are often spotted south of Jenner at Bodega Bay's windswept Highway 1 beaches.

7 **Occidental.** Redwoods tower over this Bohemian Highway town east of Bodega Bay.

8 **Sebastopol.** East of Occidental where Highways 12 and 116 intersect, Sebastopol contains restaurants, shops, and wineries.

9 **Graton.** Sebastopol surrounds this hamlet off Highway 116 east of Occidental.

10 **Santa Rosa.** Sonoma County's largest city lies south of Healdsburg on U.S. 101.

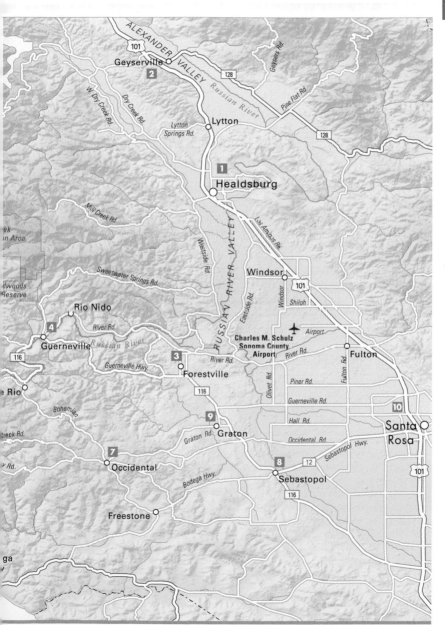

Sonoma County's northern and western reaches are a study in contrasts. Trendy hotels, restaurants, shops, and tasting rooms have transformed Healdsburg into a hot spot. Within a few miles, though, the chic yields to the bucolic, with only an occasional horse ranch, apple or peach orchard, or stand of oaks to interrupt the rolling vineyard hills.

Each of northern and western Sonoma County's regions claims its own micro-climates, soil types, and most-favored varietals, but—except for urban Santa Rosa—all have something in common: peace and quiet. This area is less crowded than the Napa Valley and southern Sonoma. Healdsburg, in particular, is hardly a stranger to overnight visitors, but you'll find less company in many of the region's tasting rooms. The Russian River, Dry Creek, and Alexander valleys are the grape-growing stars, along with the Sonoma Coast, but smaller appellations like Fort Ross–Seaview also merit investigation.

MAJOR REGIONS

Healdsburg's walkable downtown, swank hotels, and remarkable restaurant scene make it the most convenient base for exploring northern Sonoma County. The wineries here and in Geyserville to the north produce some of the country's best Pinot Noirs, Cabernet Sauvignons, Zinfandels, and Chardonnays.

In the smaller West County towns of Forestville, Guerneville, Sebastopol, Graton, and Occidental, high-style lodgings and fine dining are in shorter supply. Each

town has a few charmers, however, along with wineries worth seeking out. The western reaches of Sonoma County, extending all the way to the Pacific Ocean and the towns of Jenner and Bodega Bay, are more sparsely populated, although more and more vineyards are popping up where once stood orchards or ranches.

As the county's—and Wine Country's—largest city, workaday Santa Rosa may lack sex appeal, but it does contain the Charles M. Schulz Museum, Safari West, and other nonwine attractions, and dining and lodging options here and just to the north in Windsor tend to be more affordably priced than in the smaller towns.

Planning

When to Go

High season runs from early June through October, but even then weekday mornings find many wineries blissfully uncrowded. Summers are warm and nearly always pleasant on the coast, and though inland the temperatures often reach 90°F, this is nothing a rosé of Pinot Noir can't cure. Fall brings harvest fairs and other celebrations. Things slow down during winter, but with smaller crowds come more intimate winery visits. Roads along the Russian River are prone to flooding during heavy rains, as are a few in the Alexander Valley. Spring, when the grapevines are budding but the crowds are still thin, is a good time to visit.

Getting Here and Around

SMART (Sonoma-Marin Area Rail Transit) commuter service debuted in 2017. The train can be helpful if you're visiting the restaurants and tasting rooms of downtown Petaluma and Santa Rosa, but until the tracks are extended to Healdsburg (a few years off) it's of minimal use to wine tourists. It's possible to tour by bus, but travel by car remains the best option. One alternative is to book a group or private tour.

BUS TRAVEL

Sonoma County Transit provides transportation to all the main towns in this region, though except for the routes from Santa Rosa (which also operates its own bus line within city limits) to Healdsburg and Sebastopol, service isn't always frequent. *For more information about arriving by bus, see Bus Travel in the Travel Smart chapter. For more information about local bus service, see the Bus Travel sections for the individual towns in this chapter.*

CAR TRAVEL

Driving a car is by far the easiest way to get to and experience this region. From San Francisco, the quickest route to Northern Sonoma is north on U.S. 101 to Santa Rosa and Healdsburg. Highway 116 (aka Gravenstein Highway) heads west from U.S. 101, taking you through Sebastopol and the hamlets of Graton and Forestville before depositing you along the Russian River near Guerneville. Traffic can be slow on U.S. 101, especially around Petaluma and Santa Rosa during rush

hour and on summer weekends. Parking can be difficult in downtown Healdsburg on busy summer and early fall weekends, when you may have to park in a lot, feed a meter, or walk a few blocks.

Restaurants

Each year at the Sonoma County Harvest Festival and seasonally at local farmers' markets, the remarkable output of Northern Sonoma's farms and ranches is on display. Local chefs often scour the markets for seafood, meats, cheeses, and produce, and many restaurants have their own gardens. With all these fresh ingredients at hand, it should come as no surprise that farm-to-table cuisine predominates here, especially among the high-profile restaurants. Wood-fired pizzas are another local passion, as is modern Italian fare. Good delis and groceries abound, several of them located conveniently near wineries that allow picnics. Except in the region's most expensive restaurants, it's fine to dress casually.

Hotels

Healdsburg's hotels and inns set this region's standard for bedding down in style, with plush rooms that top $1,000 a night in a few cases. In the more affordable category are traditional bed-and-breakfast inns and small hotels, and there are even some inns and motels with down-to-earth prices. These last lodgings book up well in advance for high season, which is why Santa Rosa—just 15 miles away and home to decent chain and independent inns and hotels—is worth checking out year-round. Several secluded West County inns provide an elegant escape. Smaller properties throughout the region have two-night minimums on weekends (three nights on holiday weekends), though in winter this is negotiable.

What it Costs

	$	$$	$$$	$$$$
RESTAURANTS				
	under $16	$16–$22	$23–$30	over $30
HOTELS				
	under $201	$201–$300	$301–$400	over $400

Planning Your Time

With hundreds of wineries separated by miles of highway—Sonoma County is as big as Rhode Island—you could spend weeks here and not cover everything. To get a taste for what makes this region special, plan on a minimum of two or three days to hit the highlights. Healdsburg and the Russian River Valley are the must-sees, but it's worth venturing beyond them to the Alexander and Dry Creek valleys. If you still have time, head west toward the coast.

Appellations

Covering about 329,000 acres, the **Northern Sonoma AVA,** itself within the larger Sonoma County "appellation of origin," a geopolitical designation, and the even larger multicounty **North Coast AVA,** is divided into subappellations. Three of the most important meet at Healdsburg: the Russian River Valley AVA, which runs southwest along the river; the Dry Creek Valley AVA, which runs northwest of town; and the Alexander Valley AVA, which extends to the east and north. Also in this far northern area are smaller AVAs whose names you're more likely to see on wine labels than at the few visitable wineries within the appellations themselves: Knights Valley, Chalk Hill, and Fountaingrove, east and south of Alexander Valley; Rockpile, which slices northwest from the Dry Creek AVA to the Mendocino County line; and Pine Mountain–Cloverdale Peak, which extends from the Alexander Valley's northeastern tip into Mendocino County.

The cool climate of the low-lying **Russian River Valley AVA** is perfect for fog-loving Pinot Noir grapes as well as Chardonnay. Although three decades ago this area had as many farms, orchards, and redwood stands as vineyards, this is now one of Sonoma's most-recognized growing regions—with a significant subappellation of its own, the **Green Valley of the Russian River Valley AVA,** in the Forestville-Sebastopol area.

The **Dry Creek Valley AVA** is a small region—only about 16 miles long and 2 miles wide—but Zinfandel lovers know it well. The coastal hills temper the cooling influence of the Pacific Ocean, making it ideal for this varietal. Even more acres are planted to Cabernet Sauvignon, and you'll find Merlot, Chardonnay, Sauvignon Blanc, Syrah, and several other grape types growing in the diverse soils and climates (it's warmer in the north and cooler in the south).

Cabernet Sauvignon thrives in the warm **Alexander Valley AVA.** Sauvignon Blanc, Zinfandel, Petite Sirah, and Italian varietals such as Sangiovese do well, and certain cooler spots have proven hospitable to Chardonnay and Merlot.

Much of the **Sonoma Coast AVA,** which stretches the length of Sonoma County's coastline, lies within the Northern Sonoma AVA. The classic combination of hot summer days and cooling evening fog and breezes (in some spots even cooler than the Russian River Valley) inspired major Napa Valley wineries to invest in acreage here. The hunch paid off—Sonoma Coast Pinots and Chardonnays have become the darlings of national wine critics. Because the AVA encompasses such varied terrain—its southeastern portion edges into the comparatively warmer Sonoma Valley, for instance—some West County growers and vintners have proposed subappellations that express what they promote as the "true" Sonoma Coast geology and microclimates. One subappellation approved was the **Fort Ross–Seaview AVA,** whose hillside vineyards, mostly of Chardonnay and Pinot Noir, occupy land once thought too close to the Pacific Ocean to support grape growing. Far along in the approval process—and perhaps official by the time you read this—is the **West Sonoma Coast AVA,** which encompasses the entire Sonoma Coast but not the inland areas of the larger AVA.

Mountains surround the idyllic **Bennett Valley AVA** on three sides. Entirely in the Sonoma Valley AVA *(see Chapter 5)* and overlapping two other AVAs, it lies within the city of Santa Rosa. Coastal breezes sneak through the wind gap at Crane Canyon, making this area ideal for such cooler-weather grapes as Pinot Noir and Chardonnay, though Syrah, Cabernet Sauvignon, and Sauvignon Blanc also do well here.

Healdsburg

17 miles north of Santa Rosa.

Easily Sonoma County's ritziest town and the star of many a magazine spread or online feature, Healdsburg is located at the intersection of the Dry Creek Valley, Russian River Valley, and Alexander Valley AVAs. Several dozen wineries bear a Healdsburg address, and around downtown's plaza you'll find fashionable boutiques, spas, hip tasting rooms, and art galleries, and some of the Wine Country's best restaurants. Star chef Kyle Connaughton, who opened SingleThread Farms Restaurant to much fanfare, has motivated his counterparts all over town to up their game.

Especially on weekends, you'll have plenty of company as you tour the downtown area. You could spend a day just exploring the tasting rooms and shops surrounding

Healdsburg Plaza, but be sure to allow time to venture into the surrounding countryside. With orderly rows of vines alternating with beautifully overgrown hills, this is the setting you dream about when planning a Wine Country vacation. Many wineries here are barely visible, often tucked behind groves of eucalyptus or hidden high on fog-shrouded hills. Country stores and roadside farm stands alongside relatively untrafficked roads sell just-plucked fruits and vine-ripened tomatoes.

GETTING HERE AND AROUND

To get to Healdsburg from San Francisco, cross the Golden Gate Bridge and continue north on U.S. 101. About 65 miles from San Francisco, take the Central Healdsburg exit and follow Healdsburg Avenue a few blocks north to Healdsburg Plaza. Many hotels and restaurants are within a few blocks of the scenic town square. From Santa Rosa, the drive along U.S. 101 takes about 15 minutes in light traffic. Wineries bearing Healdsburg addresses can be as far apart as 20 miles, so you'll find a car handy. The Dry Creek Valley AVA and most of the Russian River Valley AVA are west of U.S. 101; most of the Alexander Valley AVA is east of the freeway. Sonoma County Transit Bus 60 serves Healdsburg from Santa Rosa; Bus 67, a shuttle, serves portions of downtown and vicinity but isn't convenient for winery touring.

Westside wineries: To get to wineries along Westside Road, head south on Center Street, then turn right at Mill Street. After Mill Street crosses under U.S. 101, its name changes to Westside Road. After about ½ mile, veer south to continue on Westside Road to reach the Russian River Valley wineries. Roughly following the curves of the Russian River, Westside Road passes vineyards, woods, and meadows along the way.

Eastside wineries: The route to wineries on Old Redwood Highway and Eastside Road is less scenic. Follow Healdsburg

Top Tastings and Tours

Tastings

Arista Winery, Healdsburg.
Balanced, richly textured small-lot Pinot Noirs are the specialty of this winery with a Japanese garden.

Robert Young Estate Winery, Geyserville. Other wineries purchase most of the Young family's grape harvest, but this longtime Geyserville clan retains a small percentage to make the Chardonnays and Bordeaux-style reds guests sip at its hilltop tasting space with a dramatic "infinity lawn."

Tours

Jordan Vineyard and Winery, Healdsburg. The pièce de résistance of the estate tour here is a Cabernet tasting at a 360-degree vista point overlooking acres of countryside.

Setting

Emeritus Vineyards, Sebastopol. This Russian River Valley winery's prized Hallberg Ranch Pinot Noir vines stretch carpetlike from its glass-and-metal ag-industrial tasting room.

Iron Horse Vineyards, Sebastopol. The vine-covered hills and valleys surrounding this sparkling wine producer provide such compelling views that the winery hosts all its tastings outside.

Ridge Vineyards, Healdsburg. Outdoors in good weather and indoors year-round you can enjoy views of rolling vineyards while tasting intense Zinfandels and other well-rounded wines.

Food Pairing

Silver Oak, Healdsburg. The winery pairs its several filling courses with library and current-release Cabernets, along with Pinot Noirs and other wines of the affiliated Twomey Cellars.

Just Plain Fun

Davis Family Vineyards, Healdsburg. On weekends from late spring to early fall, you can "get your BLT on" with sandwiches paired with superlative Pinot Noir, Syrah, and other wines.

Avenue south to U.S. 101. Hop on the freeway, exiting after a mile at Old Redwood Highway. Bear right as you exit, and continue south. Just past the driveway that serves both Rodney Strong and J Vineyards, turn southwest to merge onto Eastside Road.

Dry Creek Valley and Alexander Valley wineries: To reach the wineries along Dry Creek Road and West Dry Creek Road, head north from the plaza on Healdsburg Avenue. After about a mile, turn west on Dry Creek Road. Roughly parallel to Dry Creek Road is West Dry Creek Road, accessible by the cross streets Lambert Bridge Road and Yoakim Bridge Road. For Alexander Valley wineries, continue north

on Healdsburg Avenue past Dry Creek Road.

VISITOR INFORMATION

Healdsburg Chamber of Commerce & Visitors Bureau
✉ *217 Healdsburg Ave.* ✛ *At Matheson St.* ☎ *707/433–6935* ⊕ *www.healdsburg. com.*

 Sights

★ **Acorn Winery**
WINERY/DISTILLERY | A throwback to the era when a hardworking couple forsook sensible careers and went all-in to become grape growers and vintners, this low-tech yet classy operation has

Healdsburg and Northern Sonoma

Acorn Winery 35

Alexander Valley
Vineyards 26

Alley 6 Craft Distillery 28

Arista Winery 42

Christopher Creek
Winery 32

Comstock Wines 20

Copain Wines 46

David Coffaro
Estate Vineyard 3

Davis Family Vineyards ... 30

Dry Creek Peach &
Produce 6

Dry Creek Vineyard 15

Ferrari-Carano Winery 1

Foppiano Vineyards 31

Francis Ford Coppola
Winery 18

Gary Farrell
Vineyards & Winery 44

Grand Cru Custom
Crush 47

Hudson Street
Wineries 29

J Vineyards & Winery 37

Jordan Vineyard
and Winery 22

Lambert Bridge Winery ... 16

Landmark Vineyards at
Hop Kiln Estate 40

Limerick Lane Cellars 34

Locals Tasting Room 8

MacRostie Estate House .. 39

Mauritson Wines 17

Medlock Ames
Tasting Room 24

Moshin Vineyards 45

Papapietro Perry
Winery 12

Porter Creek Vineyards ... 43

Preston Farm & Winery 2

Quivira Vineyards 14

Ridge Vineyards 21

Robert Young
Estate Winery 10

Rochioli Vineyards
and Winery 41

Rodney Strong
Vineyards 36

Silver Oak 25

Stonestreet 23

Stuhmuller Vineyards 27

Trattore Farms 4

Trentadue Winery 19

Truett Hurst Winery 11

Twomey Cellars 38

Unti Vineyards 13

Virginia Dare Winery 7

Viszlay Vineyards 33

Zialena 9

Zichichi Family Vineyard ... 5

earned high praise for wines that include Cabernet Franc, Sangiovese, Zinfandel, and the rare-in-America Italian varietal Dolcetto. The gracious Betsy and Bill Nachbaur share their output in a garage-style, appointment-only tasting room amid their Alegría Vineyard. Each Acorn wine is a field blend of multiple grape varietals grown side by side and then crushed and fermented together. In the wrong hands, this old-school approach produces muddled, negligible wines, but these, made by Bill in consultation with local winemaker Clay Mauritson, soar. ⊠ *12040 Old Redwood Hwy.* ✛ *South of Limerick La.* ☎ *707/433–6440* ⊕ *acorn-winery.com* 🍷 *Tasting $15.*

Alexander Valley Vineyards

WINERY/DISTILLERY | The 1840s home-stead of Cyrus Alexander, for whom the valley is named, is the site of this winery known for Chardonnay, Cabernet Sauvignon, and a trio of Zinfandels, most notably the widely distributed Sin Zin. The standard tasting is free, but consider opting for the Reserve Seated Tasting ($15) to sample the single-vineyard Cabernet Sauvignon and the Bordeaux blend called Cyrus; a $25 wine-and-cheese pairing is also available. Tours take in the winery and wine caves dug deep into a nearby hillside. Weather permitting, you can take an invigorating vineyard hike. ■TIP➜ **The winery welcomes picnickers.** ⊠ *8644 Hwy. 128* ✛ *At Sonnikson Rd.* ☎ *707/433–7209* ⊕ *www.avvwine.com* 🍷 *Tastings free–$25, tours free–$15, vineyard hike $50.*

Alley 6 Craft Distillery

WINERY/DISTILLERY | Krystle and Jason Jorgensen make small-batch rye and single-malt whiskey, plus gin and candy-cap bitters, at the couple's industrial-park distillery 2 miles north of Healdsburg Plaza. The rye derives its overlapping flavors from its "mash bill" of rye and malted barley aged in heavily charred American oak barrels that add further layers of spice and complexity. The Jorgensens pride themselves on crafting their spirits entirely on-site, from grain milling through bottling, a process they describe with enthusiasm at their apothe-carylike tasting room, open on weekends (weekdays by appointment only). ⊠ *1401 Grove St., Unit D* ✛ *North of Dry Creek Rd.* ☎ *707/484–3593* ⊕ *www.alley6.com* 🍷 *Tasting $10.*

★ Arista Winery

WINERY/DISTILLERY | Brothers Mark and Ben McWilliams own this winery specializing in small-lot Pinot Noirs that was founded in 2002 by their parents. The sons have raised the winery's profile in several ways, most notably by hiring winemaker Matt Courtney, who has earned high praise from the *Wine Spectator* and other publications for his balanced, richly textured Pinot Noirs. Courtney shows the same deft touch with Arista's Zinfandels, Chardonnays, and a Gewürztraminer. One tasting focuses on the regions from which Arista sources its grapes, another on small-lot single-vineyard wines. Visits are by appointment only. ■TIP➜ **Guests who purchase a bottle are welcome to enjoy it in the picnic area, near a Japanese garden that predates the winery.** ⊠ *7015 Westside Rd.* ☎ *707/473–0606* ⊕ *www. aristawinery.com* 🍷 *Tastings from $35.*

Banshee Wines

WINERY/DISTILLERY | Cool-climate Sonoma Coast wines are the focus of this winery whose downtown Healdsburg store-front—reclaimed wood floors, brass pendant chandeliers, plush leather seating, window banquettes, vinyl on the turntable—feels more fancy pad than tasting room. The House Flight includes the flagship Sonoma County Pinot Noir, a Sonoma Coast Chardonnay, and Mordecai, a multivarietal blend that's always heavy on the Cabernet Sauvignon and Syrah. Given their quality, these wines represent a bargain at under $30 apiece, but to sample Banshee at its best, opt for a Reserve Flight of single-vineyard Pinot Noirs and Chardonnays. ⊠ *325 Center St.*

⊹ At North St. ☎ *707/395–0915* ⊕ *www.bansheewines.com* ⊠ *Tastings from $20.*

Christopher Creek Winery
WINERY/DISTILLERY | Petite Sirah and Syrah made this winery's reputation, but since the current owners took over in 2011, Pinot Noir and Rhône whites became an emphasis. The varied portfolio lends itself to three separate experiences. The Estate Tasting involves the whites and reds that established the winery. Guests at a Legacy Tasting sip barrel samples of Pinot Noir and place orders for "futures" available after bottle aging, and the Ultimate Tasting Experience includes barrel tastings, cheese and charcuterie, and a sip of a reserve library wine. ■TIP➔ Expect to meet one of the engaging owners at Legacy and Ultimate tastings. ⊠ *641 Limerick La. ⊹ ¼ mile east of Los Amigos Rd.* ☎ *707/433–2001* ⊕ *www.christophercreek.com* ⊠ *Tastings from $20.*

Comstock Wines
WINERY/DISTILLERY | Winemaker Chris Russi gained fans—collectors and wine critics alike—during previous stops at the Christopher Creek and Thomas George wineries, and with the high-quality purchased and estate-grown fruit at his disposal here, his posse will only expand. Refined Zinfandel is the specialty, some of it from the characterful old vines in front of the tasting room. The stunner is the Rockpile Zin, which Russi crafts in a softer, more elegant style than some of his peers. Russi also does well with purchased Pinot Noir and estate Sauvignon Blanc. Opened in 2015 in a contemporary barnlike structure, Comstock is the kind of place that encourages lingering, best done in fine weather at a Terrace Tasting, with vineyard and hillside views enhancing the pleasure of these remarkable wines. The tour and some tastings are by appointment only. ⊠ *1290 Dry Creek Rd. ⊹ 1 mile west of U.S. 101 (Dry Creek Rd. exit)* ☎ *707/723–3011* ⊕ *www.comstock-wines.com* ⊠ *Tastings from $20, tour $45 (includes tasting).*

Copain Wines
WINERY/DISTILLERY | This winery whose name means "buddies" in French makes Chardonnays, Pinot Noirs, and Syrahs. Although Copain occupies an enviable slope in northern Sonoma County—one that begs guests to sit, sip, and take in the Russian River Valley view—for years most of its wines derived from grapes grown in hillside vineyards near the coast in Monterey and Mendocino counties. In recent years Russian River Valley and Sonoma Coast fruit has joined the mix. Tastings, all by appointment, focus on single-vineyard wines. ⊠ *7800 Eastside Rd. ⊹ Near Ballard Rd.* ☎ *707/836–8822* ⊕ *www.copainwines.com* ⊠ *Tastings from $40.*

Davis Family Vineyards
WINERY/DISTILLERY | On weekends from late spring to early fall, this winery's outdoor tasting space becomes party central as guests heeding the invitation to "get your BLT on" enjoy sandwiches prepared in a food truck operated by Zazu restaurant of Sebastopol. Pinot Noir and Rhône-style wines are the specialties here. Owner-winemaker Guy Davis crafts all the Pinots the same way—aiming to let vineyard conditions and the specific clones of Pinot Noir find expression in bottle—and wine critics routinely praise the results of this humble approach. Other reds include two beautifully rendered Syrahs (great with the BLTs), a Zinfandel, and the sultry Rockpile Ridge Cabernet Sauvignon. On the lighter side Davis makes Chardonnay, a sparkling wine, sometimes rosé, and the flagship Cuvée Luke blend of Roussanne, Marsanne, and Viognier. The wine and cheese pairing is by appointment only. ⊠ *52 Front St. ⊹ At Hudson St.* ☎ *707/433–3858* ⊕ *www.davisfamilyvineyards.com* ⊠ *Tastings from $10.*

★ Dry Creek Peach & Produce
FARM/RANCH | If you happen by this farm stand in the summer, don't pass up the chance to sample the tree-ripened white

and yellow peaches, some of which may have been harvested moments before you arrived. You can buy peaches in small quantities, as well as organic peach jam. How good are these peaches? Customers include the famed Chez Panisse Restaurant in Berkeley. ■TIP→ **The stand is typically open from July to mid-September between noon and 5 on Wednesday, Friday, and the weekend. Call ahead to confirm, though.** ✉ *2179 Yoakim Bridge Rd.* ✛ *Near Dry Creek Rd.* ☎ *707/433–8121* ⊕ *www. drycreekpeach.com* ✆ *Closed mid-Sept.–June and Mon., Tues., and Thurs. July–mid-Sept.*

Dry Creek Vineyard

WINERY/DISTILLERY | Sauvignon Blanc marketed as Fumé Blanc brought instant success to the Dry Creek Valley's first new winery since Prohibition, but this area stalwart established in 1972 receives high marks as well for its Zinfandels, Bordeaux-style red blends, and Cabernet Sauvignons. In the nautical-themed tasting room—Dry Creek has featured sailing vessels on its labels since the 1980s—you can choose an all–Sauvignon Blanc flight, an all-Zinfandel one, or a mix of these and other wines. A vineyard walk and an insectary garden enhance a visit to this historic producer, a fine place for a picnic under the shade of a magnolia and several redwood trees. ■TIP→ **You can reserve a boxed lunch two days ahead through the winery, a time-saver on busy weekends.** ✉ *3770 Lambert Bridge Rd.* ✛ *Off Dry Creek Rd.* ☎ *707/433–1000, 800/864–9463* ⊕ *www.drycreekvineyard. com* ✉ *Tastings from $15, tour $30.*

Ferrari-Carano Winery

WINERY/DISTILLERY | Known for its grand Italian villa and manicured gardens—not a stray blade of grass anywhere here—this winery produces mostly Chardonnays, Sauvignon Blancs, Merlots, Zinfandels, and Cabernet Sauvignons. Although whites have traditionally been the specialty, the reds also garner attention—in particular the Bordeaux-style

blend called Trésor—and some guests come just for the dessert wines. Tours cover the wine-making facilities, underground cellar, and the gardens, where you can see a cork oak tree and learn about how cork is harvested. The tour is free and by appointment only, as are the private tastings. Walk-ins are welcome at the main tasting room and downstairs at the Enoteca tasting bar, where hosts pour reserve wines. You can also relax outside on the vineyard-view terrace and sip wine purchased by the glass or bottle. ✉ *8761 Dry Creek Rd.* ✛ *At Yoakim Bridge Rd.* ☎ *707/433–6700, 800/831–0381* ⊕ *www.ferrari-carano.com* ✉ *Tastings from $15, tour free.*

Foppiano Vineyards

WINERY/DISTILLERY | Here's the rare Russian River Valley winery where Chardonnay and Pinot Noir, though on the tasting list, don't reign supreme: the flagship wine at family-owned Foppiano is a flavorful Petite Sirah from grapes grown in a nearby, warmer-than-average section of the AVA. The winery has operated continuously since 1896; the Foppiano clan in part weathered Prohibition, when families were allowed to make up to 200 gallons a year for home consumption, by selling wine-making kits to do-it-yourself vintners. ✉ *12707 Old Redwood Hwy.* ✛ *Off U.S. 101* ☎ *707/433–7272* ⊕ *www. foppiano.com* ✉ *Tastings from $15, tours $20.*

Gary Farrell Vineyards & Winery

WINERY/DISTILLERY | Pass through an impressive metal gate and wind your way up a steep hill to reach this winery with knockout Russian River Valley views from the elegant two-tiered tasting room and terrace outside. In 2017 *Wine Enthusiast Magazine* named a Gary Farrell Chardonnay wine of the year, one among many accolades for this winery known for sophisticated single-vineyard Chardonnays and Pinot Noirs. The private Exploration Tour & Tasting, which includes a winery tour and artisanal cheeses, provides

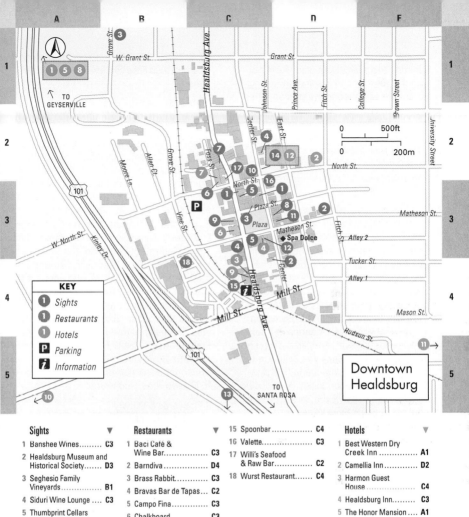

Downtown Healdsburg

KEY
- 1 Sights
- 1 Restaurants
- 1 Hotels
- P Parking
- i Information

Sights ▼

1 Banshee Wines **C3**
2 Healdsburg Museum and Historical Society **D3**
3 Seghesio Family Vineyards **B1**
4 Siduri Wine Lounge **C3**
5 Thumbprint Cellars Tasting Lounge & Art Gallery **C3**

Restaurants ▼

1 Baci Café & Wine Bar **C3**
2 Barndiva **D4**
3 Brass Rabbit **C3**
4 Bravas Bar de Tapas ... **C2**
5 Campo Fina **C3**
6 Chalkboard **C3**
7 Costeaux French Bakery **C2**
8 Downtown Bakery & Creamery............. **D3**
9 Dry Creek Kitchen **C3**
10 Guiso Latin Fusion **C2**
11 KINSmoke **D3**
12 Noble Folk Ice Cream and Pie Bar **C3**
13 Russian River Brewing Company Windsor **C5**
14 SingleThread Farms Restaurant................ **C2**
15 Spoonbar **C4**
16 Valette.................... **C3**
17 Willi's Seafood & Raw Bar............... **C2**
18 Wurst Restaurant **C4**

Hotels ▼

1 Best Western Dry Creek Inn **A1**
2 Camellia Inn **D2**
3 Harmon Guest House **C4**
4 Healdsburg Inn......... **C3**
5 The Honor Mansion **A1**
6 Hotel Healdsburg **C3**
7 Hôtel Les Mars.......... **C2**
8 Hotel Trio Healdsburg.............. **A1**
9 h2hotel **C4**
10 Madrona Manor **A5**
11 River Belle Inn **E5**
12 SingleThread Farms Inn **C2**

a solid introduction. The quicker Elevation Tasting (no tour) takes place inside or on the terrace; the Inspiration Tasting, in a private salon, concentrates on gifted winemaker Theresa Heredia's Pinot Noirs. ■ TIP→ **All visits are by appointment, but same-day Elevation reservations are usually possible during the week.** ⊠ *10701 Westside Rd.* ☎ *707/473–2909* ⊕ *www. garyfarrellwinery.com* ⊠ *Tastings from $35, tour $45.*

★ Grand Cru Custom Crush

WINERY/DISTILLERY | Wineries without production equipment of their own often make wine at communal "custom-crush" facilities. Most such places don't have tasting rooms open to the public, but by appointment at Grand Cru, just south of Healdsburg in the town of Windsor, you can reserve a Vintners' Selection of several wineries' offerings or book a private tasting with one label. If you go the latter route, **Black Kite Cellars,** a top producer of Pinot Noirs and Chardonnays from Anderson Valley (Mendocino County) and elsewhere, is worth seeking out, as is **Smith Story Wines,** which makes wines from those varietals from several appellations, along with Sauvignon Blanc, Cabernet Sauvignon, and a few others. ■ TIP→ **In some cases, the vintners or winemakers themselves host the tastings of individual wineries' offerings.** ⊠ *1200 American Way, Windsor* ✛ *From U.S. 101 Exit 496, head west on Shiloh Rd. and north on Conde La. Facility is off Conde La.* ☎ *707/687–0904* ⊕ *www.grandcrucustomcrush.com* ⊠ *Tastings from $25.*

Healdsburg Museum and Historical Society

MUSEUM | For a short break from wine tasting, visit the Healdsburg Museum and its collection of local historical objects, including baskets and artifacts from native tribes. Other exhibits cover the Mexican rancho period, the founding and growth of Healdsburg in the 1850s, and the history of local agriculture. ⊠ *221 Matheson St.* ✛ *At Fitch St.*

☎ *707/431–3325* ⊕ *www.healdsburgmuseum.org* ⊠ *Free* ⊙ *Closed Mon. and Tues.*

Hudson Street Wineries

WINERY/DISTILLERY | This under-the-radar tasting room of several family-run wineries provides a vivid snapshot of Northern Sonoma small-lot production. Reds to look for include the Kaufman Sunnyslope Vineyard Pinot Noir from Willowbrook Cellars, the Enriquez/Vökel Pinot Noir lineup, the Shippey Petite Sirahs and Zinfandels, and the Owl Ridge Dry Creek Valley Zinfandel and Alexander Valley Cabernet Sauvignon. The Shippey rosé of Petite Sirah stands out among the lighter wines. Locals, who appreciate the unfussy atmosphere and generous pours, often bring their out-of-town guests to this barnlike space in what was the cellar of one of Healdsburg's first wineries. ⊠ *428 Hudson St.* ✛ *Near Front St.* ☎ *707/433–2364* ⊕ *www. hudsonstreetwineries.com* ⊠ *Tasting $10* ⊙ *Closed Tues. and Wed.*

J Vineyards & Winery

WINERY/DISTILLERY | A top sparkling-wine maker, J also receives high marks for its Pinot Gris, Chardonnay, Pinot Noir, and other still wines. A contemporary metal-and-glass wall sculpture installed by Napa artist Gordon Huether provides visual entertainment at the stand-up Signature Bar. For a more personalized experience, indulge yourself in the Bubble Room, where wines are paired with small bites. Winery tours take place twice daily. Reservations are recommended for all visits and required for some. ■ TIP→ **From midspring through midfall, tastings are also held on a creek-side terrace.** ⊠ *11447 Old Redwood Hwy.* ✛ *At Eastside Rd.* ☎ *707/431–3646* ⊕ *www.jwine.com* ⊠ *Tastings from $20, tour $40.*

★ Jordan Vineyard and Winery

WINERY/DISTILLERY | A visit to this 1,200-acre property revolves around an impressive estate built in the early 1970s to replicate a French château. Founders

The Russian River Valley AVA extends from Healdsburg west to Guerneville.

Tom and Sally Jordan—their son, John, now runs the winery—erected the structure in part to emphasize their goal of producing Sonoma County Chardonnays and Cabernet Sauvignons to rival those in the Napa Valley and France itself. A seated Library Tasting of the current release of each varietal takes place in the château, accompanied by executive chef Todd Knoll's small bites. The tasting concludes with an older vintage Cabernet Sauvignon. The 90-minute Winery Tour & Tasting includes the above, plus a walk through part of the château. All visits are by appointment only. ■TIP→ For a truly memorable experience, splurge on the three-hour Estate Tour & Tasting, whose pièce de résistance is the Cabernet segment, which unfolds at a 360-degree vista point overlooking vines, olive trees, and countryside. ⊠ 1474 Alexander Valley Rd. ⊹ 1½ miles east of Healdsburg Ave. ☎ 800/654–1213, 707/431–5250 ⊕ www.jordanwinery.com ⊜ Library tasting $30, winery tour and tasting $40, estate tour and tasting $120 ⊗ Closed Sun. Dec.–Mar.

Lambert Bridge Winery

WINERY/DISTILLERY | Especially in spring, when its front-porch wisteria arbor blooms a nostalgia-inducing light purple, the twin-dormered Lambert Bridge winery building looks far older than its four decades. The weathered structure has matured early and well, not unlike the powerful yet polished artisanal wines produced inside. The flagship offering, the silky and supple Limited Selection Cabernet Sauvignon, is blended from the winery's best lots of Dry Creek and Alexander Valley grapes. Lambert Bridge has won praise for this and other reds but also makes excellent whites. Walk-ins can sip at the main tasting bar, hewn from a single, intricately patterned old-growth curly redwood. The seated Bordeaux Flight and the Cellar Flight for connoisseurs require an appointment. ■TIP→ Top local chefs participate in the once-a-month Chef's Table Series of food-and-wine pairings. ⊠ 4085 W. Dry Creek Rd. ⊹ ½ mile south of Lambert Bridge Rd. ☎ 707/431–4675 ⊕ www.lambert-bridge.com ⊜ Tastings from $30.

Dry Creek Valley AVA

If you drive north along Healdsburg Avenue and turn left onto Dry Creek Road, you'll soon feel as though you've slipped back in time. Healdsburg looks totally urban in comparison with the unspoiled countryside of Dry Creek Valley. The valley's well-drained, gravelly floor is planted with Chardonnay grapes to the south, where an occasional sea fog creeps in from the Russian River and cools the vineyards. Sauvignon Blanc is found in the warmer north. The red decomposed soils of the benchlands bring out the best in Zinfandel—the grape for which Dry Creek has become famous—but they also produce great Cabernet Sauvignon and Petite Sirah. And these soils seem well suited to such white Rhône varietals as Viognier, Roussanne, and Marsanne, along with Grenache, Syrah, and Mourvèdre reds. Wineries within this AVA include Dry Creek, Preston, Lambert Bridge, Mauritson, and Ridge.

Landmark Vineyards at Hop Kiln Estate

WINERY/DISTILLERY | The estate's towers rise from a 1905 stone-and-wood structure that once housed kilns for drying beer hops. Landmark, whose winery is in Kenwood, produces Chardonnays and Pinot Noirs from top California vineyards and appellations. In 2018 the winery released its first Hop Kiln Estate Pinot Noir from grapes grown just outside the tasting room. ■TIP→ **Picnickers are welcome (check the website for guidelines): enjoy your tasting inside, or head to tables throughout the property.** ⊠ *6050 Westside Rd.* ☎ *707/433–6491* ⊕ *www. hopkilnwinery.com* 🍷 *Tasting $20, tour and tasting $30.*

★ Limerick Lane Cellars

WINERY/DISTILLERY | The rocky, clay soils of this winery's northeastern sliver of the Russian River Valley combine with foggy mornings and evenings and hot, sunny afternoons to create the swoon-worthy Zinfandels produced here. The coveted 1910 Block Zinfandel comes from old-style head-trained vines planted more than a century ago. Fruit from this block adds richness and depth to the flagship Russian River Estate Zinfandel, whose grapes also come from two sets of nearby vines—one planted a decade ago, the other in the 1970s. Limerick Lane's Syrah and a Petite Sirah can be tasted along with its Zins in a restored stone farm building with views of the vineyards and the Mayacamas Mountains. ■TIP→ **Walk-ins are welcome, but it's best to make a reservation, especially on weekends.** ⊠ *1023 Limerick La.* ✛ *1 mile east of Old Redwood Hwy.* ☎ *707/433–9211* ⊕ *www.limericklanewines.com* 🍷 *Tasting $20.*

MacRostie Estate House

WINERY/DISTILLERY | A driveway off Westside Road curls through undulating vineyard hills to the steel, wood, and heavy-on-the-glass tasting space of this longtime Chardonnay and Pinot Noir producer. Moments after you've arrived and a host has offered a glass of wine, you'll already feel transported to a genteel, rustic world. Hospitality is clearly a priority here, but so, too, is seeking out top-tier grape sources—30 for the Chardonnays, 15 for the Pinots—among them Dutton Ranch, Bacigalupi, and owner Steve MacRostie's Wildcat. With fruit this renowned, current winemaker Heidi Bridenhagen downplays the oak and other tricks of her trade, letting the vineyard

The ivy-covered château at Jordan Vineyard looks older than its four-plus decades.

settings, grape clones, and vintage do the talking. Tastings, inside or on balcony terraces with views across the Russian River Valley, are all seated. ■TIP→ **Reservations, required on weekends, are a good idea on weekdays, too.** ✉ *4605 Westside Rd.* ✢ *Near Frost Rd.* ☎ *707/473–9303* 🌐 *macrostiewinery.com* 🍴 *Tastings from $25.*

★ Mauritson Wines

WINERY/DISTILLERY | Winemaker Clay Mauritson's Swedish ancestors planted grapes in what is now the Rockpile appellation in the 1880s, but it wasn't until his generation, the sixth, that wines bearing the family name first appeared. Much of the original homestead lies submerged under man-made Lake Sonoma, but the remaining acres produce the distinctive Zinfandels for which Mauritson is best known. Cabernet Sauvignon, other red Bordeaux grapes, Syrah, and Petite Sirah grow here as well, but the Zinfandels in particular illustrate how Rockpile's varied climate and hillside soils produce vastly different wines—from the soft, almost Pinot-like Westphall Ridge to the more structured and tannic Cemetery Ridge. The Mauritsons also grow grapes in Dry Creek Valley, where the winery and tasting room are located (there's a good picnic area, too), and Alexander Valley. ✉ *2859 Dry Creek Rd.* ✢ *At Lytton Springs Rd.* ☎ *707/431–0804* 🌐 *www.mauritsonwines.com* 🍴 *Tasting $30, tours $40.*

Medlock Ames Tasting Room

WINERY/DISTILLERY | Owners Chris James and Ames Morison converted a century-old country store into a contemporary showcase for the small-lot wines Ames makes from organically farmed grapes grown at their nearby Bell Mountain estate ranch. In good weather many guests sip their wine in a garden that supplies the berries and other edibles that supplement pairings of wine and artisanal cheeses. The winery, known for Bordeaux-style reds and Cabernet Sauvignon, also produces Sauvignon Blanc, Chardonnay, rosé, and Pinot Noir. ■TIP→ **To learn more about the Medlock**

Ames wine-growing philosophy, schedule a tour of the ranch and winery. ✉ 3487 Alexander Valley Rd. ✛ At Hwy. 128 ☎ 707/431–8845 ⊕ www.medlockames.com ▨ Tastings from $15, ranch tours from $40 (includes tasting).

Moshin Vineyards

WINERY/DISTILLERY | If you've ever wondered how your college math professor might fare as a winemaker, slip over to this winery known for small-lot, single-vineyard Pinot Noirs. Rick Moshin, formerly of San Jose State University's math department, started out small in 1989, but by the mid-2000s demand for his Pinots supported the construction of a four-tier, gravity-flow winery on his hillside property across Westside Road from the Russian River. Tours (by appointment only) focus on the winery's layout and Moshin's penchant for picking grapes earlier than most of his neighbors to preserve acidity, which he believes helps his wines pair well with food. In the tasting room, which always has a curated art exhibit, guests sip Pinot Noirs along with Chardonnay, Merlot, Sauvignon Blanc, Zinfandel, and other wines. ✉ 10295 Westside Rd. ✛ Off Wohler Rd. ☎ 707/433–5499, 888/466–7446 ⊕ moshinvineyards.com ▨ Tasting $15, tour $30.

Papapietro Perry Winery

WINERY/DISTILLERY | The mood is almost always upbeat at the copper-topped tasting bar as regulars and first-timers sip some of the 10 Pinot Noirs—eight from Russian River Valley grapes and one each from Sonoma Coast and Mendocino County fruit. A Russian River Valley Chardonnay and a Dry Creek Zinfandel also grace the lineup. The house style with all the wines, which include a rosé of Pinot Noir, is to pick early and shoot for elegance rather than the "overexpression" that can result from using riper fruit. Wine-and-cheese pairings (by appointment only) take place on the vineyard-view patio. ✉ 4791 Dry Creek

Rd. ✛ At Timber Crest Farms ☎ 707/433–0422, 877/467–4668 ⊕ www.papapietro-perry.com ▨ Tastings from $15.

Porter Creek Vineyards

WINERY/DISTILLERY | About as down-home as you can get—there's just a small redwood-beamed tasting room amid a modest family farm—Porter Creek makes notably good wines, some from estate biodynamically grown Chardonnay and Pinot Noir grapes. Its vineyards climb up steep hillsides of volcanic soil that is said to impart a slight mineral note to the Chardonnay; cover crops planted between the vines provide erosion control in addition to nutrients. Winemaker Alex Davis—son of George Davis, who founded the winery—also makes two distinctive wines from old-vine grapes, Carignane from Mendocino County and Zinfandel from Sonoma County, and his lineup includes Viognier and Syrah. ■TIP➔ **Look carefully for the winery's sign; the driveway is at a sharp bend in Westside Road.** ✉ 8735 Westside Rd. ☎ 707/433–6321 ⊕ www.portercreekvineyards.com ▨ Tasting $20.

Preston Farm & Winery

WINERY/DISTILLERY | **FAMILY** | The long driveway at homespun Preston, flanked by vineyards and punctuated by the occasional olive tree, winds down to farmhouses encircling a large shady yard. Year-round, organic produce grown in the winery's gardens is sold at a small shop near the tasting room; house-made bread and olive oil are also available. Owners Lou and Susan Preston are committed to organic growing techniques and use only estate-grown grapes in their wines, which include a perky Sauvignon Blanc, Barbera, Petite Sirah, Grenache, Viognier, and Zinfandel. Tours, conducted from Tuesday through Saturday, are by appointment. ■TIP➔ **Preston is a terrific place for a weekday picnic; weekends, though also enjoyable, can be crowded.** ✉ 9282 W. Dry Creek Rd. ✛ At Hartsock Rd. No. 1 ☎ 707/433–3372 ⊕ www.

prestonfarmandwinery.com 🍷 *Tasting $15, tour $30* ⏰ *No tours Sun. and Mon.*

Quivira Vineyards

WINERY/DISTILLERY | Solar panels top the modern wooden barn at Quivira, which produces Sauvignon Blanc, Zinfandel, Grenache-based rosé, and other wines using organic and biodynamic agricultural practices. The emphasis is on "growing wine"—farming grapes so meticulously that little manipulation is required in the winery. That said, winemaker Hugh Chappelle's mastery of technique is in evidence in wines such as the flagship Fig Tree Sauvignon Blanc, whose zesty yet refined characteristics derive from the combination of stainless steel and oak and acacia barrels used during fermentation. Guided tours (by appointment only) cover the farming and wine-making philosophies and offer a glimpse of the property's garden and animals. The tastings that follow include a food platter whose ingredients come from the garden. ✉ *4900 W. Dry Creek Rd. ⚓ Near Wine Creek Rd.* ☎ *707/431–8333, 800/292–8339* ⊕ *www.quivirawine.com* 🍷 *Tastings from $20, tour $40.*

★ Ridge Vineyards

WINERY/DISTILLERY | Ridge stands tall among local wineries, and not merely because its 1971 Monte Bello Cab placed first in a 30th-anniversary rematch of the famous Judgment of Paris blind tasting of California and French reds. The winery built its reputation on Cabernet Sauvignons, Zinfandels, and Chardonnays of unusual depth and complexity, but you'll also find blends of Rhône varietals. Ridge makes wines using grapes from several California locales—including the Dry Creek Valley, Sonoma Valley, Napa Valley, and Paso Robles—but the focus is on single-vineyard estate wines, such as the Lytton Springs Zinfandel from grapes grown near the tasting room. In good weather you can sit outside, taking in views of rolling vineyard hills while you sip. ■ TIP→ **The $25 tasting includes a pour**

of the top-of-the-line Monte Bello Cabernet Sauvignon from Santa Cruz Mountains grapes. ✉ *650 Lytton Springs Rd. ⚓ Off U.S. 101* ☎ *408/867–3233* ⊕ *www.ridge-wine.com/visit/lytton-springs* 🍷 *Tastings from $10, tours from $35.*

Rochioli Vineyards and Winery

WINERY/DISTILLERY | Claiming one of the prettiest picnic sites in the area, with tables overlooking the vineyards, this winery has an airy little tasting room with a romantic view. Production is small and fans on the winery's mailing list snap up most of the bottles, but the winery is still worth a stop to sample the estate Chardonnay and Pinot Noir and, when available, the Sauvignon Blanc. Because of the cool growing conditions in the Russian River Valley, the flavors of the Chardonnay and Sauvignon Blanc are intense and complex, and the Pinot Noir, which helped cement the Russian River's status as a Pinot powerhouse, is consistently excellent. Tastings are by appointment only on Tuesday and Wednesday. ✉ *6192 Westside Rd.* ☎ *707/433–2305* ⊕ *www.rochioliwinery.com* 🍷 *Tasting $20.*

Rodney Strong Vineyards

WINERY/DISTILLERY | The late Rodney Strong was among the first winemakers to plant Pinot Noir in the Russian River Valley. His namesake winery still makes Pinot Noirs, but it's known more for Cabernet. In the main tasting room (and in summer on an umbrella-shaded terrace), you can sample Cabs, Pinots, and other wines from seven Sonoma County appellations. A self-guided tour provides a good view of the fermentation tanks and machinery; guided tours also take place. ■ TIP→ **The winery hosts summer outdoor rock concerts; Michael McDonald, Melissa Etheridge, and Smokey Robinson have performed in recent years.** ✉ *11455 Old Redwood Hwy. ⚓ North of Eastside Rd.* ☎ *707/431–1533, 800/678–4763* ⊕ *www.rodneystrong.com* 🍷 *Tastings from $20, tours free.*

6

Northern Sonoma, Russian River, and West County HEALDSBURG

The focus at Ridge Vineyards is on single-vineyard estate wines.

Seghesio Family Vineyards

WINERY/DISTILLERY | In 1895 Edoardo Seghesio planted some of the Alexander Valley's earliest Zinfandel vines, some of which supply grapes for the winery's highly rated Home Ranch Zinfandel. Current Seghesio winemaker Andy Robinson crafts most of his wines—including other old-vine Zins and the Venom Sangiovese, from North America's oldest Sangiovese vineyard—using estate-grown fruit from the Alexander, Dry Creek, and Russian River valleys. The whites, from the relatively uncommon varietals Arneis and Vermentino, are special, too. You can learn about the winery's history and farming philosophy at tastings and food-wine pairings, on tours, and a few times a year on hikes of Home Ranch. The full-meal Chef's Table food-and-wine pairing is available from Friday through Sunday by appointment only. ■**TIP**➔ **When the weather's right, the tree-shaded picnic area fronting the tasting room is a sweet place to linger over wines purchased by the glass or bottle.** ⊠ *700 Grove St.* ✛ *Off W. Grant St.*

☎ *707/433–3579* ⊕ *www.seghesio.com* ⊠ *Tastings from $20.*

Siduri Wine Lounge

WINERY/DISTILLERY | Founded by two Texans with a yen for Pinot Noir, Siduri became a darling of the fruit-forward set in the mid-1990s and never looked back. The winery, named for the Babylonian goddess of wine, showcases its 20-Pinot (and counting) lineup in a casual lounge steps south of Healdsburg Plaza. Collectively, the wines—all of them good—reveal their varietal's diversity, but watch in particular for bottlings from the Lingenfelder (Russian River Valley), Pisoni (Santa Lucia Highlands), and Clos Pepe (Sta. Rita Hills) vineyards. ⊠ *241 Healdsburg Ave.* ✛ *Near Matheson St.* ☎ *707/433–6000* ⊕ *www.siduri.com* ⊠ *Tastings from $20.*

★ Silver Oak

WINERY/DISTILLERY | The views and architecture are as impressive as the wines at the Sonoma County outpost of the same-named Napa Valley winery. In 2018, six years after purchasing a 113-acre parcel with 73 acres planted to grapes, Silver Oak debuted its ultramodern, environmentally sensitive winery and glass-walled tasting pavilion. As in Napa, the Healdsburg facility produces just one wine each year: a robust, well-balanced Alexander Valley Cabernet Sauvignon aged in American rather than French oak barrels. The walk-in tasting includes the current Alexander Valley Cabernet and Napa Valley Bordeaux blend plus an older vintage. Tours, worth taking to experience the high-tech winery, are by appointment. The winery's chef prepares several courses (enough to serve as lunch) paired with library and current Cabernets plus two or more wines of sister operation Twomey Cellars, which produces Sauvignon Blanc, Pinot Noir, and Merlot. ⊠ 7370 Hwy. 128 ☎ 707/942–7082 ⊕ www.silveroak.com ⌑ Tastings from $20, tours and tastings from $30.

Stonestreet

WINERY/DISTILLERY | From the broad patio that fronts the Stonestreet Alexander Mountain Estate's stablelike building you can see some of the steep, rugged terrain where grapes for the winery's full-bodied Chardonnays and wild-as-a-stallion Cabernet Sauvignons are grown. At 5,100 acres (900 planted), this is among the world's largest mountain vineyards. Farming these steep hills is difficult and labor-intensive, but the hard-won output finds its way into top boutique wines in addition to Stonestreet's. You can taste a flight of whites, reds, or a combination; for stunning views and to experience the vineyards close up, take the mountain tour (by appointment only; morning tour includes lunch). ■ TIP→ **Stonestreet also has a tasting room in downtown Healdsburg.** ⊠ 7111 Hwy. 128 ⊹ Off W. Sausal La. ☎ 800/355–8008 ⊕ www.stonestreetwines.com ⌑ Tastings from $40, mountain tour from $150.

Stuhlmuller Vineyards

WINERY/DISTILLERY | Chardonnay and Cabernet Sauvignons from estate-grown grapes are the specialty of this slightly off-the-beaten-path winery whose tasting room and production facility occupy a stained-redwood former barn. Standout wines include the Summit Chardonnay and, from vines more than 30 years old, the Block 12 Estate Cabernet Sauvignon. Another wine to look for is the Russian River Valley Pinot Noir from the Starr Ridge Vineyard. Tastings (reservations recommended but not required) take place in a room adjoining the aging cellar, and in good weather you can sip outdoors on a gravel patio near the vineyards. One tasting surveys current releases, the other older vintages. ■ TIP→ **Picnickers are welcome at this dog-friendly winery.** ⊠ 4951 W. Soda Rock La. ⊹ Off Alexander Valley Rd. ☎ 707/431–7745 ⊕ www.stuhlmullervineyards.com ⌑ Tastings from $20.

Thumbprint Cellars Tasting Lounge & Art Gallery

WINERY/DISTILLERY | With its exposed-brick walls and contemporary art exhibits, this stylish tasting room on Healdsburg Plaza's southern edge has the feel of a hip San Francisco loft. Owner-winemaker Scott Lindstrom-Drake, who believes in selecting good fruit and applying minimal manipulation during fermentation and aging, specializes in single-vineyard Cabernet Franc, Cabernet Sauvignon, Pinot Noir, and Zinfandel. He also makes white, rosé, and red blends with alluring names such as Arousal, Four Play, and Three Some. The grapes come primarily from the Russian River, Dry Creek, Knights, and Alexander valleys. ■ TIP→ **A welcoming space during the day, the lounge often hosts comedy and other events in the evening.** ⊠ 102 Matheson St. ⊹ At Healdsburg Ave. ☎ 707/433–2393 ⊕ www.thumbprintcellars.com ⌑ Tastings from $10.

Truett Hurst Winery

WINERY/DISTILLERY | Zinfandel and Petite Sirah grow in the 15 acres surrounding Truett Hurst's lively, high-ceilinged tasting

The Russian River Valley's hot summer days and cool nights create ideal conditions for growing Chardonnay and Pinot Noir.

room. In addition to wines from those grapes, look for Pinot Noir, Cabernet Sauvignon, and the Dark Horse GPS (Grenache, Syrah, Mourvèdre, and Petite Sirah). Walk-ins can sip inside daily and on weekdays in the adjacent patio without an appointment; patio seating on weekends is by reservation. During the week, you can also sit on the tree-shaded Dry Creek shoreline sipping wine in red Adirondack chairs—a sublime experience when the weather's fine—though on weekends wine-club members have first dibs. Also on-site is the mellower tasting room of the affiliated **VML Winery** which focuses on Russian River Valley Chardonnay and Pinot Noir. ✉ *5610 Dry Creek Rd.* ✛ *2 miles south of Canyon Rd.* ☎ *707/433–9545 Ext. 100* ⊕ *www.truet-thurstwinery.com* 🍷 *Tastings from $15.*

Twomey Cellars

WINERY/DISTILLERY | The draws at the Sonoma County location of this winery founded by the owners of Silver Oak include California and Oregon Pinot Noirs, a Merlot crafted using a

centuries-old French technique, and vineyard and Mayacamas Mountains views from the glass-walled tasting room. The Pinot Noirs, from grapes grown in prime locales, are made by Erin Miller, also responsible for the Sauvignon Blanc. The extremely supple Merlot is made at Twomey's Calistoga winery employing the *soutirage traditionnel* method of transferring the wine from oak barrel to oak barrel multiple times during aging to soften the tannins and intensify the aromas. A reservation is needed for all visits except the walk-in tasting at the bar. ■TIP➔ **If the weather's nice, you can taste on the patio and enjoy its splendid views.** ✉ *3000 Westside Rd.* ✛ *¼ mile south of Felta Rd.* ☎ *707/942–7026* ⊕ *www. twomey.com/healdsburg* 🍷 *Tastings from $15.*

Unti Vineyards

WINERY/DISTILLERY | There's a reason why Unti, known for Zinfandel and wines made from sometimes obscure Rhône and Italian varietals, often bustles even when business is slow elsewhere in Dry

Creek: this is a fun, casual place. You'll often find the sociable cofounder, Mick Unti, who manages the winery, chatting up guests and pouring wine in the rustic-not-trying-to-be-chic tasting room. Tastings usually begin with Cuvée Blanc, a blend of Vermentino, Grenache Blanc, and Picpoul grapes, followed by another white or the winery's top seller, a dry Provençal-style rosé made from estate Grenache and Mourvèdre. Reds might include Barbera, Sangiovese, Syrah, or the Segromigno blend of estate-grown Sangiovese and Montepulciano. **■ TIP→ Visits here require appointments, but it's usually possible to get one on short notice.** *✉ 4202 Dry Creek Rd. ✣ ¾ mile north of Lambert Bridge Rd. ☎ 707/433–5590 🌐 www.untivineyards.com 🎫 Tastings from $15.*

Viszlay Vineyards

WINERY/DISTILLERY | In 2010 Chicagoan John Viszlay purchased 10 acres along Limerick Lane, where the climate, terrain, and sun exposure are so variable the owner-winemaker has won awards for wines as diverse as Prosecco and a Cabernet-based Bordeaux-style blend—all of whose grapes grow within rows of each other. Tastings take place indoors amid looming stacks of oak aging barrels or on a concrete patio in view of the grapevines. Although it's possible to taste at this small operation without an appointment, it's best to call ahead. **■ TIP→ Visiting Viszlay plus neighboring Limerick Lane Cellars and Christopher Creek Winery makes for an engaging, easy-to-navigate afternoon of tasting.** *✉ 929 Limerick La. ✣ ½ mile east of Los Amigos Rd. ☎ 707/481–1514 🌐 www.viszlayvineyards.com 🎫 Tastings from $15.*

★ Zichichi Family Vineyard

WINERY/DISTILLERY | Most winery owners would love to be in Steve Zichichi's shoes: his wines are largely sold out before they're bottled, and in one case while the grapes are still on the vine. As a result, customers of this northern Dry Creek Valley operation taste out of the barrel and purchase "futures"—wines available for shipping or pickup after aging is complete. The highlight, not always available for tasting, is the Old Vine Zinfandel, some of whose vines were planted in the 1920s during Prohibition, when many vineyard owners switched over to other crops. Zichichi makes another estate Zinfandel and an estate Petite Sirah, and a 100% Cabernet from the Chalk Hill appellation. **■ TIP→ Cabernet bottles are usually still available for purchase at the time of a visit.** *✉ 8626 W. Dry Creek Rd. ✣ At Yoakim Bridge Rd. ☎ 707/433–4410 🌐 www.zichichifamilyvineyard.com 🎫 Tasting $15.*

🍴 Restaurants

Baci Café & Wine Bar

$$$ | **ITALIAN** | A neighborhood trattoria with cream-yellow walls, zinc-top tables, and colorful artwork and banners, Baci bustles with tourists during high season (when reservations are recommended), but after things die down, locals continue dropping by for pizza, pastas, and osso buco, saltimbocca, and other stick-to-your-ribs Italian standards. The Iranian-born chef, Shari Sarabi, applies a Pan-Mediterranean sensibility to area-sourced, mostly organic ingredients, and his dishes satisfy without being overly showy. **Known for:** wine selection by Lisbeth Holmefjord, chef's sommelier wife; enthusiastic owners; many gluten-free dishes. *[$] Average main: $29 ✉ 336 Healdsburg Ave. ✣ At North St. ☎ 707/433–8111 🌐 www.bacicafeandwinebar.com ⏲ Closed Tues. and Wed. No lunch.*

★ Barndiva

$$$$ | **AMERICAN** | Music plays quietly in the background while servers ferry the inventive seasonal cocktails of this restaurant that abandons the homey vibe of many Wine Country spots for a more urban feel. Make a light meal out of yellowtail tuna crudo or Dungeness crab salad, or settle in for the evening with pan-seared king salmon with caviar and crème fraîche or sautéed rack of lamb with gnocchi. **Known for:** cool cocktails; stylish cuisine; open-air patio. $ *Average main: $34* ✉ *231 Center St.* ✛ *At Matheson St.* ☎ *707/431–0100* ⊕ *www. barndiva.com* ◷ *Closed Mon. and Tues.*

Brass Rabbit

$$$ | **MODERN AMERICAN** | Exposed-brick walls, leather banquettes by a designer of hot-rod interiors, and a local artisan's stained-wood furnishings and wall art set a jaunty tone at this narrow storefront restaurant. For dinner, start with a salad or soup (clam chowder for sure if available) or something from the raw bar before moving on to an entrée like nettle and ricotta dumplings, Liberty Farms duck confit, or king salmon. **Known for:** same executive chef as nearby Chalkboard; weekend brunch's kid-friendly items; by-the-glass wine picks. $ *Average main: $25* ✉ *109 Plaza St.* ✛ *Near Healdsburg Ave.* ☎ *707/473–8580* ⊕ *the-brassrabbithealdsburg.com* ◷ *No lunch Mon.–Thurs.*

Bravas Bar de Tapas

$$$ | **SPANISH** | Spanish-style tapas and an outdoor patio in perpetual party mode make this restaurant, headquartered in a restored 1920s bungalow, a popular downtown perch. Contemporary Spanish mosaics set a perky tone inside, but unless something's amiss with the weather, nearly everyone heads out back for flavorful croquettes, paella, jamón, *pan tomate* (tomato toast), duck egg with chorizo cracklings, grilled octopus, skirt steak, and crispy fried chicken. **Known for:** casual small plates; specialty cocktails, sangrias, and beer; sherry flights. $ *Average main: $27* ✉ *420 Center St.* ✛ *Near North St.* ☎ *707/433–7700* ⊕ *www. barbravas.com.*

Campo Fina

$$ | **ITALIAN** | Chef Ari Rosen showcases his contemporary-rustic Italian cuisine at this converted storefront that once housed a bar notorious for boozin' and brawlin'. Sandblasted red brick, satin-smooth walnut tables, and old-school lighting fixtures strike a retro note for a menu built around pizzas and gems such as Rosen's variation on his grandmother's tomato-braised chicken with creamy-soft polenta. **Known for:** outdoor patio and boccie court out of an Italian movie set; lunch sandwiches; wines from California and Italy. $ *Average main: $20* ✉ *330 Healdsburg Ave.* ✛ *Near North St.* ☎ *707/395–4640* ⊕ *www.campofina. com.*

★ Chalkboard

$$$ | **MODERN AMERICAN** | Unvarnished oak flooring, wrought-iron accents, and a vaulted white ceiling create a polished yet rustic ambience for executive chef Shane McAnelly's playfully ambitious small-plate cuisine. Starters such as pork-belly biscuits might seem frivolous, but the silky flavor blend—maple glaze, pickled onions, and chipotle mayo playing off feathery biscuit halves—signals a supremely capable tactician at work. **Known for:** festive happy hour; pasta "flights" (choose three or six styles); The Candy Bar dessert. $ *Average main: $30* ✉ *Hotel Les Mars, 29 North St.* ✛ *West of Healdsburg Ave.* ☎ *707/473–8030* ⊕ *www.chalkboardhealdsburg.com.*

Costeaux French Bakery

$ | **FRENCH** | Breakfast, served all day at this bright-yellow French-style bakery and café, includes the signature omelet (sun-dried tomatoes, applewood-smoked bacon, spinach, and Brie) and French toast made from thick slabs of cinnamon-walnut bread. French onion soup, salad Niçoise, and smoked-duck, cranberry-turkey, and French dip sandwiches are among the lunch favorites. **Known for:** breads, croissants, and fancy pastries; quiche and omelets; front patio (arrive early on weekends). $ *Average main: $14* ✉ *417 Healdsburg Ave.* ✛ *At North St.* ☎ *707/433–1913* ⊕ *www.costeaux. com* ◷ *No dinner.*

Downtown Bakery & Creamery

$ | BAKERY | To catch the Healdsburg spirit, hit the plaza in the early morning for a cup of coffee and a fragrant sticky bun or a too darlin' *caneló*, a French-style pastry with a soft custard center surrounded by a dense caramel crust. Until 2 pm from Friday through Monday, you can also go the full breakfast route: pancakes, granola, poached farm eggs on polenta, or perhaps the dandy mushroom-and-cheese pizza. **Known for:** morning coffee and pastries; lunchtime pizzas and calzones; fresh-fruit galettes. ⓢ *Average main: $8* ✉ *308A Center St.* ✛ *At North St.* ☎ *707/431-2719* ⊕ *www.downtownbakery.net* ⊘ *Closed Tues. No dinner.*

Dry Creek Kitchen

$$$$ | MODERN AMERICAN | Chef Charlie Palmer's ultramodern restaurant—pastel walls, soft lighting, contemporary artworks, and a gently vaulted ceiling meant to evoke a wine cave—enchants diners with clever combinations of flavors and textures in dishes based on seasonal, often local ingredients. Summer might bring a warm local peaches-and-beets appetizer with carrot-top pesto, with similar complexity achieved in late-fall main courses like Sonoma lamb loin with crispy lamb *bisteeya* (lamb in a flaky pastry). **Known for:** sophisticated cuisine; chef's tasting menu; no corkage fee (two bottles max) on wines from Sonoma County vineyards. ⓢ *Average main: $33* ✉ *Hotel Healdsburg, 317 Healdsburg Ave.* ✛ *Near Matheson St.* ☎ *707/431-0330* ⊕ *www.drycreekkitchen.com* ⊘ *No lunch.*

Guiso Latin Fusion

$$$ | LATIN AMERICAN | Three years after graduating from Santa Rosa Junior College's culinary arts program, chef Carlos Mojica opened this warmly lit Latin American–Caribbean restaurant with a handful of linen-dressed tables. Fish tacos, *pescado con coco* (fish sautéed in sweet coconut), *pupusas* (corn tortillas stuffed with cheese and pork or vegetables), and

oven-roasted slices of sweet corn on the cob with Jamaican jerk butter and garlic are among the dishes regulars return for. **Known for:** attentive service; intimate space; neighborhood feel. ⓢ *Average main: $28* ✉ *117 North St.* ✛ *Near Center St.* ☎ *707/431-1302* ⊘ *Closed Mon. No lunch.*

KINSmoke

$ | BARBECUE | Beef brisket and St. Louis ribs are the hits at this saloon-like, order-at-the-counter joint whose house-made sauces include espresso barbecue, North Carolina mustard, and the sweet-and-sourish KIN blend. Along with the expected sides of potato salad, cornbread muffins, and baked beans (the latter bourbon infused), the spiced sweet-potato tater tots and Granny Smith–and-horseradish slaw stand out. **Known for:** upbeat crew; pulled smoked chicken with Alabama white sauce; beer selection and sensibly priced local wines. ⓢ *Average main: $14* ✉ *304 Center St.* ✛ *At Matheson St.* ☎ *707/473-8440* ⊕ *www.kinsmoke.com.*

★ Noble Folk Ice Cream and Pie Bar

$ | BAKERY | Seasonal pies including blood-orange custard with graham-cracker crust are the specialty of this white-walled, brightly lit pie palace with a few tables and barstool window seating. The bakers use heritage grains like buckwheat and farro in the crusts, filling them with local fruits and other ingredients, and, if desired, topping the ensemble with ice cream in flavors from Swiss chocolate and vanilla bean to root beer, almond-cardamom, cornflake-maple, and other obscurities. **Known for:** sarsaparilla floats; house-made waffle cones; exiting customers with smiles on their faces. ⓢ *Average main: $8* ✉ *116 Matheson St.* ✛ *Near Center St.* ☎ *707/395-4426* ⊕ *www.thenoblefolk.com.*

Russian River Brewing Company Windsor

$$ | AMERICAN | The makers of Pliny the Elder and Younger operate this cavernous brewpub with a vast garden on the site

of the state-of-the-art brewing facility they opened in 2018. Choose among 20 beers on tap to wash down updated beer-compatible pub grub including chicken wings (honey-chili glaze), a malted-bacon burger with cheddar fondue, fish and Kennebec chips, a half chicken, and several salads. **Known for:** year-round and seasonal beers; guided and self-guided brewery tours; separate tasting room with 8–10 beers on tap. [$] *Average main: $18* ✉ *700 Mitchell La., Windsor* ✣ *7 miles south of Healdsburg Plaza off U.S. 101 (Shiloh Rd. Exit) at Conde La.* ☎ *707/545–2337* 🌐 *russianriverbrewing.com.*

★ SingleThread Farms Restaurant

$$$$ | **ECLECTIC** | The seasonally oriented, multicourse Japanese dinners known as *kaiseki* inspired the prix-fixe vegetarian, meat, and seafood menu at the spare, elegant restaurant—redwood walls, walnut tables, mesquite-tile floors, muted-gray yarn-thread panels—of internationally renowned culinary artists Katina and Kyle Connaughton (she farms, he cooks). As Katina describes the endeavor, the 72 microseasons of their farm—5 acres at a nearby vineyard plus SingleThread's rooftop garden of fruit trees and microgreens—dictate Kyle's rarefied fare, prepared in a theatrically lit open kitchen. **Known for:** culinary precision; new online reservation slots released on first of month; impeccable wine pairings. [$] *Average main: $275* ✉ *131 North St.* ✣ *At Center St.* ☎ *707/723–4646* 🌐 *www.singlethreadfarms.com* ⏲ *No lunch weekdays.*

Spoonbar

$$$ | **MODERN AMERICAN** | Midcentury-modern furnishings, concrete walls, and an acacia-wood communal table create an urbane setting for the h2hotel restaurant's contemporary California cuisine, and cantina doors make Spoonbar especially appealing in summer when a breeze wafts in. The seasonally changing selections might include pan-seared Alaskan halibut, Tuscan-style rib-eye, or leek-and-cheese mezzaluna, one of several pasta dishes. **Known for:** craft cocktails; seafood preparations; fried-chicken Wednesdays. [$] *Average main: $23* ✉ *h2hotel, 219 Healdsburg Ave.* ✣ *At Vine St.* ☎ *707/433–7222* 🌐 *spoonbar.com* ⏲ *No lunch.*

★ Valette

$$$$ | **MODERN AMERICAN** | Northern Sonoma native Dustin Valette opened this homage to the area's artisanal agricultural bounty with his brother, who runs the high-ceilinged dining room, its playful contemporary lighting tempering the austerity of the exposed concrete walls and butcher-block-thick wooden tables. Charcuterie is an emphasis, but also consider the signature day-boat scallops *en croûte* (in a pastry crust) or dishes that might include Liberty duck breast with blackberry gastrique or Padrón-pepper-crusted Alaskan halibut. **Known for:** intricate cuisine; "Trust me" (the chef) tasting menu; well-chosen mostly Northern California wines. [$] *Average main: $34* ✉ *344 Center St.* ✣ *At North St.* ☎ *707/473–0946* 🌐 *www.valettehealdsburg.com* ⏲ *No lunch.*

Willi's Seafood & Raw Bar

$$$ | **SEAFOOD** | Often crowded on Fridays and weekends, when reservations aren't taken, Willi's occupies a corner storefront with street-side outdoor seating and a compact dining room that curls around the full bar. The warm Maine lobster roll with garlic butter and fennel remains a hit among the small, mostly seafood-oriented plates, with the ceviches, barbecued local oysters and bacon-wrapped scallops, and "kale Caesar!" with toasted capers among its worthy rivals. **Known for:** gluten-, dairy-, nut-, and seed-free options; outdoor seating area; caramelized banana split and other desserts. [$] *Average main: $27* ✉ *403 Healdsburg Ave.* ✣ *At North St.* ☎ *707/433–9191* 🌐 *www.willisseafood.net.*

Wurst Restaurant

$ | AMERICAN | "The Wurst is the best" is the motto of this glass-fronted fast-food joint with a menu of sausages and dogs with specific toppings like the Detroit Polish with sauerkraut, beer mustard, and onion rings or augmented with (choose two) caramelized onions, sweet peppers, hot peppers, or kraut. Burgers are another specialty, with the blue-cheese and blackened-barbecue ones from a local beef purveyor among the top sellers patrons enjoy at communal and single tables inside and on the front patio. **Known for:** onion rings and fries; Midwestern pop (soda) selection; turkey and falafel burgers. $ *Average main: $9 ⊠ 22 Matheson St. ✦ Near Healdsburg Ave.* ☎ 707/395–0214 ⊕ *wurstrestaurant. com.*

Hotels

Best Western Dry Creek Inn

$ | HOTEL | Easy access to downtown restaurants, tasting rooms, and shopping, as well as outlying wineries and bicycle trails, makes this Tuscan-themed motel near U.S. 101 a good budget option. **Pros:** laundry facilities; pools, whirlpool spas, fire pit, outdoor fireplaces; convenient to dozens of wineries. **Cons:** thin walls; traffic noise audible in many rooms; some rooms have highway and parking-lot views. $ *Rooms from: $149 ⊠ 198 Dry Creek Rd.* ☎ 707/433–0300, 800/222–5784 ⊕ *www.drycreekinn.com* ⇨ *163 rooms* ¶◎¶ *Breakfast.*

Camellia Inn

$$ | B&B/INN | In a well-preserved 1869 Italianate Victorian, this colorful bed-and-breakfast sits on a quiet residential street 2½ blocks from Healdsburg Plaza. **Pros:** large Roman-shaped backyard pool; late-afternoon wine-and-cheese sessions; within easy walking distance of restaurants. **Cons:** a few rooms have a shower but no bath; all rooms lack TVs; no fitness center. $ *Rooms from: $235 ⊠ 211 North St.* ☎ 707/433–8182

⊕ *www.camelliainn.com* ⇨ *9 rooms* ¶◎¶ *Breakfast.*

★ Harmon Guest House

$$ | HOTEL | A boutique sibling of the h2hotel two doors away, this downtown delight debuted in late 2018 having already earned LEED Gold status for its eco-friendly construction and operating practices. **Pros:** rooftop bar's cocktails, food menu, and views; connecting rooms and suites; convenient to Healdsburg Plaza action. **Cons:** minor room-to-room noise bleed-through; room gadgetry may flummox some guests; minimum-stay requirements some weekends. $ *Rooms from: $264 ⊠ 227 Healdsburg Ave.* ☎ 707/922–5262 ⊕ *harmonguesthouse. com* ⇨ *39 rooms* ¶◎¶ *Free Breakfast.*

Healdsburg Inn

$$$ | B&B/INN | A genteel antidote to Healdsburg's mania for tech-chic accommodations, this inn occupies a 19th-century office building whose former tenants include a Wells, Fargo & Co. Express office and stagecoach stop. **Pros:** central location; freshly baked cookies in common room; late-afternoon wine and hors d'oeuvres. **Cons:** garish room lighting; slightly impersonal feel for this type of inn; street noise audible in plaza-facing rooms. $ *Rooms from: $329 ⊠ 112 Matheson St.* ☎ 800/431–8663 ⊕ *www.healdsburginn.com* ⇨ *12 rooms* ¶◎¶ *Breakfast.*

★ The Honor Mansion

$$$ | B&B/INN | There's a lot to like about the photogenic Honor Mansion, starting with the main 1883 Italianate Victorian home, the beautiful grounds, the elaborate breakfasts, and the home-away-from-home atmosphere. **Pros:** homemade sweets available at all hours; pool, putting green, and boccie, croquet, tennis, and basketball courts; secluded vineyard suites with indoor soaking tubs, outdoor hot tubs. **Cons:** almost a mile from Healdsburg Plaza; walls can seem thin; weekend minimum-stay requirement includes Thursday. $ *Rooms from:*

$380 ✉ 891 Grove St. ☎ 707/433–4277, 800/554–4667 🌐 www.honormansion.com ⏲ Closed 2 wks at Christmas 🛏 13 rooms 🍴 Breakfast.

Hotel Healdsburg

$$$ | RESORT | Across the street from the tidy town plaza, this spare, sophisticated full-service hotel has an upscale restaurant, a gourmet pizzeria, a spa, a pool, and a fitness center. **Pros:** several rooms overlook the town plaza; comfortable lobby with a small attached bar; extremely comfortable beds. **Cons:** exterior rooms get some street noise; rooms could use better lighting; some rooms could use a refresh. [$] *Rooms from: $382 ✉ 25 Matheson St. ☎ 707/431–2800, 800/889–7188 🌐 www.hotelhealdsburg.com 🛏 55 rooms 🍴 Breakfast.*

★ Hôtel Les Mars

$$$$ | HOTEL | This Relais & Châteaux property takes the prize for opulence with guest rooms, spacious and elegant enough for French nobility, furnished with 18th- and 19th-century antiques and reproductions, canopy beds dressed in luxe linens, and gas-burning fireplaces. **Pros:** large rooms; just off Healdsburg's plaza; room service by Chalkboard restaurant. **Cons:** very expensive; minimum-stay requirement on weekends; no pool or spa. [$] *Rooms from: $540 ✉ 27 North St. ☎ 707/433–4211 🌐 www.hotellesmars.com 🛏 16 rooms 🍴 Free Breakfast.*

Hotel Trio Healdsburg

$$ | HOTEL | Named for the three major wine appellations—the Russian River, Dry Creek, and Alexander valleys—whose confluence it's near, this Residence Inn by Marriott a mile and a quarter north of Healdsburg Plaza and its many restaurants and shops caters to families and extended-stay business travelers with spacious rooms equipped with full kitchens. **Pros:** cute robot room service; full kitchens; rooms sleep up to four or six. **Cons:** 30-minute walk to downtown; slightly corporate feel; pricey in high season. [$] *Rooms from: $209 ✉ 110 Dry Creek Rd. ☎ 707/433–4000 🌐 www.hoteltrio.com 🛏 122 rooms 🍴 Free Breakfast.*

h2hotel

$$$ | HOTEL | Eco-friendly touches abound at this hotel, from the plant-covered "green roof" to wooden decks made from salvaged lumber. **Pros:** stylish modern design; free bikes for use around town; complimentary breakfast at ground-floor Spoonbar restaurant. **Cons:** least expensive rooms lack bathtubs; fitness facility a block away at Hotel Healdsburg; gets pricey in high season. [$] *Rooms from: $349 ✉ 219 Healdsburg Ave. ☎ 707/922–5251 🌐 www.h2hotel.com 🛏 36 rooms 🍴 Breakfast.*

Madrona Manor

$$$ | B&B/INN | The centerpiece of this 8-acre estate of wooded and landscaped grounds is an 1881 mansion that in its early decades is said to have been Healdsburg's finest residence. **Pros:** old-fashioned and romantic (especially Rooms 203 and 204); pretty veranda perfect for a cocktail; destination restaurant. **Cons:** pool open only in high season; geared more toward couples than families; two-night minimum some weekends. [$] *Rooms from: $305 ✉ 1001 Westside Rd. ☎ 707/433–4231, 800/258–4003 🌐 www.madronamanor.com 🛏 22 rooms 🍴 Breakfast.*

★ River Belle Inn

$$ | B&B/INN | An 1875 Victorian with a storied past and a glorious colonnaded wraparound porch anchors this boutique property along the Russian River. **Pros:** riverfront location near a dozen-plus tasting rooms; cooked-to-order full breakfasts; attention to detail. **Cons:** about a mile from Healdsburg Plaza; minimum-stay requirement on weekends; lacks on-site pool, fitness center, and other amenities. [$] *Rooms from: $250 ✉ 68 Front St. ☎ 707/955–5724 🌐 www.riverbelleinn.com 🛏 12 rooms 🍴 Free Breakfast.*

★ SingleThread Farms Inn

$$$$ | B&B/INN | A remarkable Relais & Châteaux property a block north of Healdsburg Plaza, SingleThread is the creation of husband-and-wife team Kyle and Katina Connaughton, who operate the ground-floor destination restaurant and the four guest rooms and a suite above it. **Pros:** multicourse breakfast; in-room amenities from restaurant; rooftop garden. **Cons:** expensive year-round; no pool or fitness center (free passes provided to nearby facility with both); no spa, but in-room massages available. $ *Rooms from: $1000* ✉ *131 North St.* ✛ *At Center St.* ☎ *707/723–4646* ⊕ *www.singlethreadfarms.com* ⊷ *5 rooms* ❘◎❘ *Breakfast.*

Nightlife

Bear Republic Brewing Company

BARS/PUBS | Lovers of the brew make pilgrimages to Bear Republic to sample the flagship Racer 5 IPA, the Hop Rod Rye, the mighty Big Bear Black Stout, and many other offerings at this craft-beer pioneer. The brewery's spacious pub is an okay stop for a casual lunch or dinner. ✉ *345 Healdsburg Ave.* ✛ *At North St.* ☎ *707/433–2337* ⊕ *www.bearrepublic. com.*

Duke's Spirited Cocktails

BARS/PUBS | Fruity and savory "farm-to-bar" cocktails, many powered by local artisanal spirits and organically farmed ingredients, are among the specialties of this bar on Healdsburg Plaza's northern periphery. The old-school-in-a-fresh-setting vibe suits the inventive libations, but the owner-mixologists who run this happenin' hangout fashion the classics with equal aplomb. ✉ *111 Plaza St.* ✛ *Near Healdsburg Ave.* ☎ *707/431–1060* ⊕ *www.drinkatdukes.com.*

Performing Arts

Raven Performing Arts Theater

ARTS CENTERS | The Raven Players theater group is the resident company of this venue that also presents comedy and, in June, Healdsburg Jazz Festival performances. ✉ *115 North St.* ✛ *At Center St.* ☎ *707/433–6335* ⊕ *www.raventheater. org.*

🛍 Shopping

ART GALLERIES

★ Gallery Lulo

ART GALLERIES | A collaboration between a local artist and jewelry maker and a Danish-born curator, this gallery presents changing exhibits of jewelry, sculpture, and objets d'art. ✉ *303 Center St.* ✛ *At Plaza St.* ☎ *707/433–7533* ⊕ *www. gallerylulo.com.*

BOOKS

Copperfield's Books

BOOKS/STATIONERY | In addition to magazines and best-selling books, this store, part of a local indie chain, stocks a wide selection of discounted and remaindered titles, including many cookbooks. ✉ *106 Matheson St.* ✛ *Near Healdsburg Ave.* ☎ *707/433–9270* ⊕ *www.copperfields-books.com/healdsburg.*

CLOTHING

Looking Glass Luxe

CLOTHING | Sip sparkling wine from Sonoma and beyond while perusing this exposed-brick shop's cool couture from Rag & Bone, Love Shack Fancy, Frēda Salvador, and other top women's clothing designers. ✉ *332 Healdsburg Ave.* ✛ *Near North St.* ☎ *707/433–7033* ⊕ *www. lookingglassluxe.com.*

CRAFTS

★ One World Fair Trade

CRAFTS | Independent artisans in developing countries create the clothing, household items, jewelry, gifts, and toys sold in this bright, well-designed shop whose owners have a shrewd eye for fine craftsmanship. ⊠ *353 Healdsburg Ave.* ✛ *Near North St.* ☎ *707/473–0880* ⊕ *www.oneworldfairtrade.net.*

FOOD AND WINE
Dry Creek General Store
FOOD/CANDY | The Dry Creek Valley is so picture-perfect, it would be a shame to pass up the opportunity to picnic at one of the wineries. For breakfasts, sandwiches, bread, cheeses, and picnic supplies, stop by the general store, established in 1881 and still a popular spot for locals to hang out on the porch or in the bar. ⊠ *3495 Dry Creek Rd.* ✛ *At Lambert Bridge Rd.* ☎ *707/433–4171* ⊕ *www.drycreekgeneralstore1881.com.*

Healdsburg Farmers' Market
OUTDOOR/FLEA/GREEN MARKETS | The long-running Saturday market, held from late spring into the fall, showcases locally produced cheeses, breads, herbs, meats, and oils, in addition to the usual (ultratasty) fruits and vegetables. The flavors and smells arouse the senses, and the passion of the participating artisans warms the heart. On Tuesday mornings from late May through August, a second, smaller edition takes place in Healdsburg Plaza. ⊠ *North and Vine Sts.* ✛ *1 block west of Healdsburg Plaza* ☎ *707/431–1956* ⊕ *www.healdsburgfarmersmarket.org.*

★ Jimtown Store
FOOD/CANDY | The Alexander Valley's best picnic-packing stop has great espresso and a good selection of deli items, including sandwiches like a banh mi and a ham and Brie. While you're here, take a few minutes to browse the gifts, which include housewares and old-fashioned toys like sock monkeys. ⊠ *6706 Hwy. 128* ✛ *Near W. Sausal La.* ☎ *707/433–1212* ⊕ *www.jimtown.com.*

Oakville Grocery
WINE/SPIRITS | The Healdsburg branch of this Napa-based store is filled with wine, condiments, and deli items, and sells sandwiches and other picnic fixings. A terrace with ample seating makes a good place for an impromptu meal, but you might want to lunch early or late to avoid the crowds. ⊠ *124 Matheson St.* ✛ *At Center St.* ☎ *707/433–3200* ⊕ *www.oakvillegrocery.com.*

HOUSEHOLD ITEMS AND FURNITURE
Saint Dizier Home
HOUSEHOLD ITEMS/FURNITURE | With its selection of furniture and contemporary items for the home, this shop reminds mere mortals why the universe provides us with decorators and designers—they really do know best. ⊠ *259 Center St.* ✛ *At Matheson St.* ☎ *707/473–0980* ⊕ *www.saintdhome.com.*

SPAS
★ Spa Dolce
SPA/BEAUTY | Owner Ines von Majthenyi Scherrer has a good local rep, having run a popular nearby spa before opening this stylish facility just off Healdsburg Plaza. Spa Dolce specializes in skin and body care for men and women, and waxing and facials for women. Curved white walls and fresh-cut floral arrangements set a subdued tone for such treatments as the exfoliating Hauschka body scrub, which combines organic brown sugar with scented oil. There's a romantic room for couples to enjoy massages for two. ■ **TIP→ Many guests come just for the European-style facials, which range from a straightforward cleansing to an anti-aging peel.** ⊠ *250 Center St.* ✛ *At Matheson St.* ☎ *707/433–0177* ⊕ *www.spadolce.com* ✉ *Treatments $60–$355.*

The Spa Hotel Healdsburg
SPA/BEAUTY | Taking a page from its restaurant's farm-to-table approach, the Hotel Healdsburg's spa also sources many of its treatments' ingredients from area farms. Swedish-style massage is central to the Healdsburg Signature Massage, which also involves aromatic oils. Deep-tissue and hot-stone massages are among the other modalities. The signature facial uses biodynamic botanicals

and concludes with a cool stone facial massage. As with the facials, there are nail treatments for men and women. Some spa treatments are available in-room for hotel guests. ✉ *327 Healdsburg Ave.* ✛ *At Matheson St.* ☎ *707/433–4747* ⊕ *www.hotelhealdsburg.com/spa* ✉ *Treatments $55–$310.*

 Activities

BALLOONING
Up & Away Ballooning

BALLOONING | Being so close to the coast means that if the balloon you're in gets high enough, you'll have ocean views on a sunny day. You'll also take in plenty of vineyard vistas. Journeys begin with coffee and pastries and conclude with breakfast and a sparkling-wine toast. ✉ *Healdsburg* ☎ *707/836–0171* ⊕ *www.up-away.com* ✉ *$239 per person.*

BICYCLING
★ Wine Country Bikes

BICYCLING | This shop several blocks southeast of Healdsburg Plaza is perfectly located for single or multiday treks into the Dry Creek and Russian River valleys. Bikes, including tandems, rent for $39–$145 per day. One-day tours start at $139. ■**TIP→ The owner and staff can help with bicycling itineraries, including a mostly gentle loop, which takes in Westside Road and Eastside Road wineries and a rusting trestle bridge, as well as a more challenging excursion to Lake Sonoma.** ✉ *61 Front St.* ✛ *At Hudson St.* ☎ *707/473–0610, 866/922–4537* ⊕ *www.winecountrybikes.com.*

BOATING
Russian River Adventures

BOATING | This outfit open from mid-April through mid-November rents inflatable canoes for self-guided, full- and half-day trips down the Russian River. Pack a swimsuit and a picnic lunch and shove off. You'll likely see wildlife on the shore and can stop at fun swimming holes and even swing on a rope above the water.

The fee includes a shuttle ride back to your car. The full-day trip is dog-friendly. ✉ *20 Healdsburg Ave.* ✛ *At S. University St.* ☎ *707/433–5599, 800/280–7627* ⊕ *www.russianriveradventures.com* ✉ *From $50.*

Geyserville

8 miles north of Healdsburg.

Several high-profile Alexander Valley AVA wineries, including the splashy Francis Ford Coppola Winery, can be found in the town of Geyserville, a small part of which stretches west of U.S. 101 into northern Dry Creek. Not long ago this was a dusty farm town, and downtown Geyserville retains its rural character, but the restaurants, shops, and tasting rooms along the short main drag hint at Geyserville's growing sophistication.

GETTING HERE AND AROUND
From Healdsburg, the quickest route to downtown Geyserville is north on U.S. 101 to the Highway 128/Geyserville exit. Turn right at the stop sign onto Geyserville Avenue and follow the road north to the small downtown. For a more scenic drive, head north from Healdsburg Plaza along Healdsburg Avenue. About 3 miles north, jog west (left) for a few hundred feet onto Lytton Springs Road, then turn north (right) onto Geyserville Avenue. In town the avenue merges with Highway 128. Sonoma County Transit Bus 60 serves Geyserville from downtown Healdsburg.

VISITOR INFORMATION
Geyserville Chamber of Commerce
✉ *Geyserville* ☎ *707/276–6067* ⊕ *www.geyservillecc.com.*

 Sights

David Coffaro Estate Vineyard
WINERY/DISTILLERY | Easily one of the Dry Creek Valley's least pretentious wineries, David Coffaro specializes in red blends

Three AVAs in a Single Day

Cover three AVAs in a single day on a scenic loop drive that begins in downtown Healdsburg. Before departing, break your fast at **Costeaux French Bakery,** then pick up everything you need for a picnic there or at **Oakville Grocery.** Thus prepared, hop in the car and head south on Healdsburg Avenue.

Russian River Valley AVA

A few blocks south of Healdsburg Plaza, stay left to avoid U.S. 101. About ½ mile past the bridge over the Russian River, Healdsburg Avenue becomes Old Redwood Highway. Just past the driveway for the J and Rodney Strong wineries—by all means stop at one of them if you're eager to start tasting—make a right onto Eastside Road and continue past Copain Wines to Wohler Road and turn right. Before long you'll cross the rusting, highly photogenic Wohler Bridge. At Westside Road, turn north (right) to reach **Arista Winery.** After tasting there, continue north on Westside Road about 6½ miles.

Dry Creek Valley AVA

A sign along Westside Road indicates your passage into the Dry Creek Valley AVA. Turn northwest at Kinley Road, follow it 1½ miles to Dry Creek Road, and turn west (left). In 2½ miles you'll reach **Mauritson Wines,** where you can sip the type of Zinfandels that made Dry Creek famous and perhaps pick up a bottle to enjoy while picnicking on the property. Another good option in the AVA, Dry Creek Vineyard, is about ¾ mile farther along Dry Creek Road, at Lambert Bridge Road.

Alexander Valley AVA

From Dry Creek Road, head east on Lytton Springs Road to reach the Alexander Valley. After passing under the freeway, head north and east on Lytton Station Road, east on Alexander Valley Road, and southeast (right) on Highway 128. After ¾ mile, you'll arrive at **Silver Oak,** which makes a quintessential Alexander Valley Cabernet. If you're still game for more tasting, follow Highway 128 west to downtown Geyserville's **Locals Tasting Room,** which (for no charge) pours the wines of numerous small producers.

Enjoy dinner at **Diavola Pizzeria & Salumeria** or **Catelli's** in Geyserville, or take the scenic route back to Healdsburg, south on Geyserville Avenue, briefly east (left) onto Lytton Springs Road, and south on Healdsburg Avenue.

and single-varietal wines from grapes grown on a 20-acre estate. Zinfandel and Petite Sirah are strong suits, but Coffaro and his team also make wines using Lagrein, Aglianico, and other less familiar grapes, which also find their way into his unique blends, including the Rhône-style Terra Melange, with Peloursin and Carignane added to the usual Grenache, Syrah, and Mourvèdre mix. ⊠ *7485 Dry Creek Rd.* ⚓ *Near Yoakim Bridge Rd.* ☎ *707/433–9715* ⊕ *www.coffaro.com* ⊠ *Tasting free.*

Francis Ford Coppola Winery
WINERY/DISTILLERY | **FAMILY** | The fun at what the film director calls his "wine wonderland" is all in the excess. You may find it hard to resist having your photo snapped standing next to Don Corleone's desk from *The Godfather* or beside other memorabilia from Coppola films (including some directed by his daughter, Sofia). A bandstand reminiscent of one in *The Godfather Part II* is the centerpiece of a large pool area where you can rent a changing room, complete with shower, and spend the afternoon lounging poolside, perhaps ordering food from the adjacent café. A more elaborate restaurant, Rustic, overlooks the vineyards. As for the wines, the excess continues in the cellar, where several dozen varietal wines and blends are produced. ⊠ *300 Via Archimedes* ⚓ *Off U.S. 101* ☎ *707/857–1400* ⊕ *www.franciscoppo-lawinery.com* ⊠ *Tastings free–$25, tours $50, pool pass from $40.*

★ Locals Tasting Room
WINERY/DISTILLERY | If you're serious about wine, Carolyn Lewis's tasting room alone is worth a trek 8 miles north of Healdsburg Plaza to downtown Geyserville. Connoisseurs who appreciate Lewis's ability to spot up-and-comers head here regularly to sample the output of a dozen or so small wineries, most without tasting rooms of their own. There's no fee for tasting—extraordinary for wines of this quality—and the

extremely knowledgeable staff are happy to pour you a flight of several wines so you can compare, say, different Cabernet Sauvignons. ⊠ *21023A Geyserville Ave.* ⚓ *At Hwy. 128* ☎ *707/857–4900* ⊕ *www. tastelocalwines.com* ⊠ *Tasting free.*

★ Robert Young Estate Winery
WINERY/DISTILLERY | Panoramic Alexander Valley views unfold at Scion House, the stylish yet informal knoll-top tasting space this longtime Geyserville grower opened in 2018. The first Youngs began farming this land in the mid-1800s, raising cattle and growing wheat, prunes, and other crops. In the 1960s the late Robert Young, of the third generation, began cultivating grapes, eventually planting two Chardonnay clones now named for him. Grapes from them go into the Area 27 Chardonnay, noteworthy for the quality of its fruit and craftsmanship. The reds—small-lot Cabernet Sauvignons plus individual bottlings of Cabernet Franc, Malbec, Merlot, and Petit Verdot—shine even brighter. Tastings at Scion House, named for the fourth generation, whose members built on Robert Young's legacy and established the winery, are by appointment, but the winery accommodates walk-ins when possible. ⊠ *5120 Red Winery Rd.* ⚓ *Off Hwy. 128* ☎ *707/431–4811* ⊕ *www.ryew. com* ⊠ *Tastings from $25* ⊙ *Closed Tues.*

Trattore Farms
WINERY/DISTILLERY | The tectonic shifts that created the Dry Creek Valley reveal themselves at this winery atop one of several abruptly rolling hills tamed only partially by grapevines and olive trees. All tastings include selections of olive oils milled on-site, but the main events are the valley views and the lineup of Rhône-style whites, among them an exotic Marsanne-Roussanne blend, and reds that range from estate Grenache to the Proprietor's Reserve GSM (Grenache, Syrah, Mourvèdre). You'll get a feel for the rollicking terrain on the fun (by appointment only) Get Your Boots

Dirty vineyard and olive orchard and mill tour in a Kawasaki 4x4. ■TIP→ **For a real treat on a fair-weather weekend, book a seated outdoor tasting.** ✉ *7878 Dry Creek Rd.* ✛ *¾ mile north of Yoakim Bridge Rd.* ☎ *707/431-7200* ⊕ *www.trattorefarms. com* 🍴 *Tastings from $20, tour $70.*

Trentadue Winery

WINERY/DISTILLERY | Sangiovese, Zinfandel, and La Storia Cuvée 32 (a Super Tuscan–style blend of Sangiovese, Merlot, and other grapes) are among the strong suits of this Alexander Valley stalwart established in 1959 by the late Leo and Evelyn Trentadue, who planted the first vines in the Geyserville area since the Prohibition era. The diverse lineup also includes Sauvignon Blanc, a Sangiovese rosé, Merlot, Cabernet Sauvignon, Petite Sirah, Zinfandel, and dessert wines, all moderately priced. Tastings take place inside an ivy-covered villa, in a courtyard, and under an arbor. Some tastings and the tour require an appointment. ✉ *19170 Geyserville Ave.* ✛ *Off U.S. 101* ☎ *707/433-3104* ⊕ *www.trentadue.com* 🍴 *Tastings from $10, tour and tasting $25.*

Virginia Dare Winery

WINERY/DISTILLERY | Leave it to vintner-filmmaker Francis Ford Coppola to fashion a playful excursion out of the interlocking tales of the New World's first European child—Virginia Dare of the ill-fated 16th-century Roanoke Colony—and the once-prominent 20th-century wine brand named for her. Cheery staffers fill in the story while pouring modestly priced wines with labels reflecting these themes. Notable reds include The Lost Colony—a recent vintage comprising Syrah, Malbec, Petite Sirah, Cabernet Franc, and Petit Verdot—and the equally adventurous Manteo. The Virginia Dare Russian River Chardonnay also impresses. The winery's restaurant, Wero, emphasizes "American native" dishes such as bison ribs. ■TIP→ **Stars of Hollywood's golden age tout Virginia Dare**

wines of yore in amusing magazine ads adorning the elevator ("'Vintage Schmintage,' says Bert Lahr," aka the Cowardly Lion). ✉ *22281 Chianti Rd.* ✛ *At Canyon Rd.* ☎ *707/735-3500* ⊕ *www.virginiadarewinery.com* 🍴 *Tasting $25* ⊙ *Closed Mon.–Thurs.*

★ Zialena

WINERY/DISTILLERY | Sister-and-brother team Lisa and Mark Mazzoni (she runs the business, he makes the wines) debuted their small winery's first vintage in 2014, but their Italian-American family's Alexander Valley wine-making heritage stretches back more than a century. Mark—whose on-the-job teachers included the late Mike Lee of Kenwood Vineyards and Philippe Melka, a premier international consultant—specializes in smooth Zinfandel and nuanced Cabernet Sauvignon. Most of the grapes come from the 120-acre estate vineyard farmed by Lisa and Mark's father, Mike, who sells to Jordan and other big-name wineries. Other Zialena wines include a Sauvignon Blanc and Cappella, a Zin-based blend Lisa describes as "Mark's fun wine." Tastings take place in a contemporary stone, wood, and glass tasting room amid the family's vineyards. Tours, one focusing on production, the other on the vineyards, are by appointment only. ✉ *21112 River Rd.* ✛ *Off Hwy. 128* ☎ *707/955-5992* ⊕ *www.zialena.com* 🍴 *Tastings from $15, tours $50.*

🍽 Restaurants

★ Catelli's

$$ | ITALIAN | Cookbook author and *Iron Chef* judge Domenica Catelli teamed up with her brother Nicholas to revive their family's American-Italian restaurant, a Geyserville fixture. Contemporary abstracts, reclaimed-wood furnishings, and muted gray and chocolate-brown walls signal the changing times, but you'll find good-lovin' echoes of traditional cuisine in the sturdy meat sauce that accompanies the signature lasagna dish's

Alexander Valley AVA

Most of California's major grape varietals thrive in the disparate terrains and microclimates of Sonoma County's northern section, among them Zinfandel, which Italian immigrants such as Edoardo Seghesio planted in the Alexander Valley in the 1890s. Some of these vines survive to this day, but they were not the first grapes planted up this way. Five decades earlier, Cyrus Alexander, from whom the valley takes its name, planted grapevines on land now part of Alexander Valley Vineyards.

As recently as the 1980s the Alexander Valley was mostly planted to walnuts, pears, plums, and bulk grapes, but these days fruit for premium wines,

mainly Cabernet Sauvignon but also Sauvignon Blanc, Merlot, and Zinfandel, have largely replaced them. Rhône varietals such as Grenache and Syrah, along with Sangiovese, Barbera, and other Italian grapes, also make great wines here.

The Alexander Valley extends northeast of Healdsburg through Geyserville all the way to Mendocino County. Driving through the rolling hills along Highway 128, you're as likely to have to slow down for tandem bicyclists as for other drivers. And you might find a handful of visitors at most in the tasting rooms of some of the small, family-owned wineries.

paper-thin noodles and ricotta-and-herb-cheese filling. **Known for:** three-meat ravioli and other pastas; festive back patio; organic gardens. [$] *Average main: $21* ✉ *21047 Geyserville Ave.* ✛ *At Hwy. 128* ☎ *707/857–3471* ⊕ *www.mycatellis. com* ☾ *Closed Mon.*

Diavola Pizzeria & Salumeria

$$ | ITALIAN | A dining area with hardwood floors, a pressed-tin ceiling, and exposed-brick walls provides a fitting setting for the rustic cuisine at this Geyserville mainstay. Chef Dino Bugica studied with several artisans in Italy before opening this restaurant that specializes in pizzas pulled from a wood-burning oven and several types of house-cured meats, with a few salads and meaty main courses rounding out the menu. **Known for:** talented chef; smoked pork belly, pancetta, and spicy Calabrese sausage; casual setting. [$] *Average main: $20* ✉ *21021 Geyserville Ave.* ✛ *At Hwy. 128* ☎ *707/814–0111* ⊕ *www.diavolapizzeria. com.*

 Hotels

Geyserville Inn

$ | HOTEL | Clever travelers give the Healdsburg hubbub and prices the heave-ho but still have easy access to outstanding Dry Creek and Alexander Valley wineries from this modest, motel-like inn. **Pros:** outdoor pool; second floor rooms in back have vineyard views; picnic area. **Cons:** rooms facing pool or highway can be noisy; not much style; some maintenance issues. [$] *Rooms from: $179* ✉ *21714 Geyserville Ave.* ☎ *707/857–4343, 877/857–4343* ⊕ *www. geyservilleinn.com* ⤴ *41 rooms* ⦿ *No meals.*

 Nightlife

Geyserville Gun Club Bar & Lounge

BARS/PUBS | Two doors down from Diavola pizzeria (same ownership), this long, skinny bar in Geyserville's Odd Fellows Building wows locals and tourists with Sazeracs, Gibsons, and other classic cocktails and a bar menu of international comfort food. Hardwood floors, exposed brick, taxidermied animals, and contempo lighting set the mood at this cool spot. ⊠ *21025 Geyserville Ave.* ⊹ *At Hwy. 128* ☎ *707/814–0036* ⊕ *www. geyservillegunclub.com.*

Forestville

13 miles southwest of Healdsburg.

To experience the Russian River AVA's climate and rusticity, follow the river's westward course to the town of Forestville, home to a highly regarded restaurant and inn and a few wineries producing Pinot Noir from the Russian River Valley and well beyond.

GETTING HERE AND AROUND
To reach Forestville from U.S. 101, drive west from the River Road exit north of Santa Rosa. From Healdsburg, follow Westside Road west to River Road and then continue west. Sonoma County Transit Bus 20 serves Forestville.

 Sights

★ Hartford Family Winery
WINERY/DISTILLERY | Pinot Noir lovers appreciate the subtle differences in the wines Hartford's Jeff Stewart crafts from grapes grown in four Sonoma County AVAs, along with fruit from nearby Marin and Mendocino counties and Oregon. Stewart also makes highly rated Chardonnays and old-vine Zinfandels. If the weather's good and you've made a reservation, you can enjoy a flight of five or six wines on the patio outside the opulent main winery building. Indoors, at seated private library tastings, guests sip current and older vintages. ■**TIP➜ Hartford also has a tasting room in downtown Healdsburg.** ⊠ *8075 Martinelli Rd.* ⊹ *Off Hwy. 116 or River Rd.* ☎ *707/887–8030, 800/588–0234* ⊕ *www.hartfordwines. com* ✉ *Tastings from $25.*

Joseph Jewell Wines
WINERY/DISTILLERY | Micah Joseph Wirth and Adrian Jewell Manspeaker founded this winery whose name combines their middle ones. Pinot Noirs from the Russian River Valley and Humboldt County to the north are the strong suit. Wirth, who worked for seven years for vintner Gary Farrell, credits his interactions with Farrell's Russian River growers, among them the owners of Bucher Vineyard and Hallberg Ranch, with easing the winery's access to prestigious fruit. Manspeaker, a Humboldt native, spearheaded the foray into Pinot Noir grown in the coastal redwood country. Joseph Jewell's playfully rustic storefront tasting room in downtown Forestville provides the opportunity to experience what's unique about the varietal's next Northern California frontier. The bonuses: a Zinfandel from 1970s vines and two Chardonnays. ⊠ *6542 Front St.* ☎ *707/820–1621* ⊕ *www.josephjewell.com* ✉ *Tastings from $10, tours from $105 per couple ($500 tour is in a helicopter).*

Russian River Vineyards Tasting Lounge, Kitchen & Farm
WINERY/DISTILLERY | The lengthy moniker of this operation specializing in single-vineyard Russian River Valley Pinot Noirs hints at the bustle taking place: wine tasting indoors and out, early-evening restaurant dining on Friday and Saturday, and organic farming in nearby fields. In good weather, most guests sip wine in the courtyard under pergolas, shade trees, and umbrellas as woodpeckers pilfer acorns from nearby oaks, caching their booty in the redwood roof of the property's hop-barn-style structure. The rustic setting has been known to induce "couch lock," causing patrons to while away hours sipping wine and nibbling on cheese, charcuterie, and other snackables, even settling in with a book. ■**TIP➜ The tasting lounge stays open later than most, making this a good last stop of the day.** ⊠ *5700 Hwy. 116 N* ⊹ *¾ mile south of town* ☎ *707/887–2300* ⊕ *www.*

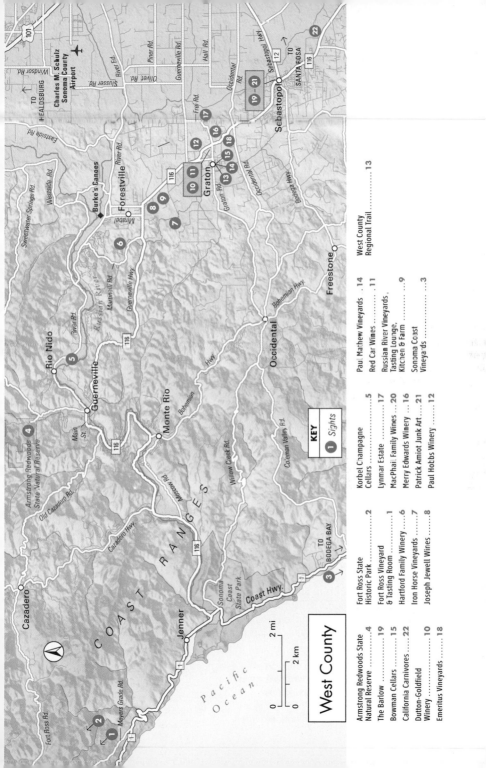

West County

KEY

| **1** Sights |

Armstrong Redwoods State
Natural Reserve 4

The Barlow 19

Bowman Cellars 15

California Carnivores 22

Dutton-Goldfield
Winery 10

Emeritus Vineyards 18

Fort Ross State
Historic Park 2

Fort Ross Vineyard
& Tasting Room 1

Hartford Family Winery 6

Iron Horse Vineyards 7

Joseph Jewell Wines 8

Korbel Champagne
Cellars 5

Lynmar Estate 17

MacPhail Family Wines ... 20

Merry Edwards Winery ... 16

Patrick Amiot Junk Art ... 21

Paul Hobbs Winery 12

Paul Mathew Vineyards . 14

Red Car Wines 11

Russian River Vineyards,
Tasting Lounge,
Kitchen & Farm 9

Sonoma Coast
Vineyards 3

West County
Regional Trail 13

russianrivervineyards.com ⊠ *Tastings from $25.*

 Restaurants

Backyard

$$$ | MODERN AMERICAN | The folks behind this casually rustic modern American restaurant regard Sonoma County's farms and gardens as their "backyard" and proudly list their purveyors on the menu. Dinner entrées, which change seasonally, might include herb tagliatelle with goat sausage or chicken pot pie. **Known for:** buttermilk fried chicken with buttermilk biscuits to stay or go; poplar-shaded outdoor front patio in good weather; Monday locals'-night specials, plus live music. $ *Average main: $26* ⊠ *6566 Front St./Hwy. 116* ✛ *At 1st St.* ☎ *707/820–8445* ⊕ *backyardforestville. com* ⊘ *Closed Tues.–Thurs.*

★ The Farmhouse Inn

$$$$ | FRENCH | Longtime executive chef Steve Litke produces three-, four-, and five-course French-inspired prix-fixe meals at the inn's romantic, softly lit destination restaurant inside a restored 19th-century farmhouse. The signature "Rabbit Rabbit Rabbit," which involves rabbit prepared three ways, is both rustic and refined, as are dishes that may include wild Alaskan halibut with Meyer lemon risotto and Chardonnay beurre blanc; the sommelier's set wine pairings, from a list that favors Sonoma County producers but roams the globe, are flawless. **Known for:** sophisticated cuisine; romantic dining; favorite of wine-industry crowd. $ *Average main: $99* ⊠ *7871 River Rd.* ✛ *At Wohler Rd.* ☎ *707/887–3300, 800/464–6642* ⊕ *www.farmhouseinn. com* ⊘ *Closed Tues. and Wed. No lunch.*

Twist

$ | AMERICAN | A lunch-only spot on Forestville's blink-and-you'll-miss-it main drag, Twist serves sandwiches like moms of yore made, only better: Cajun meat loaf, pulled pork with house-made

barbecue sauce, and a local-favorite BLT when tomatoes are in season. The sandwich of grilled yams, eggplant, red peppers, and other seasonal ingredients on a focaccia roll with sun-dried tomatoes and goat cheese wows the no-meat-for-me set. **Known for:** all-day egg scrambles; gluten-free soups; good beers, wines, and soft drinks. $ *Average main: $14* ⊠ *6536 Front St.* ✛ *Near Railroad Ave.* ☎ *707/820–8443* ⊕ *www.twisteatery. com* ⊘ *Closed Sun. and Mon. No dinner.*

Hotels

★ The Farmhouse Inn

$$$$ | B&B/INN | With a farmhouse-meets-modern-loft aesthetic, this low-key but upscale getaway with a pale-yellow exterior contains spacious rooms filled with king-size four-poster beds, whirlpool tubs, and hillside-view terraces. **Pros:** fantastic restaurant; luxury bath products; full-service spa. **Cons:** mild road noise audible in rooms closest to the street; two-night minimum on weekends; pricey, especially during high season. $ *Rooms from: $545* ⊠ *7871 River Rd.* ☎ *707/887–3300, 800/464–6642* ⊕ *www.farmhouseinn. com* ⊃ *25 rooms* ⦿ *Breakfast.*

Activities

Burke's Canoe Trips

CANOEING/ROWING/SKULLING | You'll get a real feel for the Russian River's flora and fauna on a leisurely 10-mile paddle downstream from Burke's to Guerneville. A shuttle bus returns you to your car at the end of the journey, which is best taken from late May through mid-October and, in summer, on a weekday—summer weekends can be crowded and raucous. ⊠ *8600 River Rd.* ✛ *At Mirabel Rd.* ☎ *707/887–1222* ⊕ *www.burkescanoetrips.com* ⊠ *$78 per canoe.*

Russian River Valley AVA

As the Russian River winds its way from Mendocino to the Pacific Ocean, it carves out a valley that's a near-perfect environment for growing certain grape varietals. Because of the low elevation, sea fog pushes far inland to cool the soil, yet in summer it burns off, giving the grapes enough sun to ripen properly. Fog-loving Pinot Noir and Chardonnay grapes are king and queen in the Russian River Valley AVA, which extends from Healdsburg west to the town Guerneville. The namesake river does its part by slowly carving its way downward through many layers of rock, depositing a deep layer of gravel that in parts of the valley measures 60 or 70 feet. This gravel forces the roots of grapevines to go deep in search of water and nutrients. In the process, the plants absorb trace minerals that add complexity to the flavor of the grapes.

Guerneville

7 miles northwest of Forestville; 15 miles southwest of Healdsburg.

Guerneville's tourist demographic has evolved over the years—Bay Area families in the 1950s, lesbians and gays starting in the 1970s, and these days a mix of both groups, plus techies and outdoorsy types—with coast redwoods and the Russian River always central to the town's appeal. The area's most famous winery is Korbel Champagne Cellars, established nearly a century and a half ago. Even older are the stands of trees that except on the coldest winter days make Armstrong Redwoods State Natural Reserve such a perfect respite from wine tasting.

GETTING HERE AND AROUND

To get to Guerneville from Healdsburg, follow Westside Road south to River Road and turn west. From Forestville, head west on Highway 116; alternatively, you can head north on Mirabel Road to River Road and then head west. Sonoma County Transit Bus 20 serves Guerneville.

VISITOR INFORMATION

Guerneville Visitor Center

⊠ *16209 1st St.* ✛ *At Armstrong Woods Rd.* ☎ *707/869–9000* ⊕ *www.russianriver.com.*

Sights

★ **Armstrong Redwoods State Natural Reserve**

NATIONAL/STATE PARK | FAMILY | Here's your best opportunity in the western Wine Country to wander amid *Sequoia sempervirens,* also known as coast redwood trees. The oldest example in this 805-acre state park, the Colonel Armstrong Tree, is thought to be more than 1,400 years old. A half mile from the parking lot, the tree is easily accessible, and you can hike a long way into the forest before things get too hilly. ■ TIP→ **During hot summer days, Armstrong Redwoods's tall trees help the park keep its cool.** ⊠ *17000 Armstrong Woods Rd.* ✛ *Off River Rd.* ☎ *707/869–2958 for visitor center, 707/869–2015 for park headquarters* ⊕ *www.parks.ca.gov* ⊠ *$8 per vehicle, free to pedestrians and bicyclists.*

Korbel Champagne Cellars
WINERY/DISTILLERY | The three brothers Korbel (Joseph, Francis, and Anton) planted Pinot Noir grapes in the Russian River Valley in the 1870s, pioneering efforts that are duly noted on 50-minute tours of the well-known brand's Guerneville facility. Tours include a clear explanation of the *méthode champenoise* used to make the company's sparkling wines, a walk through ivy-covered 19th-century buildings, and tastings of Korbel's bubblies and still wines. You can also taste without touring. ■ **TIP→ If you have the time, stroll through the rose garden, home to more than 250 varieties.** ✉ *13250 River Rd.* ✥ *West of Rio Nido* ☎ *707/824–7000* 🌐 *www.korbel.com/winery* 🎟 *Tasting and tour free* 🕓 *No garden tours mid-Oct.–mid-Apr.*

🍴 Restaurants

Big Bottom Market
$ | **MODERN AMERICAN** | Foodies love this culinary pit stop and grocery for its breakfast biscuits, clever sandwiches, and savory salads to go or eat here. Everything from butter and jam and mascarpone and honey to barbecue pulled pork with pickles and slaw accompanies the biscuits, whose mix made Oprah's Favorite Things 2016 list, and the stellar sandwiches include the Colonel Armstrong (curried chicken salad with currants and cashews on brioche). **Known for:** biscuits and heartier breakfast fare; by-glass wines; excellent for a quick bite. [$] *Average main: $11* ✉ *16228 Main St.* ✥ *Near Church St.* ☎ *707/604–7295* 🌐 *www.bigbottommarket.com* 🕓 *Closed Tues. No dinner.*

★ **boon eat+drink**
$$$ | **MODERN AMERICAN** | A casual storefront restaurant on Guerneville's main drag, boon eat+drink has a menu built around small, "green" (salads and cooked vegetables), and main plates assembled for the most part from locally produced organic ingredients. Like many of chef-owner Crista Luedtke's dishes, the signature polenta lasagna—creamy ricotta salata cheese and polenta served on greens sautéed in garlic, all of it floating upon a spicy marinara sauce—deviates significantly from the lasagna norm but succeeds on its own merits. **Known for:** adventurous culinary sensibility; all wines from Russian River Valley; local organic ingredients. [$] *Average main: $23* ✉ *16248 Main St.* ✥ *At Church St.* ☎ *707/869–0780* 🌐 *eatatboon.com* 🕓 *Closed Wed.*

★ **Seaside Metal Oyster Bar**
$$$ | **SEAFOOD** | Chef Michael Selvera, who made his name at San Francisco's Bar Crudo (he's still an owner), displays a subtly elegant touch with seafood: oysters, clams, mussels, octopus, and hot and cold crudo. Diners at his small downtown Guerneville restaurant's centerpiece L-shaped marble counter have the perfect perch to witness the creation of dishes like scallops with radishes and English peas and hot buttered oysters with roasted chili and garlic that impress for their ultrafreshness and gentle spicing. **Known for:** mussels, squid, and shrimp chowder; seafood-friendly wines and beers; happy hour (5 pm–6 pm) nibbles. [$] *Average main: $28* ✉ *16222 Main St.* ✥ *Near Armstrong Woods Rd.* ☎ *707/604–7250* 🌐 *seasidemetal.com* 🕓 *Closed Tues. No lunch.*

🛏 Hotels

Applewood Inn and Spa
$$ | **B&B/INN** | On a knoll sheltered by towering redwoods, this three-building mission revival–style inn is a short drive from downtown Guerneville. **Pros:** secluded location; some rooms have fireplaces, private balconies, and hot tubs; massages and facials at spa. **Cons:** may feel too remote to some; noise from neighboring rooms can be an issue in the oldest building; some rooms look careworn. [$] *Rooms from: $275* ✉ *13555 Hwy. 116* ☎ *707/869–9093* 🌐 *www.applewoodinn.com* 🛏 *19 rooms* 🍽 *Breakfast.*

On a hot summer day the shady paths of Armstrong Redwoods State Natural Reserve provide cool comfort.

AutoCamp Russian River

$$ | B&B/INN |FAMILY | Guests at this spot along the Russian River camp (well, sort of) in luxury under the redwoods in cute-as-a-button Airstream trailers decked out with top-notch oh-so-contemporary beds, linens, and bath products. **Pros:** hip, retro feel; comfortable down beds; campfire and barbecue pit for each trailer. **Cons:** lacks room service and other hotel amenities; fee for housekeeping; tents (versus trailers) late spring–mid-fall only, with two-guest maximum including children. $ *Rooms from: $300* ✉ *14120 Old Cazadero Rd.* ☎ *888/405–7553* ⊕ *autocamp. com/locations* ⤳ *24 trailers* ⍝ *No meals.*

boon hotel+spa

$ | HOTEL | Redwoods, Douglas firs, and palms supply shade and seclusion at this lushly landscaped resort ¾ mile north of downtown Guerneville. **Pros:** memorable breakfasts; pool area and on-site spa; complimentary bikes. **Cons:** lacks amenities of larger properties; pool rooms too close to the action for some guests; can be pricey in high season. $ *Rooms*

from: $195 ✉ *14711 Armstrong Woods Rd.* ☎ *707/869–2721* ⊕ *boonhotels.com* ⤳ *15 rooms* ⍝ *Breakfast.*

Cottages on River Road

$ | B&B/INN |FAMILY | Redwoods on a steep slope tower above this tidy roadside complex of single and duplex cottages separated by a grassy lawn. **Pros:** family business run with care; affordable rates; five two-bedroom cottages good for families and groups. **Cons:** books up far in advance in summer; lacks upscale amenities; some road noise audible (ask for a cottage under the trees). $ *Rooms from: $99* ✉ *14880 River Rd.* ✛ *1¼ miles east of town* ☎ *707/869–3848* ⊕ *www. cottagesonriverroad.com* ⤳ *19 cottages* ⍝ *Breakfast.*

Nightlife

El Barrio

BARS/PUBS | Mescal and classic tequila margaritas are the mainstays of this bar—a festive spot to begin or end the evening or to park yourself while waiting for a table at owner Crista Luedtke's nearby boon eat+drink. La Jefa (artisanal rye, ancho reyes chili, lemon, maple, egg white, and bitters) and more fanciful creations also await at this serape-chic watering hole. ✉ *16230 Main St.* ✛ *Near Church St.* ☎ *707/604–7601* ⊕ *www. elbarriobar.com.*

Jenner

13 miles west of Guerneville; 11 miles north of Bodega Bay.

The Russian River empties into the Pacific Ocean at Jenner, a wide spot in the road where houses dot a mountainside high above the sea. Facing south, the village looks across the river's mouth to Goat Rock State Beach, part of Sonoma Coast State Park. North of the village, Fort Ross State Historic Park provides a glimpse into Russia's early-19th-century foray into California. A winery named for the fort grows Chardonnay and Pinot Noir above the coastal fogline.

GETTING HERE AND AROUND

Jenner is north of Bodega Bay on Highway 1 and west of Guerneville on Highway 116 (River Road). Mendocino Transit Authority (⊕ *mendocinotransit. org*) Route 95 buses stop in Jenner and connect with Bodega Bay, Santa Rosa, and other coastal towns.

Sights

Fort Ross State Historic Park

NATIONAL/STATE PARK | FAMILY | With its reconstructed Russian Orthodox chapel, stockade, and officials' quarters, Fort Ross looks much the way it did after the Russians made it their major California coastal outpost in 1812. Russian settlers established the fort on land they leased from the native Kashia people. The Russians hoped to gain a foothold in the Pacific coast's warmer regions and to produce crops and other supplies for

their Alaskan fur-trading operations. In 1841, with the local marine mammal population depleted and farming having proven unproductive, the Russians sold their holdings to John Sutter, later of gold-rush fame. The land, privately ranched for decades, became a state park in 1909. One original Russian-era structure remains, as does a cemetery. The rest of the compound has been reconstructed to look much as it did during Russian times. An excellent small museum documents the history of the fort, the Kashia people, and the ranch and state-park eras. Note that no dogs are allowed past the parking lot and picnic area. ✉ *19005 Hwy. 1* ✛ *11 miles north of Jenner* ☎ *707/847–3437* ⊕ *www.fortross.org* 🖃 *$8 per vehicle.*

Fort Ross Vineyard & Tasting Room

WINERY/DISTILLERY | The Russian River and Highway 116 snake west from Guerneville through redwood groves to the coast, where Highway 1 twists north past rocky cliffs to this windswept ridge-top winery. Until recently many experts deemed the weather this far west too chilly even for cool-climate varietals, but Fort Ross Vineyard and other Fort Ross–Seaview AVA wineries are proving that Chardonnay and Pinot Noir can thrive above the fog line. The sea air and rocky soils here produce wines generally less fruit-forward than their Russian River Valley counterparts but equally sophisticated and no less vibrant. Many coastal wineries are appointment-only or closed to the public; with its rustic-chic, barnlike tasting room and wide outdoor patio overlooking the Pacific, Fort Ross provides an appealing introduction to this up-and-coming region's wines. ✉ *15725 Meyers Grade Rd.* ✛ *Off Hwy. 1, 6 miles north of Jenner* ☎ *707/847–3460* ⊕ *www.fortross-vineyard.com* 🖃 *Tasting $25* ⊘ *Closed Tues. and Wed.*

🍴 Restaurants

Coast Kitchen

$$$ | **MODERN AMERICAN** | On a sunny afternoon or at sunset, glistening ocean views from the Coast Kitchen's outdoor patio and indoor dining space elevate dishes emphasizing seafood and local produce both farmed and foraged. Starters like a baby gem lettuce Caesar and grilled salmon wings precede entrées that may include seared scallops and aged rib eye. **Known for:** ocean-view patio (frequent whale sightings in winter and spring); Sonoma County cheeses, wines, and produce; bar menu 3 pm–5 pm. *[$] Average main: $28 ✉ Timber Cove, 21780 Hwy. 1 ✥ 3 miles north of Fort Ross State Historic Park ☎ 707/847–3231 🌐 www.coastkitchensonoma.com.*

River's End

$$$$ | **AMERICAN** | The hot tip at this low-slung cliff's-edge restaurant is to come early or reserve a window table, where the Russian River and Pacific Ocean views alone, particularly at sunset, might make your day (even more so if you're a birder). Seafood is the specialty—during the summer the chef showcases local king salmon—but filet mignon, duck, elk, a vegetarian napoleon, and pasta with prawns are often on the dinner menu. **Known for:** majestic setting; international wine list; burgers, sandwiches, fish-and-chips for lunch. *[$] Average main: $32 ✉ 11048 Hwy. 1 ☎ 707/865–2484 🌐 www.ilovesunsets.com/restaurant.*

🛏 Hotels

★ Timber Cove Resort

$$$ | **RESORT** | Restored well beyond its original splendor, this resort anchored to a craggy oceanfront cliff is by far the Sonoma Coast's coolest getaway. **Pros:** dramatic sunsets; grand public spaces; destination restaurant. **Cons:** almost too cool for the laid-back Sonoma Coast; pricey ocean-view rooms; far from nightlife. *[$] Rooms from: $314 ✉ 21780 Hwy. 1 ☎ 707/847–3231 🌐 www.timbercoveresort.com 🛏 46 rooms 🍴 No meals.*

Bodega Bay

11 miles south of Jenner.

From this working town's busy harbor west of Highway 1, commercial boats pursue fish and Dungeness crab. In 1962 Alfred Hitchcock shot *The Birds* in the area. The Tides Wharf complex, an important location, is no longer recognizable, but a few miles inland, in Bodega, you can find Potter Schoolhouse, now a private residence.

GETTING HERE AND AROUND

To reach Bodega Bay from Jenner, drive south on Highway 1. Mendocino Transit Authority (🌐 *mendocinotransit.org*) Route 95 buses serve Bodega Bay.

👁 Sights

Sonoma Coast Vineyards

WINERY/DISTILLERY | This boutique winery with an ocean view tasting room makes cool-climate Chardonnays and Pinot Noirs from grapes grown close to the Pacific. The Antonio Mountain and Balistreri Family Vineyards Pinot Noirs stand out among wines that also include a mildly oaky Sauvignon Blanc, a Syrah, and a well-balanced sparkler. *✉ 555 Hwy. 1 ☎ 707/921–2860 🌐 www.sonomacoast-vineyards.com 🎫 Tastings from $25.*

⛱ Beaches

★ Sonoma Coast State Park

BEACH—SIGHT | The park's gorgeous sandy coves stretch for 17 miles from Bodega Head to 4 miles north of Jenner. **Bodega Head** is a popular whale-watching perch in winter and early spring, and **Rock Point, Duncan's Landing,** and **Wright's Beach,** at about the halfway mark, have good picnic areas. Rogue waves have swept people off the rocks at Duncan's Landing

Overlook, so don't stray past signs warning you away. Calmer **Shell Beach,** about 2 miles north, is known for beachcombing, tidepooling, and fishing. Walk part of the bluff-top **Kortum Trail** or drive about 2½ miles north of Shell Beach to **Blind Beach.** Near the mouth of the Russian River just north of here at **Goat Rock Beach,** you'll find harbor seals; pupping season is from March through August. Bring binoculars and walk north from the parking lot to view the seals. During summer lifeguards are on duty at some beaches, but strong rip currents and heavy surf keep most visitors onshore. **Amenities:** parking (fee); toilets. **Best for:** solitude; sunset; walking. ✉ *Park Headquarters/Salmon Creek Ranger Station, 3095 Hwy. 1* ✥ *2 miles north of Bodega Bay* ☎ *707/875–3483* 🌐 *www.parks.ca.gov* 🎫 *$8 per vehicle.*

Restaurants

Spud Point Crab Company
$ | **SEAFOOD** | Crab sandwiches, New England or Manhattan clam chowder, and homemade crab cakes with roasted red pepper sauce star on the brief menu of this shacklike operation. Place your order inside, and enjoy your meal to go or at one of the marina-view picnic tables outside. **Known for:** family-run operation; opens at 9 am; seafood cocktails, superb chowder. [$] *Average main: $10* ✉ *1910 Westshore Rd.* ☎ *707/875–9472* 🕒 *No dinner.*

★ Terrapin Creek Cafe & Restaurant
$$$$ | **MODERN AMERICAN** | Intricate but not fussy cuisine based on locally farmed ingredients and *fruits de mer* has made this casual yet sophisticated restaurant with an open kitchen a West County darling. Start with raw Marin Miyagi oysters, rich potato-leek soup, or (in season) Dungeness crabmeat ragout before moving on to halibut or other fish pan-roasted to perfection. **Known for:** intricate cuisine of chefs Liya and Andrew Truong; top Bay Area–foodies' choice; starters and salads. [$] *Average main: $32* ✉ *1580 Eastshore Rd.* ☎ *707/875–2700* 🌐 *www.terrapincreekcafe.com* 🕒 *Closed Tues. and Wed. No lunch.*

Hotels

Bodega Bay Lodge
$$$ | **HOTEL** | Looking out to the ocean across a wetland, the lodge's shingle-and-river-rock buildings contain Bodega Bay's finest accommodations. **Pros:** ocean views; spacious rooms; fireplaces and patios or balconies in most rooms. **Cons:** pricey in-season; parking lot in foreground of some rooms' views; fairly long drive to other fine dining. [$] *Rooms from: $350* ✉ *103 Coast Hwy. 1* ☎ *707/875–3525* 🌐 *www.bodegabaylodge.com* 🛏 *83 rooms* 🍴 *No meals.*

Bodega Harbor Inn
$ | **HOTEL** | As humble as can be, this is one of the few places on this stretch of the coast with rooms for around $100 a night. **Pros:** budget choice; rooms for larger groups; ocean views from public areas and some rooms. **Cons:** older facility; nondescript rooms; behind a shopping center. [$] *Rooms from: $99* ✉ *1345 Bodega Ave.* ☎ *707/875–3594* 🌐 *www.bodegaharborinn.com* 🛏 *16 rooms* 🍴 *No meals.*

Activities

Bodega Bay Sailing Adventures
WHALE-WATCHING | Part salty dog and part jolly entertainer, Captain Rich conducts three-hour Bodega Bay tours on his 33-foot sailboat. Whales are often sighted from winter into early spring, and sea lions and harbor seals commonly appear. The sunset tour is especially fun. ✉ *1418 Bay Flat Rd.* ✥ *Meeting place near sport fishing center* ☎ *707/318–2251* 🌐 *www.bodegabaysailing.org* 🎫 *From $95.*

Occidental

11 miles south of Guerneville; 14 miles east of Bodega Bay.

A village surrounded by redwood forests, orchards, and vineyards, Occidental is a former logging hub with a bohemian vibe. The small downtown, which contains several handsome Victorian-era structures, has a whimsically decorated bed-and-breakfast inn, two good restaurants, and a handful of art galleries and shops worth poking around.

GETTING HERE AND AROUND

From Guerneville, head west on Highway 116 for 4 miles to the town of Monte Rio, then turn south on Church Street and travel past the old Rio Theater and over the bridge spanning the Russian River. At this point the road is signed as the Bohemian Highway, which takes you into town, where the road's name changes to Main Street. From Bodega Bay, head south and then east on Highway 1, continuing east on Bodega Highway at the town of Bodega; at Freestone, head north on the Bohemian Highway. Public transit is not a convenient way to travel here.

🍴 Restaurants

★ Hazel
$$ | **MODERN AMERICAN** | Pizza and pastries are the specialties of this tiny restaurant whose owner-chefs, Jim and Michele Wimborough, forsook their fancy big-city gigs for the pleasures of small-town living. Jim's mushroom pizza, adorned with feta, mozzarella, and truffle oil, and the pie with sausage and egg are among the headliners, with Michele's sundae with salted caramel and hot fudge among the enticements for dessert. **Known for:** flavorful seasonal cuisine; roasted chicken with lemon vinaigrette entrée; Sunday brunch (try the beignets). [$] *Average main: $22* ✉ *3782 Bohemian Hwy.* ✣ *At Occidental Rd.* ☎ *707/874–6003* 🌐 *www.restauranthazel.com* ⏲ *Closed Mon. No lunch Tues.–Sat.*

Howard Station Cafe
$ | **AMERICAN** | The mile-long list of morning fare at Occidental's neo-hippie go-to breakfast and weekend brunch spot (cash only, no reservations) includes huevos rancheros, omelets, eggs Benedict, waffles, pancakes, French toast, and "healthy alternatives" such as oatmeal made several ways, house-made granola, and quinoa and brown rice bowls with kale and eggs. Soups, salads, burgers, and monstrous sandwiches are on the menu for lunch at this laid-back space with seating inside a 19th-century gingerbread Victorian and outside on its wooden porch. **Known for:** mostly organic ingredients; juice bar; vegetarian and gluten-free items. [$] *Average main: $11* ✉ *3611 Main St./Bohemian Hwy.* ✣ *At 2nd St.* ☎ *707/874–2838* 🌐 *www.howardstationcafe.com* 💳 *No credit cards* ⏲ *No dinner.*

Wild Flour Bread
$ | **BAKERY** | The sticky buns at jovial Jed Wallach's Wild Flour are legendary in western Sonoma—on weekends they're often all gone by the early afternoon—as are the rye breads and sock-it-to-me scones in flavors like double chocolate, espresso, and hazelnut. There's a long table inside, but most patrons enjoy their baked goods (cash only) on the benches outside. **Known for:** pastry lineup; fougasse (Provençal flatbread), rye, and other breads; cookies and biscotti. [$] *Average main: $5* ✉ *140 Bohemian Hwy., Freestone* ✣ *At El Camino Bodega, 4 miles south of Occidental* ☎ *707/874–2938* 🌐 *www.wildflourbread.com* 💳 *No credit cards* ⏲ *Closed Tues.–Thurs. No dinner.*

🛏 Hotels

The Inn at Occidental
$$ | **B&B/INN** | Quilts, folk art, and original paintings and photographs fill

this colorful and friendly inn up the hill from the shops and restaurants of tiny Occidental. **Pros:** whimsical decor; most rooms have private decks and jetted tubs; full gourmet breakfast and evening wine and cheese. **Cons:** not for those with minimalist tastes; not for kids; no pool or fitness center. $ *Rooms from: $259* ⊠ *3657 Church St.* ☎ *707/874–1047, 800/522–6324* ⊕ *www.innatoccidental. com* ⇌ *17 rooms* ❘○❘ *Breakfast.*

Activities

Sonoma Canopy Tours

ZIP LINING | Zip through the trees with the greatest of ease—at speeds up to 25 mph—at this ziplining center 2½ miles north of Occidental. Friendly guides prepare guests well for their 2½-hour natural high. ■**TIP**→ **Participants must be at least 10 years old and weigh between 70 and 250 pounds.** ⊠ *6250 Bohemian Hwy.* ☎ *888/494–7868* ⊕ *www.sonomacanopytours.com* ⊠ *From $99.*

Sebastopol

6 miles east of Occidental; 7 miles southwest of Santa Rosa.

A stroll through downtown Sebastopol—a town formerly known more for Gravenstein apples than for grapes but these days a burgeoning wine hub—reveals glimpses of the distant and recent past and perhaps the future, too. Many hippies settled here in the 1960s and 70s and, as the old Crosby, Stills, Nash & Young song goes, they taught their children well: the town remains steadfastly, if not entirely, countercultural. (Those hankering for a 1960s flashback can truck on over to Main Street's Grateful Bagel, complete with Grateful Dead logo.)

Sebastopol has long had good, if somewhat low-profile, wineries, among them Iron Horse, Lynmar Estate, and Merry Edwards. With the replacement in 2016 of the town's beloved Fosters Freeze location with a vaguely industrial-chic venue for California coastal cuisine and the continuing evolution of the cluster of artisanal producers at the Barlow, the site of a former apple-processing plant, the town always seems poised for a Healdsburg-style transformation. Then again, maybe not—stay tuned (in, not out).

GETTING HERE AND AROUND

Sebastopol can be reached from Occidental by taking Graton Road east to Highway 116 and turning south. From Santa Rosa, head west on Highway 12. Sonoma County Transit Buses 20, 22, 24, and 26 serve Sebastopol.

VISITOR INFORMATION
Sebastopol Visitor Center
⊠ *265 S. Main St.* ✛ *At Willow St.* ☎ *707/823–3032* ⊕ *www.sebastopol.org.*

Sights

The Barlow

MARKET | A multibuilding complex on the site of a former apple cannery, The Barlow celebrates Sonoma County's "maker" culture with tenants who produce or sell wine, beer, spirits, crafts, clothing, art, and artisanal food and herbs. Only club members and guests on the allocation waiting list can visit the anchor wine tenant, Kosta Browne, but MacPhail, Pax, and Friedeman have tasting rooms open to the public. Crooked Goat Brewing and Woodfour Brewing Company make and sell ales, and you can have a nip of vodka, gin, sloe gin, or wheat and rye whiskey at Spirit Works Distillery. A locally renowned mixologist teamed up with the duo behind nearby Lowell's and Handline restaurants to open Fern Bar, whose zero-proof (as in nonalcoholic) cocktails entice as much as the traditional ones. ⊠ *6770 McKinley St.* ✛ *At Morris St., off Hwy. 12* ☎ *707/824–5600* ⊕ *www.thebarlow.net* ⊠ *Complex free; tasting fees at wineries, breweries, distillery.*

California Carnivores

GARDEN | Its cool collection of carnivorous plants, said to be the world's largest, makes this nursery a diverting stop. The colors are sublime, and the mechanics of the plants are fascinating. Venus flytraps and several insect-nabbing relatives are on display and for sale; shipping is easily arranged. Even more effective than the Venus plants are the American pitchers, whose flashy leaves take down flies but also wasps. ⊠ *2833 Old Gravenstein Hwy. ✛ Off Gravenstein Hwy. (Hwy. 116)* ☎ *707/824–0433* ⊕ *www.californiacarnivores.com* ⬛ *Free* ⊙ *Closed Tues. and Wed.*

★ Dutton-Goldfield Winery

WINERY/DISTILLERY | An avid cyclist whose previous credits include developing the wine-making program at Hartford Court, Dan Goldfield teamed up with fifth-generation farmer Steve Dutton to establish this small operation devoted to cool-climate wines. Goldfield modestly strives to take Dutton's meticulously farmed fruit and "make the winemaker unnoticeable," but what impresses the most about these wines, which include Pinot Blanc, Chardonnay, Pinot Noir, and Zinfandel, is their sheer artistry. Among the ones to seek out are the Angel Camp Pinot Noir, from Anderson Valley (Mendocino County) grapes, and the Morelli Lane Zinfandel, from grapes grown on the remaining 1.8 acres of an 1880s vineyard Goldfield helped revive. Tastings often begin with Pinot Blanc, a white-wine variant of Pinot Noir, proceed through the reds, and end with a palate-cleansing Chardonnay. ⊠ *3100 Gravenstein Hwy. N/Hwy. 116 ✛ At Graton Rd.* ☎ *707/827–3600* ⊕ *www.duttongoldfield.com* ⬛ *Tastings from $20.*

Emeritus Vineyards

WINERY/DISTILLERY | Old-timers recall the superb apples grown at Hallberg Ranch, but since a 2000 replanting this dry-farmed property has evolved into an elite Pinot Noir vineyard. Owner Brice Jones coveted this land for its temperate climate and layer of Goldridge sandy loam soil atop a bed of Sebastopol clay loam, a combination that forces vine roots to work hard to obtain water, which in turn produces berries concentrated with flavor. Some grapes are sold to other wineries, with the remainder used to craft the flagship Emeritus Hallberg Ranch Pinot Noir and other wines. The winery also makes a sometimes even more acclaimed wine from its nearby Pinot Hill vineyard. You can taste both in a structure whose floor-to-ceiling windows are retracted in good weather to create an extended open-air space. The tour is by appointment only; tasting reservations are recommended. ⊠ *2500 Gravenstein Hwy. N ✛ At Peachland Ave.* ☎ *707/823–9463* ⊕ *www.emeritusvineyards.com* ⬛ *Tasting $20, tour and tasting $30.*

★ Iron Horse Vineyards

WINERY/DISTILLERY | A meandering one-lane road leads to this winery known for its sparkling wines and estate Chardonnays and Pinot Noirs. The sparklers have made history: Ronald Reagan served them at his summit meetings with Mikhail Gorbachev; George H. W. Bush took some along to Moscow for treaty talks; and Barack Obama included them at official state dinners. Despite Iron Horse's brushes with fame, a casual rusticity prevails at its outdoor tasting area (large heaters keep things comfortable on chilly days), which gazes out on acres of rolling, vine-covered hills. Regular tours take place on weekdays at 10 am. Tastings and tours are by appointment only. ■TIP→ **When his schedule permits, winemaker David Munksgard leads a private tour by truck at 10 am on Monday.** ⊠ *9786 Ross Station Rd. ✛ Off Hwy. 116* ☎ *707/887–1507* ⊕ *www.ironhorsevineyards.com* ⬛ *Tasting $30, tours from $50 (includes tasting).*

Lynmar Estate

WINERY/DISTILLERY | *Elegant* and *balanced* describe Lynmar's landscaping and

Iron Horse produces sparklers that make history.

contemporary architecture, but the terms also apply to the wine-making philosophy. Expect handcrafted Chardonnays and Pinot Noirs with long, luxurious finishes, especially on the Pinots. The attention to refinement and detail extends to the tasting room, where well-informed pourers serve patrons enjoying garden and vineyard views through two-story windows. Consistently performing well is the Quail Hill Pinot Noir, a blend of some or all of the 14 Pinot Noir clones grown in the vineyard outside. Also exceptional are the Pinnacle Tier, a Chardonnay (La Sereinité) and three Pinot Noirs (Five Sisters, Anisya's Blend, and Lynn's Blend). Most wines can be bought only by belonging to the allocation list or at the winery, which offers seasonal food-and-wine pairings. Tastings are by appointment only. ⊠ *3909 Frei Rd.* ⊹ *Off Hwy. 116* ☎ *707/829-3374* ⊕ *www. lynmarestate.com* ✉ *Tastings from $30* ⊙ *Closed Tues.*

MacPhail Wines

WINERY/DISTILLERY | A two-story cascade of crumpled ruby-red Radio Flyer wagons meant to mimic wine pouring out of a bottle grabs immediate attention inside this swank industrial space in The Barlow food, art, and wine complex. Consulting winemaker Matt Courtney, who also makes the wines at Arista, crafts the lineup of bright, classy Pinots, no two tasting alike. The grapes come from vineyards that include Mendocino County's Anderson Valley and several prime Sonoma County appellations. The winery also makes Chardonnay and rosé (of Pinot Noir, of course). ⊠ *The Barlow, 6761 McKinley St.* ⊹ *Off Morris St.* ☎ *707/824-8400* ⊕ *macphailwine.com* ✉ *Tastings from $20* ⊙ *Closed Tues.*

★ Merry Edwards Winery

WINERY/DISTILLERY | Winemaker Merry Edwards has long described the Russian River Valley as "the epicenter of great Pinot Noir," and the winery that bears her name produces single-vineyard and blended wines that express the unique characteristics of the soils, climates, and grape clones from which they derive. (Edwards's research into Pinot Noir clones has been so extensive that one was named after her.) Edwards preferred the Russian River as a growing site, believing that the warmer-than-average daytime temperatures encouraged more intense fruit, with the evening fogs mitigating the extra heat's potential adverse effects. The winery also makes a Sauvignon Blanc that's lightly aged in old oak. Tastings end, rather than begin, with this singular white wine so as not to distract guests' palates from the Pinot Noirs. ⊠ 2959 Gravenstein Hwy. N/Hwy. 116 ✛ Near Oak Grove Ave. ☎ 707/823–7466, 888/388 9050 ⊕ www.merryedwards. com ☒ Tastings free (call winery to confirm).

Patrick Amiot Junk Art

PUBLIC ART | The whimsical sculptures of local junk artist Patrick Amiot and his wife, Brigitte Laurent (he creates them, she paints them), can be seen all over Sonoma County, but you can see many works on **Florence Avenue** three blocks west of Main Street. Amiot reclaims old car parts, abandoned appliances, and the like, refashioning them into everything from pigs, dogs, and people to mermaids and Godzilla. ⊠ Sebastopol ✛ Florence Ave. between Bodega Ave. (Hwy. 12) and Healdsburg Ave. ☎ 707/824–9388 ⊕ www.patrickamiot.com.

Paul Hobbs Winery

WINERY/DISTILLERY | Major wine critics routinely bestow high-90s scores on the Chardonnays, Pinot Noirs, Cabernet Sauvignons, and a Syrah produced at this appointment-only winery set amid gently rolling vineyards in northwestern Sebastopol. Owner-winemaker Paul Hobbs's university thesis investigated the flavors that result from various oak-barrel toasting levels, and he continued his education—in both vineyard management and wine making—at the Robert Mondavi Winery, Opus One, and other

storied establishments before striking out on his own in 1991. Tastings take place in a space designed by winery specialist Howard Backen's architectural firm. Guests on a Signature Tasting visit the winery and sip several wines; the Vineyard Designate Experience includes the tour plus small bites paired with limited-edition single-vineyard wines. ⊠ 3355 Gravenstein Hwy. N ✛ Near Holt Rd. ☎ 707/824–9879 ⊕ www.paulhobbswinery.com ☒ Tastings from $65 ⦾ Closed weekends and holidays.

Red Car Wines

WINERY/DISTILLERY | Some movie folks started Red Car, naming it for Los Angeles's old streetcars and producing wines out of Southern California before moving to Sonoma County a decade ago. Coastal, cool-climate wines are the specialty. Wines that consistently shine include the Ritchie Vineyard Chardonnay, the rosé of Pinot Noir, the Platt Vineyard Pinot Noir, and the Estate Vineyard Pinot Noir and Syrah. The tasting room's hip rustic-casual decor pairs well with the upbeat rock playlist and the hosts' low-key vibe. On a sunny afternoon the shaded outdoor patio is the place to be. The tour (reservation required) is an excursion to a vineyard in Freestone, 8 or so miles away. ■TIP➔ **Red Car shares a parking lot with Dutton-Goldfield, making this a good two-for-one stop.** ⊠ 8400 Graton Rd. ✛ At Gravenstein Hwy. (Hwy. 116) ☎ 707/829–8500 ⊕ redcarwine.com ☒ Tastings from $20, tour $40.

🍴 Restaurants

Fork Roadhouse

$$$ | AMERICAN | Pork-belly-and-fried-egg tacos, polenta bowls with chèvre and a poached egg, and thick French toast served with seasonal fruit, whipped cream, and maple syrup draw the breakfast crowd to this cheerful, low-slung, multiroom haven 3 miles west of downtown Sebastopol. Salads, grass-fed burgers, and fried-chicken sandwiches

are lunchtime lures, with artichoke, fennel, and leek ragout and slow-roasted and grilled baby back ribs typical dinner fare. **Known for:** many organic ingredients; alfresco dining on creek-side patio; those groovy West County locals. $ *Average main: $24 ⊠ 9890 Bodega Hwy./Hwy. 12 ✛ Near Montgomery Rd.* ☎ *707/634-7575* ⊕ *www.forkcatering.com/the-roadhouse* ⊗ *Closed Mon.–Wed.*

Gravenstein Grill

$$$ | **MODERN AMERICAN** | Tablecloths, cut flowers, and the soft glow of liquid paraffin candles and strings of lights overhead draw most diners to this casual-elegant restaurant's expansive outdoor patio. For meals served indoors or out, chef Bob Simontacchi relies on mostly local sources for the organic, sustainable ingredients in dishes like vegan coconut curry, Liberty duck confit, wild-caught petrale sole, and a town-fave burger with white-cheddar pimento cheese. **Known for:** Monday–Thursday prix-fixe menu; Sonoma-centric wine list; weekend brunch's eggs Florentine, brioche French toast. $ *Average main: $28 ⊠ 8050 Bodega Ave.* ✛ *At Pleasant Hill Ave. N* ☎ *707/634-6142* ⊕ *www.gravensteingrill. com.*

Handline Coastal California

$ | **MODERN AMERICAN** |**FAMILY** | Lowell Sheldon and Natalie Goble, who also run a fine-dining establishment (Lowell's) a mile away, converted Sebastopol's former Foster's Freeze location into a 21st-century fast-food palace that won design awards for its rusted-steel frame and translucent panel-like windows. Their menu, a paean to coastal California cuisine, includes oysters raw and grilled, fish tacos, ceviches, tostadas, three burgers (beef, vegetarian, and fish), and, honoring the location's previous incarnation, chocolate and vanilla soft-serve ice cream for dessert. **Known for:** upscale comfort food; outdoor patio; sustainable seafood and other ingredients. $ *Average main: $14 ⊠ 935 Gravenstein Hwy.*

S ✛ *Near Hutchins Ave.* ☎ *707/827–3744* ⊕ *www.handline.com.*

★ Lowell's

$$ | **MODERN AMERICAN** | Occupying a light-filled storefront with a small dining room and open kitchen (there's also seating in an adjoining, plant-filled courtyard), this downtown Sebastopol restaurant whose owners grow much of its produce takes its inspiration from classic rustic-Italian cuisine. Juxtaposing flavors is the chef's strong suit—local Gravenstein apples in a recent pork-belly starter, for instance, provided sweetness and mild acidity that heightened the savory notes of the accompanying tomatillo sauce. **Known for:** pasta made in-house daily; "Gemischter" salad with spicy greens and goat cheese; macro bowls and vegan pizza variations. $ *Average main: $22 ⊠ 7385 Healdsburg Ave.* ✛ *At Florence Ave.* ☎ *707/829–1077* ⊕ *lowellssebastopol.com.*

★ Pascaline Patisserie & Café

$ | **CAFÉ** | Delicate pastries and quiches, croques monsieur, and other bistro bites have made locals as passionate about this Highway 116 café as its executive and pastry chefs, who previously worked at prestigious establishments in Paris, San Francisco, and elsewhere, are about their cuisine and hospitality. Pastel-green walls, a wood-burning stove, and tables from unpainted reclaimed wood lend the small interior space a French-country feel; on sunny days there's more seating on a wooden deck outside. **Known for:** kouign amann (a Breton pastry); French-style coffee; joyous atmosphere. $ *Average main: $11 ⊠ 4552 Gravenstein Hwy. N* ✛ *Almost to Forestville* ☎ *707/823–3122* ⊕ *pascalinepatisserieandcafe.com* ⊗ *No dinner.*

★ Ramen Gaijin

$$ | **JAPANESE** | Inside a tall-ceilinged, brick-walled, vaguely industrial-looking space with reclaimed wood from a coastal building backing the bar, the chefs in Ramen Gaijin's turn out richly flavored ramen bowls brimming with

The views, wine, and architecture make a visit to Paul Hobbs Winery special.

crispy pork belly, woodear mushrooms, seaweed, and other well-proportioned ingredients. *Izakaya* (Japanese pub grub) dishes like *donburi* (meat and vegetables over rice) are another specialty, like the ramen made from mostly local proteins and produce. **Known for:** craft cocktails by renowned mixologist Scott Beattie, Japanese whiskeys; gluten-free, vegetarian dishes; pickle, karage (fried-chicken thigh), and other small plates. $ *Average main: $17* ✉ *6948 Sebastopol Ave.* ✛ *Near Main St.* ☎ *707/827–3609* ⊕ *www.ramengaijin.com* ⊗ *Closed Sun. and Mon.*

Screaming Mimi's

$ | **AMERICAN** |**FAMILY** | Pink on the outside, with tutti-frutti walls on the inside and colorful chairs painted by a local artist, Sebastopol's hands-down favorite for all-natural ice cream and sorbet often appears in feature stories listing the nation's best shops. Mimi's Mud (espresso-ice-cream cookies, chocolate, and homemade fudge) and strawberry made from local fruit are among the popular ice creams, with grapefruit Campari, lemon, and raspberry among the top palate-cleansing sorbets. **Known for:** egg creams and ice-cream floats; espresso coffee drinks; seasonal blackberry fudge. $ *Average main: $5* ✉ *6902 Sebastopol Ave./Hwy. 12* ✛ *At Petaluma Ave./Hwy. 116* ☎ *707/823–5902* ⊕ *www.screamin-mimisicecream.com.*

Zazu Kitchen + Farm

$$$ | **MODERN AMERICAN** | Raised gardens on Zazu's patio supply produce and spices for chef Duskie Estes's pig-centric cuisine, which incorporates salumi by her husband and co-owner, John Stewart, along with ingredients the two farm or raise. When lifted, the vast industrial-looking space's garagelike doors admit a breeze; indoors or out, make a meal of small plates like Korean chicken wings and fried oysters or sample a few appetizers before moving on to a bacon burger or porcini-noodle-and-mushroom stroganoff. **Known for:** chef a Food Network regular; creative craft cocktails; ethical protein sourcing. $ *Average main:*

$27 ✉ The Barlow, 6770 McKinley St., No. 150 ✣ Off Morris St. ☎ 707/523–4814 🌐 www.zazukitchen.com ⏲ Closed Tues. No lunch Mon., Wed., and Thurs.

Hotels

★ Avalon Luxury Inn

$$$ | **B&B/INN** | Set amid redwoods and impeccably furnished, the Tudor-style Avalon provides romance, luxury, and seclusion in a creek-side setting. **Pros:** lavish breakfasts; woodsy, romantic setting; fireplaces in all rooms. **Cons:** two-person maximum occupancy; two-night minimum for some stays; atmosphere may be too low-key for some. *[$] Rooms from: $319 ✉ 11910 Graton Rd. ☎ 707/824–0880 🌐 avalonluxuryinn.com 🛏 3 rooms 🍴 Breakfast.*

Fairfield Inn & Suites Santa Rosa Sebastopol

$ | **HOTEL** | A safe West County bet that often has availability when other inns and hotels are full, the three-story Fairfield, a bit south of Sebastopol's core, is a competently run chain hotel. **Pros:** convenient to West County wineries and Santa Rosa; good-size outdoor pool and spa; frequent Internet specials. **Cons:** hardly a unique Wine Country experience; occasional service letdowns; sometimes overpriced during high season. *[$] Rooms from: $195 ✉ 1101 Gravenstein Hwy. S ☎ 707/829–6677 🌐 www.winecountryhi.com 🛏 82 rooms 🍴 Breakfast.*

Graton

½ mile west of Sebastopol.

Mere steps from Sebastopol and not far from Occidental, the tiny hamlet of Graton has a one-block main drag one can stroll in two minutes—although it's possible to while away a few hours at the block's artist-run gallery, nostalgia-inducing antiques shop, tasting rooms, and two notably fine restaurants. For more strolling, you can hit the local hiking trail.

GETTING HERE AND AROUND

To reach Graton from Sebastopol, head west from Highway 116 a half-mile on Graton Road. Sonoma County Transit Bus 20 passes through Graton.

Sights

Bowman Cellars

WINERY/DISTILLERY | Winemaker Alex Bowman learned his craft as a lad, making hobby wines with his father, an electrical contractor with deep West County roots. By his late 20s the wine-making bug had bitten Alex hard, inspiring him to make wines "for real." His debut wine won a double-gold ribbon at the local county fair, prompting him to draw on the experience of several wine-industry relatives to establish Bowman Cellars with his wife, Katie. The two pour their wines in a rustic-casual tasting room fronted by a sunny patio twice as large and, on sunny weekends, thrice as crowded. Alex shows a light but knowing touch with Russian River Valley Chardonnay and Pinot Noir, the winery's two stars. **■ TIP→ The while-it-lasts Nosh menu includes items like local cheeses, gourmet potato chips, and caprese salad.** *✉ 9010 Graton Rd. ✣ At Edison St. ☎ 707/827–3391 🌐 bowmancellars.com 🍷 Tasting $15 ⏲ Closed Mon.–Wed.*

Paul Mathew Vineyards

WINERY/DISTILLERY | With experience that includes stints as a winery tour guide, cellar rat, sales rep, vineyard developer, and finally winemaker, owner Mat Gustafson of Paul Mathew Vineyards knows how to make and market his single-vineyard Pinot Noirs and other wines. Gustafson specializes in spare, low-alcohol, food-friendly Russian River Valley Pinots and makes Chardonnay, Gewürztraminer, and Viognier whites along with Cabernet Franc and Syrah. On a hot summer day his rosé of Pinot Noir makes for delightful sipping in the picnic area behind the tasting room, which occupies a century-old Edwardian storefront. ✉ 9060 Graton Rd. ✥ At Ross Rd. ☎ 707/861–9729 🌐 www.paulmathewvineyards.com 🍷 Tasting $15 ⏲ Closed Mon.–Wed.

West County Regional Trail

TRAIL | Oaks, poplars, and other trees shade this trail that winds north from Graton through land once used by the local railway line. In summer you'll see plenty of blackberries (and sometimes local pickers) along the 3-mile stretch between Graton and Forestville. The path is so quiet it's hard to believe that nearby in 1905 the Battle of Sebastopol Road raged between crews of two rival rail lines. ■ **TIP→ There's free trailhead parking behind the old Graton Fire Station.** ✉ *Graton* ✥ *Entrance off Graton just west of Ross Rd.* ☎ *707/565–2041* 🌐 *parks.sonomacounty.ca.gov* 🎟 *Free.*

🍴 Restaurants

★ Underwood Bar & Bistro

$$$ | MODERN AMERICAN | Run by the same people who operate the Willow Wood Market Cafe across the street, this restaurant with a Continental atmosphere has a seasonal menu based on smaller and larger dishes. The petite offerings might include anything from hoisin-glazed ribs and seared tuna crudo to Chinese broccoli; depending on the season, osso buco, mushroom-leek ravioli, or Provençal fish stew might be among the entrées. **Known for:** varied menu; old-style cocktails, ports, and cognacs; Cobb salad, Thai curry prawns, and sandwiches for lunch. [$] *Average main: $27* ✉ *9113 Graton Rd.* ✥ *About ½ mile west of Hwy. 116* ☎ *707/823–7023* 🌐 *www.underwoodgraton.com* ⏲ *Closed Mon. No lunch Sun.*

Willow Wood Market Cafe

$$ | MODERN AMERICAN | This café across the street from the Underwood Bar & Bistro serves simple, tasty soups, salads, and sandwiches. Brunch is elaborate, but even breakfast—specialties include hot, creamy polenta and house-made granola—is modern-American down-home solid. **Known for:** casual setting; outdoor back patio; ragouts on polenta. [$] *Average main: $18* ✉ *9020 Graton Rd.* ✥ *About ½ mile west of Hwy. 116* ☎ *707/823–0233* 🌐 *willowwoodgraton.com* ⏲ *No dinner Sun.*

Santa Rosa

6 miles east of Sebastopol; 55 miles north of San Francisco.

Urban Santa Rosa isn't as popular with tourists as many Wine Country destinations—which isn't surprising, seeing as there are more office parks than wineries within its limits. Nevertheless, this hardworking town is home to a couple of interesting cultural offerings and a few noteworthy restaurants and vineyards. The city's chain motels and hotels can be handy if you're finding that everything else is booked up, especially since Santa Rosa is roughly equidistant from Sonoma, Healdsburg, and the western Russian River Valley, three of Sonoma County's most popular wine-tasting destinations.

GETTING HERE AND AROUND

To get to Santa Rosa from Sebastopol, drive east on Highway 12. From San Francisco, cross the Golden Gate Bridge and continue north on U.S. 101. Santa Rosa's hotels, restaurants, and wineries are spread over a wide area; factor in extra time when driving around the city, especially during morning and evening rush hour. To get here from downtown San Francisco, take Golden Gate Transit Bus 101. Several Sonoma County Transit buses serve the city and surrounding area.

VISITOR INFORMATION

Visit Santa Rosa

✉ *9 4th St.* ✛ *At Wilson St.* ☎ *800/404–7673* ⊕ *visitsantarosa.com.*

 Sights

Balletto Vineyards

WINERY/DISTILLERY | A few decades ago Balletto was known for quality produce more than for grapes, but the new millennium saw vineyards emerge as the core business. About 90% of the fruit from the family's 650-plus acres goes to other wineries, with the remainder destined for Balletto's estate wines. The house style is light on the oak, high in acidity, and low in alcohol content, a combination that yields exceptionally food-friendly wines. On a hot summer day, sipping a Pinot Gris, rosé of Pinot Noir, or brut rosé sparkler on the outdoor patio can feel transcendent, but the superstars are the Chardonnays and Pinot Noirs. ■ **TIP➜ Look for the Teresa's unoaked and Cider Ridge Chardonnays and the Burnside Road, Sexton Hill, and Winery Block Pinots, but all the wines are exemplary—and, like the tastings, reasonably priced.** ✉ *5700 Occidental Rd.* ✛ *2½ miles west of Hwy. 12* ☎ *707/568–2455* ⊕ *www.ballettovineyards.com* 🍷 *Tasting $10.*

★ Benovia Winery

WINERY/DISTILLERY | Winemaker Mike Sullivan's nuanced Chardonnays and Pinot Noirs would taste marvelous even in a toolshed, but guests to Benovia's subtly chic ranch house will never know. Appointment-only tastings of his critically acclaimed wines take place by the brown-hued space's fireplace, at a few tables, or on the open-air patio. From any vantage point, the views of the estate Martaella Vineyard all the way to Napa's Mt. St. Helena draw the eye. Opting for a minimalistic approach in two Chardonnays from Martinelli family grapes, Sullivan allows the minerality of the Three Sisters Vineyard wine, from the coastal Fort Ross–Seaview AVA, to lead but lets a hint of California ripeness express itself in the Zio Tony from the warmer Russian River Valley. The same scenario plays out with the estate Tilton Hill and Cohn Pinot Noirs, the former from cooler Freestone, the latter from fruit grown farther inland. ✉ *3339 Hartman La.* ✛ *Off Piner Rd.* ☎ *707/921–1040* ⊕ *benoviawinery.com* 🍷 *Tastings $30.*

Carol Shelton Wines

WINERY/DISTILLERY | It's winemaker Carol Shelton's motto that great wines start in the vineyard, but you won't see any grapevines outside her winery—it's in an industrial park 4 miles north of downtown Santa Rosa. What you will find, and experience, are well-priced Zinfandels from grapes grown in vineyards Shelton, ever the viticultural sleuth, locates from Mendocino to Southern California's Cucamonga Valley. With coastal, hillside, valley, inland, and desert's-edge fruit the Zins collectively reveal the range and complexity of this varietal that so arouses Shelton's passion. Although Zinfandel gets most of the attention, Shelton also makes Cabernet Sauvignon, Carignane, and Petite Sirah reds, and whites that include Chardonnay, Viognier, and the Rhône-style Coquille Blanc blend. ✉ *3354-B Coffey La.* ✛ *Off Piner Rd.* ☎ *707/575–3441* ⊕ *www.carolshelton.com* 🍷 *Tasting $10.*

Charles M. Schulz Museum

MUSEUM | **FAMILY** | Fans of Snoopy and Charlie Brown will love this museum dedicated to the late Charles M. Schulz, who lived his last three decades in Santa Rosa. Permanent installations include a re-creation of the cartoonist's studio, and temporary exhibits often focus on a particular theme in his work. ■ **TIP➜ Children and adults can take a stab at creating cartoons in the Education Room.** ✉ *2301 Hardies La.* ✛ *At W. Steele La.* ☎ *707/579–4452* ⊕ *www.schulzmuseum.org* 🍷 *$12* ☉ *Closed Tues. early Sept.–late May.*

DeLoach Vineyards

WINERY/DISTILLERY | Best known for its Russian River Valley Pinot Noirs, DeLoach also produces Chardonnays, old-vine Zinfandels, and a few other wines. Some of the reds are made using open-top wood fermentation vats that have been used in France for centuries to intensify a wine's flavor. Tours focus on these and other wine-making techniques and include a stroll through certified biodynamic and organic gardens and vineyards. You can also take a wine-blending seminar, compare California and French Chardonnays and Pinot Noirs, or (depending on the time of year) taste Pinots by a fireplace or enjoy a gourmet picnic. Tours and some tastings are by appointment. ■TIP→ The sparklers and still wines of the affiliated JCB label are poured in a separate on-site tasting room and a swank space (320 Center Street) in Healdsburg. ⊠ 1791 Olivet Rd. ⊹ Off Guerneville Rd. ☎ 707/526–9111 ⊕ www.deloachvineyards.com ⧉ Tastings from $25, tour and tasting $50.

Inman Family Wines

WINERY/DISTILLERY | "The winemaker is in," reads a driveway sign when owner Kathleen Inman, who crafts her winery's Chardonnay, Pinot Noir, and other western Russian River Valley wines, is present. She's often around, and it's an extra treat to learn directly from the source about her farming, fermenting, and aging methods. Her restrained, balanced wines complement sophisticated cuisine so well that top-tier restaurants include them on their lists. Inman shows equal finesse with rosé of Pinot Noir, sparkling wines, and Pinot Gris. Her zeal to recycle is in evidence everywhere, most conspicuously in the tasting room, where redwood reclaimed from an on-site barn was incorporated into the design, and crushed wine-bottle glass was fashioned into the bar. Tastings, some held on an outdoor patio, are by appointment only. ⊠ 3900 Piner Rd. ⊹ At Olivet Rd. ☎ 707/293–9576 ⊕ www.inmanfamilywines.com ⧉ Tastings from $20.

La Crema Estate at Saralee's Vineyard

WINERY/DISTILLERY | The high-profile brand's multistory tasting space occupies a restored early-1900s redwood barn used over the years for hops, hay storage, and as a stable. With its cool Russian River Valley maritime climate, the celebrated Saralee's Vineyard, named for a former owner, fits the preferred La Crema profile for growing Chardonnay and Pinot Noir. You can sample wines from set flights, or staffers will customize one based on your preferences. Seated private Nine Barrel tastings of the best wines require reservations, as does the golf cart tour of the property and its vines, lake, and wildlife. ■TIP→ On sunny days the barn's decks and patio and the nearby Richard's Grove, with its broad lawn and diverse foliage, attract much attention. ⊠ 3575 Slusser Rd., Windsor ⊹ ¾ mile north of River Rd. ☎ 707/525–6200 ⊕ www.lacrema.com ⧉ Tastings from $15, tour $65.

Luther Burbank Home & Gardens

GARDEN | Renowned horticulturist Luther Burbank lived and worked on these grounds and made great advances using the modern techniques of selection and hybridization. The 1.6-acre garden and greenhouse showcase the results of some of Burbank's experiments to develop spineless cactus and such flowers as the Shasta daisy. ■TIP→ Use your cell phone on a free self-guided garden tour, or from April through October take a docent-led tour (required to see the house). ⊠ 204 Santa Rosa Ave. ⊹ At Sonoma Ave. ☎ 707/524–5445 ⊕ www.lutherburbank.org ⧉ Gardens free, tour $10 ⊙ No house tours Nov.–Mar.

★ Martinelli Winery

WINERY/DISTILLERY | In a century-old hop barn with the telltale triple towers, Martinelli has the feel of a traditional country store, but the sophisticated wines made here are anything but old-fashioned. The winery's reputation rests on its complex Pinot Noirs, Syrahs, and Zinfandels,

A familiar-looking hat provides shade at the Charles M. Schulz Museum.

including the Jackass Hill Vineyard Zin, made with grapes from 130-year-old vines. Noted winemaker Helen Turley set the Martinelli style—fruit-forward, easy on the oak, reined-in tannins—in the 1990s, and the current team continues this approach. You can sample current releases at a walk-in tasting at the bar or reserve space a couple of days ahead for a seated tasting on the vineyard-view terrace. Rarer and top-rated vintages are poured at appointment-only sessions. ✉ *3360 River Rd., Windsor ✢ East of Olivet Rd.* ☎ *707/525–0570, 800/346–1627* ⊕ *www.martinelliwinery.com* ✉ *Tastings from $25.*

Matanzas Creek Winery

WINERY/DISTILLERY | The visitor center at Matanzas Creek sets itself apart with an understated Japanese aesthetic, extending to a tranquil fountain, a koi pond, and a vast field of lavender. The winery makes Sauvignon Blanc, Chardonnay, Merlot, Pinot Noir, and Cabernet Sauvignon under the Matanzas Creek name, and three equally well-regarded wines—a Bordeaux red blend, a Chardonnay, and a Sauvignon Blanc—bearing the Journey label. No reservation is required for the pairing of small-lot wines and local artisanal cheeses, offered in the tasting room. The winery encourages guests to enjoy a picnic on the property with a bottle or glass of Matanzas wine. ■ **TIP➜ An ideal time to visit is in May and June, when lavender perfumes the air.** ✉ *6097 Bennett Valley Rd.* ☎ *707/528–6464, 800/590–6464* ⊕ *www.matanzascreek. com* ✉ *Tastings from $15.*

Paradise Ridge Winery

WINERY/DISTILLERY | The winery lost its tasting room and other buildings in the October 2017 Wine Country wildfires but is hoping to reopen by late 2019. During reconstruction, occasional events will take place on the 156-acre estate, most notably popular parties on summer Wednesday evenings, when locals and tourists sip wine by the glass or bottle, catch the sunset, listen to local bands, and sample food from area vendors. Until the estate hospitality center reopens (and even afterward), wine tastings will take place at Paradise Ridge's longtime tasting room in Kenwood. ✉ *4545 Thomas Lake Harris Dr.* ✣ *Off Fountaingrove Pkwy.* ☎ *707/528–9463* 🌐 *www.prwinery.com* 🕒 *Closed except for occasional events (call or check website).*

Railroad Square Historic District

HISTORIC SITE | The location of Santa Rosa's former Northwestern Pacific Railroad depot—built in 1903 by Italian stonemasons and immortalized in Alfred Hitchcock's coolly sinister 1943 film *Shadow of a Doubt*—provides the name for this revitalized neighborhood west of U.S. 101. The depot is now a visitors center, and 4th Street between Wilson and Davis Streets contains restaurants, bars, and antiques and thrift shops worth checking out, as do nearby lanes. ✉ *California Welcome Center, 9 4th St.* ✣ *At Wilson St.* ☎ *707/577–8674* 🌐 *visitsantarosa.com/welcome-center.*

Safari West

NATURE PRESERVE | **FAMILY** | An unexpected bit of wilderness in the Wine Country, this preserve with African wildlife covers 400 acres. Begin your visit with a stroll around enclosures housing lemurs, cheetahs, giraffes, and rare birds like the brightly colored scarlet ibis. Next, climb with your guide onto open-air vehicles that spend about two hours combing the expansive property, where more than 80 species—including gazelles, cape buffalo, antelope, wildebeests, and zebras—inhabit the hillsides. **■ TIP→ If you'd like to extend your stay, lodging in swank Botswana-made tent cabins is available.** ✉ *3115 Porter Creek Rd.* ✣ *Off Mark West Springs Rd.* ☎ *707/579–2551, 800/616–2695* 🌐 *www.safariwest.com* 🎟 *From $83.*

SOFA Santa Rosa Arts District

NEIGHBORHOOD | Street murals, galleries, and shops carrying works by local artisans make this compact enclave worth the half-mile stroll from the Railroad Square Historic District. The arts district takes its name from its main drag, South A Street. Most of the murals can be found on Art Alley, which starts just south of the **Santa Rosa Arts Center** exhibition space at 312 South A Street. Be sure to pop into the well-curated **JaM JAr** shop at No. 320 to see crafts, vintage items, and artworks, including paintings by one owner and jewelry by the other. ✉ *S. A St. and Sebastopol Ave.* ☎ *707/526–0135 arts center* 🌐 *santarosaartscenter.org.*

🍴 Restaurants

Bird & The Bottle

$$$ | **ECLECTIC** | The owners of Willi's Seafood, Bravas Bar de Tapas, and other Sonoma County favorites operate this "modern tavern" serving global bar bites and comfort food in a multiroom, nostalgic yet contemporary space that evokes home, hearth, and good cheer. Shrimp wontons, chicken-skin cracklings, fried cheddar-cheese curds, matzo-ball soup, Cobb salad, crispy pork riblets, and skirt steak all go well with the astute "Booze" menu of cocktails, wines, and artisanal beers, ciders, and spirits. **Known for:** small bites, full meals; happy hour (Sunday–Thursday); neighborhood feel. [$] *Average main: $26* ✉ *1055 4th St.* ✣ *Near College Ave.* ☎ *707/568–4000* 🌐 *birdandthebottle.com.*

★ Bistro 29

$$$ | **FRENCH** | Chef Brian Anderson prepares steak frites, cassoulet, duck confit, and sautéed fish with precision at his perky downtown restaurant—rich-red walls, white tile floors, and butcher paper atop linen tablecloths set the mood—but the mixed-greens salad with Dijon vinaigrette best illustrates his understated approach: its local produce bursts with freshness, and the dressing delicately balances its savory and acidic components. Start with escargots or bay scallops with béchamel, finishing with beignets or orange crème brûlée for dessert. **Known for:** midweek prix-fixe menu; sweet and savory crepes; beer selection,

Luther Burbank Home and Gardens showcases the results of its namesake's many botanical experiments.

Sonoma County and French wines.
$ *Average main: $27* ⊠ *620 5th St.*
⊹ *Near Mendocino Ave.* ☎ *707/546–2929*
⊕ *www.bistro29.com* ⊗ *Closed Sun. and Mon. No lunch Sat.*

★ Bollywood Bar & Clay Oven

$$ | INDIAN | Although its cinematic name conjures images of glitz and excess, this exposed-brick downtown Santa Rosa restaurant surprises patrons with subtly spiced dishes and artisanal cocktails so attuned to the cuisine you might opt for a different one with each course instead of wine or beer. The wide-ranging menu includes everything from steamed green millet stuffed with tiny beet cubes to pork-belly vindaloo and other voluptuous curries. **Known for:** clay-oven entrées and naan; family-style tasting menu; vegetarian, vegan, and gluten-free options.
$ *Average main: $17* ⊠ *535 4th St.* ⊹ *At Old Courthouse Sq.* ☎ *707/535–0700*
⊕ *bollywoodbar.net* ⊗ *No lunch.*

Gerard's Paella y Tapas

$ | SPANISH | Gregarious, ubiquitous local caterer Gerard Nebesky boosted his culinary fortunes besting celeb chef Bobby Flay in a 2008 paella "Throwdown," and his fame may surge yet again following the 2019 release of the Amy Poehler–Tina Fey pic *Wine Country,* with a character based on him. At his down-to-earth, order-at-the-counter restaurant, a sort of Chipotle of paella, Gerard serves moist and delectable versions of that dish plus small bites. **Known for:** beer, wine, "shrub" vinegar sodas; Spanish baguette sandwiches; papas bravas (crispy potatoes). $ *Average main: $13*
⊠ *701 4th St.* ⊹ *At D St.* ☎ *707/708–8686*
⊕ *www.gerardspaella.com/restaurant.*

Rosso Pizzeria & Wine Bar

$$ | PIZZA | Ask local wine pourers where to get the best pizza, and they'll often recommend lively Rosso, a sprawling strip-mall restaurant whose chefs hold center stage in the large open kitchen. Two perennial Neapolitan-style pizza favorites are the Moto Guzzi, with house-smoked mozzarella and spicy Caggiano sausage, and the Funghi di Limone, with oven-roasted mixed mushrooms and

Taleggio and fontina cheese. **Known for:** diverse California wine selection; crispy double-fried chicken with pancetta bits and sweet-and-sour sauce; salads and gluten-free dishes. [$] *Average main: $19* ✉ *Creekside Center, 53 Montgomery Dr.* ✣ *At Brookwood Ave.* ☎ *707/544–3221* 🌐 *www.rossopizzeria.com.*

Sazon Peruvian Cuisine

$$$ | **PERUVIAN** | Join Peruvian locals enjoying a taste of back home at this strip-mall restaurant whose name means "flavor" or "seasoning." Several ceviche appetizers—including one with ponzu sauce for a Japanese twist—show the range of tastes the lead chef and owner, José Navarro, conjures up, as does the *arroz con mariscos,* a velvety, turmeric-laced seafood paella. **Known for:** skillfully spiced Peruvian food; small and large plates to share family-style; deli annex with salads, sandwiches to stay or go. [$] *Average main: $24* ✉ *1129 Sebastopol Rd.* ✣ *At Roseland Ave.* ☎ *707/523–4346* 🌐 *www.sazonsr.com.*

SEA Thai Bistro

$$ | **ASIAN** | The initials in this upscale strip-mall bistro's name stand for "Southeast Asian," reflecting the cuisines beyond Thailand's the chef prepares. Glass chandeliers of jellyfish and schools of fish glow softly above patrons who sit at dark-wood tables or the rectangular onyx bar, enjoying comfort food like spring rolls and "street fair" rice noodles with chicken, bacon, and vegetables before diversely spiced entrées. **Known for:** culinary mashups like Thai bruschetta with prawns, avocado, and peanut sauce; many seafood dishes; worthy beer and wine list. [$] *Average main: $21* ✉ *2350 Midway Dr.* ✣ *At Farmers La.* ☎ *707/528–8333* 🌐 *www.seathaibistrobar.com.*

★ **The Spinster Sisters**

$$$ | **MODERN AMERICAN** | Modern, well-sourced variations on eggs Benedict and other standards are served at this concrete-and-glass hot spot's weekday breakfast and weekend brunch. Lunch might bring carrot soup, wilted kale salad, or a *banh mi* sandwich, with dinner consisting of shareable bites and small and large plates—think kimchi-and-bacon deviled eggs, vegetable *fritto misto,* and grilled hanger steak. **Known for:** local and international wines; happy hour (Tuesday–Friday 4 pm–6 pm) small bites; horseshoe-shaped bar a good perch for dining single, picking up gossip. [$] *Average main: $26* ✉ *401 S. A St.* ✣ *At Sebastopol Ave.* ☎ *707/528–7100* 🌐 *thespinstersisters.com* 🕒 *No dinner Sun. and Mon.*

Stark's Steak & Seafood

$$$$ | **STEAKHOUSE** | The low lighting, well-spaced tables, and gas fireplaces at Stark's create a congenial setting for dining on steak, seafood from the raw bar, and sustainable fish. With entrées that include a 20-ounce, dry-aged rib eye and a 32-ounce porterhouse for two, there's not a chance that meat eaters will depart unsated, and nonsteak options such as tamarind barbecue prawns and halibut with cherry-tomato confit surpass those at your average temple to beef. **Known for:** thick steaks; high-quality seafood; steak house atmosphere. [$] *Average main: $34* ✉ *521 Adams St.* ✣ *At 7th St.* ☎ *707/546–5100* 🌐 *www.starkssteakhouse.com* 🕒 *No lunch weekends.*

★ **Walter Hansel Wine & Bistro**

$$$$ | **FRENCH** | Tabletop linens and lights softly twinkling from this ruby-red roadhouse restaurant's low wooden ceiling raise expectations the Parisian-style bistro cuisine consistently exceeds. A starter of cheeses, oyster ceviche, or escargots awakens the palate for entrées like chicken cordon bleu, steak au poivre, or what this restaurant does best: seafood dishes that might include pan-seared scallops or subtly sauced wild Alaskan halibut. **Known for:** romantic setting for classic cuisine; French and California wines; profiteroles with Valrhona chocolate sauce. [$] *Average main: $31* ✉ *3535 Guerneville Rd.* ✣ *At Willowside*

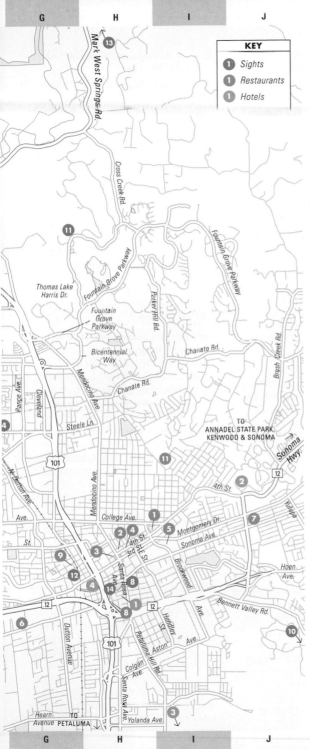

6

Northern Sonoma, Russian River, and West County **SANTA ROSA**

KEY

1	Sights
1	Restaurants
1	Hotels

Sights ▼

1	Balletto Vineyards	**A9**
2	Benovia Winery	**B4**
3	Carol Shelton Wines	**F5**
4	Charles M. Schulz Museum	**F6**
5	DeLoach Vineyards	**A6**
6	Inman Family Wines	**A5**
7	La Crema Estate at Saralee's Vineyard	**A3**
8	Luther Burbank Home & Gardens	**H7**
9	Martinelli Winery	**B3**
10	Matanzas Creek Winery	**J8**
11	Paradise Ridge Winery	**G3**
12	Railroad Square Historic District	**G8**
13	Safari West	**H1**
14	SOFA Santa Rosa Arts District	**H8**

Restaurants ▼

1	Bird & The Bottle	**I7**
2	Bistro 29	**H7**
3	Bollywood Bar & Clay Oven	**H7**
4	Gerard's Paella y Tapas	**H7**
5	Rosso Pizzeria & Wine Bar	**I7**
6	Sazon Peruvian Cuisine	**G8**
7	SEA Thai Bistro	**J7**
8	The Spinster Sisters	**H8**
9	Stark's Steak & Seafood	**G7**
10	Walter Hansel Wine & Bistro	**B6**
11	Willi's Wine Bar	**I6**

Hotels ▼

1	Astro Motel	**H8**
2	Flamingo Conference Resort & Spa	**J6**
3	Gables Wine Country Inn	**I9**
4	Hyatt Regency Sonoma Wine Country	**H8**
5	Vintners Inn	**E3**

Rd., 6 miles northwest of downtown ☎ *707/546–6462* 🌐 *walterhanselbistro.com* 🕑 *Closed Mon. and Tues. No lunch.*

Willi's Wine Bar
$$$ | **ECLECTIC** | Among the few restaurants to perish in the Wine Country's 2017 wildfires, Willi's was slated to reopen in 2019 in a Santa Rosa strip mall, still serving up inventive globe-trotting small plates paired with international wines. Dishes like pork-belly pot stickers represent Asia, with Tunisian roasted local carrots and Moroccan-style lamb chops among the Mediterranean-inspired foods. **Known for:** patio seating; inspired wine selection; 2-ounce pours so you can pair a new wine with each dish. [$] *Average main: $29* ✉ *1612 Terrace Way* ✥ *Near Town and Country Dr.* ☎ *707/526–3096* 🌐 *williswinebar.net.*

Hotels

★ Astro Motel
$ | **HOTEL** | **FAMILY** | The Sixties are back splashier than ever at this tastefully and whimsically restored motel diagonally across from the Luther Burbank Home & Gardens. **Pros:** vintage midcentury-modern furnishings; well-designed rooms; near local arts district. **Cons:** no pool, gym, spa, and other amenities; about a mile from Railroad Square Historic District; surrounding neighborhood mildly scruffy. [$] *Rooms from: $170* ✉ *323 Santa Rosa Ave.* ☎ *707/200–4655* 🌐 *theastro.com* 🛏 *34 rooms* 🍴 *No meals.*

Flamingo Conference Resort & Spa
$ | **HOTEL** | If Don Draper from *Mad Men* popped into this 1950s motel-hotel hybrid 2¼ miles northeast of downtown Santa Rosa, he'd feel right at home. **Pros:** cool pool Jayne Mansfield partied at; retro vibe; two children under 12 stay free in same room as parents. **Cons:** 30-minute walk to downtown; standard rooms can feel cramped; shows its age in some spots. [$] *Rooms from: $169* ✉ *2777 4th St.* ☎ *707/545–8530, 800/848–8300* 🌐 *www.flamingoresort.com* 🛏 *170 rooms* 🍴 *No meals.*

★ Gables Wine Country Inn
$$ | **B&B/INN** | Guests at this circa-1887 Gothic Victorian inn set on 3½ bucolic acres slip back in time inside high-ceilinged, period-decorated pastel-painted rooms, some with four-poster beds and all with comfortable mattresses and high-quality sheets. **Pros:** Victorian style and hospitality; three-course gourmet breakfasts; country vibe yet 4 miles from Railroad Square Historic District. **Cons:** period look may not work for all guests; slightly off the beaten path; weekend minimum-stay requirement April–mid-November. [$] *Rooms from: $209* ✉ *4257 Petaluma Hill Rd.* ☎ *707/585–7777* 🌐 *www.thegablesinn.com* 🛏 *9 rooms* 🍴 *Free Breakfast.*

Hyatt Regency Sonoma Wine Country
$$ | **HOTEL** | Relentlessly corporate but easy on the eyes, the Hyatt wins points for its convenient downtown location, decent-size pool, courteous staff, and arbor-lined sculpture garden. **Pros:** full-service hotel with restaurant, pool, spa, and fitness center; convenient to Railroad Square dining and shopping; frequent online specials. **Cons:** the many events booked here detract from the leisure-traveler experience; corporate feel; may not seem worth it at full price. [$] *Rooms from: $249* ✉ *170 Railroad St.* ☎ *707/284–1234* 🌐 *hyatt.com* 🛏 *253 rooms* 🍴 *No meals.*

Vintners Inn
$$ | **HOTEL** | With a countryside location, a sliver of style, and spacious rooms with comfortable beds, the Vintners Inn further seduces with a slew of amenities and a scenic vineyard landscape. **Pros:** John Ash & Co. restaurant; jogging path through the vineyards; online deals pop up year-round. **Cons:** occasional noise from adjacent events center; trips to downtown Santa Rosa or Healdsburg require a car; pricey on summer and fall weekends. [$] *Rooms from: $295* ✉ *4350*

Matanzas Creek Winery is a star of the tiny Bennett Valley AVA.

Barnes Rd. ☎ 707/575–7350, 800/421–
2584 ⊕ www.vintnersinn.com ➲ 78
rooms ⦿ No meals.

 Nightlife

BREWPUBS

★ **Russian River Brewing Company**
BREWPUBS/BEER GARDENS | It's all about
Belgian-style ales, "aggressively hopped
California ales," and barrel-aged beers at
this famous brewery's Santa Rosa pub.
The legendary lineup includes Pliny the
Elder (and Younger, but only in February),
Blind Pig I.P.A., Supplication sour (aged
12 months in used Pinot Noir barrels),
and many more. ■**TIP→ A second, larger**
location (more seats, more beers) opened
in late 2018 at Conde and Mitchell Lanes
in Windsor. ⊠ 725 4th St. ⊕ Near D St.
☎ 707/545–2337 ⊕ www.russianriver-
brewing.com.

CASINO

Graton Resort & Casino
CASINOS | Slots predominate at this spiffy
casino. Blackjack, baccarat, and a few

other table games are also available.
Dining options include Chinese and pizza
restaurants and a pricey food court. The
resort's hotel has 200 rooms, a Vegaslike
pool area, and a full-service spa. ⊠ 288
Golf Course Dr. W, Rohnert Park ⊕ West
off U.S. 101 ☎ 707/588–7100 ⊕ www.
gratonresortcasino.com.

🎟 **Performing Arts**

Green Music Center
ARTS CENTERS | The center's principal,
acoustically sophisticated Joan and
Sanford I. Weill Hall hosts classical (Santa
Rosa Symphony), jazz (Kenny Barron
Quintet), avant-garde (Kronos Quartet),
and other ensembles, as well as performers from Martha Redbone and Joan Baez
to Ice-T and Joshua Bell. During summer
the hall's back wall opens out for Summer at the Green concerts on a terraced
lawn. The curved walls of the intimate
240-seat Schroeder Hall were designed
to enhance the sounds of the room's
1,248-pipe organ ■**TIP→ If driving,**
park in Lots L–O (included in ticket price).

✉ *Sonoma State University, Rohnert Park Expwy. and Petaluma Hill Blvd., Rohnert Park* ✛ *East off U.S. 101* ☎ *866/955–6040* ⊕ *gmc.sonoma.edu.*

Luther Burbank Center for the Arts

ARTS CENTERS | This cultural hub, configured theater-style or open-floor depending on the performance, books acts and ensembles as varied as Celtic Thunder, Anjelah Johnson, and the risk-taking local theater group Left Edge. ✉ *50 Mark West Springs Rd.* ✛ *East off U.S. 101* ☎ *707/546–3600* ⊕ *www.lutherburbankcenter.org.*

 Activities

Annadel State Park

HIKING/WALKING | More than 40 miles of hiking, mountain biking, and equestrian trails lace this day-use park that swarms with locals in April and May when the wildflowers bloom around Lake Ilsanjo. The rest of the year you can take to the trails or fish for black bass or bluegill (state fishing license required). ✉ *6201 Channel Dr., off Montgomery Dr.* ☎ *707/539–3911* ⊕ *www.parks.ca.gov* 🎫 *$8 per vehicle.*

Getaway Adventures

TOUR—SPORTS | Owner Randy Johnson and his energetic crew lead kayaking excursions down the Russian River and conduct biking and hiking tours to wineries, organic farms, and other locales. ✉ *Santa Rosa* ☎ *707/568–3040, 800/499–2453* ⊕ *www.getawayadventures.com* 🎫 *From $159 for 1-day trip.*

Index

A

Abbot's Passage Supply Co., 152, 156
Acacia House by Chris Cosentino ✕, 127
Accommodations, 33. ⇨ see also Hotels
Acorn Winery, 190, 192
Acres Home and Garden (shop), 131
Acumen Wine Gallery, 73–74
Ad Hoc ✕, 99
Adobe Road Winery, 179
Aerena Galleries & Gardens, 131
Aging, 53, 61
Air travel, 30, 42
Alexander Valley AVA, 188, 214
Alexander Valley Vineyards, 192
Alexander Valley wineries, 190
Alexis Baking Company and Café ✕, 85
All Seasons Bistro ✕, 139
Alley & Craft Distillery, 192
Anaba Wines, 156
Andaz Napa ☲, 89
Angèle ✕, 85
Annadel State Park, 246
Apartment and house rentals, 33
Appellations, 54, 56–57
Napa Valley, 56–57, 71–73
Northern Sonoma County, Russian River, and West County appellations, 188–189, 198, 214, 217, 221
Sonoma Valley, 151
Applewood Inn and Spa ☲, 222
Archer Hotel Napa ☲, 89–90
Arista Winery, 74, 190, 192
Armstrong Redwoods State Natural Reserve, 221
Art galleries. ⇨ see Museums and art galleries
Astro Motel ☲, 244
Artesa Vineyards & Winery, 74
Ashes and Diamonds Winery, 24, 74
Atlas Peak AVA, 73
Auberge du Soleil ☲, 116
Auberge Sonoma ☲, 166
Auction Napa Valley, 43
AutoCamp Russian River ☲, 223
Avalon Luxury Inn ☲, 234

B

B Cellars, 98, 107
B.R. Cohn, 171
B Spa Therapy Center, 104–105
B Wise Vineyards Cellar, 174–175, 177
Baci Café & Wine Bar ✕, 205
Backyard ✕, 220
Balletto Vineyards, 236
Balloon rides, 8
Napa Valley, 66, 93, 106–107, 144

Northern Sonoma County, Russian River, and West County, 213
Balloons Above the Valley, 93
Banshee Wines, 192–193
Bardessono ☲, 103
Barlow, The, 228
Barndiva ✕, 205–206
Barnett Vineyards, 116–117
Barrel fermentation, 61
Bars, 18–19
Baths at Roman Spa, 143
Beaches, 13, 225–226
Bear Republic Brewing Company, 211
Beaulieu Vineyard, 110
Bedrock Wine Co., 156
Beltane Ranch ☲, 174
Bennett Lane Winery, 133
Bennett Valley AVA, 151, 189
Benovia Winery, 236
Benziger Family Winery, 152, 170
Beringer Vineyards, 117
Best Western Dry Creek Inn ☲, 209
Best Western Plus Elm House Inn ☲, 90
Best Western Plus Stevenson Manor ☲, 141
Best Western Sonoma Valley Inn ☲, 166
Bicycling, 13, 30
Napa Valley, 106, 132, 144
Northern Sonoma County, Russian River, and West County, 184, 213
Sonoma Valley, 169, 179, 246
tours, 106, 169
Big Bottom Market ✕, 222
Big Easy, The (music club), 182
Biodynamic farming, 60, 61
Bird & The Bottle ✕, 239
Bistro Don Giovanni ✕, 85
Bistro Jeanty ✕, 99–100
Bistro 29 ✕, 239–240
Black Kite Cellars, 196
Blackbird Inn ☲, 90
Blending, 61
Blue Note Napa (club), 91
Boat travel, 30, 42
Boating, 10, 94, 213, 220, 226, 246
Bodega Bay, 184, 225–226
Bodega Bay Lodge ☲, 226
Bodega Bay Sailing Adventures, 226
Bodega Harbor Inn ☲, 226
Bodega Head, 225
Bollywood Bar & Clay Oven ✕, 240
Books and films about, 26–27
boon eat+drink ✕, 222
Boon Fly Café ✕, 85
boon hotel+spa ☲, 223
Bottega ✕, 100
Bottle aging, 53
BottleRock Napa Valley (festival), 43
Bouchaine Vineyards, 74
Bouchon Bistro ✕, 100
Bounty Hunter Wine Bar & Smokin' BBQ ✕, 85

Bowman Cellars, 234
Boxcar Fried Chicken & Biscuits ✕, 163
Brannan Cottage Inn ☲, 141
Brass Rabbit ✕, 206
Brasswood Bar + Bakery + Kitchen ☲, 107
Bravas Bar de Tapas ✕, 206
Brewsters Beer Garden ✕, 181
Brian Arden Wines, 133–134
Bud break, 57
Buena Vista Winery, 152, 156, 171, 177
Bungalows of Calistoga ☲, 141
Burke's Canoe Trips, 220
Bus travel, 30–31, 42, 69, 149, 187
Buster's Southern BarBeQue & Bakery ✕, 139

C

Ca' Toga Galleria d'Arte, 23, 134
Cade Estate Winery, 117–118
Cadet Wine + Beer Bar, 91
Café Citti ✕, 177 168
Cafe La Haye ✕, 163
Cakebread Cellars, 110
Caldwell Snyder (gallery), 131
California Carnivores (nursery), 229
Calistoga, 66, 132–144
Calistoga AVA, 72
Calistoga Balloons, 144
Calistoga Bikeshop, 144
Calistoga Inn Restaurant & Brewery ✕, 139
Calistoga Motor Lodge ☲, 142
Calistoga Pottery, 143–144
Calistoga Ranch ☲, 142
Camellia Inn ☲, 209
Cameo Cinema, 131
Campo Fina ✕, 206
Canoeing, 10, 220
Canopy tours, 228
Car tours
Napa Valley, 98, 101
Northern Sonoma County, Russian River, and West County, 214
Sonoma Valley, 177
Car travel and rentals, 31, 42, 69–70, 149–150, 187
Carbon dioxide, 54–55
Carneros Resort & Spa ☲, 90
Carol Shelton Wines, 236
Carpe Diem Wine Bar ✕, 85–86
Castello di Amorosa, 134
Catelli's ✕, 214, 216–217
Caymus Vineyards, 110
Central Market ✕, 181
Chalkboard ✕, 206
Charles Krug Winery, 118
Charles M. Schulz Museum, 236
Charmat process, 55
Charter Oak ✕, 127
Château Montelena, 134
Chateau St. Jean, 175
Chateau Sonoma, 168

Children, attractions for, *28*
Chiles Valley AVA, *73*
Christopher Creek Winery, *193*
CIA at Copia, *74–75*
Ciccio ✕, *100–101*
Clif Family Bruschetteria Food Truck ✕, *127*
Clif Family Tasting Room, *118*
Cliff Lede Vineyards, *95*
Clos du Val, *75*
Coast Kitchen ✕, *225*
Coles Chop House ✕, *86*
Compline ✕, *86*
Comstock Wines, *193*
Cook St. Helena ✕, *127*
Coombsville AVA, *72*
Copain Wines, *193*
Copperfield's Books, *92, 211*
Corison Winery, *118*
Cornerstone Sonoma, *156–157*
Costeaux French Bsakery ✕, *206*
Cottage Grove Inn 🛏, *142*
Cottage Inn & Spa 🛏, *166*
Cottages of Napa Valley 🛏, *90*
Cottages on River Road 🛏, *223*
Crocker & Star, *119*
Crocodile French Cuisine ✕, *181*
Cru @ The Annex, *75*
Crush pad, *51*
Culinary Institute of America at Copia, *74–75*
Culinary Institute of America at Greystone, *119*
Cuvaison Estate Wines, *75*
Cuvée, *55, 62*

D

Darioush, *75, 77*
David Coffaro Estate Vineyard, *213, 215*
Davis Estates, *134–135*
Davis Family Vineyards, *190, 193*
Dean & Deluca (shop), *131*
Deerfield Ranch Winery, *175*
DeLoach Vineyards, *237*
Di Rosa Center, *22, 77*
Diamond Mountain District AVA, *73*
Diavola Pizzeria and Salumeria ✕, *214, 217*
Dining, *16–17.* ⇨ *see also Restaurants*
Disgorging, *55*
Distilleries.* ⇨ *see Wineries*
Dr. Wilkinson's Hot Springs Resort, *144*
Domaine Carneros, *24, 77–78*
Domaine Chandon, *95*
Donum Estate, *22, 25, 152, 157*
Dosage, *55*
Downtown Bakery & Creamery ✕, *207*
Dry Creek General Store, *212*
Dry Creek Kitchen ✕, *207*
Dry Creek Peach & Produce, *193–194*
Dry Creek Valley AVA, *188, 198, 214*

Dry Creek Valley wineries, *190*
Dry Creek Vineyard, *194*
Duckhorn Vineyards, *119*
Duke's Spirited Cocktails, *18, 211*
Duncan's Landing, *225*
Dutton-Goldfield Winery, *229*

E

Eastside wineries, *189–190*
Ehlers Estate, *119*
El Barrio (bar), *19, 223–224*
El Bonita Motel 🛏, *129–130*
El Dorado Hotel 🛏, *166*
El Dorado Kitchen ✕, *163*
El Molino Central ✕, *163–164*
El Pueblo Inn 🛏, *167*
Elizabeth Spencer Winery, *110–111*
Embrace Calistoga 🛏, *142*
Emeritus Vineyards, *190, 229*
Enjoy Napa Valley, *93*
Enoteca Wine Shop, *144*
Ernie's Tin Bar, *18, 182*
Etude Wines, *78*
Evangeline ✕, *139*

F

Fairfield Inn & Suites Santa Rosa Sebastopol 🛏, *234*
Fairmont Sonoma Mission Inn & Spa 🛏, *167*
Families, attractions for, *28*
Far Niente, *107–108*
Farmer's markets
  Napa Valley, *80, 92, 106*
  Northern Sonoma County, Russian River, and West County, *212*
  Sonoma Valley, *168, 169*
Farmhouse Inn, The ✕ 🛏, *220*
Farmstead at Long Meadow Ranch ✕, *127–128*
Fat Pilgrim & Harvest Home (shop), *168*
Fermentation
  barrel, *61*
  malolactic ("malo"), *52, 63*
  yeast, *54, 64*
Fermenters, *52*
Ferrari-Carano Winery, *194*
Festival Napa Valley, *43*
Festivals and seasonal events, *43–44*
Fig Cafe ✕, *172*
Film, *131*
Filtering, *52*
Finesse, the Store, *105*
Fining, *52*
Flamingo Conference Resort & Spa 🛏, *244*
Flavor! Napa Valley (festival), *43*
Florence Avenue, *231*
Food pairings, *152*
Foppiano Vineyards, *194*
Forestville, *184, 218–220*
Fork Roadhouse ✕, *231–232*
Fort Ross-Seaview AVA, *189*

Fort Ross State Historic Park, *224*
Fort Ross Vineyard & Tasting Room, *224*
Francis Ford Coppola Winery, *23, 215*
Francis House 🛏, *142*
Frank Family Vineyards, *135*
French Laundry ✕, *101*
Frenchie Picnics and Provisions ✕, *164*
Frog's Leap, *111*
Fruit set, *57*

G

Gables Wine Country Inn 🛏, *244*
Gaige House 🛏, *174*
Gallery Lulo, *211*
Gardens, *156–157, 172, 229, 237*
Gary Farrell Winery, *194, 196*
Gatehouse Restaurant ✕, *128*
General Vallejo's Home, *160*
Geology, *57*
Getaway Adventures (tour), *246*
Geyserville, *184, 213–218*
Geyserville Gun Club Bar & Lounge, *19, 217–218*
Geyserville Inn 🛏, *217*
Girl & the Fig ✕, *164*
Glen Ellen, *146, 169–174*
Glen Ellen Star ✕, *172–173, 177*
Gloria Ferrer Caves and Vineyards, *157*
Glossary, *60–64*
Goat Rock Beach, *226*
Gondola Servizio, *94*
Goose & Gander ✕, *19, 128*
Goosecross Cellars, *95, 95*
Gordon Huether Studio, *78*
Gott's Roadside ✕, *128*
Grace's Table ✕, *86*
Graton, *184, 234–235*
Grafton Resort & Casino, *245*
Gran Eléctrica ✕, *86*
Grand Cru Custom Crush, *196*
Grapes, *55–56*
Gravenstein Grill ✕, *232*
Green Music Center, *245–246*
Green Valley of the Russian River Valley AVA, *188*
G's General Store, *168–169*
Guerneville, *184, 221–225*
Guiso Latin Fusion ✕, *207*

H

Hall St. Helena, *22, 119, 121*
Hampton Inn Petaluma 🛏, *181–182*
Handline Coastal California ✕, *232*
Handwritten Wines, *97*
Hanson of Sonoma Organic Vodka, *157–158*
Haraszthy, Agoston, *158*
Hare & Hatter Sausage Emporium ✕, *164, 177*
Harmon Guest House 🛏, *209*

Hartford Family Winery, *218*
Harvest, *57, 60*
Harvest Inn by Charlie Palmer
⊡ , *130*
Harvest Moon Cafe ✕ , *164*
Harvest Table ✕ , *128*
Hazel ✕ , *227*
Healdsburg and Northern Sonoma,
184, 189–213
Healdsburg Farmers' Market, *212*
Healdsburg Inn ⊡ , *209*
Healdsburg Museum and Historical
Society, *196*
Health and safety, *34–35, 42*
Health Spa Napa Valley, *131–132*
Hess Collection, *78, 98*
Hiking, *101, 235, 246*
Hill Family Estate, *97*
History, *82, 115, 117, 158*
Honig Vineyard & Winery, *111*
Honor Mansion, The ⊡ , *209–210*
Hotel Healdsburg ⊡ , *210*
Hôtel Les Mars ⊡ , *210*
Hotel Petaluma ⊡ , *182*
Hotel Trio Healdsburg ⊡ , *210*
Hotel Villagio ⊡ , *103*
Hotel Yountville ⊡ , *103*
Hotels, *33*
Napa Valley, *33, 70, 89–91, 103–104, 116,*
129–131, 141–143
Northern Sonoma County, Russian River,
and West County hotels, 33, 187,
208–211, 217, 220, 222–223, 225, 226,
227–228, 234, 244–245
prices, *33, 150, 188*
Sonoma Valley, *33, 150, 166–167, 174,*
178, 181–182
House rentals, *33*
Howard Station Cafe ✕ , *227*
Howell Mountain AVA, *73*
H2hotel ⊡ , *210*
Hudson Street Wineries, *196*
Hunter Gatherer (shop), *105*
Hyatt Regency Sonoma Wine Country
⊡ , *244*
Hydro Bar & Grill, *143*

I

Immunizations, *32*
Incavo Wine Lounge & Collective,
182
Indian Springs Resort and Spa ⊡ ,
142–143
Indian Springs Spa, *144*
Inglenook, *24, 111*
Ink House ⊡ , *130*
Inman Family Wines, *237*
Inn at Occidental, The ⊡ , *227–228*
Inn at Sonoma ⊡ , *167*
Inn on First, The ⊡ , *90*
Inn on Randolph ⊡ , *90–91*
Inn St. Helena ⊡ , *130*
Inns, *33*
Iron Horse Vineyards, *25, 190, 229*
Itineraries, *36–41*

Ivy, Twig & Twine (shop), *92*

J

J Vineyards and Winery, *196*
Jack London State Historic Park,
171, 177
JaM Cellars, *92*
JaM JAr (shop), *239*
Jan de Luz (shop), *132*
JCB Tasting Salon, *97, 98*
Jenner, *184, 224–225*
Jericho Canyon Vineyard, *135*
Jessup Cellars, *97–98*
Jimtown Store, *212*
John Anthony Vineyards Tasting
Room, *78–79*
Johnny's Restaurant & Bar ✕ ,
139–140
Jordan Vineyard and Winery, *190,*
196–197
Joseph Jewell Wines, *218*
Joseph Phelps Vineyards, *24, 121*

K

Kayaking, *10, 93, 240*
Keller Estate, *179–180*
Kelly's Filling Station and Wine
Shop, *105*
Kenwood, *146, 174–179*
Kenwood Inn and Spa ⊡ , *178*
Kenwood Vineyards, *175*
Kenzo ✕ , *86*
KINSmoke ✕ , *207*
Kitchen Door ✕ , *87*
Kivelstadt Cellars, *171*
Kollar Chocolates (shop), *105–106*
Korbel Champagne Cellars, *222*
Kortum Trail, *226*
Kunde Estate Winery & Vineyards,
152, 175

L

La Crema at Saralee's Vineyard, *237*
La Rochelle Winery, *176*
La Torque ✕ , *87*
Labels, *54*
Lagunitas Brewing Company, *180*
Laird Family Estate, *79*
Lambert Bridge Winery, *197*
Landmark Vineyards, *175–176, 198*
Las Alcobas Napa Valley ⊡ , *130*
LaSalette Restaurant ✕ , *164*
Lasseter Family Winery, *171–172*
Laurel Glen Vineyard, *172*
Lavender Inn ⊡ , *103*
Ledson Hotel ⊡ , *167*
Ledson Winery & Vineyards, *176*
Limerick Lane Cellars, *25, 176, 198*
Locals Tasting Room, *214, 215*
Lodging, *33.* ⇨ *see also Hotels*
London, Jack, *171, 173, 177*
Long Meadow Ranch General Store
& Cafe ✕ , *121*

Looking Glass Luxe (shop), *211*
Los Carneros AVA, *71–72, 151*
Lovina ✕ , *140*
Lowell's ✕ , *232*
Loxton Cellars, *172*
Luther Burbank Center for the
Arts, *246*
Luther Burbank Home and Gardens,
237
Lynmar Estate, *229–230*

M

MacArthur Place Hotel & Spa
⊡ , *167*
MacPhail Family Wines, *231*
MacRosie Estate House, *198–199*
Made Fritz Brewing Co., *121*
Madrona Manor ⊡ , *210*
Maison Fleurie ⊡ , *103*
Makers Market, *92*
Malolactic fermentation ("malo"), *52*
Mark Herold Wines, *79*
Market ✕ , *128, 129*
Martinelli Winery, *237–238*
Matanzas Creek Winery, *238*
Maturation, *53*
Mauritson Wines, *199*
McEvoy Ranch, *152, 180*
Meadowlark Country House ⊡ , *143*
Meadowood Napa Valley ⊡ , *130*
Mecox (shop), *92*
Medlock Ames Tasting Room,
199–200
Merry Edwards Winery, *25, 230–231*
Merryvale Vineyards, *121–122*
Milliken Creek Inn ⊡ , *91*
Miminashi ✕ , *87*
Model Bakery ✕ , *129*
Money matters, *35*
Moon Mountain District Sonoma
County AVA, *151*
Morimoto Napa ✕ , *87*
Moshin Vineyards, *200*
Mount Veeder AVA, *72–73*
Mount View Hotel & Spa ⊡ , *143*
Mumm Napa, *22, 111–112*
Museums and art galleries, *22–23*
Napa Valley, *66, 73–74, 75, 77, 78, 80–81,*
98–99, 111–112, 119, 121, 124, 131,
134, 136
Northern Sonoma County, Russian River,
and West County, 196, 203, 211, 231,
236, 239
Sonoma Valley, *160*
Must, *63*
Mustards Grill ✕ , *101–102*
Mystic Theatre & Music Hall, *182*

N

Napa, *66, 73–93*
Napa Bookmine, *92*
Napa Palisades Saloon, *19*
Napa River Inn ⊡ , *91*
Napa Valley, *14, 66–144*

appellations, 56–57, 71–73
Calistoga, 66, 132–144
exploring, 73–83, 95–99, 107–109,
  110–112, 114–115, 116–129, 133–139
hotels, 33, 70, 89–91, 103–104, 116,
  129–131, 141–143
Napa, 66, 73–94
nightlife and the arts, 34, 91–92, 131, 143
Oakville, 66, 107–109
outdoor activities and sports, 93–94,
  106–107, 132, 144
restaurants, 70, 85–89, 99–103, 109,
  115–116, 139–140
Rutherford, 66, 109–116
shopping, 34, 92–93, 104–106, 131–132,
  143–144
St. Helena, 66, 116–132
spas, 66, 90, 92–93, 106, 131–132,
  142–143, 144
transportation, 30–31, 69–70, 73, 107,
  110, 116
visitor information, 73, 116, 133
when to go, 69
Yountville, 66, 94–107
Napa Valley Aloft, 106
Napa Valley Balloons, 106–107
Napa Valley Bike Tours, 106
Napa Valley Distillery, 79
Napa Valley Lodge ⌂, 104
Napa Valley Olive Oil Manufacturing
  Company ✕, 132
Napa Valley Railway Inn ⌂, 104
Napa Valley Wine Train, 9, 79–80
Nichelini Family Winery, 122
Nickel & Nickel, 108
Nightlife and the arts, 34
Napa Valley, 34, 91–92, 131, 143
Northern Sonoma County, Russian River,
  and West County nightlife and the arts,
  34, 211, 217–218, 223–224, 245–246
Sonoma Valley, 34, 168, 182
Noble Folk Ice Cream and Pie Bar
  ✕, 207
Norman Rose Tavern ✕, 87–88
North Block Hotel ⌂, 104
North Block Spa, 106
North Coast AVA, 188
Northern Sonoma AVA, 188
Northern Sonoma County, Russian
  River, and West County, 14,
  184–246
appellations, 188–189, 198, 214, 217, 221
beaches, 225–226
Bodega Bay, 184, 225–226
exploring, 190, 192–194, 196–205,
  213–216, 218, 221–222, 225, 226,
  228–231, 234–235, 236–239
Forestville, 184, 218–220
Geyserville, 184, 213–218
Graton, 184, 234–235
Guerneville, 184, 221–225
Healdsburg and Northern Sonoma, 184,
  189–213
hotels, 33, 187, 208–211, 217, 220,
  222–223, 225, 226, 227–228, 234,
  244–245
Jenner, 184, 224–225
nightlife and the arts, 34, 211, 217–218,
  223–224, 245–246
Occidental, 184, 227–228

outdoor activities and sports, 213, 220,
  226, 228, 247
restaurants, 187, 205–209, 216–217, 220,
  222, 225, 226, 227, 231–234, 235,
  239–241, 244
Santa Rosa, 184, 235–246
Sebastopol, 184, 228–235
shopping, 34, 211–212
spas, 212–213, 222
transportation, 30–31, 187
visitor information, 190
West County, 14

O

Oak barrels, 53
Oak Knoll District of Napa Valley
  AVA, 72
Oakville, 66, 107–109
Oakville AVA, 72
Oakville Grocery, 109, 212
O'Brien Estate, 80
Occidental, 184, 227–228
Oenotri ✕, 88
Olea Hotel ⌂, 174
One World Fair Trade (shop), 211–212
Organic wine, 60
Oso Sonoma ✕, 164–165
Ottimo ✕, 102
Outdoor activities and sports
Napa Valley, 93–94, 106–107, 132, 144
Northern Sonoma County, Russian River,
  and West County outdoor activities and
  sports, 213, 220, 226, 228, 247
Sonoma Valley, 169, 179
Oxbow Public Market, 80

P

Packing, 35
Pairings, 71, 152
Palooza Gastropub & Wine Bar
  ✕, 178
Pangloss Cellars Tasting Lounge, 158
Papapietro Perry, 200
Paradise Ridge Kenwood Tasting
  Room, 176, 238–239
Paris Wine Tasting, 82
Parks, state
Napa Valley, 135
Northern Sonoma County, Russian River,
  and West County, 221, 224, 225–226,
  246
Sonoma Valley, 171, 179, 180
Pascaline Patisserie & Cafe ✕, 232
Passports, 32
Patrick Amiot Junk Art, 23, 231
Patz & Hall, 25, 152, 159, 177
Paul Mathew Vineyards, 234–235
Pearl ✕, 181
Pearl Wonderful Clothing (shop), 132
Pestoni Family Estate Winery,
  122–123
Petaluma, 146, 179–182
Petaluma Adobe State Historic
  Park, 180
Petaluma Gap AVA, 151
Piña Napa Valley, 112

Pinot on the River (festival), 44
PlumpJack Winery, 108
Poetry Inn ⌂, 104
Porter Creek Vineyards, 200
Prager Winery & Port Works, 123
Press, 52
Press ✕, 129
Preston Farm & Winery, 200–201
Prices, 33, 150, 188
Pride Mountain Vineyards, 123
Prisoner Wine Company, The, 123
Protéa Restaurant ✕, 102
Provenance Vineyards, 112
Pruning, 57
Public transportation, 30–31

Q

Quarryhill Botanical Garden, 172
Quivira Vineyards and Winery, 201

R

R+D Kitchen ✕, 102
Racking, 52
RAD Napa, 22, 80
Railroad Square Historic District, 239
Ramen Gaijin ✕, 232–233
Ram's Gate Winery, 159
Ravenswood Winery, 159
Raymond Vineyards, 123–124
Red Car Wines, 231
Red wine, 50–51
Redd Wood ✕, 102
Reservations, 33
Restaurant at Auberge du Soleil
  ✕, 115
Restaurant at CIA Copia ✕, 88
Restaurant at Meadowood, The
  ✕, 129
Restaurants
Napa Valley, 70, 85–89, 99–103, 109,
  115–116, 139–140
Northern Sonoma County, Russian River,
  and West County, 187, 205–209,
  216–217, 220, 222, 225, 226, 227,
  231–234, 235, 239–241, 244
prices, 33, 150, 188
Sonoma Valley, 150, 163–166, 172–173,
  177–178, 181
RH Yountville (museum), 98–99
RH Yountville ✕, 102
Rhône Room, 159
Riddling, 55
Ride sharing, 31
Ridge Vineyards, 25, 190, 201
River Belle Inn ⌂, 210
RiverHouse by Bespoke Collection,
  81–82
Robert Louis Stevenson Museum, 124
Robert Louis Stevenson State
  Park, 135
Robert Mondavi Winery, 108
Robert Sinskey Vineyards, 99
Robert Young Estate Winery, 25,
  190, 215

Rochioli Vineyards and Winery, 201
Rock Point, 225
Rodney Strong Vineyards, 201
Rombauer Vineyards, 124–125
Romeo Vineyards & Cellars, 135–136
Rosé wine, 55
Rosso Pizzeria & Wine Bar ✕, 240–241
Round Pond Estate, 112
Russian River, 14. ⇨ see also Northern Sonoma County, Russian River, and West County
Russian River Adventures, 213
Russian River Brewing Company ✕, 207–208, 245
Russian River Valley AVA, 188, 214, 221
Russian River Vineyards Tasting Lounge Kitchen & Farm ✕, 218, 220
Rutherford, 66, 109–116
Rutherford AVA, 72
Rutherford Grill ✕, 115–116

S

Safari West, 239
Safety, 34–35, 42
Sailing, 226
Saint, The (wine bar), 131
St. Clair Brown Winery, 82
Saint Dizier Home (shop), 212
St. Francis Winery, 152, 176, 177
St. Helena, 66, 116–132
St. Helena AVA, 72
St. Helena Cyclery, 132
St. Supéry Estate Vinyards & Winery, 114
Saintsbury, 81
Salt & Stone ✕, 178
Sam's Social Club ✕, 140
Santa Rosa, 184, 235–246
Santa Rosa Arts Center, 239
Santé ✕, 165
Sazon Peruvian Cuisine ✕, 241
Schramsberg, 24, 136
Screaming Mimi's ✕, 233
Scribe, 25, 152, 160
SEA Thai Bistro ✕, 241
Seaside Metal Oyster Bar ✕, 222
Seasonal events, 43–44
Sebastiani Theatre, 168
Sebastopol, 184, 228–235
Seghesio Family Vineyards, 202
Senza Hotel 🏨, 91
Sequoia Grove, 112, 114
Settling tanks, 52
Shackford's Kitchen Store, 92
Sharpsteen Museum of Calistoga History, 136
Shell Beach, 226
Shipping, 35
Shopping, 11, 34
Napa Valley, 34, 92–93, 104–106, 131–132, 143–144

Northern Sonoma County, Russian River, and West County, 34, 211–212
Sonoma Valley, 34, 168–169, 178
Siduri Wine Lounge, 202
Sigh (bar), 18, 168
Silver Oak, 25, 98, 108–109, 190, 202–203, 214
SingleThread Farms Inn 🏨, 211
SingleThread Farms Restaurant ✕, 208
Sky & Vine (bar), 19
Smith Story Wines, 196
Smith-Madrone Winery, 24, 125
Sofa Santa Rosa Arts District, 23
Sojourn Cellars, 160
Solage Calistoga 🏨, 143
Solbar ✕, 140
Sonoma, 146, 151–169
Sonoma Barracks, 160
Sonoma Canopy Tours, 228
Sonoma Coast AVA, 151, 188–189
Sonoma Coast State Park, 225–226
Sonoma Coast Vineyards, 225
Sonoma County Harvest Fair, 43
Sonoma Creek Inn 🏨, 167
Sonoma Mission, 160
Sonoma Mountain AVA, 151
Sonoma Plaza, 160–161
Sonoma Portworks, 180–181
Sonoma State Historic Park, 160
Sonoma TrainTown Railroad, 161
Sonoma Valley, 14, 146–182
appellations, 151
exploring, 152, 156–163, 170–172, 174–177, 179–181
Glen Ellen, 146, 169–174
hotels, 33, 150, 166–167, 174, 178, 181–182
Kenwood, 146, 174–179
nightlife and the arts, 34, 168, 182
outdoor activities and sports, 169, 179
Petaluma, 146, 179–182
restaurants, 150, 163–166, 172–173, 177–178, 181
shopping, 34, 168–169, 178
Sonoma, 146, 151–169
spas, 166, 167, 169, 178
transportation, 30–31, 149–150
visitor information, 151, 179
Sonoma Valley AVA, 151
Sonoma Valley Bike Tours, 169
Sonoma Valley Certified Farmers Market, 168
Southside Yountville Cellars ✕, 103
Spa at Kenwood Inn, 178
Spa at Napa River Inn, 92–93
Spa at The Estate, The, 106
Spa Dolce, 212
Spa Hotel Healdsburg, The, 212–213
Spa Solage, 144
Sparkling wine, 54–55
Spas, 12
Napa Valley, 66, 90, 92–93, 106, 142–143, 144
Northern Sonoma County, Russian River, and West County, 212–213
Sonoma Valley, 166, 167, 178

Spinster Sisters, The ✕, 241
Spoonbar ✕, 208
Sports. ⇨ see Outdoor activities and sports
Spring Mountain AVA, 72–73
Spring Mountain Vineyard, 125
Opud Point Olub Oompany ✕, 225
Stags Leap District AVA, 72
Stag's Leap Wine Cellars, 81
Stags' Leap Winery, 82
Stark's Steak & Seafood ✕, 241
Starling Bar Sonoma, 168
Stemmer-crusher, 51–52
Sterling Vineyards, 136
Stewart Cellars, 98, 99
Stonestreet, 203
Stony Hill Vineyard, 24, 125
Store at CIA Copia, 93
Storybook Mountains Vineyard, 136
Studio by Feast it Forward, 83
Stuhlmuller Vineyards, 203
Sugarloaf Ridge State Park, 179
Sunflower Caffé ✕, 165, 177
Sushi Mambo ✕, 140
Susie's Bar, 19, 143
Sweet Scoops ✕, 165–166
Swiss Hotel (bar), 168

T

Tamber Bey Vineyards, 137
Tannins, 64
Tarla Mediterranean Grill ✕, 88
Tasco Tasco Portuguese Tapas Restaurant & Wine Bar ✕, 166
Taste of Sonoma (festival), 43
Tasting, 46–48
Napa Valley, 66, 71, 82, 118
Northern Sonoma County, Russian River, and West County, 190, 199–200, 203, 215, 218, 220, 224
Sonoma Valley, 146, 152, 158, 159, 174–175, 176
Tasting rooms, 48–49
Taxes, 31
Tedeschi Family Winery, 137
Terrapin Creek Cafe & Restaurant ✕, 226
Thinning the fruit, 57
Three Sticks Wines, 25, 161
Thumbprint Cellars Tasting Lounge & Art Gallery, 203
Timber Cove Resort 🏨, 225
Timing the visit, 32
Tipping, 35
Tips Roadside ✕, 178
Tom Eddy Winery, 137
Torc ✕, 88
Tours
Napa Valley, 71, 98, 101
Northern Sonoma County, Russian River, and West County, 190, 214
Sonoma Valley, 152, 169
Tra Vigne Pizzeria and Restaurant ✕, 129
Train travel, 31, 42

Transportation, *30–31*
Napa Valley, 69–70, 73, 107, 110, 116
Northern Sonoma County, Russian River,
and West County, 187
Sonoma Valley, 149–150
Trattore Farms, *215–216*
Trefethen Family Vineyards, *24, 83*
Trentadue Winery, *216*
Tres Sabores Winery, *125–126*
Trinchero Napa Valley, *126*
Truchard Vineyards, *83*
Truett Hurst Winery, *203–204*
T-Vine Winery, *136–137*
Twist ✕, *220*
Twomey Cellars, *137–138, 204*

U

Underwood Bar & Bistro ✕, *235*
Unti Vineyards, *204–205*
Up & Away Ballooning, *213*
Uptown Theatre, *92*

V

V Marketplace, *106*
Valette ✕, *208*
Valley of the Moon Certified Farm-
ers' Market, *168*
Varietals, *64*
Vella Cheese Company (shop), *169*
Venge Vineyards, *24, 138*
Veraison, *57*
Veraison ✕, *140*
Vermeil Wines, *138*
VGS Chateau Potelle, *24, 126*
Vincent Arroyo Winery, *138*
Vineyards. ➪ *see* Wineries
Vintage House 🏨, *104*
Vintners Inn 🏨, *244–245*
Virginia Dare Winery, *216*
Visas, *32*
Viszlay Vineyards, *205*
Viticulture, *64*
VJB Cellars, *176–177*
VML Winery, *204*
Von Strasser Family of Wines,
138–139

W

Walt Wines, *161, 163*
Walter Hansel Wine & Bistro ✕,
241, 244
West County, *14.* ➪ *see also Northern*
Sonoma County, Russian River, and
West County
West County Regional Trail, *235*
West of West Wine Festival, *28*
West Sonoma Coast AVA, *189*
Westin Verasa Napa 🏨, *91*
Westside wineries, *189*
Whale-watching, *226*
When to go, *32*
Whetstone Wine Cellars, *83*
White wine, *49–50, 52–53*

Wild Flour Bread ✕, *227*
Wild Horse Valley AVA, *73*
Willi's Seafood & Raw Bar ✕, *208*
Willi's Wine Bar ✕, *244*
Willow Stream Spa at Fairmont
Sonoma Mission Inn & Spa, *169*
Willow Wood Market Cafe ✕, *235*
Wine
appellations, 54, 56–57, 71–73
bars, 85–86, 131, 166, 178, 182
biodynamic, 60
clubs, 48
history, 82, 115, 117, 158
labels, 54
making of 43–52
organic, 60
red, 50–51
rosé, 55
sparkling, 54–55
tasting, 46–48, 66, 71, 82, 118, 146, 152,
158, 159, 174–175, 176, 190, 199–200,
203, 215, 218, 220, 224
varietals, 64
viticulture, 64
vocabulary for, 60–64
white, 49–50, 52–53
Wine & Food Affair (festival), *44*
Wine Country Bikes, *213*
Wine Country Cyclery, *169*
Wine Country Inn 🏨, *130–131*
Wine Road Wine Barrel Tasting Week-
ends, *43*
Wineries, *24–25*
Abbot's Passage Supply Co., 152, 156
Acorn Winery, 190, 192
Acumen Wine Gallery, 73–74
Adobe Road Winery, 179
Alexander Valley Vineyards, 192
Alexander Valley wineries, 190
Alley & Craft Distillery, 192
Anaba Wines, 156
Arista Winery, 74, 190, 192
Artesa Vineyards & Winery, 74
Ashes and Diamonds, 24, 74
B Cellars, 98, 107
B.R. Cohn, 171
B Wise Vineyards Cellar, 174–175
Balletto Vineyards, 236
Banshee Wines, 192–193
Barnett Vineyards, 116–117
Beaulieu Vineyard, 110
Bedrock Wine Co., 156
Bennett Lane Winery, 133
Benovia Winery, 236
Benziger Family Winery, 153, 170
Beringer Vineyards, 117
Black Kite Cellars, 196
Bouchaine Vineyards, 74
Bowman Cellars, 234
Brian Arden Wines, 133–134
Buena Vista Winery, 152, 156, 171
Cade Estate Winery, 117–118
Cakebread Cellars, 110
Carol Shelton Wines, 236
Castello di Amorosa, 134
Caymus Vineyards, 110
Charles Krug Winery, 118
Château Montelena, 134
Chateau St. Jean, 175
Christopher Creek Winery, 193
Clif Family Tasting Room, 118

Cliff Lede Vineyards, 95
Clos du Val, 75
Comstock Wines, 193
Copain Wines, 193
Corison Winery, 118
Crocker & Star, 119
Cru @ The Annex, 75
Cuvaison Estate Wines, 75
Darioush, 75, 77
David Coffaro Estate Vineyard, 213, 215
Davis Estates, 134–135
Davis Family Vineyards, 190, 193
Deerfield Ranch Winery, 175
DeLoach Vineyards, 237
Domaine Carneros, 24, 77–78
Domaine Chandon, 95
Donum Estate, 22, 25, 152, 157
Dry Creek Valley Wineries, 190
Dry Creek Vineyard, 194
Duckhorn Vineyards, 119
Dutton-Goldfield Winery, 229
Ehlers Estate, 119
Elizabeth Spencer Winery, 110–111
Emeritus Vineyards, 190, 229
Etude Wines, 78
Far Niente, 107–108
Ferrari-Carano Winery, 194
Foppiano Vineyards, 194
Fort Ross Vineyard & Tasting Room, 224
Francis Ford Coppola Winery, 23, 215
Frank Family Vineyards, 135
Frog's Leap, 111
Gary Farrell Winery, 194, 196
Gloria Ferrer Caves and Vineyards, 157
Goosecross Cellars, 95, 97
Grand Cru Custom Crush, 196
Hall St. Helena, 22, 119, 121
Handwritten Wines, 97
Hanson of Sonoma Organic Vodka,
157–158
Hartford Family Winery, 218
Hess Collection, 78, 98
Hill Family Estate, 97
Honig Vineyard & Winery, 111
Hudson Street Wineries, 196
Inglenook, 24, 111
Inman Family Wines, 237
Iron Horse Vineyards, 25, 190, 229
J Vineyards and Winery, 196
JaM Cellars, 92
JCB Tasting Salon, 97, 98
Jericho Canyon Vineyard, 135
Jessup Cellars, 97–98
John Anthony Vineyards Tasting Room,
78–79
Jordan Vineyard and Winery, 190, 196–197
Joseph Jewell Wines, 218
Joseph Phelps Vineyards, 24, 121
Keller Estate, 179–180
Kenwood Vineyards, 175
Kivelstadt Cellars, 171
Korbel Champagne Cellars, 222
Kunde Estate Winery & Vineyards, 152,
175
La Crema at Saralee's Vineyard, 237
La Rochelle Winery, 176
Lagunitas Brewing Company, 180
Laird Family Estate, 79
Lambert Bridge Winery, 197
Landmark Vineyards, 175–176, 198
Lasseter Family Winery, 171–172
Laurel Glen Vineyard, 172
Ledson Winery & Vineyards, 176

Limerick Lane Cellars, 25, 176, 198
Locals Tasting Room, 214, 215
Loxton Cellars, 172
Lynmar Estate, 229–230
MacPhail Family Wines, 231
MacRosie Estate House, 198–199
Mad Fritz Brewing Co., 121
Mark Herold Wines, 79
Matanzas Creek Winery, 238
Mauritson Wines, 199
Medlock Ames Tasting Room, 199–200
Merry Edwards Winery, 25, 230–231
Merryvale Vineyards, 121–122
McEvoy Ranch, 180
Moshin Vineyards, 200
Mumm Napa, 22, 111–112
Napa Valley Distillery, 79
Nichelini Family Winery, 122
Nickel & Nickel, 108
O'Brien Estate, 80
Papapietro Perry, 200
Paradise Ridge Kenwood Tasting Room, 176, 238–239
Patz & Hall, 25, 152, 159, 177
Paul Mathew Vineyards, 234–235
Pestoni Family Estate Winery, 122–123
Piña Napa Valley, 112
PlumpJack Winery, 108
Porter Creek Vineyards, 200
Prager Winery & Port Works, 123
Preston Farm & Winery, 200–201
Pride Mountain Vineyards, 123
Prisoner Wine Company, The, 123
Provenance Vineyards, 112
Quivira Vineyards and Winery, 201
Ram's Gate Winery, 159
Ravenswood Winery, 159
Raymond Vineyards, 123–124
Red Car Wines, 231
Rhône Room, 159
Ridge Vineyards, 25, 190, 201
Robert Mondavi Winery, 108
Robert Sinskey Vineyards, 99
Robert Young Estate Winery, 25, 190, 215
Rochioli Vineyards and Winery, 201
Rodney Strong Vineyards, 201
Rombauer Vineyards, 124–125
Romeo Vineyards & Cellars, 135–136
Round Pond Estate, 112
Russian River Vineyards Tasting Lounge Kitchen & Farm, 218, 220
St. Clair Brown Winery, 82
St. Francis Winery, 152, 176, 177
St. Supéry Estate Vinyards & Winery, 114
Saintsbury, 81
Schramsberg, 24, 136
Scribe, 25, 152, 160
Seghesio Family Vineyards, 202
Sequoia Grove, 112, 114
Siduri Wine Lounge, 202
Silver Oak, 25, 98, 108–109, 190, 202–203, 214
Smith Story Wines, 196
Smith-Madrone Winery, 24, 125
Sojourn Cellars, 160
Sonoma Coast Vineyards, 225
Sonoma Portworks, 180–181
Spring Mountain Vineyard, 125
Stag's Leap Wine Cellars, 81
Stags' Leap Winery, 82
Sterling Vineyards, 136
Stewart Cellars, 98, 99
Stonestreet, 203

Stony Hill Vineyard, 24, 125
Storybook Mountains Vineyard, 136
Studio by Feast it Forward, 83
Stuhlmuller Vineyards, 203
Tamber Bey Vineyards, 137
Tedeschi Family Winery, 135
Three Sticks Wines, 25, 161
Thumbprint Cellars Tasting Lounge IV Art Gallery, 203
Tom Eddy Winery, 137
Trattore Farms, 215–216
Trefethen Family Vineyards, 24, 83
Trentadue Winery, 216
Tres Sabores Winery, 125–126
Trinchero Napa Valley, 126
Truchard Vineyards, 83
Truett Hurst Winery, 203–204
T-Vine Winery, 136–137
Twomey Cellars, 137–138, 204
Unti Vineyards, 204–205
Venge Vineyards, 24, 138
Vermeil Wines, 138
VGS Chateau Potelle, 24, 126
Vincent Arroyo Winery, 138
Virginia Dare Winery, 216
Viszlay Vineyards, 205
VJB Cellars, 176–177
VML Winery, 204
Von Strasser Family of Wines, 138–139
Walt Wines, 161, 163
Westwood Estate, 163
Whetstone Wine Cellars, 83
Yao Family Wines, 126
ZD Wines, 114–115
Zialena, 216
Zichichi Family Vineyard, 205
Westwood Estate, 163
Whetstone Wine Cellars, 83
Winter Wineland (festival), 43
Woodhouse Chocolate (shop), 132
Wright's Beach, 225
Wurst Restaurant ✕ , 209
Wydown Hotel ⌒ , 131

Y

Yack & Yeti ✕ , 88
Yao Family Wines, 126
Yeast, 64
Yeti Restaurant ✕ , 173
Yountville, 66, 94–107
Yountville AVA, 72

Z

Zazu Kitchen + Farm ✕ , 233–234
ZD Wines, 114–115
Zialena, 216
Zichichi Family Vineyard, 205
Ziplining, 226
ZuZu ✕ , 89

Photo Credits

Front Cover: Jared Ropelato/Shutterstock [Description: Fall color drapes the rolling hills of Napa and Sonoma Valleys in California.] Back cover, from left to right: Lee Jorgensen; Courtesy Glen Ellen Star; Courtesy of Napa Valley Wine Train. Interior, from left to right: Ljupco Smokovski/Shutterstock (1). Rebecca Gosselin Photography (2-3). Jill Krueger (5). Chapter 1: Experience Napa and Sonoma: Courtesy of Inglenook (6-7). Michael Warwick/Shutterstock (8-9). I8V-Israel Valencia (9). Courtesy of the Napa Valley Wine Train (9). Mariana Marakhovskaia/Shutterstock (10). Courtesy of Sonoma County Tourism (10). Courtesy of Wine Country Botanicals (10). Longmeadow Ranch (10). Joseph Phelps Vineyards (11). Nat and Cody Gantz 2018/Hanson of Sonoma Distillery (11). CIA at Copia (12). PlumpJack Winery (12). Donum Estate (12). Valentina_G/Shutterstock (12). Courtesy of Sonoma County Tourism (13). Zack Frank/Shutterstock (13). Gama Nine (16). Lisovskaya Natalia/Shutterstock (16). Jeff Bramwell (16). Steven Freeman (16). 2018 Robert McClenahan (17). Richard Ault (17). New Africa/Shutterstock (17). Tubay Yabut Photography (17). Garrett Rowland (18). Ernie's Tin Bar (18). Harmon Guesthouse (18). Natalie and Cody Gantz (18). Courtesy of Sky & Vine Rooftop Bar (19). El Barrio Bar (19). Courtesy of Sonoma County Tourism (19). Christophe Genty Photography/Goose & Gander (19). Jay Jeffers (20). Zeljko Radojko/Shutterstock (20). Courtesy of Makers Market (20). Carlos Yudica/Shutterstock (20). McEvoy Ranch (20). Natalia Svistunova/Shutterstock (21). Nikovfrmoto | Dreamstime.com (21). McEvoy Ranch (21). Victor M. Samuel Photography (21). Napa Wine Candles (21). Sara Sanger 2017 (22). Infinity Visuals (23). Chapter 3: Visiting Wineries and Tasting Rooms: Courtesy of Three Sticks Wines (45). Megan Reeves Photography (49). Courtesy of Napa Valley Balloons, Inc. (50). Andy Dean Photography / Shutterstock (56). Chapter 4: Napa Valley: Courtesy of the Napa Valley Wine Train (65). Courtesy of the Napa Valley Wine Train (72). Avis Mandel (77). Robert Holmes (81). Di Rosa (89). Victor M. Samuel (93). cheng cheng/Shutterstock (94). Openkitchenphotography (100). Jason Tinacci (105). Far Niente+Dolce+Nickel & Nickel (109). Olaf Beckman (114). Courtesy of Long Meadow Ranch (122). Scott Chebagia (124). Smcfeeters | Dreamstime.com (133). Calistoga Ranch (141). Chapter 5: Sonoma Valley and Petaluma: Wildly Simple Productions (145). Rocco Ceselin/Ram's Gate Winery (153). Julie Vader/Shutterstock (161). Leo Gong (165). Benziger Family Winery (170). Chapter 6: Northern Sonoma, Russian River, and West County: Joe Becerra/Shutterstock (183). Joe Becerra/Shutterstock (197). Matt Armendariz (199). Robert Holmes (202). Warren H. White (204). Sonoma County Tourism (223). Laurence G. Sterling/Iron Horse Vineyards (230). Mitch Tobias, courtesy of Paul Hobbs Winery (233). Joe Shlabotnik/Flickr, [CC BY-ND 2.0] (238). Jeffrey M. Frank/Shutterstock (240). Matanzas Creek (245). About Our Writer: Danny Mangin, Courtesy of J Rodby.

Fodor's NAPA AND SONOMA

Editorial: Douglas Stallings, *Editorial Director;* Margaret Kelly, Jacinta O'Halloran, *Senior Editors;* Kayla Becker, Alexis Kelly, Amanda Sadlowski, *Editors;* Teddy Minford, *Content Editor;* Rachael Roth, *Content Manager;* Jeremy Tarr, *Fodors.com Editorial Director;* Rachael Levitt, *Fodors.com Managing Editor*

Design: Tina Malaney, *Design and Production Director;* Jessica Gonzalez, *Production Designer*

Maps: Rebecca Baer, *Senior Map Editor;* David Lindroth, Mark Stroud (Moon Street Cartography), *Cartographers*

Photography: Jill Krueger, *Senior Photo Editor;* Ashok Kumar, *Photo Researcher*

Production. Jennifer DePrima, *Editorial Production Manager;* Carrie Parker, *Senior Production Editor;* Elyse Rozelle, *Production Editor*

Business & Operations: Chuck Hoover, *Chief Marketing Officer;* Robert Ames, *General Manager;* Stephen Horowitz, *Director of Business Development and Revenue Operations;* Tara McCrillis, *Director of Publishing Operations*

Public Relations and Marketing: Joe Ewaskiw, *Manager;* Esther Su, *Marketing Manager*

Writers: Daniel Mangin

Editor: Margaret Kelly (lead editor)

Editorial Contributors: Linda Cabasin, Laura M. Kidder

Production Editor: Carrie Parker

Production Design: Liliana Guia

3rd Edition

ISBN 978-1-64097-138-7

ISSN 2375–9453

Library of Congress Control Number 2018914618

SPECIAL SALES

This book is available at special discounts for bulk purchases for sales promotions or premiums. For more information, e-mail SpecialMarkets@fodors.com.

PRINTED IN THE UNITED STATES OF AMERICA

10 9 8 7 6 5 4 3 2 1

About Our Writer

 Daniel Mangin returned to California, where he's maintained a home for three decades, after two stints at the Fodor's editorial offices in New York City, the second one as the Editorial Director of Fodors.com and the Compass American Guides. While at Compass he was the series editor for the *California Wine Country* guide and commissioned the *Oregon Wine Country* and *Washington Wine Country* guides. A wine lover whose earliest visits to Napa and Sonoma predate the Wine Country lifestyle, Daniel is delighted by the evolution in wines, wine making, and hospitality. With several dozen wineries less than a half-hour's drive from home, he often finds himself transported as if by magic to a tasting room bar, communing with a sophisticated Cabernet or savoring the finish of a smooth Pinot Noir.